The Praeger Handbook of Education and Psychology

Volume 1

Edited by JOE L. KINCHELOE AND
RAYMOND A. HORN Jr.

Shirley R. Steinberg, *Associate Editor*

Westport, Connecticut
London

Library of Congress Cataloging-in-Publication Data

The Praeger handbook of education and psychology / edited by Joe L. Kincheloe and
Raymond A. Horn Jr.
    v. cm.
    Includes bibliographical references and index.
    ISBN 0–313–33122–7 (set : alk. paper)—ISBN 0–313–33123–5 (vol 1 : alk. paper)—
    ISBN 0–313–33124–3 (vol 2 : alk. paper)—ISBN 0–313–34056–0 (vol 3 : alk. paper)—
    ISBN 0–313–34057–9 (vol 4 : alk. paper)   1. Educational psychology—Handbooks, manuals, etc.
    I. Kincheloe, Joe L. II. Horn, R. A. (Raymond A.)
  LB1051.P635   2007
  371.4–dc22   2006031061

British Library Cataloguing in Publication Data is available.

Library of Congress Catalog Card Number: 2006031061
ISBN: 0–313–33122–7 (set)
      0–313–33123–5 (vol. 1)
      0–313–33124–3 (vol. 2)
      0–313–34056–0 (vol. 3)
      0–313–34057–9 (vol. 4)

First published in 2007

Praeger Publishers, 88 Post Road West, Westport, CT 06881
An imprint of Greenwood Publishing Group, Inc.
www.praeger.com

Printed in the United States of America

The paper used in this book complies with the
Permanent Paper Standard issued by the National
Information Standards Organization (Z39.48–1984).

10 9 8 7 6 5 4 3 2 1

Contents

VOLUME 2

PART III   ISSUES IN EDUCATION AND PSYCHOLOGY

Constructivism

Creativity

Criticality

Culture/Cultural Studies

Developmentalism

Memory

Mind

Psychoanalysis

Race, Class, and Gender

VOLUME 4

Situated Cognition

Teaching

PART I

Introduction

CHAPTER 1

Introduction: Educational Psychology—Limitations and Possibilities

JOE L. KINCHELOE

The great Russian psychologist Lev Vygotsky writing in the 1930s maintained that scholars in the discipline of psychology were drifting into the polar camps of behaviorism and phenomenology. There was no doubt that Vygotsky clearly saw into the future of psychology in general as well as its associated discipline, educational psychology. Indeed, the field of educational psychology would reflect these polar camps but the mainstream of the field was undoubtedly positioned within the behavioristic (or as time passed, the mechanistic) camp. Even after the decline of behaviorism as a school of psychological thought in the 1960s and 1970s, mainstream educational psychology would hang on to numerous behavioristic trappings while embracing the most mechanistic and rationalistic aspects of emerging schools of psychological thought (see Kozulin's [1997] Introduction in Vygotsky's *Thought and Language*).

THE EMERGENCE OF EDUCATIONAL PSYCHOLOGY: DIVERGENT TRADITIONS

This handbook begins with this insight, as the editors and authors explore the nature of educational psychology at the beginning of the twenty-first century. In this process they seek to examine and formulate new approaches to the subject that are practical, just, critical, and scholarly rigorous enough to address the complexity of the domain of study. The mechanistic tradition of educational psychology from behaviorism to cognitivism has emphasized the quantifiable behavior of groups of individuals—focusing in particular on producing generalizable empirical data about these aggregates of people. The contributors and editors of this handbook have not found this dominant mechanistic tradition to be very helpful in contributing to the improvement of teaching and learning. Indeed, we have often found the social, political, pedagogical, economic, and philosophical influences of this dominant impulse to be profoundly harmful to those— especially those marginalized because of race, class, gender, national origin, ethnicity, geographic place, etc.—who are vulnerable to its power.

Thus, the contributors to this volume find the roots of their disciplinary orientation more within the traditions of cultural and interpretive psychology where the focus is less on producing generalizable empirical data and more on the process of meaning making. In these alternative traditions the effort to understand phenomena in relation to the processes and contexts of which they are a part takes precedence over identifying causal relations between discrete variables (see Smith [1998]). Thus, in this introduction I will explore the different traditions of educational psychology, focusing on the root belief structures that shape them. Following this effort I will analyze the contributions of the interpretivist tradition, in the process describing a *critical* interpretivist approach. Such analysis will emphasize the explanatory benefits of interpretivism while embracing the critical concerns with the role of power in human affairs and the ways it operates in relation to issues of oppression and social justice.

We see the results of the dominance of the mechanistic tradition, as Mary Frances Agnello points out in her chapter on scientific literacy testing, in the emergence and influence of IQ and other forms of testing and measurement as well as the demand that research in educational psychology be conducted only as a verifiable and statistics-based human science. Agnello goes on to assert that in this mechanistic tradition the focus on the measurement of "human responses to various stimuli" led to a split between those mechanists who would not study consciousness and those interpretivists who would. Picking up on this theme, Kathleen Berry in her chapter on memory traces the mechanistic perspective back to the science of Rene Descartes who positioned the study of cognition in biology as an analysis of the physiology of the brain. Memory, thus, was viewed as an object existing materially within the container of the brain. Memory and mind were viewed as fundamentally separate from body and spirit. (In this context see Richard Prawat's chapter on diverse historical understandings of the nature and location of mind.) In the Cartesian context the biologically grounded, cause and effect tradition of mechanism exercised its power over the interpretive tradition, positioning human beings more as objects than as subjects.

The debate between the two traditions of educational psychology, as Patricia Whang points out in her chapter on Buddhism and educational psychology, may be best exemplified historically in the early twentieth-century debate between mechanist Edward Thorndike and interpretivist John Dewey. In the eyes of the educational psychologists Thorndike won the argument, tying educational psychology to quantification and laboratory studies of teaching and learning. Thorndike's victory, Mark Garrison maintains in his chapter on psychometrics, meant that the knowledge produced by the testing technologies of educational psychology could be used to justify forms of oppression based on particular individuals being designated as less than human. Obviously, this is one of the negative social effects of the mechanistic tradition previously referenced.

Psychology is a child of the Age of Reason, the Western European Enlightenment of the seventeenth and eighteenth centuries. What scholars refer to as modernity arose out of this Scientific Revolution. Traditional sources of meaning were swept aside in the modernist tsunami and psychology emerged as a discourse designed in part to restore meaning in new social and intellectual conditions. The hope was that by placing our faith in the scientific method and its objectively produced knowledge that human beings could move beyond arbitrary authority. They would have the knowledge to make rational and moral decisions about their lives and the world around them. In later centuries we can see this same impulse at work as educational psychology would be used as a scientific means of determining educational purpose.

In the mindset of mechanistic educational psychology, educators do not determine their purposes based on larger understandings of justice and meaning as they interact with the demands of particular social, political, and cultural contexts. Instead, such educators derive purpose from the empirical studies of educational psychology. Objective knowledge in this context is used to guide what teachers and students should be doing in terms of efficiency and smooth functioning of bureaucratic organizations. In this context the work of those who study the political, social, cultural, and economic contexts of education in relation to larger philosophical and theoretical systems of meaning is irrelevant to the work of schools. The modes of knowledge constructed in these contexts are not viewed as legitimate in the mechanistic educational psychological cosmos.

PSYCHOLOGY/EDUCATIONAL PSYCHOLOGY AS THE MOST MODERN AND MECHANISTIC OF ALL THE SCIENCES

In the mechanistic articulation of educational psychology that emerged from Cartesian science, the life of the mind is constituted mainly by the cognitive process of formulating representations of the world that exists "out there" apart from human perception. A key dimension of the emerging educational psychological tradition here involves viewing cognitive activity as the act of the mind reflecting external reality. As many of the authors writing in this handbook contend, such a viewpoint rests on many problematic and unsupported assumptions. In an ontological context— ontology is the branch of philosophy that deals with being in the world—such a psychological perspective assumes that an objective reality exists apart from human agents. In an epistemological context—epistemology is the branch of philosophy that deals with the nature of knowledge and truth—it assumes that if we use the correct methods of knowledge production, we will assure that we "reflect" this objective reality correctly.

To be viewed by the high-status physical sciences as truly scientific, psychologists believed that they had to adopt such mechanistic, computational views of the mind. It is ironic that in the twenty-first century after many physical and social scientists are questioning the radical empiricism of mechanistic and computational modes of science, it is the field of psychology— educational psychology—in particular that is holding down the fort of mechanistic reductionism. What I mean by the term mechanistic reductionism involves the view that the mind can best be studied in contextual isolation in lab settings and that mathematical symbols and logic provide the best vehicles for researching and expressing the nature of cognitive activity. Such mechanistic reductionism views human psychology as an individual experience that can best be appreciated by uncovering the general laws of cognition that shape all human psychological activity now and forever (see Pickering [1999]).

Thus, psychology/educational psychology is the most "modern-ist" science—reflecting the original principles of the Scientific Revolution of the seventeenth and eighteenth centuries. Understanding this dimension to the psychological sciences, those coming from the interpretivist tradition in psychology and other fields of study try to convince the mechanists that so-called scientific views of cognition are not objective but are shaped by the social context, the historical era in which scientists operate. Often the assumptions embedded within our lived worlds are not visible until hundreds of years have passed. At that point what seemed simple and straightforward can be understood as riddled with problematic assumptions about human beings, selfhood, intelligence behavior, progress, and social values. With this established, interpretivists insist that psychology is produced by culture and concurrently culture is produced by psychology. This coconstructive process is always operating, making it difficult for individuals operating in a place and time shaped by psychology's belief structures to separate such *beliefs* from objective reality.

Thus, educational psychology's beliefs in the centrality of the individual as the primary locus of behavior, on the superiority of Western forms of rationality, on intelligence as what one scores on an IQ test, etc. may look very silly and even primitive in only a few decades. The discomfort mechanistic psychology has exhibited in considering other cultural ways of operating in and constructing the world as legitimate, and even intelligent, may soon be viewed as manifestations of callous and narcissistic forms of ethnocentrism. With these possibilities in mind, advocates of the alternative interpretivist tradition contend, it is important for educational psychologists to engage in philosophical and social theoretical analysis of their discipline.

Philosophical research, as I define it in my work on the *bricolage* (see Kincheloe and Berry [2004]), involves inquiring into the numerous assumptions that shape a field or a body of knowledge. In the professional education of educational psychologists such important activities are not to be found in the mechanistic curriculum. Such philosophical research is long overdue in this domain. To function effectively in an informed and ethical way, educational psychologists must come to understand the ways the knowledge they are taught to accept as true are shaped by dominant power interests and ideologies. Such forces move educational psychologists to produce knowledge and engage in activities that often reward the socially, politically, and economically privileged and punish the marginalized (see Richardson and Woolfolk [1994]). In this context Ray Horn and myself and the authors included in this book emphasize the need for educational psychologists to carefully examine what passes as reason and validated research in the mechanistic tradition, in the process asking in a *critical* sense whose interests this most modernist of sciences serves.

In this context a central question of psychology/educational psychology emerges. How we answer it shapes the way in which we approach the field. How do humans represent and make meaning of the events that take place around them? Mechanistic psychologists maintain that the world is represented by symbols that are material (have substance) in some neuron-based or biochemical manner. In a more interpretive psychology the symbol processing that takes place is more conceptual and less biochemical. These symbols in interpretive psychology are very complex and cannot be separated from sociocultural and political contexts or situation-specific intentions, moods, and meaning constructions. In this context symbolic representation of the world and its events always connect the mind to micro (individualisitic) and macro (social) contexts. Thus, as we will emphasize throughout the handbook, educational psychology cannot be studied as simply an individualistic phenomenon.

Making these distinctions in relation to the question about representation and meaning making, it is important to note that a central task of educational psychology involves developing a theory of learning. It is necessary but not sufficient for educational psychologists to possess a theory of representation and meaning making. The field has a more difficult task—to find out not how individuals learn but how they learn in particular sociocultural settings, e.g., school, work, leisure, etc. Such a task, interpretivists posit, cannot be accomplished by only studying quantitatively measured behavior of groups of individuals that can then be generalized universally. Instead, individuals must be studied in their natural settings (not labs) using a bricolage of research methods including ethnography, phenomenology, history, life history, semiotics, and many others. Unfortunately, the most modern of sciences in its mechanistic articulation has not been comfortable using such research orientations. As a result, our understanding of how individuals represent and make meaning of the world and how they use these processes to learn about the world, themselves, and others has been profoundly compromised.

BORN IN THE USA: MODERNITY, MECHANISM, AND REGULATION

Thus, modern psychology and its educational psychological *nephew* were born in a Eurocentric, patriarchal, individuated, and decontextualized academic domain. The founding *fathers* within this mechanistic cosmos had faith that studying the abstracted, self-contained individual would lead them to an understanding of human life in general. Patricia Whang in her chapter in this volume extends this assertion contending that it is important to question "how the contributions made by educational psychologists have been constrained by the largely male and Euro-American perspectives, values, and traditions held by influential members of the field."

Since psychology emerged in movement from Western traditional to modern social orders, it was caught in the change of emphasis from the community and the household to the separate individual. In the premodern West, individuals were inseparable from the sociocultural context in which they were born and raised. Premodern westerners were simply not able to remove themselves from their social location and role(s) in order to try on new ways of being or new behaviors. To exist outside the local community was to "not be," to cease to exist. One's meaning was to be found in the life of the community—not in one's individual longings. As modernity slowly unfolded in Western Europe in the fifteenth, sixteenth, and seventeenth centuries, individualism emerged as the construct around which society was grounded. Psychology could not escape this defining dimension of modernity, and without conscious notice embraced it in its own self-construction.

When the ed psych nephew was emerging in the United States, in the early twentieth century, this individualistic dynamic played an important role in focusing the discipline's attention on young people in particular who were struggling to deal with drastic social changes such as industrialization, urbanization, and immigration. In this context, disciplinary experts determined that one of central functions of the field had to involve providing social order in this period of change. Such ordering could be brought about via the use of educational psychology as an instrument of normalization and regulation. The poor, the non-white, and the immigrant were the individuals who were in most need of regulation because of what was perceived as the danger they presented to the larger society. Thus, educational psychology was there to "prove" that these individuals did not possess the intellectual ability to succeed in school and therefore needed to be socially regulated so they would not stain the social fabric.

In this multicultural, industrialized context the notion of education for an educated citizenry took a back seat to the goal of education as protecting the social order. With its emerging intelligence testing and professed ability to rank order people's worth, mechanistic educational psychology became a central technology of social regulation. As Patricia Whang points out in her chapter here, ed psych's regulatory function became an important dimension of the United States' educational efficiency movement of the first couple of decades of the twentieth century in which individuals were socialized to work in the boring factory work of mass production. In this mechanistic social context behavioral psychology with its emphasis on the regulation of human behavior emerged. In many ways behaviorism was the highest expression of the mechanistic psychological orientation as it viewed humans as passive beings who could be shaped by a system of rewards and punishments to meet the demands of dominant forms of social, political, and scholarly behaviors.

TECHNOLOGIES OF SOCIAL REGULATION: THE POWER OF THE MECHANISTIC PARADIGM

We cannot understand the social role of psychology and educational psychology outside of a context dominated by measuring, evaluating, sorting, training, resocializing, and regulating. The discipline gained tremendous power as it came to "educate" political leaders, educators, and business leaders about what constituted the most important social problems of the day. In the process psychology/educational psychology began to take over social functions once reserved for the church. Instead of employing divine authority to claim the truth of its knowledge and its works, psychology claims scientific validation. There is simply no clear boundary line separating the inner world of psychology from the outer world of cultural politics—both domains often serve power interests that are not working for the best interests of individuals falling outside various dominant groups. As a form of regulatory power educational psychology operates to discover universal "truths" about individuals that can be used to determine their worth to the social order. Those who score low on the standardized tests, for example, cannot enter into the land of sociopolitical decision makers.

Even many of the most important reform movements in psychology have failed to challenge this regulatory feature. Humanistic psychology is in the end a regulatory technology as its concern with oppression avoids questioning the existing sociopolitical order. The psychology of Carl Rogers—as appealing as it may have looked to many—never understood this blurred boundary between the social and the individual. Rogers never appreciated the ways that social power helped produce subjectivity/consciousness. A central point in educational psychology, thus, involves the power of the interaction between the individual and society, between macroregulatory practices and microregulatory practices. Thus, no matter what types of reforms are proposed in the discipline, if they don't eventually address these power dynamics then they will leave the regulatory status quo intact. In this context simply being learner-centered and focusing on the needs of the learner does not create an emancipatory educational psychology. Outside of these power concerns educational psychology consistently operates to support the regulation and control of various individuals.

In this context it is important to note that power doesn't only operate by denying individuals the "right" to engage in empowering activities. Power is often productive in that it produces particular forms of both things and people. For example, mechanistic educational psychology attempts to produce individuals who seek particular forms of regulation and control. Educational psychology's management of behavior in schools becomes more and more a technology of the self. As in *hegemony* operating at the macrolevel, students via psychological techniques are induced to regulate themselves, to grant their consent to the status quo. Of course, just like hegemony such regulatory strategies can be unsuccessful with particular individuals and groups. On the other hand, it can be (and has been) wildly successful.

Since educational psychology has been the dominant disciplinary discourse shaping schooling over the last century, education has been profoundly shaped by the regulatory power described above. Such power has promoted the dominance of patriarchy, whiteness, and class elitism and the ways of seeing and being they promote. One encounters these power inscriptions in the educational psychology validated teaching methods, classroom management procedures, content standards, official lesson plans, and testing procedures found in contemporary schools. Mary Frances Agnello extends this theme in her chapter here as she traces the impact of educational psychology on the control of teachers' work. Indeed, such control has never been stronger than in the middle of the first decade of the twenty-first century. As Mark Garrison points out in his chapter, the words measure, measures, or measurement can be found at least 135 times in the No Child Left Behind legislation. Every dimension of life in schools has been subjected to the testing technologies of educational psychology in the twenty-first century, in the process leaving nothing to chance. Mechanistic regulation has become more powerful than ever.

The authors of this handbook are deeply concerned with these power-driven regulatory dimensions of educational psychology. Sandra Racionero and Rosa Valls, for example, argue in their chapter that the social decontextualization of the mechanist paradigm assures that existing power relations are maintained and dominant culture continues to be viewed as superior to all others. In his compelling chapter on educational psychology in South Africa, J. E. Akhurst writes that during apartheid mechanistic educational psychology helped produce a theory of "deviance" where the "culturally different" learner was viewed as a dangerous person who was capable of challenging the dominant (white) culture. Teachers were induced to identify and "reorient" such young people. Not unlike their contemporary U.S. counterparts, South African educators under apartheid were given preconstructed syllabi to follow that were tied to carefully inspected textbooks. Administrators would not tolerate teacher divergence from this official curriculum and monitored teacher behavior via the administration of a system of standardized tests.

Only a multidisciplinary psychology with social, economic, cultural, political, and philosophical dimensions will help educational psychology come to understand its oppressive dimensions. In this context educational psychologists will come to understand that the content of the curriculum holds dramatic consequences and is not simply background noise to the brain activity under study. Analyzing the political implications of particular ways of thinking about educational psychology is not an outsider interruption to the "real work" of the discipline. Such analysis is central to the very purpose of studying cognition, selfhood, learning, and teaching in the first place. In particular, teachers, students, and the public need to understand these broader dimensions of the work of educational psychology so they can evaluate how democratic and just the discipline's influence on teaching and learning actually is. The power of decontextualized, allegedly nonpolitical ed psych has dominated those around it for far too long.

MECHANISTIC VICTORIES: HARD SCIENCE GRANTS US THE "TRUTH" ABOUT THE HUMAN MIND

Thus, mechanistic psychology won victory after victory over more interpretive varieties, in the process securing the right to shape both educational psychology and school practice. Deploying the metaphor as human as machine, educational psychology promoted mind as a mechanism of mystery that operated in its own particular manner. Finding its philosophical roots as far back as Plato, mechanistic educational psychology organizes the world according to similarities and differences among phenomena as well as cause and effect relationships. This mechanism or philosophical realism runs through behaviorism and contemporary cognitive science. In contemporary mainstream ed psych, the mechanistic metaphor of choice is the mind as computer.

What began in the mid-twentieth century as an effort to employ computers as a means of mimicking the workings of the mind ended up describing the human mind as a computer. In effect, a method for making sense of the mind transmogrified into the end product, manifesting in the process both a flawed form of reasoning and a reductionistic understanding of humanness and the cognitive process. As Leila Villaverde puts it in her chapter on memory and educational psychology, "The world and human beings were believed to mimic machines and the object was to focus on the discreet parts of the larger operating system." The parts of the system worthy of note in this context involved the ways the brain encodes, stores, and retrieves data. Learning in such a context, she concludes, became characterized by rote and recall.

With its focus on obtaining scientific legitimacy, mechanistic educational psychology forged ahead with its lab studies and explorations of animal learning. Hard science—as in biology, chemistry, and physics—was viewed as sitting at the head of the scientific table. We are the *men* of science and our way of seeing the human mind is the only valid and worthwhile one, the mechanists proclaimed. Mary Frances Agnello captures this spirit well in her chapter in this volume when she contends that mechanists believed that mental activities were ordered by the same system of laws as those Sir Isaac Newton attributed to the physical universe. These ways of seeing dominated the field for decades, dispelling most challenges with a wave of the wand of hard science.

Since Thorndike convinced the field that Dewey's interpretivist concerns were irrelevant in the second and third decades of the twentieth century, it was only in the 1970s and 1980s that situated cognition began to make inroads into the mechanistic playground. Deborah Brown tells us in her chapter in this volume on action research that significant progress was made in questioning mainstream assumptions at the Institute for Research on Teaching at Michigan State University during the last three decades of the twentieth century. When this work was combined with a variety of expressions of sociocognition, critical pedagogy, reconceptualized curriculum theory, cultural psychology, feminist critiques of developmentalism, and critical educational psychology, the foundation for a new conversation in educational psychology was constructed.

This is not to say that a new paradigm emerged or that the victories of the mechanistic perspective were reversed. In the middle of the twenty-first century mechanism still rules the ed psych roost and with the help of governmental initiatives such as No Child Left Behind is gaining renewed power in many venues. Operating as if mechanistic and reductionistic scientific practices have never been challenged, many proponents of contemporary mechanistic educational psychology assume that there is only one way of viewing phenomena such as cognition or intelligence. Of course, this holds profound consequences when students—often from the social, cultural, and economic margins—are judged to be deficient or incapable of productive thinking or activity. Far too often such deficiency is nothing more than a way of operating that falls outside the purview of the mechanistic imagination. An *epistemological* pluralism, a diversity of paradigmatic perspectives, is direly needed in mainstream educational psychology for both catalyzing the advance of the discipline as well as saving "different students" from the label of "failure" and the justification of their marginalization. The editors and authors of this handbook believe that it is more important than ever to challenge the victories of mechanism.

MECHANISTIC PSYCHOLOGY AND NAÏVE REALISM

The great cognitive psychologist Jerome Bruner uses the phrase "empty mechanism" to describe the decontextualizing, individuating educational psychology that has resulted in universal pronouncements about the nature and development of the human mind. (See Lise Bird's powerful chapter on developmental appropriateness in this context.) The naïve realist epistemological stance of the mechanistic position unquestioningly believes that its findings are

- transhistorical and transcultural truths
- descriptions of the mind that correspond to a natural reality
- political neutral pronouncements about the psychological world (see Kenneth Gergen [1997]).

Even when particular scholars such as Jean Piaget operated outside the mechanistic context, the naïve realism of field induced educational psychologists to discount such transgressions and emphasize the most reductionistic dimensions of such work (see Burman [1994]). The reasoning of the mechanistic paradigm is universalistic, unhampered by those pesky differences of culture. Thus, the unquestioned epistemological assumptions of mechanism tacitly shaped what aspects of the mind psychologists could or could not see. And this is one of the key points of this handbook: structures, unseen and ignored by mainstream psychology, have profoundly shaped what passes as our knowledge of the subject matter of educational psychology.

In his own brilliant way John Dewey in *How We Think* in 1933 exposed the deficiencies of an epistemology of naïve realism. Such a form of empiricism, he contended, leads to "mental inertia, laziness, [and] unjustifiable conservatism." In psychology such a lack of rigor, albeit in the name of hard science, induces scholars to invent "fantastic and mythological explanations" for cognitive processes. Thus, inventions such as Spearman's "g"—the internal force that propels mental ability—or IQ or multiple intelligences are assumed to be "real." In this process belief in such scientific phantasms becomes disciplinary dogma and the rigor of subsequent research and theorizing is actually subverted. In the end we are not nearly as smart as we think we are as scientific and rational beings. With the help of this naïve realism the heart of psychology was extracted and consumed in the ritual of modernist science.

Thus, we come to the more fallible and tentative psychology of interpretivism. We begin to see that all psychological assertions are interpretations of a complex reality and that those who articulate a view of the mind with the claim of truth are victims of the sirens of realism and *positivism*. Such truth mongers fail to discern the social, cultural, discursive, epistemological, and ideological construction of our sense of reality. Naïve realism/positivism in this context fails to account for the fact that all entities are parts of larger processes that change over time. Mechanistic psychologists caught in the trap of these epistemological webs do not understand that when we view particular psychological phenomena in light of different contexts, we may see them in entirely new ways. Indeed, the supply of such contexts is infinite.

In the practice of mechanistic educational psychology the belief that experts have developed the proper *way* to view psychological phenomena, the proper space from which to observe them becomes quite problematic when considered in relation to the infinite supply of observational contexts (see Bredo [1994]). Let's think of intelligence from a 487th contextual perspective. Using research techniques such as factor analysis to reduce the complexity of a wide array of variables to a few ostensibly related ones, mechanistic educational psychologists find "the answer," or at least "correlations." As with Richard Herrnstein and Charles Murray (1994) in their best-selling *The Bell Curve*, fancy methodological footwork turns correlations between African-Americans and low IQ scores into attributions of causality and truth. Statistical correlations between African-Americans and low IQ scores are magically transformed into genetic inferiority and is the cause of African-Americans' low intelligence. If it didn't serve to hurt so many people, such an assertion would be humorous. This is where we begin to discern the tragedy of the naïve realism of mechanistic educational psychology.

With these naïve ways of seeing so firmly implanted in educational psychology, numerous practitioners in the field find administering tests, determining academic grade levels, and assessing the developmental progress to be their main activities. Depending upon their scores and levels, students will be directed to particular vocations and life paths—I was told I should be a piano tuner because I was not "academic material" but had an interest in music. If such practitioners of ed psych come to question the validity and effects of their tests and measurements, they often do so on their own initiatives—few who taught them ask social and political questions of the process. Without such hard questions and without monkey wrenches thrown into the gears of such mechanisms, the poor and marginalized will continue to be relegated to unchallenging and unrewarding life paths while the socioeconomically privileged will assume the good jobs and interesting pursuits. These privileged students will continue to succeed in education and will learn the predigested knowledges of schooling because they have been assured that there is a future benefit to learning such material. Such students are not "smarter" than their less privileged peers; they simply have a different social relationship to school and its role in their lives.

Certainly one of the most important dimensions of mechanistic educational psychology involves the dismissal of the importance of studying psychological phenomena in social, cultural, political, economic, and philosophical context. We see the results of such dismissal in the examples previously provided. Buoyed by this contextualization, thinking can no longer be viewed as a mere individual computational process. As Dewey argued, such a mechanistic perspective demeans the complex nature of thought. Thought is not simply a procedure that follows rules and instructions. Even the most controlled bureaucrats can become brilliant rule benders and creative exploiters of the regulations they are given. They will learn to negotiate the demands of their bosses with the needs of their clients. Thus, their thinking is shaped by numerous forces that must be encountered and dealt with in their immediacy.

These ideas about contextualization and the complexity of everyday cognitive activity are profoundly important as we consider the history of educational psychology. As psychology moved from behaviorism to cognitivism in the middle of the twentieth century, it worked to present a less passive view of the human. Yet, despite the effort, learning continued to be viewed as a mechanistic act with an end product of neat solutions to well-defined problems. In cognitivist-based educational psychology classes in teacher education, students were taught that learning was a technical, linear, and rationalistic process. Such students were induced to believe that teaching involved primarily the act of inputting data into the students' "processing mechanisms." Here it is translated into symbols, inserted into memory banks, and made ready for future usage. Though it was a reform movement, cognitivism adeptly retained the mechanism in mechanistic educational psychology. The mainstream scholarship and teaching of the discipline retains this mechanism in the twenty-first century.

THE ORIGINS AND PURPOSES OF INTERPRETIVIST PSYCHOLOGY

What I am calling interpretivist psychology is concerned with research into the meanings of human action and expressions as well as developing insight into beliefs about the self and the "other" in particular historical and cultural settings. In interpretivism's more critical guise it is also concerned with the social construction of the self and the ways discourses, ideologies, and other power structures help construct the meanings humans give to the world in ways that hurt particular groups and individuals. Over the last three centuries the roots of this interpretivist tradition can be traced to such thinkers as Vico, Lazarus, Wundt, the Russian school shaped by Leontiev, Luria, and Vygotsky, and the American pragmatists Peirce, James, and Dewey. John Dewey captured the spirit of interpretivism with his analysis of the two dimensions of learning theory. As Douglas Simpson and Xinoming Liu describe in their chapter on Dewey's contribution to educational psychology in this volume, the great pragmatist viewed learning theory from two angles—the micro and the macro.

In Dewey's formulation the micro perspective focused primarily on the student, while the macro focused on the teacher, other students and the more general environment that surrounds the student. In the micro-context Dewey connected the student's native appetites, instincts, and impulses to the general impulse to activity, thus constructing learning as a natural addendum to being a human being. This dimension of learning was then connected to places, subjects, ideas, emotions, and any other social dynamic that exerts an influence on the student. In this context Dewey maintained that learning always involved the student's interaction with the environment. The role of the teacher was to make sure that such interactions could develop in ways that would eventuate in personal, social, and moral growth. Like Dewey scholars such as Lev Vygotsky and many others would focus on the continual interactions between biology and culture. In the case of Dewey and Vygotsky the message was clear: for educational psychology to become a rigorous, practical, socially responsible discipline, it would have to broaden its modes of analysis. As Patricia Whang maintains in her chapter in this volume, the field would have to broaden its "sources of influence."

In the 1970s and 1980s such broadening began to take place with the emergence of *situated cognition* and *complexity theory*. With these perspectives were combined critical pedagogy, multiculturalism, *postcolonialism*, and interdisciplinary approaches to research—an alternative knowledge base for educational psychology was taking shape (see Beth Blue Swadener and Kagendo Mutua's important chapter on decolonizing research in educational psychology). As Montserrat Castello and Luis Botella argue in their chapter, "Constructivism and Educational Psychology," the new paradigm of the discipline draws upon this knowledge base always focusing on the integration of the social and the cognitive. Such integration, they posit, allows educational psychologists to consider both individual representations and the social situations where education and cognitive activity occur. The editors and authors of this handbook believe that these perspectives can help make contemporary educational psychology a more emancipatory domain that helps teachers make education a more democratic form of social practice.

As Lois Shawver maintains in this volume, the old universal meta-narratives of educational psychology cannot survive the electronic hyperreality of fingertip knowledge. Faith in a Cartesian–Newtonian explanation of cognition cannot be maintained in the contemporary era. Indeed, informed by a bricolage of diverse, multidisciplinary knowledges, interpretivist educational psychologists of the twenty-first century know too much to perpetuate the status quo of the discipline. Drawing upon feminism and the post-discourses, interpretivists reject mechanism because they understand

- the connection of the knower to what is known—thus, there is no privileged vantage point to gain objective truth about human cognition.

- the necessity of side-stepping the mechanist tendency to decontextualize the subjects of research and the researcher from their sociohistorical context—thus, no individual activity exists in simple isolation.
- the impact of the psychologist's values on how he or she sees the world—the frames we bring shapes the knowledge we produce.
- the inseparable nature of language and data in the field—no psychological data is pure and objective.
- the elitist nature of the relationship between educational psychologists and the consumers of the knowledges they produce—psychological knowledge production must always involve a democratic dialogue between producer and consumers of information.

Such insights allow interpretivists the empowerment to free ed psych from its status as a "nonsocial social science." Operating on the multilogical, multidisciplinary terrain of interpretivism, scholars represented by the authors operating in this volume work to bring the psyche and consciousness back to center stage in the discipline. Always positioning this move in a variety of larger contexts, the editors and the authors work to view subjectivity in more complex frames than the automatic processes and quantitative constructs of the mechanists. It is Ray Horn's and my interpretation that mechanistic psychology has failed to construct a compelling description of what it means to be human. To describe cognitive processes without an understanding of the construction of identity and selfhood or devoid of insight into the nature of consciousness provides little help in the larger effort to make sense of human beings and their relationship to the processes of teaching and learning.

Mechanists, interpretivist educational psychologists maintain, have provided a cornucopia of fragmented information about the brain. In this process they have failed to carefully examine the larger theoretical dimensions of their mission. Such a failure has moved them to discern their goal as producing a final, fixed, universal notion of *the mind*—one that works as well today as it will in the year 2525 and in every sociocultural context. Psychological theorizing, interpretivists contend, should not involve such decontextualized, monological pronouncements nor should it be considered objective knowledge that can simply be transferred directly to practice. Knowledge production and usage are far more complex activities. Thus, interpretivists argue that educational psychologists have to start at the beginning and actually rethink what it is that we are trying to do in the first place.

THE INTERPRETIVIST RETHINKING OF EDUCATIONAL PSYCHOLOGY

Such a rethinking involves the difficult and long neglected task of asking what shapes our view of what a science such as educational psychology should be trying to accomplish. The goal is not, interpretivists argue, the attempt to gather pieces of the larger jigsaw puzzle of the mind so that one day we will know all there is about it. Instead, interpretivist educational psychology posits that we must expose the often-occluded background assumptions on which psychologists draw to help them shape their professional activities. The science of psychology found its roots in the common cultural, social, political, and philosophical assumptions of the historical epoch in which it developed. In this context there were unquestioned ways of seeing men and women, white people and those not considered white, the rich and the poor, the sexually "normal" and the sexually "deviant," the intelligent and the stupid, etc. Many find such insights very disturbing because of their exposure of the ways hard sciences reflect the biases and prejudices of their *Zeitgeists*. Indeed, they are disturbed by the disrespect for scientific authority such expose might foster.

Without this interpretivist expose, living human beings—in particular, students—will continue to be reduced to transhistorical and transcultural central processing mechanisms. In the mechanistic context culture and psychology were separated like roosters at a Balinese cockfight. With uncritical modes of sociological and anthropological analysis focused at the institutional level and mechanistic psychology focused at the technical level, there was no place for the interpretivists concerned with the interaction of the macro-meso-micro levels to go. Bricolage, offering a way out with its emphasis on interrelationship and multilogicality, displays a quest for different ways of knowing and inquiring. In the bricolage educational psychologists come to know diverse ways of being human—especially the subjugated ones—and employ them in their understandings of the divergent construction of humanness. In this way they will be more sensitive to multiple ways of being humane and intelligent. Such insights will subvert mechanistic psychological tendencies to certify one's own ways of thinking and being as the superior ones around which all others should be evaluated (see Elizabeth Tisdell's chapter on spirituality and interconnectedness in this volume).

Employing multicultural ways of seeing from subjugated and indigenous traditions and multiple methodological insights from a variety of schools of thought is central to the critical interpretivist rethinking of educational psychology. In the spirit of the bricolage a methodology such as phenomenology—long abandoned after the victory of behaviorism and technicist cognitivism—provides a way to bring the value of subjective human experience to the ed psych table. At the same time, hermeneutics—in Gestalt psychology a central analytical tool—can be resuscitated for great value in a critical interpretivist reconceptualization of educational psychology. Few analytical discourses could do more than phenomenology and hermeneutics to catalyze educational psychology's search for answers to questions about meaning, self-awareness, and the influence of social context. Such tools will help interpretivists focus their attention on issues of human dignity, freedom, power, authority, regulation, and social responsibility.

In their struggle to recast ed psych the interpretivists seek old and new ways to enhance their ability to contextualize humanness—as hermeneutics puts it, to see the discipline in light of numerous horizons. In this *modus operandi* history, cultural studies, linguistics, sociology, and communications to name just a few become requisite disciplines in the psychological bricolage—educational psychological studies. In this configuration educational psychology becomes a multilogical, interactive, ever-evolving, always in process pursuit where individuals and their relationships to each other and the world around them become central foci of professional attention. Human meaning making is seen here as inseparable from lived experiences and multiple contexts and can take place in the body as well as the head. Thus, the study of any psychological phenomenon cannot be removed from contexts in which they take place. The effort to study memory in a lab using human recall of nonsense syllables is misguided (see Villaverde and Berry in this volume). When framed outside issues of context, purpose, disposition, meaning, etc., the study of memory is a waste of time (see Smith [1998] for an expansion of these ideas).

EPISTEMOLOGY AND EDUCATIONAL PSYCHOLOGY

Let us pause to clarify the epistemological dynamics that are central to our paradigmatic concerns in this handbook. Epistemology is the branch of philosophy that studies the nature and production of knowledge. In the effort to understand why we view the world and ourselves in the ways we do, few disciplines contribute more than epistemology. Our epistemological assumptions, though we don't know they are there, are always working to shape our construction of the world and subsequently our actions in it. Naming and exposing epistemological assumptions is a central dimension of the critical interpretivist psychology explored in this volume. In this context we can better understand the importance of what Montserrat Castello and Luis Botella are telling us in their chapter on constructivism in this volume. Epistemological perspectives, they contend, provide psychologists with criteria to choose among competing theoretical perspectives. In a mechanistic paradigm epistemological questions are deemed irrelevant because knowledge is simply a representation of the world "out there," and as such is judged on the basis of its truth value. This is the end of the epistemological story in mechanism—there is no need to bother with further epistemological deliberations.

Interpretivists, however, are not so lucky. They struggle with the relationship between knowledge and the world around us. They understand that the arguments we make cannot be separated from the epistemological positions we accept both consciously and unconsciously. Simply put, mechanistic educational psychology has tacitly accepted a correspondence epistemology—a naïve realism as we labeled it above—that asserts that there is a single reality that can be discovered via the Cartesian–Newtonian scientific method. Viewing epistemological issues as much more complex, interpretivist educational psychologists see this correspondence perspective as dangerous and misleading. With this in mind interpretivists seek to expose the ways ideology shapes our view of the world, language tacitly constructs it, and sociohistorical context renders certain views natural and others unnatural. (See Stephen Brookfield's important chapter, "The Ideological Formation and the Oppositional Possibilities of Self-Directed Learning," for insight into the effect of ideology in this domain.)

Thus, mechanism's correspondence and interpretivism's constructivism move the differing paradigms to adopt divergent metaphors to ground their psychological labors. Because of this they ask different questions about the mind and selfhood and construct varying interpretations of cognitive activities. Knowing this, John Shotter (1993) argues that mechanistic psychology promotes the idea that

Everything intelligent we do involves a "cognitive process" working in terms of "inner" mental representations of the "external" world, and that the way to study such processes is by modeling them in computational terms. (73–74)

Shotter believes that the miscalculations of correspondence epistemology will lead to the destruction of the dominance of mechanism. More and more scholars will come to see the ways mainstream mechanistic psychologists have misled themselves. What they have labeled as intelligence and set out to measure with great pomp and precision is less a "real" entity that corresponds to the external world than a human construction that resonates with the cultural beliefs and social needs of people operating at a particular time and in a specific place.

From the mechanist perspective the constructivist epistemology of interpretivism is relativistic. If we do not establish a strict correspondence between truth and external reality, mechanistis argue, interpretivists will be unable to discern between truth and falsity (see Thayer-Bacon [2000]). Interpretivists deny this charge, maintaining that psychologists can develop criteria for developing interpretations of the psychological world that fall neither into relativism or some form of correspondence absolutism. If educational psychologists accept a correspondence epistemology, knowledge becomes a warehouse of representations. Cognition becomes an act of ordering these representations. Teaching in this epistemological context becomes a process of efficiently transferring true knowledge into students' brains. When the representations in minds of students match those of the teacher, learning has taken place.

Thus, knowledge for mechanists consists of elements and factors (things-in-themselves)—knowledge for interpretivists involves complexes and contexts and their relationships. Such epistemological distinctions hold profound implications for pedagogy. As Cynthia Chew Nations argues in her chapter in this handbook, in the mechanistic framework the teacher becomes the source of students' knowledge of elements and factors. In a more constructivist interpretivist model, she continues, teachers create active learning environments where students learn to think critically. In a critical constructivist context thinking critically involves coming to understand the complexes, contexts, and relationships that shape the lives of diverse individuals. Knowledge in a critical interpretivist epistemology no longer simply resides in textbooks and students' brains. Instead, critical interpretivist knowledge is always being constructed, always being produced in the interaction of perspectives generated in diverse contexts. As learners examine these diverse knowledge constructions and their relationships to one another, they begin to aspire to a higher domain of cognitive thought. The process of moving to these higher levels of thinking is a powerful and exciting activity. Its promise of new insights about self and world motivate me to engage in this work on educational psychology.

MOVING TO A NEW EPISTEMOLOGICAL TERRAIN

Many scholars have argued over the last three or four decades that a correspondence epistemology promotes a misleading portrait of the process of recognition. Recognition does not consist of simply comparing two pictures with one another. The process is much more complex, as illustrated in human beings' recognition of emotional feelings, justice, and genius. One does not hold a picture of genius up to what he or she is observing in the lived world—other types of thinking are operating in this context. The individual here is producing situated and implicit knowledges that help him or her interpret the nature and meaning of the phenomenon he or she is encountering. Thus, a simple correspondence-based test cannot be used in such situations to determine if the observer has accurately represented reality.

Jeanette Bopry in her chapter on Francisco Varela extends this epistemological point. This correspondence dynamic, she asserts, does not help us understand the way dogs perceive the world. Dogs' ways of constructing the world is very different from humans but is not "wrong." Such a reality implies that there are numerous ways of making sense of the world that work for the individual or animal that constructs them. Perceptions emerge when cognitive systems interact with the environmental context surrounding them. Bopry adeptly articulates this point: "My description of a sunset is not a description of an external phenomenon as much as it is a description of my own visual field." Thus, knower and known are eternally joined together, as no constructions of reality can be made without the presence of both mind and environment.

In this context we can clearly understand the epistemological foundations on which interpretivism rests. The interaction/connection between the individual and culture and the knower and the known is central to an understanding of the learning process. Indeed, the cultural system of which one is a part profoundly shapes the ways one thinks, the ways one constructs the world around oneself. Because of the diversity of such contexts and the infinite ways they shape cognitive behavior, mechanistic efforts to generate universal general laws are futile. Guided by a constructivist epistemology, interpretivists view cognition as a contextually specific, interactive, ever-evolving process in which the person both constructs and is constructed by the various contexts enveloping him or her.

Operating on this new epistemological terrain, interpretivists understand they must be better scholars than those who preceded them in educational psychology. They must gain an interdisciplinary understanding of the cognitive process. (See Lara Lee's chapter, "Reconnecting the Disconnect in Teacher–Student Communication in Education," on the role of communications in an interdisciplinary educational psychology.) In this context they enter the bricolage, making use of diverse disciplinary tools and perspectives to gain a deeper and thicker view of these complex social, cultural, economic, political, philosophical, and psychological dynamics. Such insights dramatically reorient our pedagogical understandings, as we are empowered as scholar-teachers to discern the ways particular students in specific circumstances construct their own meanings of academic experiences (see Alison Cook-Sather's chapter "Recognizing Students among Educational Authorities"). Contrary to the pronouncements of many, such epistemological/cognitive understandings do not simply *dictate* our pedagogical strategies—instead, they *inform* them. One can still use a wide variety of teaching methodologies in light of such knowledge. Teachers by no means are condemned to teach the same way.

If we understand that learning takes place in context and in process, then we begin to appreciate the impact of the prior knowledge students bring to a classroom on the learning process. Many boys coming from working-class backgrounds, for example, may carry with them to school an understanding of academic work as an effeminate pursuit. Such prior knowledge plays a dramatic role in shaping their disposition toward learning. An educational psychologist or a teacher who does not know this operates at a severe disadvantage. Sandra Racionero and Rosa Valls in their chapter on dialogic learning are well aware of such dynamics and maintain that teachers who understand them focus more attention on the nature and needs of the learner. This moves pedagogy away from the mechanistic focus on the teacher as the "unique agent in the teaching–learning process." Again, such insight does not dictate pedagogical method. To focus on the nature and needs of the learner does not mean that teachers do not ever confront students with bodies of knowledge. There is still much analysis to do on just what it means to be more attentive to the nature and needs of the learner.

To be attentive to the nature and needs of the learner in a critical interpretivist sense does not mean that we focus our attention on natural and ready-made students. It also does not mean that we attend to the learner so we can "normalize" him or her—fit him or her to the needs of dominant institutions. Here is where critical interpretivists have to be very careful. We can develop the most child-centered pedagogies possible that not only focus our attention on the nature and needs of the learner but allow the learner to produce his or her own knowledge about the world. If such knowledge is not problematized, subjected to ideological, discursive, and cultural analysis, then we may empower students to become hegemonized by the needs of the dominant culture. While critical interpretivists most definitely want students who actively participate in the world, we also want students with the ability to ask hard questions of the knowledges they encounter and even the knowledges they produce. Such a goal requires even more of the teacher who must understand the nature and needs of the student in a larger sociocultural and political context. Such a teacher must always be aware of the political consequences of particular epistemologies, psychologies, and pedagogies.

MECHANISM AND THE CENTRAL PROCESSING MECHANISM

With these epistemological understandings in mind one is better equipped to understand how mechanistic educational psychology has come to "believe in" a central processing mechanism (CPM). Indeed, the primary task of such a paradigm is to delineate the nature of this hidden mechanism and how it operates. To study it mechanists must remove it from everything else and then in its isolation delineate exactly how it represents the real world, categorizes the different aspects of the world, draws on stored memories, learns, etc. This mechanism stands apart from everything on which it operates and must be described in this way—the focus is on its universal properties. The capacity or efficiency of this CPM is what mechanists claim to be measuring when they administer psychological tests. Of course, the problem is that since we don't have any clear understanding of what the CPM is and little understanding of what exactly constitutes its high-level and efficient operation, then we're not exactly sure what such tests are measuring. When we bring our epistemological insights to bear in this situation, we can uncover further confusion about the relation of the CPM to social, cultural, political, economic, and philosophical context.

Mark Garrison in his chapter on psychometrics extends these observations, maintaining that there is an irrational dimension to the measurement work of mechanistic psychology. Garrison contends that the psychometric project can be better understood as a political theory that attempts to assign worth to human beings. A key aspect of its operation as a political theory is that it constantly argues that there is nothing political about its operations. In this context it can be understood as a conservative political theory that attempts to assert the just nature of the status quo. Mechanistic psychology in the work of psychometrics claims that it facilitates the efficiency of the democratic sociopolitical process that allows people of superior intellect to attain power. Psychological tests become more important in the mechanistic context than an individual's real-life performance. If I illustrate great intellectual achievement, for example, but my IQ is low, my worth as an intelligent, high-functioning person can be diminished by the label "overachiever."

The results of psychometric tests speak with the voice of scientific authority. They move through psychometrics to education where they are accepted as the final truth about psychological issues and the worth of individuals. "This student who scored low on the aptitude tests," mechanists tell us, "is not college material." Using this narrow, brain-centered, test-driven view of the quality one's CPM, mechanistic educational psychology assures us that individuals who don't receive their blessing in the form of high-test scores simply are incapable of learning. They must be relegated to the dustbin of society. It is a powerful political theory that can make such decisions with the imprimatur of scientific authority. Yet, it is grounded on a house of epistemological cards, for it applies numerical values to objects that Mark Garrison maintains do not even have a referent in a constructed real world. Even if we assume the truth of a correspondence epistemology, we still don't know the nature of the CPM.

Jerome Bruner, one of the most important interpretivist educational psychologists of the last third of the twentieth century and the first decade of the twenty-first century, rejects the notion of a CPM, asserting that the field should look instead for "cultural amplifiers" of cognition. Bruner wants to know what situations and contexts help us think better and more clearly and how do we bring them into the educational process. In the psychometric approach the focus of measurement of the CPM is pursued to the exclusion of other dimensions of intelligence. In many ways it might be described as a psychology of nihilism, as it assumes that nothing that can be done to improve the intelligence of those with low IQ. Even such elusive constructs as creativity, Jane Piirto argues in her chapter in this volume, have been addressed by psychometrics. In such a process our understanding of creativity—like intelligence—has been undermined. In this conceptual context Julia Ellis's chapter, "Creative Problem Solving," provides educational psychologists and teachers with both a powerful theoretical insight into creativity as well as a masterful microanalysis of practical ways of integrating such understandings into classroom practice.

HURT: MECHANISTIC PSYCHOLOGY AND THE DEFICIT MODEL

In its roles as the purveyor of truth about the workings of the brain and the great social regulator, mechanistic educational psychology has often unleashed great harm on children. George Dei and Stanley Doyle-Wood in their chapter in this volume make this point dramatically when they illustrate the ways mechanistic ed psych helps create a "deep curriculum" of Eurocentrism that many times forces minority students into a "disembodied silence." Indeed, students whose abilities and selfhood are dismissed by the mechanists are hurt badly. This is one way that student subjectivity is produced, as countless students learn from the deep curriculum that they are "stupid." Over the last thirty years I have interviewed numerous students who have clearly learned the most important lesson of mechanistically driven schools: they are not capable of doing academic work.

In the mechanistic context many psychologists teach teachers that not all students can learn. This is the deficit model of psychology and pedagogy that undermines so many young lives. The academic and social failure that results from such oppressive assumptions, Kathryn Herr writes in her chapter on problem teens, is viewed as a personal failing. Mechanistic psychology's personalization of failure is viewed outside of any larger social or cultural context and then is used to construct a crisis of youth. In this context Herr describes the growth industry of "kid fixing" with its emphasis on different types of intervention for different categories of young people. For middle-class children/youth with health insurance, therapy is offered; for poor and minority young people prison is the solution of choice.

Picking up on Herr's insights, Scot Evans and Isaac Prilleltensky insist in their chapter, "Literacy for Wellness, Oppression, and Liberation," that educational psychologists in this context should avoid "psychologizing problems and victim-blaming approaches." Such approaches illustrate yet again the decontextualizing tendencies of mechanistic psychology, as they substitute individual remedies for larger social problems. Evans and Prilleltensky maintain that psychologists must learn how social violence is manifested in the lives of individual young people. Such a task is difficult, however, in a field that is obsessed with labeling and categorizing children and young people. Recognizing such troubling disciplinary tendencies, Beth Blue Swadener and Kagendo Mutua in their chapter, "Beyond Schools as Data Plantations: Decolonizing Education Research," maintain that an interdisciplinary field of educational psychology must not be used to pathologize young people and their families. In the contemporary neoliberal culture of labeling and assessment, Swadener and Mutua insist, many educational psychologists and school leaders simply ignore the way in which categories of child and youth pathology and "risk" are socially constructed.

In the pathologizing and victim-blaming deficit model of contemporary educational psychology, the hurtful practices of the mechanistic approach to the discipline can be seen in crystal clarity. Indeed, the reasons young people fail rest as more in the social, philosophical/epistemological, cultural, economic, and political configurations of the society than in his or her individual deficiencies. How is failure defined? How is aptitude constructed? What is the process by which success gains its meaning in diverse cultures? As interpretivist educational psychologists operating in the multidisciplinary bricolage attempt to answer these questions, we begin to understand the complex ways in which such meanings gain widespread acceptance. I would maintain that the effort to understand the origins of a deficit psychology and its influence in the twenty-first century cannot be understood outside of a larger historical understanding of race and class politics in macro- and micro-contexts.

MACRO-HISTORICIZATION: THE IMPORTANT "RECOVERY" ROLE OF MECHANISTIC PSYCHOLOGY

The mechanistic victim bashing of the late twentieth and early twenty-first century can be better understood as a part of a larger reactionary sociopolitical impulse of the era. Though it seems far away and detached from contemporary psychological practice, the context constructed by the last 500 years of European colonialism in the world is central to our understanding of present practices. After centuries of exploitation the early twentieth century began to witness a growing impatience of colonized peoples with their sociopolitical, economic, and educational status. A half millennium of colonial violence had convinced Africans, Asians, Latin Americans, and indigenous peoples around the world that enough was enough. Picking up steam after World War II, colonized peoples around the world threw off colonial governmental strictures and set out on a troubled journey to independence. The European colonial powers, however, were not about to give up such lucrative socioeconomic relationships so easily. With the United States leading the way, Western societies developed a wide array of neocolonial strategies for maintaining many of the benefits of colonialism. This neocolonial effort continues unabated and in many ways with a new intensity in an era of transnational corporations and the "war on terror" in the twenty-first century.

Though most Americans are not aware of it, the anticolonial rebellion initiated the liberation movements of the 1960s and 1970s that shook the United States and other Western societies. Indeed, the civil rights movement, the women's movement, the anti-Vietnam War movement, the Native American rights movement, and the gay rights movement all took their cue from the anticolonial struggles of individuals around the world. For example, Martin Luther King wrote his dissertation on the anticolonial rebellion against the British led by Mohandas Gandhi in India. King focused his scholarly attention on Gandhi's nonviolent resistance tactics, later drawing upon such strategies in the civil rights movement.

By the mid-1970s a conservative counterreaction—especially in the United States—to these liberation movements was taking shape with the goals of "recovering" what was perceived to be lost in these movements (see Gresson [1995]). Thus, the politics, cultural wars, and educational and psychological debates, policies, and practices of the last three decades cannot be understood outside of these efforts to "recover" white supremacy, patriarchy, class privilege, heterosexual "normality," Christian dominance, and the European intellectual canon. They are the defining macro-concerns of our time, as every topic is refracted through their lenses. Any view of educational psychology, curriculum development, or professional education conceived outside of this framework ends up becoming a form of ideological mystification.

Mechanistic educational psychology is enjoying contemporary success in its testing and labeling functions in part because it plays such an important role in "recovering" what was perceived to have been lost in the anticolonial liberation movements. One of the psychological dimensions of what was perceived to be lost was the notion of Western or white intellectual supremacy. No social mechanism works better than intelligence/achievement testing to "prove" Western supremacy over the peoples of the world. Psychometricians operating in their ethnocentric domains routinely proclaim the intellectual superiority of Western white people. Richard Herrnstein and Charles Murray, for example, in their best-selling book, *The Bell Curve*, write unabashedly that the average IQ of African peoples is about 75. The fact that the concept of an intelligence test is a Western construct with embedded Western ways of understanding the world is never mentioned in this brash assertion. Thus, the contemporary psychological obsession with labeling, measuring, and victim blaming is concurrently a macro-historical, meso-disciplinary, and a micro-individual matter. Critical interpretivist educational psychologists cannot allow mechanistic reductionism to continue to subvert our understanding of the complexity of these issues.

FAILURE AND DIFFERENCE

The social dimension of the psychological process by which individuals are labeled failures is obvious. A political economy of aptitude exists that has to do with an individual's access to the psychological resources of the larger society—to Bruner's cultural amplifiers of cognition. How can we measure intellectual ability without taking into account an individual's or a group's access to such cultural tools? In light of the Eurocentrism and reductionism embedded in mechanistic ways of viewing the psychological realm, we begin to understand that those individuals labeled as failures are often social and cultural outsiders. Their difference from the white, male, upper middle/upper class, conformist mainstream is viewed as deficiency, irremediable incompetence. Without an educational psychology and a pedagogy that find insights in diverse traditions, epistemologies, worldviews, and macro-histories, these attributions of the failure of those different from the Eurocentric center will continue to rule the day.

As George Dei and Stanley Doyle-Wood contend in their chapter in this handbook, "we must all develop an anticolonial awareness of how colonial relations are sustained and reproduced in schooling practices." Since the macro always intersects with and shapes the micro, the power of colonialism and the neocolonialism of the twenty-first century is always embedded in the individual mind. Taking a cue from Dei and Doyle-Wood, critical interpretivists employ anticolonial knowledges and epistemologies in the effort to reconstruct educational psychology. Brenda Cherednichenko's insights in her chapter, "Teacher Thinking for Democratic Learning," extend these ideas into the everyday life of the classroom. In this context she writes that many teachers hold a cultural and socioeconomic class affinity with many of their successful students. As a result these are the chosen ones who are provided a "more complex, challenging, and intellectual curriculum." Because marginalized students lack access to the intellectual tools of high culture—Bruner's cultural amplifiers—they are deemed unworthy of help.

In the present era of standardized curricula and top-down content standards the pronouncements of Dei, Doyle-Wood, and Cherednichenko too often fall on deaf ears. In this conceptual context Sandra Racionero and Rosa Valls remind readers that when educational psychologists and teachers fail to consider difference, school culture takes on hegemonic purposes. In this hegemony of whiteness boys and girls from minority contexts realize that academic success demands that they give up their ethnic and cultural identities. Indeed, they must work to become as much like individuals from dominant cultures as possible. What is sad is that even such an effort doesn't assure them of acceptance and attributions of success in the scholarly domain. Delia Douglas expands these racial dynamics in her chapter on the everyday educational practices of white superiority.

Even after they jump though all the scholarly and advanced degree-mandated hoops, they often find that such certification is not enough. They must prove themselves again and again to those from the elite halls of racial, class, gendered, and ethnic privilege. Educational psychologists in a reconceptualized discipline can play a key role in researching the ways these hurtful dynamics manifest themselves in school setting, Scot Evans and Isaac Prilleltensky maintain in their chapter here. To accomplish such a goal, Evans and Prilleltensky conclude, educational psychologists must develop a sensitivity to power and structures of inequality. It is in this way that educational psychologists can help alleviate the suffering caused by equating difference with deficiency. In the context of these structures of inequality Rochelle Brock's two highly creative chapters on race and critical thinking expand our understanding of these dynamics.

CONSTRUCTING, SITUATING, AND ENACTING

Getting beyond the hurtful dimensions of mechanistic educational psychology demands much work and an engagement with the complexity of the discipline's domain of inquiry. The authors and editors of this handbook fervently believe such a move is possible. Numerous important breakthroughs in the last few decades have empowered critical interpretivists to move to a new terrain of educational psychology. In the next few sections of this introduction I will lay out one path to such a terrain. Via the understandings of constructivism, situated cognition, and enactivism, I believe that the field of educational psychology can be transformed. Drawing upon the insights generated from these discourses and interpreting them in the bricolage of multidisciplinary understandings, critical interpretivists can move to a domain that Ray Horn and I have described as postformalism. In no way do we proclaim that postformalism is the end of psychological history—of course not. We do suggest, however, it might suggest an important stop on our journey to a more just, power-sensitive, and scholarly rigorous articulation of educational psychology.

Our earlier epistemological analysis of constructivism lays the foundation for our critical interpretivist trek. Constructivist epistemology leads us to a vantage point where we begin to understand the interaction of individual and context as the construction of more a *process* than a *thing-in-itself.* As a process this individual-context interaction results more in an ever-changing mutual modification than an act of producing a "finalized something." Thus, individual and context are coconstructed, as they enter into a dynamic interactive process—the human being changes as does the environment in which he or she operates. Jeanette Bopry in her chapter here clarifies our understanding of this coconstructivism as she describes perceptions as emerging from the interaction of a cognitive system with its environment. This interaction in the language of complexity theory is labeled "structural coupling." Such a process, Bopry maintains, is recursive "in that changes in A triggered by B will trigger changes in B which will trigger changes in A." Tara Fenwick in her chapter draws upon her own important work in complexity theory to highlight these insights. The systems shaped by the structural coupling, she maintains, are inseparable as they create "a new transcendent unity of action and identities." Such insights hold profound implications for the future of educational psychology and pedagogy.

For example, the field of neuroscience, John Weaver writes in his chapter on "Neuropolitics," illustrates the biological and cognitive importance of structural coupling of the individual and the environment. Every neuron in the brain is constructed to engage in a particular activity. Yet, at birth, Weaver contends, all neurons can be employed to perform any task regardless of their predisposition. Thus, human beings are capable of creating new neural networks to facilitate their insight into the surrounding cosmos. Educational psychologists can make good use of this neuroscientific understanding to help teachers and students create new neural matrixes by exposing them to new and diverse ways of seeing the world. In many ways this is an amazing scientific insight in that it subverts mechanistic forms of cognitive essentialism that insist humans cannot "learn intelligence," that they cannot teach themselves to become smarter. Thus, structural couplings connecting students with diverse contexts and sociocultural processes produce neurological, cognitive, political, and ethical benefits. Critical interpretivists use this knowledge in their larger effort to reconceptualize educational psychology, in the process creating a psychology and subsequently a pedagogy of optimism and hope.

Thus, this educational psychology of optimism and hope focuses on the importance of these insights into the interaction of individual and context, the macro and the micro. As David Hung, Jeanette Bopry, Chee Kit Looi, and Thiam Seng Koh maintain in their chapter, "Situated Cognition and Beyond: Martin Heidegger on Transformations in Being and Identity," the whole is not made up of discrete things-in-themselves but is an interaction of intimately connected dynamics. The relationship connecting these entities, Hung, Bopry, Looi, and Koh posit, shapes the meanings they assume. No meaning exists outside of these interrelationships. Indeed, the mind is shaped by these structural couplings and cognitive activity comes to be understood in terms of this individual-contextual relationship and the coconstructive process that modifies both. Knowing in this configuration is always a social process seeking to interpret the meaning of diverse relationships. Teachers and learners in this complex process always know that there is no final interpretation. Epistemologically savvy, they realize that they must be humble for all of their interpretations are incomplete and flawed in ways not discernible in the present sociohistorical context.

In this interpretivist context, learning, Tara Fenwick in her chapter reminds us, is viewed as a "continuous invention and exploration, produced through the relations among consciousness, identity, action and interaction, objects, and structural dynamics of complex systems." Relationship in this domain takes on an importance previously unimagined in the psychological sciences. A quick return to some previously addressed concepts is appropriate in this context. Our previous discussion of epistemology and positivism's unquestioned acceptance of a naïve realism becomes very important in this context. Intimately connected to the positivist epistemology is a positivist *ontology* that views the world as a simplistic domain composed of things-in-themselves that lend themselves to precise empirical measurement. Such an epistemology and ontology allow psychologists and teachers to evade a confrontation with complexity and operate in the shadow of reductionism. Such naivete undermines the scholarly rigor of educational psychology, rendering acts of penetrating insight, contextual analysis, and interpretive genius irrelevant. Knowledge is produced by following positivist procedure not by analyzing phenomena in new contexts and as parts of unseen processes.

Psychologists who embrace these positivist epistemologies and ontologies study an objective world and its contents as isolated phenomena. In this naïve realist framework things-in-themselves wait around like belles at the ball for a knower to arrive and "discover" them via use of the correct research method. Such a system shapes not only the production of knowledge but the reception of knowledge as well. Naïve realism fosters the faith that knowledge discovery is the end of the research and learning process. After researchers, teachers, and students "know" one of these things-in-themselves, they have nothing more to learn. Thus, in this epistemological and ontological context the purpose of learning is to obtain the "truths" already certified and commit them to memory.

In the world of mechanistic psychology's naïve realism all of our work on the interaction of whole and parts, process, structural coupling, complexity, interrelationship, power, and justice is irrelevant to the real work of the discipline. Returning to Tara Fenwick's important contributions to these ideas, the interpretivist concerns laid out here set up the possibility of inspired human action. The more teachers and learners understand about the interactions of complex systems, the more empowered they are to participate in creative shared action. What I have referred to elsewhere as a "critical ontology" holds particular importance in this context. If we better understand the constructed, situated, and enacted nature of humans "being-in-the-world," then we appreciate that—in the words of Hung, Bopry, Looi, and Koh—we construct "the world by living in it."

Being-in-the-world demands that we constantly learn and interpret. Critical interpretivist educational psychologists take these ideas seriously as they attempt to better understand both the knowledge production and learning processes. These tasks cannot be performed rigorously and justly without engaging diverse and multiple levels of analysis. Scot Evans and Isaac Prilleltensky are helpful in their delineation of what these levels involve: "personal, interpersonal, organizational, community, and social." For teachers and students to learn, to develop a sense of democratic sensitivity and social justice, and to develop a satisfactory balance of a wide variety of needs, they must engage with all of these levels. It is disconcerting to note that mechanistic psychology, operating in its positivistic framework, excludes such interaction as an act of degradation to the sanctity of scientific work.

INTERPRETIVISTS DRAWING ON THE POWER OF SITUATED COGNITION

Critical interpretivists carefully study and learn numerous lessons from situated cognition which emerged in the 1980s as a challenge to mechanistic cognitivism. Led by psychologists such as Jean Lave and Etienne Wenger, situated cognition insisted that we would learn far more about the cognitive process if we focused more attention on practical forms of thinking found among everyday people in everyday pursuits. Such research is important on many levels, not the least of which it would help move such psychologists away from their obsession with the computer model of the human mind. In this context situated cognitivists examined on the cognitive processes of workers engaged in vocational pursuits around the world. In these imminently practical contexts situated cognitivists came to understand in great clarity the way that mechanistic educational psychologists had become obsessed with producing a model of the vehicle in which cognitive activity takes place, in the process missing the activity itself.

Central to the situated cognitivist position is the understanding that the cognitive activity always takes place in a community of practice. As Diana Ryan and Jeanette Bopry contend in their chapter, "Stakeholder-Driven Educational Systems Design: At the Intersection of Educational Psychology and Systems," community members develop ways of doing things that are mutually valued and in so doing, they learn from each other." Picking up on these situated cognitivist concerns, Hugh Munby, Nancy Hutchinson, and Peter Chin in their chapter on workplace learning and education posit that the concern with practical learning forces educational psychologists to rethink our notions of teaching, learning, and knowledge. After an encounter with situated cognition and its interest in how individuals learn in the workplace, we can never think about cognition in the same way again. Indeed, cognitive studies in the situated cognitivist configuration, Munby, Hutchinson, and Chin tell us, would be better off to focus its attention on practical forms of reasoning that eventuate in action (knowing how) rather than on theoretical reasoning that leads to the development of declarative knowledge (knowing that).

While this is a complex issue, after the work of the proponents of situated cognition one would think that only dyed-in-the-wool mechanists would unproblematically privilege the value of knowing that over knowing how. Yet, as Munby, Hutchinson, and Chin assert, there is a political economic dimension to these knowledges that exerts a profound impact on how they are represented and valued. The declarative knowledge of knowing that possesses a higher status in Western societies as it is associated with professions such as law and medicine. The professional curriculum for law and medicine, of course, is filled with data banks of declarative knowledge.

This is not to say that law and medicine don't require knowing in action—of course they do. Entry into the field, however, is patrolled by tests demanding particular forms of declarative knowledge. Thus, Munby, Hutchinson, and Chin insist that the question posed by situated cognition to students of educational psychology and pedagogy is profound: Is the schools' emphasis on declarative/decontextualized knowledge misguided? These are central questions for the field of educational psychology. Again, while there are no simple answers, the effort to address them leads us all to new insights into the nature of cognition and its relationship to teaching and learning. Critical interpretivists take these inquiries very seriously. Situated cognition obviously avoids privileging monological forms of declarative knowledge as the most important form of knowledge and its commitment to memory as the ultimate objective of the educational process.

As Hung, Bopry, Looi, and Koh describe it in their chapter here, situated cognition views knowing as a social process where learners seek to understand interrelated phenomena. Concurrently, these same learners, argue the proponents of situated cognition, have to understand their own historicity—their construction in a particular historical context—and the ways it shapes their multiple relationships to the learning process and what is being learned. Here the individual-context relationship is reconceptualized. The learner is no longer merely seen as operating in an environment; the person and environment join together as portions of coconstructed wholes. To separate them is to destroy them. Learning is embedded in these coconstructed wholes and emerges in the actions that occur in these contexts. The knowledge learned is not transmitted in some simple sense from teacher to learner. Again, critical interpretivists see no easy and obvious lesson about the nature of teaching to be derived from situated cognition. They do, however, find it to be essential knowledge for those attempting to design revolutionary new forms of educational psychology and pedagogy.

INTERPRETIVISTS DRAWING ON THE POWER OF ENACTIVISM

Picking up on the work of the Santiago school of cognitive theory, we now examine enactivism as an important contribution to the cognitive theoretical bricolage engaged by critical interpretivist educational psychologists. Embracing constructivism as their intellectual ancestor, Humberto

Maturana and Francisco Varela argue that the world we know is not pre-given but enacted. Thus, in the spirit of constructivism, they maintain that the act of cognition does not primarily involve the Cartesian effort to commit to memory "*mental* reflections" of the real world. Instead of attempting to reconstruct "true" mental reflections of the "real world," learners should focus on our actions *in relation* to the world. Observing the mind from biological and psychology perspectives, enactivists undertake the struggle to repair the damage unleashed by mechanism's reduction and fragmentation of the psychological world.

When we add enactivist insights to critical interpretivism's theoretical bricolage of critical theory/critical pedagogy, feminism, constructivism, and complexity theory, we gain a powerful theoretical recipe for a new educational psychology. As Erica Burman, Issac Prilleltensky, Valerie Walkerdine, Jerome Bruner, Jean Lave, Etienne Wenger, John Pickering, Ken Gergen, James Wertsch, Roy Pea, and many others have argued over the last few years in the spirit of Lev Vygotsky, cognition is a socially situated dynamic that always takes place in specific historical contexts. Enactivism profoundly contributes to the work of these scholars, contending that it is in this specific sociohistorical context that humans realize who they are and what they can become. A central contribution of enactivism involves its assertion that humans realize their highest cognitive abilities in specific everyday circumstances—in the enaction of cognitive activity in the lived world.

Francisco Varela argues that individuals engage in a higher order of thinking when they learn to utilize knowledge and feelings from a circumstance where particular ways of thinking and acting are deemed intelligent and transfer them to more complex situations where intelligent action is deemed ambiguous. Thus, intelligent behavior in an enactivist context does not involve a form of reasoning where universal rules are followed—divergent contexts will demand diverse modes of intelligence. In this context intelligent and even ethical action may seem logically contradictory to those operating at Piaget's *formal level of cognition*. Varela (1999) uses the Vajrayana Buddhist tradition's notion of "crazy wisdom" to denote someone who has learned to operate at the level of ambiguity and complexity. At another point in his work he refers to such abilities as "intelligent awareness." Teachers, educators, and educational psychologists who operate in the critical interpretivist framework perform their teaching and research with an appreciation of crazy wisdom and intelligent awareness.

In the enactivist frame we crawl outside the conceptual window and move into the postmechanistic psychological cosmos. In a biological context we come to understand that throughout the world of animals all beings possess knowledge that is constituted in the concrete situation. In this context we grasp Varela's (1999) point in *Ethical Know-How*: "What we call general and abstract are aggregates of readiness-for-action" (p. 18). This means that students don't manifest their intelligence simply by developing efficient mental file cabinets for storing data; it tells us that various knowledges are important as we discern their meanings and relationships and become empowered to use them in the improvisation demanded by particular circumstances. In an academic setting the particular circumstance might involve making an argument, defending a position, figuring out how to use knowledge of oppression to help an individual who is suffering, or a teacher struggling to deal with a student who is having difficulty in a math class.

Appreciating these enactivist insights educational psychologists and teachers are ready for another cognitive theoretical step forward. As we come to understand these enactivist concepts concerning the realization of our cognitive abilities in concrete circumstances, we return to the complex dynamics of self-production. In critical interpretivism the understanding of how the self is produced and how this process shapes how we construct the world becomes profoundly important. In modes of teaching and researching where this feature is omitted, nothing can be done to make up for the exclusion. Enactivism refuses to ignore the disjunction between what cognitive psychology has traditionally confirmed vis-à-vis our immediate experience, consciousness, or awareness of selfhood. At times in the recent history of cognitive psychology—for example, in behaviorism—scientists insisted that consciousness did not exist because it did not lend itself to empirical measurement. Other cognitive perspectives, while not denying its existence three times before the cock crowed, simply ignored it. Obviously, such approaches to consciousness, immediate experience, and awareness of selfhood left an unfillable theoretical hole in its wake. Why, Varela asks, do humans experience the self so profoundly? Just ignoring the hole will not make it go away.

Informed by enactivism we ask what is the nature of the disjunction between scientifically validated cognitive theory and our experience of consciousness. Operating on the grounding of our understanding of consciousness construction, we follow Varela's description of the emergent and self-organizing dimensions of selfhood, his notion of the virtual self. The emergent, virtual self arises out of a maze of relationships—in much the same way hermeneutics describes the emergence of meaning in the relationships produced by the hermeneutic circle. It has no definable CPM, no "brain command" where control is coordinated. Consider this cognitive dynamic in light of our understanding of the cultural politics of the construction of the self. Such a process operates to create new social, cultural, political, and economic relationships to produce new and more market-compliant, consumer selves. In this context we begin to understand the pedagogical implications of the emergent self. The self is infinitely more malleable, more open to change than we had previously imagined. Given one's motivation, of course, this dimension of selfhood can be mobilized for great benefit or manipulated for great harm.

Buoyed by these insights, we enter the arena with a new insight into what can be. We know that despite the power of generations of cognitive determinists operating under the flag of IQ, human beings can learn to become more intelligent. Individuals can *construct* their own intelligence in a supportive context. And in this context such people understand that selfhood is even more of a miraculous phenomenon than many had imagined. In the emergent context we gain a perspective; indeed, to live is to have a point of view. A critical teacher or researcher, however, gains numerous levels of understanding on the origins of his or her perspective.

Varela writes of a moment-to-moment monitoring of the nature of our selfhood. Such monitoring involves gaining meta-awareness of the various connections we make to diverse dimensions of the sociophysical world around us. It involves isolating and letting go of an egocentrism that blinds us to the virtual and relational nature of our selfhood. In a critical interpretivist educational psychological context it means avoiding those definitions of higher-order thinking that view it as an egocentric manifestation of the combative proponent of rationality. In the process we also elude the cultural and gender inscriptions such perspectives drag along with them. With these knowledges we are prepared for the struggle to reconceptualize educational psychology.

So critical interpretivists begin to play more focused attention to the ways complex systems display emergent properties by way of the interaction of simple elements. The structural couplings that develop in this interaction make possible such emergence. Thus, as Jeanette Bopry posits in her chapter on Varela, the human nervous system does not pick up information from the environment. Instead, it makes meaning, it interprets its interaction with its context. This is why enactivists assert that they don't see the external environment but their own visual field. To figure out the significance of what they see in their fields, human beings—according to the enactivists—must reach out to others for help. How do my perceptions mesh with the perceptions of others? As Bopry puts it, "we share a reality because we have cospecified it through the coordination of our actions with the actions of others." The development of a view of reality takes place in social interaction—such a view emerges from individuals talking to one another about what they see in their visual fields.

In Western societies our language constructs a view of worldviews and knowledge about the world as a "thing" that one deposits in the container of the mind. Thus, knowledge is viewed as something contained in vocabulary, written documents, databases, etc. Drawing on Varela and Bopry, critical interpretivists understand knowledge is too complex to be simply contained. Bopry puts it succinctly: "Within the enactive framework knowledge is effective action within a domain." Indeed, knowledge is always constructed (enacted) within a context. Thus, this enacted view of knowledge reshapes our view of intelligence. Intelligence is no longer equated simply with the ability to solve pre-given and well-structured problems. In an enactivist context it involves one's capacity to construct frameworks of understanding that resonate with and extend the insights of others. Bopry is quick to point out in this context that the networks created in this context do not have to be the same as everyone else's. There is room for disagreement and diversity of the worlds of understanding that human beings create. The key point is that the frameworks of insight different individuals create resonate, that is, it engenders thought and positive interchange among groups of interpreters.

Given our epistemological insights critical interpretivists understand that this enactivist understanding of intelligence with its frameworks of insight does not mean that intelligent people recover a pre-given, objective reality. Thus, as Varela insists, cognition is constructed not by representations of true reality but by embodied action in lived contexts. This means that the world is enacted, made in the everyday activities of human beings interacting with their environments. The everyday world of humans is a cosmos of situated individuals, perpetually having to devise their next steps in light of the contingency of the next moment.

Contrary to mechanistic psychological precepts, this ongoing configuration of what to do is not a rationalistic selection process among a pre-given smorgasbord of possible courses of action. It can more accurately be described as a never-ending improvisational performance in an ever-changing environment. Definitions of intelligence and even ethical action do not amount to much if they are merely abstract principles that are separated from the necessity of figuring out what to do in immediate situations. Outside of these immediate contexts definitions of intelligence, precepts for professional performance, and rules for ethical action become stale utterances and banal homilies of the cloistered scholastic. Such pronouncements like the seed of Onan fall on barren ground.

MOVING TO THE CRITICAL: POSTFORMALISM

Drawing upon the innovations delineated by the long tradition of interpretivism, the psychological work of John Dewey and Lev Vygotsky, cultural psychology, the paradigmatic analyses of Ken Gergen, constructivism, situated cognition, and enactivism, Shirley Steinberg and I have worked over the last fifteen years to develop a critically grounded foundation for educational psychology. Incorporating insights from feminist theory, African-American ways of seeing, *subjugated knowledges*, the ethical concerns of liberation theology, and a variety of critical theories from the Frankfurt School, Paulo Friere, and critical pedagogy to particular *post-discourses*, we have sought to provide a contemporary critical interpretivist educational psychology grounded on a multilogical version of scholarly rigor and a concern for social justice.

This postformalism also draws on the work of Jean Piaget, although parting company with him around the importance of the social and questions of the universality of Western science. Piaget's formal thinking implies an acceptance of a mechanistic worldview that is caught in a linear, reductionistic, cause–effect form of reasoning. Unconcerned with questions of power relations and the way they structure our consciousness, Piaget's "higher-order formal operational thinkers" accept an objectified, unpoliticized way of knowing that breaks a social, educational, or psychological system down into its component parts in order to understand how it works. Aggrandizing certainty and prediction, formal thinking organized certified facts into universal theories. The facts that do not fit into the theory are jettisoned, and the theory developed is the one best suited to limit contradictions in the knowledge produced. Thus, formal thinking operates on the assumption that resolution must be found for all contradictions. Schools and standardized testmakers, assuming that formal operational thought represents the highest level of human cognition, focus their efforts on its cultivation and measurement. Students and teachers who move beyond such cognitive formalism are often unrewarded and sometimes even punished in educational contexts.

Humble in their debt to the above-mentioned sociopsychological discourses, postformalists attempt to politicize cognition. In this context they attempt to remove themselves from the alleged universalism of particular sociopersonal norms and ideological expectations. The postformal concern with questions of meaning, emancipation via ideological disembedding, and attention to the process of self-production moves beyond the formal operational level of thought with its devotion to proper procedure. Postformalism grapples with purpose, focusing attention to issues of human dignity, freedom, authority, scholarly rigor, and social responsibility. Many have argued that postformalism with its bricoleur's emphasis on multiple perspectives will necessitate an ethical relativism that paralyzes social action. A critical postformalism grounded on an *evolving criticality* refuses to cave in to relativistic inaction. In this context postformalism promotes a conversation between critical theory and a wide range of social, psychological, and philosophical insights. This interaction is focused on expanding and constructing self-awareness, new forms of critical consciousness, and more effective modes of social action.

Thus, in the spirit of John Dewey and Lev Vygotsky postformalism is about learning to think and act in ways that hold pragmatic consequence—the promise of new insights and new modes of engaging the world. In this context students in postformal schools encounter bodies of knowledge, not for the simple purpose of committing them to memory but to engage, grapple with, and interpret them in light of other data. At the same time such students are confronting such knowledges they are researching and interacting with diverse contexts. They are focused on the process of making meaning and then acting on that meaning in practical and ethically just ways (see Sharon Solloway and Nancy Brooks' important chapter on postformalism and spirituality in this volume).

Postformal Thinking: Toward a Complex Cognition

Indeed, such students are becoming students of complexity and processes. Postformal students move beyond encounters with "formal" properties of subject matter. Cartesian logic and the mechanistic education it supported focused attention on the formal dynamics of defining subject matter, subdividing it, and classifying it. As Dewey put it in the 1930s in *How We Think*: in formal thinking and teaching "the mind becomes logical only by learning to conform to an external subject matter" (p. 82). The student in this context is told to meticulously reproduce material derived from arithmetic, geography, grammar, or whatever. The concepts of meaning making or use in context are irrelevant in the formal context. Thus, as complexity theory would posit decades after Dewey's work on cognition: objects in the rearview mirror are more complex than they may appear.

In the spirit of complexity postformalists understand that since what we call reality is not external to consciousness, cognition operates to construct the world. It is more important than we ever imagined (see Horn [2004]). Like cream in a cup of dark roast Columbian coffee, complexity theory blends well with Dewey's critique of formalism. Cognitive activity, knowledge production, and the construction of reality are simply too complex to be accomplished by following prescribed formulae. The reductionistic, obvious, and safe answers produced by formalist ways of thinking and researching are unacceptable to postformalists. What are the epistemological and ideological processes, postformalists ask, that operate to confirm such knowledge claims while disconfirming others? Understanding the pluralistic nature of epistemology, postformalists see beyond the one-truth reductionism of formalism. Understanding, for example, that there are many ways to define and measure intelligence moves postformalists to engage in a more rigorous analysis of such a phenomenon.

The procedure-based, decontextualized, epistemologically naïve formalist way of approaching educational psychology is the method of beginners not of seasoned, rigorous scholars. Just as physics and biology have retreated from formalist efforts to search for subatomic particles and genes as the ultimate organizational components of matter and life, psychologists of a postformal stripe see the mind less as a compilation of neurons and more of a complex set of processes operating in diverse contexts. Such reductionistic formalist obsessions emerge when research topics are dehistoricized and decontextualized. This is why postformalists are dedicated to the study of context. Without such contextualization Abraham Maslow's hierarchy of needs is put forth as a universal truth, just as relevant for a nineteenth-century woman in an isolated tribe in an Amazon rainforest as it is for Prime Minister John Howard in twenty-first-century Australia. Without postformalism's contextual intervention, Piaget's formal operational thinking becomes the standard for measuring the highest order of intelligence for African tribespeople in rural Namibia as well as for affluent students from the Upper East Side in New York City. Needs and concepts of higher-order thinking, once historicized and culturally contextualized, emerge as social constructions. It is hard to discern the footprints of social construction in the formalist haze.

Picking up on Tara Fenwick's delineation of experiential learning, postformalists deepen their appreciation of the importance of experience in the intersection of constructivism, situated cognition, and enactivism. Carefully examining the interaction of experiential learning in everyday contexts with particular critical theoretical insights, postformalism traverses a terrain of complexity leading to new insights about cognition and the forces that shape it. Respecting Fenwick's admonitions, postformalists refuse deterministic and elitist orientations that view individuals as "blind dupes" of social structures. Instead postformalists learn from people's everyday lived experiences, always appreciating the need to question anyone's experience—their own included—for the role power plays in refracting it. No experience—no matter the context in which it is embedded, no matter how "theoretically sophisticated" it is deemed to be—is free from the influence of power. Drawing on insight from experience in postformalism is always accompanied by the hermeneutic act of interpreting the meanings of such experience in light of particular contexts and processes. There is nothing simple about experiential learning in postformalism.

The postformal effort to deal with the complexity of experience is intimately connected to the previously discussed multilogicality of the bricolage. One of the central dimensions of this multilogicality involves the effort to overcome the monological limits of formalistic science and its companion, hyperreason. In this context postformalists point out the ways that mechanistic notions of intelligence and ability have dismissed the insights and contributions of the socially and economically marginalized and alternative ways of developing found in differing cultural contexts. Formalism's lack of respect for those who fall outside its boundaries is unacceptable in the contemporary world; in this context postformalism constantly pushes the boundaries of cognition and knowledge production with its emphasis on subjugated knowledges and indigenous ontologies. In postformalism complexity theory breaks bread with a literacy of power. In the process a powerful synergy is constructed that shines a new light on the field of educational psychology.

In postformalism critical social theory works in the trenches with diverse discourses in the process expanding our understanding of complexity and challenging critical theory itself. In this context critical theory sees itself in terms of an evolving criticality that is perpetually concerned with keeping the critical tradition alive and fresh. Such theoretical moves challenge educational psychology to ask how it is shaped by its own culture. Postformalism is the uninvited guest in the summer house of cognitive studies that keeps pressuring the discipline's elite to understand that mechanistic psychology is an ideology with devastating effects on those not in the country club of modernity. Pointing out that mechanism operates in the low-affect social world of naïve realism, postformalists chart its values of neutrality and amoral technicism. We keep politics out of psychology, psychometricians insist, and we just objectively measure human intelligence and that has nothing to do with the cultural realm. In a neosocial Darwinist era where survival-of-the-fittest perspectives find wide acceptance, these formalist educational psychologies once again provide justification for the failure of the socially, economically, culturally, and politically marginalized. Postformalism will not allow such reductionism to stand.

Postformalism, Complexity, and Multiple Perspectives

In this context postformalists turn their critical lenses on the complexity of the interrelationship between consciousness and culture. Culture makes personhood possible with the preexisting world it has constructed. Such a cosmos is made up of ideas, various constructions of the physical world, interpretations, linguistic structures, and emotional registers. Such dynamics are embedded in various social institutions, discursive practices, social relationships, aesthetic forms, and technologies. Individuals construct their lives with the assistance of these cultural inheritances—the concept of identity itself is meaningless without them. Thus, again the point needs to be made: the domain of psychology is more complex than it seems in the mechanistic portrayal. Any psychology, postformalists maintain, that claims predictive ability in the complexity of everyday life does not appreciate the complications of mind, consciousness, culture, and power.

For example, a mechanistic psychology that assumes IQ can predict the future academic performance of students and uses it in this way misses numerous important points of great relevance to postformalists. On one simplistic level there is a predictive element to IQ and academic performance, as long as particular conditions are held constant. As long as students do not learn about the social, cultural, political, and economic structures of both IQ testing and schools and schools continue to emphasize IQ test type skills, there is a correlation between test scores and academic performance. The assumption here is that students be kept in the dark about the panoply of forces that help shape their relation to the test. Thus, in order for this predictive dimension to work we must keep test takers as ignorant as possible about what exactly the test reflects about the relationship between the student and dominant culture.

When students are informed about these complex dynamics, they can begin to reshape that relationship. Also, the predictive dimension rests on the assumption that no curricular innovation will take place that will focus students' attention more on meta-understandings of curriculum and the construction of knowledge. As long as these dynamics are ignored and the curriculum is viewed as a body of previously produced truths to be committed to memory, then the logic behind both IQ and curriculum are similar. Students tend to act and react similarly to situations grounded on this formalist logic. When such formalist logic is challenged and more interpretive, complex, and activity-based cognition is demanded, the predictive dimension of IQ testing evaporates into the mechanistic mist.

Thus, questions concerning the predictive capacity of IQ and other forms of standardized testing are much more complex than mechanistic educational psychology has claimed. Thus, postformalists call for a far more complex understanding of the cognitive act as well as its measurement and evaluation. In the spirit of complexity postformalists promote the ability to both appreciate and deal with uncertainty and ambiguity. In this context they are aware of the underside of the mechanistic quest for certainty and the social and personal damage such a trek produces. Given the vast array of abilities human beings can possess and the infinite diversity of contexts in which to develop and apply them, the mechanistic tendency to label individuals as simply "intelligent" or "not intelligent" is an insult both to the field of psychology and the individuals affected by such crass labels.

Intelligence in the postformal articulation is *not* a description of the hereditary dimensions of the CPM and the efficiency of its operation. Understanding complexity, postformalists maintain that intelligence is more a local than a universal phenomenon. As such, postformalist intelligence involves diverse individuals responses to challenges that face them in light of particular contexts, access to cultural amplifiers, cultural capital, and particular tools and artifacts, specific values, social goals and needs, patterns of construction, linguistic dynamics, and traditions of meaning making. Thus, the postformal mind is shaped by specific contexts and is constructed by particular interrelationships in certain domains. It is enacted into existence—that is, it emerges as it acts in relation to these contexts and domains. Understanding the functioning of this mind is never certain and easy and measuring it in some quantitative manner is even harder. But that's okay, postformalists are comfortable with such complications in the zone of complexity.

Central to this postformalist appreciation of complexity is the general task of understanding both the situatedness of mind in general and our selves in particular. (See Wolff-Michael Roth's powerful chapter, "Situating Situated Cognition," on the nature of this situatedness of mind.) In this context we embrace our postformal humility because we come to appreciate just how limited by time and space, by history and culture our perspectives are. A scholar of any discipline would always be humbled if she had access to a time machine that allowed her to view scholars from the twenty-fifth century reading and commenting on her work. And hers was work that was deemed of sufficient quality to merit comment in 2477! This is one of many reasons that postformalists value the effort to seek multiple perspectives on everything they do. As I have argued previously in this introduction, the more diverse the experiences and the *positionalities* of those issuing the multiple perspectives the better. In the spirit of subjugated knowledges it is important to gain the views of individuals from groups that have been marginalized and dismissed from the mainstream scholarly process.

Thus, complexity demands that postformalists pursue multiple perspectives and multilogical insights into scholarly production. One dimension of such multilogicality involves tracing the developmental history of ideas. How was it shaped by tacit assumptions and contextual factors such as ideology, discourse, linguistics, and particular values? These dynamics are central tasks in postformal scholarship and pedagogy. Indeed, students' ability to understand the ways that ideas and concepts are constructed by a variety of forces and how power is complicit with which interpretations are certified and which ones are rejected is central to being a rigorous educated person. Of course, a central contention of postformalism is that hegemonic educational structures operate to undermine the presence of multiple perspectives in the school. Indeed, one of the most important goals of many of the educational reforms championed by right-wing groups in Western societies over the last few decades has been the elimination of such "dangerous" perspectives from the school. With the victory of these forces in the United States embodied in the appointment of George W. Bush to the presidency in 2000, policies based on these exclusionary practices have been institutionalized.

Thus, the multilogical goals of postformalism have suffered a setback. As George Dei and Stanley Doyle-Wood and Montserrat Castello and Luis Botella maintain in their chapters in this volume, educational psychology must realize the limitations and monologicality of traditional sources within the discipline. In this context Susan Gerofsky in her chapter on research in educational psychology writes of the need for interdisciplinarity to broaden the field's access to diverse perspectives. The point in all of these chapters fit into the postformalist critical interpretivist notion of the future of educational psychology. To move forward the field must see the psychological domain from outside of a white, Eurocentric, patriarchal, class elitist position. Some of the most important positions may be the ones with which mainstream educational psychology is the most unfamiliar. Employing these knowledges postformalism provides a way out, an escape from the ideological blinders of the mechanistic worldview.

Postformalism and the Basis for a Political Educational Psychology

In a hegemonized and colonized educational system the role of educational psychology becomes even more important than it has been—and it has historically played a central role in shaping educational policy and practice. Postformalism is deeply concerned with exposing the importance of mechanistic educational psychology and its real life consequences. As Ellen Essick points out in her chapter, "Gender and Educational Psychology," women are regulated via the "performance of femininity." Essick's powerful argument helps readers understand the way these politics of gender shape and are shaped by educational psychology. Taking a cue from Essick, postformalists call for a political educational psychology that studies not only the performance of femininity but also power-shaped performances in the domains of race, class, ethnicity, sexuality, etc.

Erica Burman's powerful chapter on the gendering of childhood extends these power and gender themes, as it traces the way they inform even the way we theorize the development of children. (In this context take a look at Nicole Green's fascinating account of the problems of mechanistic developmentalism in "Homeschooling: Challenging Traditional Views of Public Education.") In Burman's analysis of developmentalism, the child manifests cognitive development by embracing a masculine rationalistic gender model. In this same manner mechanistic descriptions of higher order thinking have privileged a cultural masculinity. Power operates not only in these ways in ed psych but is connected to all dimensions of the domain. Every theory, every research method, every interpretive construct in the field is a contested concept that is intimately connected to issues of power. How psychologists and their discipline is historically and socially situated is a dynamic of power—moreover, the way we interpret this situatedness is affected by power. (See Rochelle Brock and Joe Kincheloe's chapter on the politics of educational psychology, "Educational Psychology in a New Paradigm: Learning a Democratic Way of Teaching.")

In his chapter, "Reclaiming Critical Thinking as Ideology Critique," Stephen Brookfield argues in the spirit of critical theorist Herbert Marcuse that "the struggle to think conceptually is always a political struggle." He follows this notion with the assertion—central to postformalism's notion of a political educational psychology—that "political action and cognitive movement are partners . . . in the development of a revolutionary consciousness." In this spirit postformalists reassert the inseparability of the political and the psychological. How we teach individuals to think in a rigorous manner is highly political. What we teach them to think about is infused with politics. There is no way to escape this power dynamic, no matter how hard many mechanists say they have tried.

When we construct a curriculum, power is involved. When we evaluate student performance, power is involved. When we embrace certain educational goals and reject others, power is involved. Some educational psychologists suggest that intelligence involves knowing your way around. Postformalists ask: where is it that we want to know our way around and what is it we want to do after we know our way around. Both of these questions are both constructed by and answered in relation to issues of power. As critical interpretivists have taught us, cognition does not take place in a vacuum. Do we work to get to know our way around the country club so we can cultivate business contacts and improve our personal socioeconomic status? Or do we get to know our way around the political structures of the city so we can work to help individuals struggling to survive the poverty they face daily?

A political educational psychology asks and answers these types of questions. Francisco Varela asks in this political psychological context: how can compassionate concern be fostered in an egocentric culture that is taught to avoid such an orientation. Taking Varela's question seriously, postformalists merge their critical orientation with enactivism. Combining their power literacy with an enactivist effort to enact compassion in the specificity and immediacy of everyday life, postformalists struggle to transcend egocentrism and move psychological scholarship to a new domain of political understanding and informed action. At this point Varela's insights dovetail synergistically with the cognitive theory of John Dewey.

Dewey was always concerned with connecting the ability to think critically with issues of ethical sensibility and social reform. Indeed, he was impatient with scholars who sought to develop grandiose theories and abstract truths outside of any connection to the real life problems of human beings. Cognitive studies in this critical context can never retreat to the privileged position of mere contemplation—there must always be an active, operative grounding to such scholarship. Had they been contemporaries Dewey and Varela could have engaged in a fascinating conversation around the issue of enacting reflective, contextualized, and critical forms of thinking. Montserrat Castelló and Luis Botella in this volume challenge educational psychologists to take up these political challenges, maintaining that any form of ethical practice demands that they engage in the social debates of their time and place.

One might ask why do relatively few professionals operating in the field of educational psychology connect their work to such social debates. Obviously, the epistemological and paradigmatic dynamics discussed throughout this introduction contribute to such inactivity. The political tasks of postformalism are often hidden from overt view by the power wielders of the contemporary electronic social condition. In the information saturation of *hyperreality* power shapes information and access to dangerous information that challenges the status quo in a covert manner. Michelle Stack writes in her chapter in this volume about the power of television to represent the world in particular but in hidden ideological ways. As Stephen Brookfield writes in "Reclaiming Critical Thinking as Ideology Critique," we often operate in the midst of ideology without ever knowing it. Indeed, educational psychologists and many teachers unfamiliar with critical power theory will often deny the political nature of their professional work. I'm just measuring student academic performance, psychometricians will tell us. It is the role of postformalists to help such professionals understand the discursive, ideological, and regulatory dimensions of their work.

Such an effort to bring individuals to a literacy of power is delicate and complex. It must be undertaken with great respect for the many talents the learner possesses and the unique knowledges he or she brings to the table. Just as one learns mathematical literacy or technological literacy, the individual engaged in developing a literacy of power enters into particular power relationships with the critical teacher. The critical teacher must always be sensitive to the ways this relationship can be abused and be represented as a simplistic hierarchy as one "in the know" and one who is ignorant. Postformalists are radical in their pursuit of humility in their efforts to engage various individuals in a literacy of power in general and in the psychological domain in particular. It must sensitively and carefully lay out the way that particular ways of conceptualizing cognition and the role of educational psychology produce a power illiteracy.

As Scot Evans and Isaac Prilleltensky maintain in their chapter here, such an illiteracy renders individuals unable to "challenge dominant ideas about what society should be like." Indeed, they posit, psychological counselors, for example, who lack a power literacy often engage unconsciously in psychologizing problems in ways that socially and politically decontextualize their interventions. Such psychologizing leads to strategies that blame the victim for his or her oppression. Understanding these political dynamics, counselors can operate with an understanding of connecting the macro and the micro, the social and the individual. Beckoning the spirit of Dewey, Patricia Whang extends Evans and Prilleltensky's insights by reminding readers in her chapter in this volume that education always performs for better or worse particular social functions. A literacy of power moves us to see beyond the blinders of mechanism's abstract individualism.

Postformalists thus develop new purposes for educational psychology. They ponder questions of "what could be" in addition to questions of "what is." They ask what difference my work can make at both the social and the individual levels. The development of a critical consciousness becomes central to the educational psychological enterprise, as professionals carefully analyze what it means to see behind the curtain of everyday life. As they see behind the curtain they begin to understand the tacit forces invisible to mechanistic eyes. Defining critical consciousness as the process of individuals working together to gain awareness of repressive political conditions, Cathy Glenn in her chapter in this volume discusses the process of respectfully engaging students in a negotiation of what it might mean to gain and act on a critical consciousness.

In Glenn's pedagogical process students and teachers work together to interrupt the operations of dominant power in ways that expose their respective complicity in supporting such frameworks. While Glenn's understanding of this delicate process does not necessitate a particular form of pedagogy, it does demand that students not be treated as passive receptacles of expert produced truths concerning the nature and effects of power. This theme of the multiplicity of pedagogies available to accomplish such a delicate educational psychological task is a theme that runs throughout this handbook. These are complex and ambiguous issues that demand rigorous study, experiential insights, and profound interpretive labors in our effort to develop effective strategies. Glenn's nuanced discussion of the complex pedagogical implications of teaching for the purpose of developing a critical consciousness constitutes one of the high points of this handbook.

Smartin' Up: Postformalism and the Quest for New Orders of Cognition

Postformalism understands that intelligence, justice, emotion, activity, disposition, context, access, power, justice, tools, process, and ethics ad infinitum cannot be separated in the study of educational psychology. With these connections in mind postformalists warn scholars about the complexity of the scholarly process they're about to get into when they seek to engage in postformal educational psychology. Much is asked of those who enter into this realm. In their chapter on situated cognition David Hung, Jeanette Bopry, Chee Kit Looi, and Thiam Seng Koh provide great insight into the complexity of this scholarly process. Indeed, postformalists urge adherents at every level of theory and practice to enter into research groups, to develop lifelong learning relationships with those interested in the multiple dimensions of postformal psychology.

As I write about the process of becoming a bricoleur in my work on social, educational, and psychological research, the multidisciplinarity and multiperspectival demands of the brico-lage cannot be learned in an undergraduate, master's or PhD. program. Becoming a scholar of postformalism—like becoming a scholar of the bricolage—is a lifelong learning process. Every-time I enter a new dimension of postformalism, I feel as if I need to put myself through another self-taught doctoral program. Lifelong interactive learning relations with other individuals make the process much easier. My motivation to engage myself and others in this process never wanes, for we are dealing with one of the central processes of humanness—making ourselves smarter, more ethical, more sensitive to the needs of others, more active in helping alleviate those needs, and more aware of the nature of our connections and interrelationships with various dimensions of the world around us. I want "smartin' up" in all the complexity that our study of these multiple and interrelated domains informs us.

In this postformal context as we transcend the "rational irrationality" of formalism and mech-anism, we help students get in touch with what John Dewey called their own "vital logical movement." In the history of mechanistic educational psychology it was these forms of analysis that were denigrated and replaced by formalist logical procedures. In the memorization of these cut-and-dried logical steps millions of children and young people lost their passion for learning and growing. Indeed, they dedicated their lives to getting out of learning situations, in the process relinquishing their disposition to explore themselves and the world around them. Do not mistake this rejection of dry formalistic procedure as a call for a "return to nature" and the hereditary natural developmental process of the child. (See Lise Bird Claiborne's compelling chapter on developmentalism and developmental appropriateness to gain a textured understanding of the complexity of the developmental process.)

The vital logical movement of individuals can be facilitated by good teachers and by entry into Vygotsky's zone of proximal development (ZPD) where students learn by association with skilled others. Thus, as is generally the case with postformalism, we seek to expand cognitive abilities in ways that are informed by multiple insights while avoiding dogmatic blueprints for how to do it. Formal reasoning is profoundly different from everyday thinking. Formal thinking embraces a subject matter that is impersonal as algebraic formulae and consciously operates to remove itself from the subjectivity, the dispositions, and intentions of the thinker. Postformalism categorically rejects this type of cognition and seeks to connect with and understand all that formal reasoning seeks to exclude.

In the postformal context we get smarter by creating our own multilogical ZPDs. In these contexts we construct our own community of experts—whether virtually by reading their work or by interacting with them personally. In our self-constructed ZPDs we build new intellectual and action-based relationships and structurally couple with multiple minds. Schools, postformalists argue, should be grounded on these types of cognitive principles—not on the psychometric, abstract individual, decontextualized, and personally disconnected models of the no-child-left-behind ilk. We can teach students to be lifelong learners who understand that intelligence is not a fixed, hereditarian concept but a fluid, socially constructed construct that can be learned when individuals are exposed to dynamic and challenging new contexts—for example, teacher and/or self-constructed ZPDs. Viewed in this context postformalism is a psychology of hope than transcends the nihilism of mechanism. Postformalists refuse to believe that human beings are condemned to academic hell because of the infallibility and intractability of test scores.

Thus, as a critical discourse, postformalism seeks an empowering notion of learning. Directly challenging mechanistic psychology's passive view of the learner, postformalism is dedicated to a respect for human dignity and the diverse range of talents and abilities that individuals operating in diverse social, cultural, geographic, and economic context develop. Indeed, postformalist look behind IQ and other standardized test scores to uncover the infinite talents that people with low-test scores develop in the idiosyncratic contexts of their lives. When mechanistic influenced pedagogies refuse to consider these amazing talents and pronounce individuals with low-test scores incapable of learning, they commit a psychological and educational crime against such students.

Postformalists in this context believe in the ingenuity of human beings, the power of individuals to learn, to create their own ZPDs. One of the most important impediments to such human agency is the ideology of mechanistic psychology. This regressive ideology works to convince individuals from marginalized backgrounds that they are incapable of learning like "normal" students. Unfortunately, mechanists do a good job of convincing such boys and girls, men and women of their "lack of ability." Over the last few decades I have interviewed scores of brilliant people who told me that they were not good at "school learning" or "book learning." Often they told me of their lack of intelligence as they were in the middle of performing difficult and complex forms of mental labor. They may not have done well in school but they had learned the most important mechanistic psychological lesson—they were not academic material.

In my conversations with those students mislabeled and abandoned by mechanistic educational psychology, I observe powerful intellectual abilities in their interactions with the world. They often illustrate a compelling ability to see things previously not discerned in domains dominated by conventional perspectives. They many times break through the tyranny of "the obvious" with insights gained by viewing a phenomenon from an angle different from the "experts." Postformalists are proud to have "friends in low places" who see schools, for example, from the perspective of those who have "failed." As a postformalist I treasure these perspectives. Indeed, they have played a central role in how I have come to understand educational institutions. Over the last couple of decades I have written extensively about what such brilliant people have taught me as I work to be a better educator, psychologist, sociologist, historian, philosopher, and student of cultural studies—in my struggle to become a bricoleur.

Postformalism and the Relational Self: Constructing a Critical Ontology

Postformalists connect these political insights to the enactivist contention that learning takes place when a self-maintaining system develops a more effective relationship with the external features of the system. In this theoretical intersection emerges the postformalist notion of a critical ontology. As previously discussed ontology is the branch of philosophy that studies the nature of what it means to be in the world. In a postformalist critical ontology we are concerned with understanding the sociopolitical construction of the self in order to conceptualize and enact new ways of being human. These new ways of being human always have to do with the critical interpretivist psychological insight that selfhood is more a relational than an individual dynamic. In this context enactivists is highlighting the profound importance of *relationship* writ large as well as the centrality of the nature and quality of the relationships an organism makes with its environment.

In a cognitive context this is an extension of Vygotsky's ZPD to the ontological realm. In the development of a critical ontology we learn from these ideas that political empowerment vis-à-vis the cultivation of the intellect demand an understanding of the system of relationships that construct our selfhood. In a postformal education these relationships always involve students' connections to cultural systems, language, economic concerns, religious beliefs, social status, and the power dynamics that constitute them. With the benefit of understanding the self-in-relationship teachers and students gain a new insight into what is happening in any learning situation. Living on the borderline between self and external system and self and other, learning never takes place outside of these relationships (see Pickering, 1999). Such knowledge changes our orientation to the goals and methods of educational psychology and pedagogy.

Thus, a critical ontology is intimately connected to a relational self. Humans are ultimately the constructs of relationships, not fragmented monads or abstract individuals. From Varela's perspective this notion of humans as constructs of relationships corresponds precisely to what he is labeling the virtual self. A larger pattern—in the case of humans, consciousness—arises from the interaction of local elements. This larger pattern seems to be driven by a central controlling mechanism that can never be located. Thus, we discern the origin of mechanistic psychology's dismissal of consciousness as irrelevant. This not only constituted throwing out the baby with the bath water but discarding the tub, the bathroom fixtures, and the plumbing as well. In this positivistic/mechanistic articulation the process of life and the basis of the cognitive act were deemed unimportant. A critical ontology is always interested in these processes because they open us to a previously occluded insight into the nature of selfhood, of human being. The *autopoiesis*, the self-making allows humans to perpetually reshape themselves in their new relationships and resulting new patterns of perception and behavior.

Postformalists understand that there is no way to predict the relationships individuals will make and the nature of the self-(re)construction that will ensue. Such uncertainty adds yet another element of complexity to the study of sociology, pedagogy, and psychology, as it simultaneously catalyzes the possibilities of human agency. It moves those critical interpretivists who enamored with postformalism yet another reason to study the inadequacies of Cartesian science to account for the intricacies of the human domain. Physical objects *don't necessarily* change their structures via their interaction with other objects. Postformalism's critical ontology understands that human beings *do* change their structures as a result of their interactions. As a result the human mind moves light years beyond the lifeless mechanist computer model of mind.

Kathryn Herr picks up on these critical ontological concepts in her chapter in this volume. Such a relational model, she writes, allows students to move from mechanistic developmental models based on separation to relational concepts that value human beings' ability to enter into positive, growth-producing relationships. With these issues in mind, Herr maintains that this relational competency catalyzes the development of creativity, autonomy, and assertion. Indeed, she posits, one comes to learn more about himself or herself via modes of affiliation and connection to other people. Such a psychology of self holds profound political dynamics, Herr concludes. The linear, autonomy-focused developmental models of Erik Erikson, for example, are designed to serve the needs of a free market economy and a "stacked deck" faux-competitive society. A critical ontology understands that affiliation is not a threat to autonomy. Instead relationship enhances our effort to build a empowering life where concern and care for others is central to everyone's best interests. Learning, of course, takes place in these relational ZPDs—not as a separate, decontextualized, competitive activity.

Enactivist concepts of structural coupling and coemergence reenter the postformalist cosmos in this relational ontological context. We are empowered to see beyond individual learners, Tara Fenwick writes in her chapter, abstracted from the processes and environmental contexts of which they are a part. "They focus on *relations*," she asserts, "not the components, of systems, for learning is produced within the evolving relationships among particularities that are dynamic and unpredictable." Our very identities are shaped by these interactions. Thus, drawing upon these relational ontological dimensions, postformalists profoundly reshape what it is that educational psychologists study. David Hung, Jeanette Bopry, Chee Kit Looi, and Thiam Seng Koh in their chapter in this handbook contribute to these ontological dimensions of educational psychology. Focusing on ontological relationship, they maintain that purposive behavior involves interconnected acts connected to physical and social contexts. Change and process are the key features of these interrelationships, which in their interaction produce a complex whole—a systematic unity that constitutes a new identity.

Postformalists help construct communities of practice to catalyze these critical ontologies, these relational selves. Understanding the subtle emergent character of this construction process, postformalists know that they cannot simply mandate particular relationships and force the construction of particular learning communities. Individual learners working together must construct their own communities of practice and their synergistic relationships. Postformal teachers also know, however, that they can operate to enhance such activities as opposed to impeding them. Understanding the notions put forth in critical interpretivist educational psychology, postformalism and critical ontology, empowers educators to enhance rather than impede. In such understanding "learning that" enters into a dialectical relationship with "learning how." As is usually the case different types of knowledge are required to accomplish particular complex tasks. Postformalists bring the knowledges discussed in this introduction into relationship with the immediacy of human beings interacting with one another in specific lived contexts.

In this epistemologically informed ontological context—simply put, understanding the way the produced knowledge shapes the nature of our being in the world—we focus our postformal attention on Hung, Bopry, Looi, and Koh's chapter here and its focus on the ontological insights of Martin Heidegger. If learning is inseparable from meaning making, they contend, then it is also inseparable from the process of identity formation (being) in a social community. Here, Hung, Bopry, Looi, and Koh contend, we can begin to distinguish between "learning *about*" and "learning *to be*." Thus, learning is as much an ontological act as it is an epistemological act. Most school learning in a mechanistic context, they continue, is about committing to memory preexisting knowledge domains—the truth of scientifically based disciplines. In learning to be, the authors maintain, individuals become members of communities of practice, in the process constructing a new relational identity. Katheryn Kinnucan-Welsch in her chapter on teacher professional development considers these ideas in relation to the effort to improve teacher education.

This relational identity plays a central role in constructing what it is that a student learns. We can see this ontological dynamic play out in schools on a daily basis as students who enter particular youth subcultures where the changes in their identities profoundly shape not only what they know about the world but also how they see both the world and themselves. This is a profound learning experience. Thus, we cannot see learning and being apart from our contexts. Thus, we are not self and world in the way coffee is in a can. The self is the world and the world is the self in a critical ontology. Human being cannot be understood outside of sociopolitical context, postformalism asserts. This is a subtle proposition. As Hung, Bopry, Looi, and Koh remind us, "although being can be phenomenologically perceived separately from the world, being exists or takes meaning only in relation to the world."

In this context the absurdity of the way IQ tests have been developed and used comes into clear focus. Constructed as measures of the individual's ability, their failure to account for the connection between the individual and the contexts of which he or she is a part renders them useless. If the individual and his or her cognitive orientations are shaped by this being-in-the-world, psychological tests miss the origins and causes of why individuals display particular cognitive characteristics. They attribute to nature what is a manifestation of particular social, political, economic, cultural, and historical relationships. Thus, postformalism views the self and the development of selfhood and cognitive ability in new and exciting ways. In his chapter on transformative learning Edward Taylor argues that these dynamics create a dramatic rupture with the past. Our relational ontological perspectives provide us with a new way of understanding the way individuals relate to the world around them.

CONCLUSION: THE LARGER STRUGGLE

As it integrates the powerful insights emerging from the interpretivist tradition in educational psychology, constructivism, situated cognition, enactivism, and multiple forms of criticality, postformal pushes the cognitive envelop. I find great hope in these ideas as they provide a compelling way out of the dead end of mechanistic educational psychology. As I write this introduction in the repressive political atmosphere of the first decade of the twenty-first century, the attempt to escape mechanistic educational psychology and the regressive, antidemocratic sociopolitical and educational system it is used to support has never been more important. Ray Horn and I along with the brilliant authors included in this volume hope that this work contributes to the effort to escape these authoritarian, antidemocratic, and inegalitarian impulses of the present era. If it does then we will have considered it a great success.

TERMS FOR READERS

Bricolage—The French word "bricoleur" describes a handyman or handywoman who makes use of the tools available to complete a task. Some connotations of the term involve trickery and cunning and are reminiscent of the chicanery of Hermes, in particular his ambiguity concerning the messages of the gods. If hermeneutics came to connote the ambiguity and slipperiness of textual meaning, then bricolage can also imply imaginative elements of the presentation of all formal research. I use the term here in the way Norman Denzin and Yvonna Lincoln (2000) employ it in *The Handbook of Qualitative Research* to denote a multimethodological form of research that uses a variety of research methods and theoretical constructs to examine a phenomenon.

Complexity theory—Posits that the interaction of many parts gives rise to characteristics not to be found in any of the individual parts. In this context complexity theory studies the rules shaping the emergence of these new characteristics and the self-organization of the system that develops in this autopoietic (self-creating) situation. As the complex system is analyzed, complexity theorists come to understand that it cannot be reduced to only one level of description.

Critical—Having to do with critical theory which is concerned with questions of power and its just distribution. (See Kincheloe [2004] for an expansion of these ideas).

Epistemology—The branch of philosophy that studies knowledge and its production. Epistemological questions include: What is truth? Is that a fact or an opinion? On what basis do you claim that assertion to be true? How do you know?

Ethnography—A form of social and cultural research that attempts to gain knowledge about a particular culture, to identify patterns of social interaction, and to develop interpretations of societies and social institutions. Ethnography seeks to make explicit the assumptions one takes for granted as a culture member. Ethnographic researchers make use of observation and interviews of culture members in their natural setting, their lived contexts.

Evolving criticality—The notion of criticality—the concern with transforming oppressive relations of power in a variety of domains that lead to human oppression finds its origins in critical theory and evolves as it embraces new critical discourses in new eras. In this context much of my work has been involved with tracing an evolving criticality that studies the ways that new times evoke new manifestations of power, new consequences, and new ways of understanding and resisting them. Concurrently this evolving criticality devises new social arrangements, new institutions, new modes of cognition, and new forms of selfhood.

Formal level of cognition—Constitutes Jean Piaget's highest order of human cognition where individuals exhibit the ability to formulate abstract conclusions, understand cause–effect relationships, and employ the traditional scientific method to explain reality.

Hegemony—Italian social theorist Antonio Gramsci theorized in the 1930s that dominant power in "democratic societies" is no longer exercised simply by physical force but through social psychological attempts to win men and women's consent to domination through cultural institutions such as the schools, the media, the family, and the church. In hegemony the power bloc wins popular to consent by way of a pedagogical process, a form of learning that engages people's conceptions of the world in such a way that transforms (not displaces) them with perspectives more compatible with those of dominant power wielders.

Phenomenology—The study of phenomena in the world as they are constructed by our consciousness. As it analyzes such phenomena it asks what makes something what it is. In this way phenomenologists "get at" the meaning of lived experience, the meaning of experience as we live it. In this effort phenomenology attempts to study what it means to be human.

Positionalities—Who people are, where they stand or are placed in the web of reality. The term connotes the historical construction of human identity.

Postcolonialism—In the most technical sense the term refers to the period after colonial rule, but there are many dimensions of postcolonialism that transcend this meaning. In a critical context one of those dimensions involves examining and working through the effects of colonialism in the political, social, cultural, economic, psychological, and educational spheres of both colonizer and colonized states and peoples.

Post-discourses—The theoretical ways of understanding that developed in the last third of the twentieth century that questioned the assumptions about the world put forth by modernist, scientific Western frameworks. They would include postmodernism, poststructuralism, postcolonialism, and postformalism.

Semiotics—The study of the nature and influence of signs, symbols, and codes.

Subjugated knowledges—Derived from dangerous memories of history and everyday life that have been suppressed and information that has been disqualified by social and academic gatekeepers, subjugated knowledge plays a central role in all critical ways of seeing. Through the conscious cultivation of these low ranking knowledges, alternative democratic visions of society, politics, education, and cognition are possible.

FURTHER READING

Bredo, E. (1994). Cognitivism, Situated Cognition and Deweyan Pragmatism. *Philosophy of Education Society Yearbook*. http://www.ed.uiuc.edu/eps/pes-yearbook/94_docs/bredo.htm.

Burman, E. (1994). *Deconstructing Developmental Psychology*. New York: Routledge.

Gergen, K. (1997). The Place of the Psyche in a Constructed World. *Theory and Society*, 7 (6).

Gresson, A. (1995). *The Recovery of Race in America*. Minneapolis: University of Minnesota Press.

Horn, R. (2004). Scholar-Practitioner Leaders: The Empowerment of Teachers and Students. In J. Kincheloe & D. Weil (Eds.), *Critical Thinking and Learning: An Handbook for Parents and Teachers*. Westport, CT: Greenwood.

Kincheloe, J. L. (2004). *Critical Pedagogy*. New York: Peter Lang.

Kincheloe, J. L. and K. S. Berry (2004). *Rigour and Complexity in Educational Research: Conceptualizing the Bricolage*. London: Open University Press.

Pickering, J. (1999). Beyond Cognitivism: Mutualism and Postmodern Psychology. http://www.csv.warwick.ac.uk/~psrev/mutualism.html.

Richardson, F. and R. Woolfolk (1994). Social Theory and Values: A Hermeneutic Perspective. *Theory and Psychology*, 4(2), 199–226.

Smith, H. (1998). Educational Psychology: A Cultural Psychological and Semiotic View. Paper Presented to the Meeting of the Australian Association for Research in Education. Adelaide. http://www.aare.edu.au/98pap/smi98134.htm.

Thayer-Bacon, B. (2000). *Transforming Critical Thinking: Thinking Constructively*. New York: Teachers College Press.

Varela, F. (1999). *Ethical Know-How: Action, Wisdom, and Cognition*. Palo Alto, CA: Stanford University Press.

CHAPTER 2

Educational Psychology Timeline

ED WELCHEL, DORIS PAEZ, AND P. L. THOMAS

Early 1800s	Jonathan Friedrich Herbart postulated that activities of the mind could be expressed mathematically. He is considered the first educational psychologist.
1883	G. Stanley Hall, aka "the Darwin of the Mind," established the first psychological laboratory in the world at the Johns Hopkins University.
	G. Stanley Hall published *The Content of Children's Minds*.
1886	J. Dewey writes a psychology textbook.
1887	G. Stanley Hall establishes the *American Journal of Psychology*.
1887	G. S. Hall, as the first president of Clark University, creates the first pedagogical seminary (workshop) focused on the scientific study of education, which led to the publishing of a journal, *Pedagogical Seminary* (eventually this became the *Journal of Genetic Psychology*), and the introduction of pedagogical courses in the psychology department at Clark by W. F. Burnham. Burnham stayed at Clark for 36 years and that is considered the first true "Educational Psychology" department.
1889	Edward L. Thorndike, considered the foremost authority on behavioral psychology, joins Teachers College faculty and remains there throughout his career.
	James Sully, *Outlines of Psychology: Theory of Education*.
1890	William James, *Principles of Psychology*.
	James McKeen Cattell coins the phrase "mental test."
1891	William James is asked by Harvard to address teachers in Cambridge, Mass. These "talks" were later published as *Talks to Teachers on Psychology*, which is considered the first educational psychology textbook.
1892	G. S. Hall calls a meeting of 26 prominent psychologists to form an association. This is considered the founding of American Psychological Association (APA).
1894	J. Dewey becomes a faculty member at the University of Chicago. He publishes an article on relative frequency of word use by young children ("The Psychology

of Infant Language" in *Psychological Review*) and founds an elementary school, considered the first university laboratory school.

1895   First course in educational psychology is taught at the University of Buffalo.

1896   Lightner Witmer establishes the first psychological clinic in the United States, at the University of Pennsylvania.

1897   Joseph Mayer Rice, considered the "father of research on teaching," presents empirical evidence on the futility of the "spelling grind" to school administrators.

1900   J. Dewey, as president of APA, gives a "presidential" address to APA members on educational issues and the building of mutually respectful relationships between educational psychologists and classroom teachers.

1905   Alfred Binet, *New Methods for the Diagnosis of the Intellectual Level of Subnormal*.

Alfred Binet and Theodore Simon design tests to quantify intelligence in children.

1906   Ivan Pavlov establishes classical conditioning in his publications.

1909   Maria Montessori, *Corso Di Pedagogia Cientifica* (*The Method of Scientific Pedagogy Applied to Child Education*).

1910   *The Journal of Educational Psychology* is founded.

John Dewey, *How We Think*.

1911   E. L. Thorndike, *Animal Intelligence*.

John B. Watson, *Psychology as the Behaviorist Views It* (1913).

E. L. Thorndike, *Educational Psychology*.

1915   Sigmund Freud, *On Repression*.

1916   Lewis M. Terman publishes *The Measurement of Intelligence*.

A complete account of E. L. Thorndike's studies is published in the Egyptian-journal *Al-Muktataf*.

1918   William H. Kilpatrick publishes "The Project Method" in *Teachers College Record*—claimed to combine Thorndike's educational psychology with Dewey's educational philosophy.

Robert S. Woodworth publishes *Dynamic Psychology*—introducing the concept of "drive."

1919   E. P. Cubberley, *Public Education in the United States*.

1920   John B. Watson and Rosalie Rayner, *Conditioned Emotional Reactions*.

1922   John Dewey, *The Human Nature and the Conduct*.

"The army intelligence tests have put psychology on the map of United States"—J. M. Cattell.

1923   Sigmund Freud, *The Ego and the Id*.

1924   Max Wertheimer, *Gestalt Theory*.

1926   The College Board sponsors the development of the Scholastic Aptitude Test (SAT) and administers the test for the first time this year.

1930   B. F. Skinner, "On the Conditions of Eliciation of Certain Eating Reflexes."

1931   L. L. Thurstone publishes *Multiple Factor Analysis*, a landmark work focusing research on cognitive abilities.

1933   Alfred Adler, *On the Sense of the Life*.

1934	Psychology begins to be a requirement in undergraduate course work.
1935	B. F. Skinner, "Two Types of Conditioned Reflex and a Pseudo-Type"—Pavlovian conditioning and operant conditioning distinguished.
1937	B. F. Skinner employs the word *operant* for the first time and applies *respondent* to the Pavlovian type of reflex.
	Anna Freud, *The Ego and the Mechanisms of Defense.*
1938	B. F. Skinner, *The Behavior of the Organisms.*
1942	Carl Rogers introduces patient-centered therapy.
1946	Harold E. Jones becomes the first president of APA's Division 15, Educational Psychology.
1947	Jerome Bruner and Cecile Goodman, *Value and Need as Organizing Factors in Perception.*
1948	B. F. Skinner, *Walden Two.*
	The C. G. Jung Institute is established in Zurich.
1949	Jerome Bruner and Leo Postman, *On the Perception of Incongruity: A Paradigm.*
1953	B. F. Skinner, *Science and Human Behavior.*
1954	Abraham Maslow, *Motivation and Personality*—introduces a hierarchical theory of human personality.
	B. F. Skinner demonstrates at the University of Pittsburgh a machine designed to teach arithmetic, using an instructional program.
	Anne Anastasi's textbook, *Psychological Testing.*
1955	Social psychologist Richard Crutchfield publishes "Conformity and Character."
	Lee J. Cronbach and Paul E. Meehl, "Construct Validity in Psychological Tests."
1956	Jerome Bruner and collaborators, *A Study of Thinking.*
	Benjamin Bloom, *Cognitive Taxonomy of Objectives.*
1957	B. F. Skinner and Charles B. Ferster, *Schedules of Reinforcement.*
	B. F. Skinner, *Verbal Behavior.*
1958	Allen Newell, Marvin E. Shaw, and Herbert A. Simon, "Elements of a Theory of Human Problem Solving"—the first exposition of the information-processing approach in psychology.
1959	Wolfgang Köhler, *Gestalt Psychology Today.*
	John W. Thibaut and Harold H. Kelley, *The Social Psychology of Groups.*
	Noam Chomsky, *Verbal Behavior*—revision of B. F. Skinner's edition.
1960	Robert Watson, "History of Psychology: A Neglected Area."
	First school of professional psychology established in Mexico.
1961	Carl Rogers, *On Becoming a Person.*
1962	Creation of bachelor courses and the profession of psychologist.
1963	J. B. Caroll publishes "A Model of School Learning" in *Teachers College Record* and *The Place of Educational Psychology in the Study of Education* ("The Discipline of Education" edited by J. Walton and J. L. Keuthe).
1964	Humanistic psychology emerges as the "third force" in psychology.
	T. W. Wann edits *Behaviorism and Phenomenology: Contrasting Bases for Modern Psychology.*

1965	Roger Brown, *Social Psychology*.
	Roger M. Gagne, *The Conditions of Learning*.
	The *Journal for the History of Behavioral Sciences* is founded.
1966	Jerome S. Bruner, *Studies in Cognitive Growth*.
1967	Robert Watson establishes the first history of psychology PhD program in the world.
1968	Abraham Maslow, *Toward a Psychology of Being*.
	Malcom Knowles presents the concept of a "learner-centered" instructional approach.
1969	Albert Bandura, *Principles of Modification of the Behavior*.
1970s	Throughout this decade, Joseph Schwab accused educators and curriculum scholars of "doctrinaire adhesion" to educational psychology.
1971	B. F. Skinner, *Beyond Freedom and Dignity*.
1972	Ron Harré and Paul Secord, *The Explanation of Social Behavior*.
1973	Karl von Frisch, Konrad Lorenz, and Nikollaas Tinbergen receive the Nobel Prize in recognition of their studies on the behavior of animals.
1975	Mary Henle, *Gestalt Psychology and Gestalt Therapy*.
Late 1970s to early 1980s	Resurgence of theories about cognitivism and knowledge acquisition.
	John Robert Anderson (1976) presents the Adaptive Control Theory (ACT), which modifies the view of cognitivism.
	D. E. Rumelhart and Donald Norman, theory of "accretion" or knowledge acquisition, which postulates that instructional design and curriculum design should match.
	David Merrill postulates the "component display theory," which emphasizes that learners should have control over the sequence of learning.
1980	M. J. Lerner, *The Belief in a Just World*.
	One of ten doctorates granted in the United States is estimated to be in psychology.
1981	American Psychological Association grows to approximately 50,500 members.
1982	D. Kahneman, P. Slovic, and A. Tversky, *Judgment under Uncertainty: Heuristics and Biases*.
	The Humanistic Psychology Institute becomes the Saybrook Institute.
1983	Howard Gardner, *Frames of Mind*.
1985	Howard Gardner, *The New Mind's Science*.
1986	China's "Humanistic Psychology Craze," especially its "Maslow Craze" gradually takes shape and, through 1989, Maslow's books sell 557,900 copies.
1990	Donald Norman, *Things That Make Us Smart*.
1991	Howard Garnder, *The Unschooled Mind*.
1992	First published work on critical postformalism, Joe L. Kincheloe, Shirley R. Steinberg, and Deborah J. Tippins, *The Stigma of Genius: Einstein and Beyond Modern Education*.
1993	Roger Sperry, "The Impact and Promise of the Cognitive Revolution."
	Joe L. Kincheloe and Shirley R. Steinberg establish postformalism as a challenge to traditional educational psychology.

1994	Richard Herrnstein and Charles Murray, *The Bell Curve*.
	Roger Sperry dies.
1996	Joe L. Kincheloe, Shirley R. Steinberg, and Aaron Gresson, *Measured Lies: The Bell Curve Examined*. The book challenges the psychometrics of Herrnstein and Murray.
1997	Kieran Egan, *The Educated Mind: How Cognitive Tools Shape Our Understanding*.
1999	Joe L. Kincheloe, Shirley R. Steinberg, and Patricia H. Hinchey, *The Postformal Reader: Cognition and Education*.
	Joe L. Kincheloe, Shirley R. Steinberg, and Lila E. Villaverde, *Rethinking Intelligence*.
	Second edition of Joe L. Kincheloe, Shirley R. Steinberg, and Deborah J. Tippins, *The Stigma of Genius*.
	Howard Gardner, *The Disciplined Mind*.
2000	Joel J. Mintzes, James H. Wandersee, and Joseph D. Novaka, *Assessing Science Understanding: A Human Constructivist View*.
2001	Seymour Saranson, *American Psychology and Schools: A Critique*.
2002	Expansion of the *Educational Psychology Series* by Academic Press reflects current issues and notable "younger" or next-generation educational psychologists.
	Joshua M. Aronson, *Improving Academic Achievement: Impact of Psychological Factors on Education*.
	Daniel J. Moran and Richard W. Malott, *Evidence-based Educational Methods*.
	Roger Marples, *The Aims of Education*.
	Susan Bentham, *Psychology and Education*.
	Robert D. Greer, *Designing Teaching Strategies: An Applied Behavior Analysis Systems Approach*.
	Joshua Aronsen, *Improving Academic Achievement: Impact of Psychological Factors on Education*.
2004	Joe L. Kincheloe, *Multiple Intelligences Reconsidered*.
	David Dai and Robert Sternberg, *Integrating Perspectives on Intellectual Functioning and Development*. (Sternberg's reflections and "newer" perspective)
	Chery Sanders and Gay Phye, *Bullying: Implications for the Classroom*. (new emphasis on bullying apparent in the literature)
	Larisa V. Shavinina and Michel Ferrari, *Beyond Knowledge: Extracognitive Aspects of Developing High Ability*.
	IDEA reauthorized as Individual with Disabilities Education Improvement Act (IDEIA), ensuring greater flexibility for assessment (e.g., eliminates need for cognitive-achievement discrepancy in learning disability identification).

PART II

Introducing Theorists Important to Education and Psychology

CHAPTER 3

Albert Bandura

SABRINA N. ROSS

Imagine two siblings (one an older brother and the other a younger sister) on a shopping trip with their mother. The older brother sees a toy he wants and continuously begs the mother to buy it until she gives in and purchases it for him. The younger sister, observing the reward her brother received for his behavior, begins to beg for a toy until she too receives one. The sister has learned to change her behavior by observing her brother's behavior and its consequences. This is the concept of observational learning developed by Albert Bandura as a major part of his Social Cognition Theory. Social cognition theory is a grand theory of human development that seeks to explain the entirety of human development and psychological functioning occurring over the life course of the individual. Bandura's theory countered commonly held views of learning through direct reinforcement by presenting humans as intelligent and adaptable learners capable of extracting complex guidelines for behavior from instances of observational learning. The reconceptualization of the process of human learning in straightforward and practical terms makes his social cognitive theory one of the few grand theories that continue to enjoy relevancy and application in contemporary times. A discussion of Albert Bandura and his development of the social cognitive theory follows.

Bandura's social cognitive theory explains the influences of social modeling, human cognition, and motivation on behavior. The development of Bandura's theory of social cognition was influenced by his early psychological research studies and also by his early life experiences. In his theory, Bandura presents humans as adaptable and agentic (i.e., capable of effecting desired change) individuals who use direct and indirect learning sources to guide their present and future actions.

Albert Bandura was born on December 4, 1925, in a small town of Alberta, Canada, the youngest and only male of six children. Bandura's belief in human agency was encouraged by his early educational experiences. He attended a small, understaffed, and inadequately resourced school in Canada that served both elementary and high school students, but although the school was underresourced, students there excelled academically. The meager staff and resources at his school made it necessary for Bandura and other students to take responsibility for their own learning. He believed the students' involvement in their own learning attributed greatly to their academic success; these early experiences instilled in Bandura the importance of self-direction and motivation in learning. These themes are emphasized in his social cognitive theory.

Bandura also recognizes in his theory the ability of individuals to react to chance encounters and fortuitous events in ways that can meaningfully alter their life course. Bandura's decision to major in psychology resulted from his reaction to one such event. He entered undergraduate school at the University of British Columbia and enrolled in an introductory psychology course because it fit an early morning time slot that he needed for his class schedule. Once in the class, he loved it and decided to major in psychology. Before taking the psychology course, he had intended to major in the biological sciences.

After receiving his bachelor's degree in 1949, Bandura attended graduate school at the University of Iowa. He received his Master of Arts degree in 1951 and his PhD in 1952; both degrees were in clinical psychology. He accepted a faculty position at Stanford University in California in 1953. He remained at Stanford for the entirety of his career.

One of Bandura's earliest projects at Stanford involved the study of hyperaggression in male adolescents from well-to-do and seemingly well-functioning households. He hypothesized that the hyperaggressive adolescents were modeling the hostile behavior of their parents. Although the parents did not allow their sons to display aggression in their homes, they encouraged aggressive behavior in school by telling the adolescents to physically defend themselves during disputes. When these adolescents got in trouble at school for their aggressive displays, their parents typically sided with them against the school administrators. Bandura hypothesized that the adolescents learned their aggressive behavior by imitating their parents' aggression. He further hypothesized that even though the adolescents were punished for behaving aggressively at home, their observation of their parents' aggression was a more powerful influence on their behavior than was the punishment. His research findings were important because they provided evidence against the popular Freudian assumption that parental punishment would discourage aggression in children. Bandura's work with aggressive adolescents demonstrated that observation of parental behavior was a more powerful influence on child behavior than was punishment. Bandura along with his first doctoral student, Richard Walters, published his findings in his first book *Adolescent Aggression* (1959). His early work on adolescent aggression and parental modeling paved the way for his concept of observational learning.

Perhaps the most famous study that Bandura conducted on observational learning and aggression was the Bobo doll study. Bandura showed kindergarten children a film in which one of his female students physically attacked a Bobo doll, an inflatable balloon that was weighted at the bottom to make it bob back and forth when struck. After viewing the film, the children were made to feel frustrated by being placed in a room full of toys that they were not permitted to touch. Finally, the children were led to a room with a Bobo doll and other toys identical to those in the film they had viewed. The majority of the kindergartners imitated the aggressive behavior they viewed in the film; almost half continued to reproduce this behavior months later. Bandura conducted many variations on the Bobo doll experiment; each resulted in a reproduction of the aggressive behavior modeled.

Bandura's findings from the Bobo doll study dispelled several assumptions about learning and aggression. At the time he began his studies, many psychologists believed that learning was simply the result of direct reinforcement. In cases of direct reinforcement, the learner is given a reward each time the desired behavior is approximated until the desired behavior is achieved. Bandura's variations on the Bobo doll experiment demonstrated that learners do not require direct reinforcement for learning to take place. Rather, learners can receive vicarious reinforcement by seeing a model rewarded for his or her behavior and change their own behavior as a result. Recall the example of the older brother and younger sister shopping with their mother; the sister observed her brother receiving reinforcement (i.e., the toy he was begging for) for his behavior and changed her own behavior as a result. This is an example of learning that takes place through vicarious reinforcement.

Another Freudian assumption popular with psychologists at the time of Bandura's early Bobo doll experiments was that viewing violent or aggressive acts would have a draining effect that reduced aggression in the individual. This assumption was termed the catharsis effect. Both Bandura's Bobo doll study and his studies with aggressive adolescent males disproved the assumptions of the catharsis effect. On the basis of these studies and others, Bandura developed a theory of observational learning and motivation that he termed social cognition theory.

In social cognition theory, Bandura presents human behavior as being largely a product of direct and indirect learning. As discussed previously, direct learning (also referred to as trial and error learning) is reinforced through the learner's receipt of rewards or punishments. Indirect learning (also called vicarious learning and observational learning) occurs when the learner alters his or her behavior without receiving rewards or punishment. Recall again the example of the brother and sister on the shopping trip with their mother. Before she began imitating her brother's begging, the sister had received no direct reinforcement for her behavior; she observed the brother beg and be rewarded, then she changed her behavior. For Bandura, observational learning had important advantages over trial and error learning. Whereas trial and error learning is risky and time-consuming, observational learning saves the learner both time and risk by allowing him or her to learn from the successes and mistakes of others. For Bandura, humans have a great capacity for symbolism; we can retain socially modeled information in the form of mental images or verbal descriptions that serve as symbols for future behavior. Through social modeling, individuals can extend their learning by using symbols from the original modeled behavior to guide future rules for action. Returning once again to the example of the brother and sister on the shopping trip, Bandura argued that the sister will be able to apply her learning to different situations. For example, having retained the symbol of her brother receiving a reward for begging his mother, she might try begging her father or grandparents for a desired toy. She might try begging her mother to allow her to spend the night at a friend's house. In each case, the learner becomes able to apply his or her observational learning to new situations in ways that guide his or her future actions.

Central to Bandura's theory of social cognition is the term triadic reciprocal causation, which describes the simultaneous influences of thoughts, feelings, and the environment on human behavior. For Bandura, human behavior results from interactions between individual biological factors (e.g., cognitive capabilities), psychological factors (e.g., emotional states), and the environment. These factors influence and are, in turn, influenced by one another; the interactions among these biological, psychological, and environmental factors produce variations in human behavior. The results of reciprocal causation are that humans are at the same time producers of and products of their environment.

For a practical example of triadic reciprocal causation, imagine that you and other college students are seated on the first day of class, waiting for your professor to arrive. As you wait, you join in small talk with the other students. The professor arrives; upon entering the room she makes eye contact and confidently announces that class will now begin. According to Bandura, the behaviors of the professor will be influenced by her emotional state (e.g., Is she excited about teaching the course? Does she believe herself to be an effective instructor?), her cognitions (e.g., her initial thoughts about the course and students), and the classroom environment. Suppose that when the professor enters the classroom you and your classmates continue with your small talk and fail to acknowledge her entrance. Your actions might create a negative classroom environment for the professor to react to. On the other hand, you and your classmates might stop talking as the professor enters and focus your attention on her, indicating that you are ready to begin class. These two very different environmental responses on your part will interact with the professor's thoughts and beliefs to influence her actions as she begins teaching the course. In turn, you and your classmates will react to the professor's subsequent behavior, possibly altering her behavior and the classroom environment as a result. In this way, the professor and the environment are continuously interacting with and influencing each other through reciprocal causation.

Three very important concepts in Bandura's social cognition theory are social modeling, the self-system, and self-regulation. The concept of social modeling, or observational learning, has been discussed previously. This concept will be discussed in greater detail now, along with the concepts of the self-system and self-regulation for greater clarity of social cognition theory.

SOCIAL MODELING

Bandura used his Bobo doll study to identify the steps involved in the process of social modeling. He hypothesized that social learning could occur through the learner's actual observation of real people, observations of the environment, or observations of television or other media. In order for learning to occur, the individual must be attentive to the modeled behavior (e.g., the sister must be actively paying attention to the brother's behavior). In addition, characteristics of both the learner and the model influence learning. For example, learner fatigue or distraction decreases learning while model attractiveness, competence, and prestige increase learning of the modeled behavior.

The learner must be able to utilize mental imagery or verbal descriptions to retain the modeled behavior so that it can be reproduced later. Reproduction involves translation of the retained images and/or descriptions into actual behavior; in order for reproduction to occur, the learner must have the ability to reproduce the behavior.

The learner must be motivated to engage in the observed behavior. For Bandura, the factors influencing motivation include past reinforcement or punishment, incentives or threats, and seeing the model of the behavior reinforced or punished (as occurred when the sister observed her brother receiving his desired toy). According to him, reinforcements are better motivators of behavior than are punishments. Unlike traditional behaviorists, he does not believe that direct or vicarious reinforcements and punishments cause learning; instead he believes that they provide reasons for the learner to demonstrate learned behaviors.

In general, children tend to engage in observational learning more than adults, and inexperienced persons do it more than those with experience. For Bandura, individuals use language and symbols to translate their observations of socially modeled behaviors into guides for future actions. The extent to which socially modeled behaviors translate into future actions for the learner depends on human motivation and self-management. He hypothesized that human motivation and management are derived from an internal structure called the self-system.

The adaptive nature of humans enables them to extend observational learning to future behaviors through the self-system. For Bandura, the self-system is a set of cognitive structures that influence perception, evaluation, and behavior regulation. Bandura developed the concept of the self-system to explain consistency in human behavior. He believes that the learner consciously engages the self-system to evaluate behavior in relation to previous experiences and future consequences. As a result of these evaluations, self-regulation occurs. Self-regulation is the individual's ability to control his or her behavior.

Self-regulation is engaged when one violates some form of previously adopted social norm or standard. It involves three steps: self-monitoring, judgment, and self-response. Self-monitoring is simply the awareness of one's own behavior. Judgment involves comparing one's behavior with personal standards (i.e., judging one's behavior against oneself) or other standards of reference. Self-response involves the internal feelings associated with judgments of individual behavior. If the judgment is favorable, a rewarding self-response (e.g., feelings of pride or satisfaction) may result, and if the judgment is unfavorable, a negative self-response (e.g., feelings of shame or inadequacy) may result. In general, individuals aim to perform actions that provide a sense of satisfaction; they tend to avoid engaging in behaviors that induce self-devaluing reactions. Over time, one's tendency to meet or fail to meet self-standards can influence perceptions of self-concept and self-efficacy. Self-concept is an individual's judgment of his or her capability. Self-efficacy is an individual's perceived ability to be effective and perform actions necessary to change one's environment.

For Bandura, self-efficacy serves as a source for human motivation across the life cycle. Self-efficacy is acquired or changed through four sources: mastery experiences (successful performance), social modeling, social persuasion, and physiological or emotional arousal. In general, successful mastery experiences increase self-efficacy while failures lower self-efficacy. Observing others succeed (social modeling) can increase self-efficacy if one perceives oneself to be like the model; observing others fail can decrease self-efficacy. Social persuasion involves the degree of praise or insult one receives for completed behaviors. Praise of the persuader can increase self-efficacy if the persuader is credible and is describing a behavior that is within the learner's ability to perform. One's physiological state also can influence self-efficacy. Whereas high levels of emotional arousal (e.g., adrenaline) can decrease performance and self-efficacy, lower levels of emotional arousal can increase performance and self-efficacy.

As mentioned earlier, Bandura's social cognition theory is a grand theory of human development that seeks to explain human behavior across the life course. For Bandura, the establishment of self-efficacy throughout various developmental "milieus" (i.e., changing situations) in the life cycle is determinant of healthy and adaptive human functioning. According to him, these milieus (i.e., infancy, family relations, peer relations, school, adolescence, adulthood, and advancing age) are commonly recognized but are not fixed stages in the Piagetian sense of human development. Bandura views development as a lifelong process, marked by individual variations in cognitive ability, environmental influence, and perception.

SOCIAL COGNITIVE THEORY AND POSTFORMAL THOUGHT

Postformal thought questions Piaget's assertions that adolescent thinking and adult thinking are qualitatively identical as well as Piaget's contention that formal operations is the final stage of cognitive development in humans. Bandura's social cognitive theory is compatible with postformal thinking in its rejection of highly fixed stages of cognitive development and its recognition of qualitatively different types of cognitive functioning that occur throughout the life cycle. For Bandura, cognitive functioning does not follow a universal or fixed path. It is multidirectional and follows diverse trajectories of change depending on individual abilities and the social context. The emphasis of social cognitive theory on the importance of context in evaluating thinking and learning outcomes discourages its adherence to fixed stages of cognitive development. Variations in social context and individual characteristics will necessarily produce variations in cognitive development.

As mentioned earlier, Bandura explains human development as the establishment and maintenance of self-efficacy resources throughout the life cycle. Such development differs according to the milieu or changing situation the individual encounters. In each milieu, Bandura identifies cognitive functioning as involving the individual's adaptation to changing situations in practical ways that enhance self-efficacy.

In infancy, adaptation involves learning that one's actions influence the social environment. The establishment of a sense of personal agency and causality result from this adaptation and enables the infant to engage in abstraction and learn to gauge likely outcomes of actions through social modeling experiences. Bandura's next milieu, the family context, provides children with ample vicarious experiences that inform the use of social and verbal behavior to alter social outcomes and enhance self-efficacy. The peer context reinforces the child's self-efficacy as the child learns coping and problem-solving behaviors through the development of peer relationships.

Particularly applicable to educational psychology and critical theory is Bandura's recognition of the importance of self-efficacy in the school milieu for successful educational outcomes. For Bandura, the school milieu is the place where individuals learn the knowledge, strategies, and skills needed for successful participation in society. Self-efficacy is critical for mastery in the school environment and the wider social environment. According to him, individuals possessing high self-efficacy at academic task mastery will perform more successfully than individuals lacking academic self-efficacy and will also perform better at activities outside the school environment. Thus, those who come to school cognitively prepared will likely be successful in school, and their academic success will increase their academic self-efficacy and motivate them to continue to do well. For those students who enter the school setting with low academic self-efficacy, however, their school experiences will likely serve to further decrease their self-efficacy and impede their development, leaving them ill-prepared for the future. Thus, while educational practices such as competitive grading and ability grouping may serve to enhance the self-efficacy of students already possessing high levels of academic self-efficacy, these practices can also decrease the self-efficacy of students entering school with low academic self-efficacy. Bandura's recognition of social influences on school performance disparities makes his theory compatible with critical theorists who recognize the bidirectional influence of children's individual characteristics and social context on their school performance.

Adolescence, the next milieu in Bandura's theory, involves cognitive skills of adaptation, avoidance of health risk behaviors, and practice of forethought regarding potential career paths. The adult milieu differs markedly from the adolescent milieu in that it involves the adoption and management of social roles involving marriage, employment, and financial management. The milieu of middle years involves stabilization of self-efficacy, but this stability is often reversed in advancing age, however, as physical functioning and memory decline. For Bandura, self-efficacy can be maintained in advancing age through reliance on differing levels of cognitive processes. For example, memory functions may decline in advanced age, but levels of information integration can remain consistent and levels of knowledge and expertise may increase.

Bandura's theory of social cognition employs a pragmatic approach to cognitive functioning that has real-world applicability; it recognizes fluidity in cognitive development whereby different cognitive processes become relevant as one's social, cultural, and temporal contexts change throughout the life cycle. Social cognition theory recognizes the context specificity of cognitive processes and allows for fluidity in the development and demonstration of cognitive functioning across the life cycle. In this way, social cognition theory is compatible with postformal thought.

CONTRIBUTIONS

By presenting human beings as reflective, self-directed, and self-managing individuals capable of adapting to changing environments with flexibility and adaptability, Bandura's social cognitive theory suggests a positive view of human existence. For him, both socially appropriate and socially inappropriate behaviors result from social cognitive learning, not childhood trauma or unconscious drives and impulses. As a result, maladaptive behaviors can be altered through appropriate social modeling. His straightforward, efficient, and effective methodology for treating socially inappropriate behaviors continues to have broad application in therapeutic and criminological contexts.

Bandura suggests that maladaptive behaviors (e.g., aggression, phobias, and depressive psychological states) arise through observational learning and persist because some reward (either vicarious or direct) is associated with the behavior. The goal of therapy, for him, is to enhance the individual's ability to self-regulate his or her own behavior in ways that are socially appropriate. He advocates therapy that changes maladaptive behavior through vicarious modeling (i.e., learner observes others successfully modeling behaviors to be adopted), cognitive modeling (i.e., learner imagines himself or herself modeling appropriate behavior), and systematic desensitization (i.e., learner performs behaviors that invoke anxiety gradually to decrease phobic reactions). The therapeutic applications of Bandura's social cognitive theory focus on small changes in behavior that can be generalized to other maladaptive behaviors in the individual.

Bandura has influenced public reform efforts as well with his social cognitive theory. He argues that the media is a symbolic environment that serves as a source of social modeling for learners. He has specifically argued that the attitudes and behaviors of children and adults can be altered through the modeling of violent television and film images. His argument for the causal link between violent media images and aggression resonated with concerned parents and educators advocating for media reform and has resulted in ongoing studies about the relationship between violent media images and aggression.

Bandura's social cognitive theory emphasizes the flexibility and adaptability of the individual and recognizes the individual capacity for planning and self-direction. Bandura's focus on individual agency and capacity for self-management makes the application of his theory particularly useful in changing times and diverse cultural settings. The far-reaching effects of globalization on society and technology have necessitated that individuals be able to adapt to quickly changing economic, social, and political environments. The application of Bandura's theory suggests that in the midst of changing times, individuals have the capacity to adapt, plan, and execute their lives in meaningful, productive ways.

Bandura's expansion of his concept of human agency to group dynamics resulted in his concept of collective agency; collective agency is the belief of groups of people in their ability to work together to produce change. This theoretical expansion broadens the application of social cognition theory to include strategies for social change.

CRITIQUES OF SOCIAL COGNITIVE THEORY

Biological theorists have been critical of Bandura's social cognitive theory, claiming that his social cognitive theory ignores the influence of genetics (e.g., individual biological states, physiological responses, differences in learning ability) on behavior. They argue that individual responses to their environment are partly genetic, and by ignoring this genetic influence, social cognitive theory ignores the role of the brain in information processing. In actuality, Bandura's social cognitive theory recognizes the influence of genetics on human behavior, but downplays this influence by arguing that social factors are a more powerful influence on behavior than are genetic factors.

HONORS AND AWARDS

To date, Albert Bandura has authored seven books and edited two additional works. In 1986 *Social Foundations of Thought and Action*, a book of his complete theories, was published. As a result of his contributions to the field of psychology, his advocacy for public reform, and his leadership and service endeavors, Bandura has received at least 16 honorary degrees and numerous awards and honors. Among his honors are the American Psychological Association Distinguished Achievement Award (1972), the William James Award from the American Psychological Society (1989), the Distinguished Lifetime Contributions Award from the California Psychological Association (1998), the Thorndike Award for Distinguished Contributions of Psychology to Education from the American Psychological Association (1999), the Lifetime Achievement Award from the Association for the Advancement of Behavior Therapy (2001), the Lifetime Achievement Award from the Western Psychological Association (2004), the James McKeen Cattell Award from the American Psychological Society (2004), and the Outstanding Lifetime Achievement Award from the American Psychological Association (2004).

REFERENCES

Bandura, A. (1997). *Self-efficacy: The Exercise of Control*. New York: W.H. Freeman.
Bandura, A. (1986). *Social Foundations of Thought and Action: A Social Cognitive Theory.* Englewood Cliffs, NJ: Prentice-Hall.
Evans, R. I. (1989). *Albert Bandura: The Man and His Ideas. A Dialogue*. New York: Praeger.

CHAPTER 4

Jerome Bruner

Jerome Bruner is still active today in the field of educational psychology. He has continued to evolve his ideas about learning and education in many books and articles. He made a large contribution to the development of curriculum theory during the 1950s and 1960s and is considered the leading figure of the "Cognitive Revolution" in the field of psychology. Most of Bruner's professional life has been spent in the northeastern section of the United States. During the 1970s, Bruner spent some time in England at Oxford University as the Watts Professor of Experimental Psychology. Since the late 1990s, Bruner has been a professor of psychology at the New York University of Law. During the 1960s, Bruner's ideas and theories on education had their greatest impact on the field of educational psychology.

Jerome Bruner was born in 1915 to a middle-class family from a suburb of New York City. At the young age of 12, Bruner's father died. After his father's death, Bruner moved around with his mother frequently, going to several different high schools. Bruner attended Duke University for his undergraduate degree in the 1930s and then went on to Harvard University for his graduate studies. At Harvard University, Bruner received his PhD. in Psychology in 1941. It was at Harvard that Bruner studied under the auspices of Gordon Allport, a leading psychologist of the time. Bruner's dissertation dealt with the impact of a leader's use of technology (i.e., the radio) upon people in society. Burton Weltman in writing about Bruner's work states, "his research focused on the relationship between propaganda, education, and public opinion" (Weltman, 1995, p. 223). Looking back at his work, Bruner claims his work was propelled by an obsession with Nazi Germany and ultimately dismisses the early years of his work (Bruner, 1983, p. 38).

During World War II, Bruner worked for the United States Army's Intelligence Corps focusing on issues of propaganda (Hevern, 2004). His interest in public opinion and eventually his concern about the world of education were given genesis during this era. Shortly after World War II, Bruner returned to Harvard as a professor to continue his life in the world of academia. During his early years at Harvard as a professor, Bruner began to study the concept of perception. It was at this time Bruner began to reject the notions of behaviorists and began his quest to discover what motivates people to learn. Throughout his work, Bruner found that people tended to see what they wanted to see (Weltman, 1995). At this time, Bruner began to work on studies in cognition.

It would be these studies in cognitive development that would propel Bruner to the forefront of educational psychology in the late 1950s.

Bruner took issue with the teachings of B. F. Skinner, a leading behavioral psychologist. Behaviorism had dominated the field of psychology, especially following the war years of the 1940s. According to Skinner, behaviorism addressed the following concepts: that individual nature could be managed by social nurturing; inherited traits could be countered by societal factors; and conditioning could help people learn or to be trained. For Bruner, the biggest problem with behaviorism is that it denied the capacity of human reason. Bruner believed that reason could control human behavior. He had a problem with people who conditioned other people. He felt that this type of conditioning was antidemocratic and too controlling. Bruner in his work began to write about how the right hand controlled the imagination and emotion of human beings and the left hand controlled the scientific and rational side of our thinking. The theory of the right hand and left hand led Bruner to think more about how meaning is constructed. It was with these theoretical writings that Bruner began to be noticed by other leaders in the field of psychology and eventually emerged as a leader.

The seminal event that brought Bruner to the national scene was the 1957 launching of the satellite Sputnik by the Soviet Union. This event caused fear in both the hearts and minds of liberal and conservative thinkers in America. The Cold War between the United States and the Soviet Union was in full momentum by the end of the 1950s. The 1950s has often been characterized by romantic imagery of the stable American family, but a level of anxiety and fear existed in most corners of America. The Sputnik launching by the Soviets gave a platform for people critical of American education to claim that we were behind the Soviets in mathematics and science. A national conference of leaders was convened to deal with this apparent educational gap. Bruner was the leader of the national conference at Woods Hole on Cape Cod in 1959. The conference was sponsored by the National Academy of Sciences and the National Science Foundation (Smith, 2002). It was from the discussions at the conference that the classic work *The Process of Education* (1960) by Jerome Bruner emerged. This book provided the research-based evidence that backed many new curriculum programs of the 1960s. It was during this period of time that Bruner became a leading figure in the cognitive revolution that would control the world of education during the 1960s. Bruner became a leading figure on many panels such as the President's Advisory Panel of Education, advisor to the Head Start Program, and president of the American Psychological Association from 1964 to 1965 (Smith, 2004).

The Woods Hole conference helped to usher in the New Curriculum movement of the 1960s. The New Curriculum movement ultimately was concerned with the fact that the United States did not produce enough top-notch scientists (Weltman, 1995). Course materials and teacher training in the sciences was blamed for the failure of American students, as compared to students in the Soviet Union. The curriculum that was developed from the conference would ultimately lead Bruner to develop "Man: A Course of Study" (MACOS) in the mid-1960s. The MACOS curriculum was more social-studies based and sought to answer the following questions: what makes a human being uniquely human and how did humans get to be this way. Bruner was the leading figure in the development of constructivist theories of learning. The constructivist theory of learning is concerned with how an individual constructs meaning. The consequences for education were that teachers should be concerned with how a learner is thinking as opposed to the material that is taught. In addition to this concern, a teacher must realize that knowledge is not independent from the experiences of the learner. By promoting constructivist theory of learning, Bruner is oft aligned with Jean Piaget and Lev Vygotsky.

Bruner used a similar framework for his ideas as Piaget but disagreed about absolute stages of development. Bruner's objection with Piaget's stages of development was his disagreement with what makes a child ready for an "adult concept" (Weltman, 1995). Piaget's theory of development had become gospel during the 1950s. Education in America had become dependent upon the biologically determined stages as outlined by Piaget. Piaget argued that pushing a child too early might be detrimental to a child's learning. Thus, the system of American education was neatly divided into grade levels and according to these grade levels different concepts would be taught. A young child would not be ready for the scientific fields of biology, chemistry, and physics until the high school setting. In Bruner's work *The Process of Education,* he outlined several key concepts for learning to take place at any level. Bruner wrote two follow-up books about his theories that he outlined in *The Process of Education.* Those books were *The Process of Education: Towards a Theory of Instruction* (1966) and *The Relevance of Education* (1971).

In *The Process of Education: Towards a Theory of Instruction,* Bruner claimed that structure in learning was essential in helping a person to master concepts. Structure for a developer of curriculum is important because it helps the curriculum developer to divide a subject matter into steps. This division of subject matter helps the learner to master the new concept. According to Bruner, the use of structure in education helps to make a student's learning more efficient, useful, and meaningful (Weltman, 1995). In Bruner's *The Process of Education: Towards a Theory of Instruction,* he defines that structure is needed in order to understand the larger body of knowledge. Structure does not necessarily include a list of basic facts or details that a learner must memorize. For Bruner the understating of subject comes from understanding the main concepts. Discovery learning uses this principle. A student in a discovery learning setting does not simply memorize the teacher's explanations of topics but instead works through examples to learn the subject's structures.

Bruner criticized that American education wasted too much time in delaying concepts that a young learner may be ready to comprehend. His term for readiness was the idea of a spiral curriculum (Smith, 2002). A spiral curriculum should always revisit ideas and build upon them until a learner has grasped the bigger picture. Within this spiral curriculum, Bruner's concept that intuition is a key element in the learning process was important. A learner can start with a hunch and then explore that hunch to validate if their intuition was correct. It is this stimulation of intuition that allows for "any subject [to] be taught effectively in some intellectually honest form to any child at any stage of development" (Bruner, 1983). For Bruner a learner could make a guess at the structures before there was a need to rationalize about them. In his writings he compares this to the way scientists often make their discoveries. A scientist makes an observation about a human characteristic. The scientist then makes an intuitive guess as to the origins of this characteristic. Finally, a scientist must conduct an experiment to determine if the guess was correct. Therefore, Bruner in his writing and thinking makes the following statement: "The schoolboy learning physics is a physicist" (Weltman, 1995, p. 196). Lastly, Bruner states that a learner must be motivated to comprehend a concept and external elements, such as grades, rarely help a learner master a concept. Discovery is important for a learner to acquire new knowledge. Through a learner's own cognitive efforts, they can relate the new material to concepts they have learned before.

In developing these theories about instruction, Bruner worked with children in much the same way as Piaget did in his studies. Later in the 1970s, Piaget was critical of Bruner's theory and Piaget rejected the idea that anything can be taught to anyone at any age. Bruner observed several stages that a child goes through in discovering and learning concepts. A child comes to master their world by going through each stage. For Bruner, these stages are not absolutes. There are no boundaries or time limits with a stage, but in order to master a concept all three stages must be used. The three stages are known as enactive, iconic, and symbolic.

The first stage that Bruner defined was the enactive stage. A young child best understands their environment by interacting with the objects around them. A child is not using words or imagery at this level. At this level the objects around a child are used to help them make sense of their world.

An observation often noted by parents is that an infant or toddler often seems more fascinated by the box a gift came in as opposed to the actual gift. In this stage of learning, a child will play with coins and paper money in order to begin their understanding of currency. The second stage a child encounters is called iconic. At this level a child begins to make perceptions of their world. Visual memory begins to be developed by the child. Continuing with the example of currency, a child can begin to look at pictures of coins and money and make the connection of their values. Many children's books are filled with pictures of objects. Sometimes a child might not be able to touch or see an elephant first hand but through the iconic representation of an elephant in a children's book about circuses, a child has an interaction with an elephant. Icons are presented to the child or developed by the child on their own. The third stage is called symbolic. At this point the perceptual way of thinking gives way to symbol systems, such as, language, words, and numbers. The symbolic stage allows for concepts to become compacted in the learner's mind. Using the symbol of the dollar sign (i.e., $) in their writing will trigger for the learner their understanding of the concept of currency. Sayings such as "a penny saved is a penny earned" begin to carry meaning for the learner on the symbolic stage because of having mastered the concept of currency.

Children learn a subject matter by moving through the stages of enactive, iconic, and symbolic. The symbolic stage becomes the dominant level of learning for most people. In teaching a new concept it makes sense to use the order of the stages. However, a teacher of mathematics might realize that a student may conceptually understand the concepts of geometry but may still fall back on the iconic stage in order to work out the geometric problems. Using Bruner's theory, knowledge becomes a process in which a learner takes part in the construction and develops comprehension. Bruner wrote in *The Process of Education* that "the task of teaching a subject to a child at any particular age is one of representing the structure of that subject in terms of the child's way of viewing things" (Bruner, 1960, p. 33). The focus on the learner is very important. Thus, Bruner's theory is very student-centered. Anyone can learn any concept as long as the enactive, iconic, and symbolic terms are developmentally appropriate.

Bruner became a leading figure in America during the 1960s. After the assassination of President Kennedy in 1963, Lyndon Johnson took over as president and during his 1964 campaign looked at Bruner's concept of the Head Start program. Bruner conceived of Head Start as a way to bridge the cultural differences between the upper and lower classes of American society. Also, Bruner conceived of Head Start as a test of compensatory education (Weltman, 1995). President Johnson decided to use the Head Start program in his War on Poverty campaign. Bruner acted as an advisor to this program (Bruner, 1983, p. 152). The other major contribution to curriculum development and educational psychology during the 1960s by Bruner occurred with the development of MACOS starting in 1962.

The curriculum of MACOS was aimed at 10-year-old students, who were at the beginning stages of symbolic thought. MACOS was designed "to promote the social sciences rather than history, and structural concepts and values instead of facts" (Weltman, 1995, p. 248). The course came prepackaged with multimedia materials that a student would use to discover the concepts. Teachers needed to be extensively trained in order to use the program. The project received funding from the National Science Foundation. Between 1964 and 1967 the materials and course curriculum were tested effectively in volunteering school districts. The course was well received by students and was considered well designed by Bruner. The course emphasized discovery learning and critical thinking in interactive classroom settings. The students were not graded on their learning experiences in order to provide a stress-free environment (Weltman, p. 251). In the early 1970s a backlash against MACOS began to appear around the United States. Conservative parents in several states challenged that the program had a liberal bias and was inappropriate for their children. In particular some parents were concerned with the graphic presentation of

Eskimos seal hunting. Eventually, the controversy over the MACOS curriculum found its way to the United States Congress. Beginning in the 1970s, the National Science Foundation had to submit to the Congress for reviewing all project curriculums under budgetary consideration. As a result, MACOS lost funding and began to be removed from the many schools that adopted the curriculum. In the 1970s, Bruner's theories began to receive criticism from across the political spectrum. Left, right, and radical writers in the field of educational psychology attacked the writings about cognition by Bruner. Shortly after the failure of the MACOS project, Bruner left the United States and began his tenure at Oxford University.

Bruner continued to develop his theories about learning in many books and novels. In his later writings, Bruner became very critical of anti-intellectualism found in public opinion. One of Bruner's concerns in education had been how to bridge the gap between the "high brows" and "low brows" by developing a higher level of culture for all groups (Weltman, p. 259). Bruner wanted children to think like a scientist and thereby causing the child to appreciate the field of science. Bruner's work helped psychologists to see the child as a social being and not as a being who developed in isolation. Bruner's original theory of the child as an active scientist has changed over the years with his growth as a scholar. His concerns and writings have been focused more on the social activism and cultural studies. In his writings today, Bruner can be viewed as a poststructuralist. He has moved away from the formalism in his earlier writings and now tends to analyze statements and writings as forms of narrative text. Bruner continues to write about the link between psychology and education. His latest concern is with cultural psychology and its impact on education.

REFERENCES

Bruner, J. (1960). *The Process of Education*. Cambridge, MA: Harvard University Press.

Bruner, J. (1983). *In Search of Mind: Essays in Autobiography*. New York: Harper & Row.

Hevern, V. W. (2004, April). Key Theorists: Jerome S Bruner. *Narrative Psychology: Internet and Resource Guide*. Retrieved on December 10, 2005, from the Le Moyne College Web Site: http://web.lemoyne. edu/~hevern/nr-theorists/bruner_jerome_s.html.

Smith, M. K. (2002). Jerome S. Bruner and the Process of Education. *The Encyclopedia of Informal Education*. Retrieved on December 10, 2005, from http://www.infed.org/thinkers/bruner.htm. Last updated: January 28, 2005.

Weltman, B. D. (1995). Debating Dewey: The Social Ideas of American Educators Since World War II an Examination of Arthur Bestor, Jerome Bruner, Paul Goodman, John Goodlad, and Mortimer Adler (Doctoral dissertation, Rutgers The State University of New Jersey, 1995). *Dissertations Abstract International, 56/09*, 3479.

CHAPTER 5

Judith Butler

RUTHANN MAYES-ELMA

Olson and Worsham quoted Butler as stating,

For me, there's more hope in the world when we can question what is taken for granted, especially about what it is to be a human ... What qualifies as a human, as a human subject, as human speech, as human desire? How do we circumscribe human speech or desire? At what cost? And at what cost to whom? These are questions that I think are important and that function within everyday grammar, everyday language, as taken-for-granted notions. We feel that we know the answers.

WHY BUTLER?

Judith Butler is a very well known theorist of gender, power, sexuality, and identity. Many academics are introduced to Butler in graduate school, thus she has been described as "one of the superstars of '90s academia, with a devoted following of grad students nationwide," according to the Web site theory.org.uk. I fell in love with Butler while I was doing my dissertation; her theories on the aforementioned were fascinating (which we will get to later) and in my opinion could help the educational system become stronger. Butler's theories fall directly in line with postformal thinking. The definition of postformalism that I work from has been set forth by Joe Kincheloe, Shirley Steinberg, and Patricia Hinchey in this important book, *The Post-Formal Reader*: "Post-formal thinking is concerned with questions of meaning, self-awareness, and the nature and function of the social context.... Post-formalism grapples with purpose, devoting attention to issues of human dignity, freedom, power, authority, domination, and social responsibility" (1999, pp. 21–22). In thinking through this lens it couldn't be more obvious that Butler fits so nice and neatly within it, although Butler would hate the idea of anything fitting nice and neatly into a box.

Although Butler's main interest and passion resides with gender, power, sexuality, and identity, many crossovers can be derived from these and used to improve our educational system. Once we understand Butler's train of thought we can use the same reasoning and apply it to the many aspects of schools today in order to change what is a purely mechanistic system with all of its testing into a postformalistic system in which each student has control of their own learning.

BUTLER'S PASSION

A true Hegelian at heart, Butler has been influenced by Hegel before she even wrote her dissertation. Thus, Hegel himself is still influencing us, but through Butler's works instead of his own. In all of Butler's books she asks questions about the formation of identity and subjectivity. She traces the process of becoming through existing power structures and asks questions of those power structures, as stated by Sara Salih in her profound book, *Judith Butler*. Butler loves to ask questions, but rarely provides us with answers to those questions. Many find Butler's works in and of themselves to be a process of becoming.

Butler's best known work to date, which has also been regarded as her most important book, would have to be *Gender Trouble* (1990, 1999). In *Gender Trouble* Butler introduces us to the concept of gender as performativity, which she states is very different from performance. According to Butler the word "performance" denotes the existence of a subject, whereas "performativity" does not. This does not mean that there isn't a subject, but instead it may be behind or before the action in question, which was and still is a radical way of discussing gender identity. The performativity is created, as Butler states, through the social or the macro. The environment in which one is in helps shape one's gendered identity. Whereas each environment is different, one can perform gender very differently within each of the various environments. According to Butler, gender is something we "do," not something we "are." Butler's approach to gender identity has been said to come from Simone de Beauvoir's (1949) highly controversial book that was ahead of its time, *The Second Sex*, in which de Beauvoir states, "One is not born, but rather becomes, a woman. No biological, psychological, or economic fate determines the figure that the human female presents in society; it is civilization as a whole that produces this creature, intermediate between male and eunuch, which is described as feminine" (p. 281). Butler agrees in this sense of becoming, not born of or into, but instead of a process. She sees gender as what she has called an "artificial unity," where people are thrown together because of either their XX or XY chromosomes, as she states in her book *Gender Trouble* (1999, p. 114). Gender is an act or many acts put together, which is always occurring and reshaping or reinventing itself. For Butler, gender is produced, not a natural and definitely not a constant.

Butler also stated in *Gender Trouble* that feminists should not look at gender and the power structures that are produced and restrained by it in order to emancipate oneself, but instead understand how the category of "woman" is produced and for what political purpose (p. 2). In her book *The Psychic Life of Power*, Butler (1997) states that how we become our gender is by submitting to power (p. 2). She believes that the power structure itself gives us power and in order to change what power we have we must first change the system. Power forms our becoming and we in turn form power; it is very fluid. Just as Butler did not like the term "performance" when dealing with gender identity because it denotes the presence of a subject she also uses this idea of a non-preexisting subject in her ideas of reshaping power systems. Since we do not preexist, but instead become—or construct our own identities—Butler believes that it is possible to subvert oppressive power systems and recreate them into emancipatory systems.

In order to reshape power, thus reshaping reality we must reshape language, according to Butler. When Wittig (1992) stated in his book, *The Straight Mind and Other Essays*, that "Language casts sheaves of reality upon the social body, stamping it and violently shaping it," Butler agreed (pp. 43–44). In *Excitable Speech* (1997) Butler noted that we can turn words in our language that have negative connotations into ones that have positive connotations. We can embrace the term "woman" or "feminine" even when others are using it as negative. We can redefine what these terms mean and in turn how they should be used.

It is no secret that some do not like or agree with Butler, but no one can deny the fact that she has influenced and had a huge impact upon many different critical and theoretical fields. In Shildrick's opinion, in his chapter on Judith Butler in Brown, Collinson, and Wilkinson's book *Blackwells Biographical Dictionary of Twentieth-Century Philosophers* (1996), Butler's theorizations of performative identity are indispensable to postmodern feminism. McNay agreed in his article "Subject, Psyche & Agency: The Work of Judith Butler" in volume 16 of the journal *Theory, Culture & Society*, when he stated that Butler has "pushed feminist theory into new terrain" (1999, p. 175). Whereas Dollimore (1996) stated in his article "Bisexuality, Heterosexuality, and Wishful Theory" in volume 10 of the journal *Textual Practice*, that Butler is brilliant; he also found her to be "hopelessly wrong" (pp. 533–535). Whatever opinion you may have of Judith Butler I am sure you have not seen or heard the last of her. As Butler states herself in *Contingency, Hegemony, Universality: Contemporary Dialogues on the Left*, which she coauthored with Laclau and Zizek, she has not "fallen asleep on the job" (2000, p. 269). She will continue to discuss the "politics of discomfort," as Salih has so eloquently stated in her book *Judith Butler* (2002, p. 151).

BUTLER APPLIED TO EDUCATION

In our schools today we have curriculums that are dictated by standardized tests, thanks to No Child Left Behind (NCLB), which I'm sure Butler would agree should be renamed All Children Left Behind. Testing, now more than ever in our history determines the educational purpose for each child and school. Everything revolves around the test!

From studies we know that certain "types" of students do poorly on standardized tests namely any child who is the "other," which is based on a concept by Michel Foucault in his best-selling book *The History of Sexuality*; which includes anyone who is not an upper/middle class, white male. Many children learn one thing from this constant testing—they are stupid, they are not as good as the other children, and they will not amount to anything in life. We then label these students as "special needs," which Butler would disagree with altogether. Putting anything into a tight, neat category is an injustice, according to Butler, but that is what our current system does to children whether they do well or do poorly on the tests. This is not just an injustice for those who don't do well; it is also for those who do well. They are being set up for failure right from the start, they might not be able to live up to the expectation that others have of them from their tests scores. This "artificial unity," as Butler (1999) has deemed it in her infamous book *Gender Trouble*, is a result of standardized testing. Students are grouped into categories dependent upon how well they did on their tests. In this group the only thing that they have in common is their test score range, which makes it an "artificial" group.

And whose knowledge has been deemed the "official knowledge" as to put children into these "artificial" groups? Butler knows that the "knowledge" on the standardized tests and the "knowledge" that is being deemed important in class is not the "others" knowledge, but instead an elitist knowledge. It is a Eurocentric, patriarchal knowledge that has been deemed important and "best." The tests that every student must take are nothing more than an attempt to brainwash and perpetuate white supremacy. The "others" or outsiders as some may call them are expected to conform, or they will be banished from the elitist system. Isn't it ironic that the public school system that Horace Mann and Henry Barnard, and later John Dewey, set out to create with their idea of the universal schooling for all, a system where ALL students could receive an education and be valued, has turned full circle into what they were trying to get away from in the beginning. If lawmakers had it their way, every child who is not the "norm" (aka a white, upper/middle class male) would not be allowed to attend public school. Instead of honoring each individual, as Butler would have, we have instead honored who we deem worthy. So it then becomes a case of those who do poorly on the tests are obviously unworthy.

Butler believes that there is no "right" and "wrong," there are no binary oppositions, instead everything is fluid because things change with the social. In other words the micro changes along with the macro; each has an affect upon the other and each changes and is changed by the other. Interpretation is the key, according to Butler. Everything is up to interpretation. It is this interpretation that tells each of us what the world around us really is; it explains our own reality—knowing that there is no such thing as one "true" reality, but instead multiple realities, each being shaped by our interpretation of the macro. What Butler believes forms our interpretations is our culture, our social, and our environment in which we have been brought up and in which we currently live. So, again our interpretations are fluid as well, the micro and macro both play a part of forming each other's "realities." Which is why minorities (and I mean ALL types of minorities: race, creed, color, culture, gender, sexual orientation, etc.) do not do well on standardized tests because their "realities" are not the same as the white guy who made the test. What may be important to Mr. White Guy may not be, and probably isn't, what minorities deem as important. Instead of having children create their own realities, as Butler would have done in schools, NCLB has mandated that every student conform to the "right" and dominant reality.

When Butler stated that we could change reality and thus the power systems that operate within by changing the language, I believe she must have known that this would hold true for education as well. The power in our educational system, much less our country, is in the hands of the "elite," or what society has deemed elite—the Eurocentric, upper/middle class male, and in accordance with that falls the language we are to use, the "proper English" we are to teach our students. In order to change this power system, the system that thinks the answers to all our problems are in tests, we must change the language. A great place to begin this transformation is in our schools and classrooms. We concentrate on test scores for individuals and make sure that each individual child listens and memorizes, instead of coming together to learn from one another. Since there is no "I" in gender as Butler (1999) has stated in *Gender Trouble*, I would like to take it one step further and state that there is no "I" in education (p. 145). Gender is a performance, fluid and free, it changes as its environment changes, so should education.

In college I took a variety of subjects and courses. Some of which were standard banking system approaches to learning, while others were far greater than anything I could have imagined; classes where I was allowed to be free, to challenge myself, and educate myself. I was allowed to disagree with those philosophers, theorists, and scientists that many would say were "the greats." I learned from those around me through projects and discussions, some of which were very heated, but what is wrong with that. I became a more well rounded, better educated, and a more critical person through my discussions and dealings with different types of individuals, individuals who had been previously silenced in my educational world because their knowledge was not deemed worthy in my school. But why did I have to wait until I was in college to have these educational experiences? Why couldn't I have had them in preschool? Butler would agree that the reason I didn't was because it is too risky for those "elite" to have people think for themselves. If I had said the things that I did or gave the opinions I gave while I was in college during my K-12 education I would have been punished, just as Butler (1999) says we are punished for "doing" our gender "incorrectly" or against the status quo, in her book *Gender Trouble*.

With standardized testing, and NCLB in the larger context, there is always a right and a wrong, a correct way and an incorrect way, which is of course based on Eurocentric, patriarchal values. There is no interpretation, only the following of a set script, which ensures upper/middle class whites succeed and others fail and pushing those who do "fail" into trade schools or worse pushing them out of school altogether. Our country's lawmakers and those specifically behind NCLB's purpose would have to be to ensure our country has white, male CEOs and minority McDonald's workers, if they are even lucky enough to get that job in these trying times.

I'm sure Butler would agree that NCLB has begun and encouraged others to believe in the propaganda that they have been trying to "sell" for quite some time now. In my opinion, just as the Nazis unleashed their propaganda against the Jews in order to demoralize them and bring their status as seen by the rest of the world down to lower than animals; NCLB is trying to do the same thing to all those children who do not fit the "correct" profile—white, upper/middle class male. All of those who do believe that standardized tests are correcting the problem are inadvertently following and perpetuating the aforementioned propaganda—the NCLB propaganda.

Butler believes that we need to empower those who are being disserviced under our current system. Instead of using what many deem the "filing cabinet system" where teachers impart wisdom, knowledge, or intelligence (whatever you want to call it) onto the students, thus mandating that they file it to memory so it can be spit out later on a test, we should actually help each other create knowledge. In this model teachers and students are all active participants, none no better than the rest. Again, they work together and learn from each other's "realities." They come into contact with "others" knowledge and grapple with it (which is part of the postformal definition used earlier) in order to interpret it for themselves in accordance with some other knowledge that they have previously interpreted and which has become a part of their own created identity. Together everyone will derive meanings of things in their own way, no right and no wrong. People just might even open their minds a bit.

Butler once spoke of an incident that happened to her in an interview she gave to Olson and Worsham (2000), which appeared in volume 20 of *The Journal of Composition Theory*, that speaks to this point of learning from each other. While she taught at Berkeley a student asked her if she was a lesbian. He asked it in such a way to make sure she knew that his definition and ideas of the word "lesbian" were negative. She did not let this deter her though. She saw this as an opportunity to educate him about her definition of the word "lesbian." She replied that she was indeed a lesbian and she said it without shame or humiliation, which stunned the student because he was obviously looking for a shameful, humiliated reaction. Butler stated, "It wasn't that I authored that term: I received the term and gave it back; I replayed it, reiterated it . . . It's as if my interrogator were saying, 'Hey, what do we do with the word *lesbian*? Shall we still use it?' And I said 'Yeah, let's use it *this* way!' Or it's as if the interrogator hanging out the window were saying 'Hey, do you think the word *lesbian* can only be used in a derogatory way on the street?' And I said 'No, it can be claimed on the street! Come join me!' We were having a negotiation" (p. 760). This of course is a very risky conversation to have according to the higher powers that run our country's educational system, but these are the kinds of conversations we need to be having, instead of having a mandated curriculum that makes children memorize "facts" (and I use that term loosely) and spit them out again on a test.

In education we need to discuss and learn from one another. We need to discuss those issues that have been deemed "taboo" in our culture, how else are we to move past them? How else are we to emancipate ourselves, change the power system, and thus change ourselves? This is real education, the type that will never occur under the NCLB legislation because it would disrupt the current macro system and that of course would just be too risky. Call me a dreamer, and maybe it is because I believe in Butler's passion, but I believe that we can have an educational system that has a positive, lasting effect upon society instead of the negative one we are now perpetuating and endorsing with our current educational system's legislation. I believe in an educational system that wipes out injustice and empowers those who are currently considered "others." We know how and what to implement in order to make this dream a reality, Butler has put forth many ideas that would help us achieve our goal, we just need to do it now.

Just as Butler loves to ask questions, we need to begin to ask questions of our educational system. We need to look at what is working and what is not working, what is damaging our children and what is empowering our children, what can help us and our descendants have a bright future, and what is keeping all of us from that future which unless we change will never be attained.

CHAPTER 6

John Dewey

DONAL E. MULCAHY

In his lifetime, John Dewey not only achieved prominence in the fields of psychology, philosophy, and education but very significantly shaped new thinking in all three. As is evidenced by the attention given in current debate to issues of assessment and testing in schools, of the insights he shared, none are more contentious and of continuing relevance today than his work in the field of educational psychology.

INTRODUCTION

From quiet, humble beginnings, and even self-doubt, John Dewey's long and highly decorated career leaves him remembered as one of the greatest thinkers of the twentieth century and a towering figure, alongside Plato and Rousseau, in the field of education. Throughout, Dewey remained a man of admirable personal qualities: a devoted husband and father, a source of succor and comfort to society's marginalized, a defender of citizens' and workers' rights, and a person of modest demeanor who dealt as nobly with pain and loss in his personal life as he did with fame and recognition. In his own life he exemplified his philosophical convictions: that theory is meaningless without action, that reason and emotions are interwoven, and that knowledge and intelligence are to serve living. Ever the pragmatist, Dewey also believed philosophy should be used to serve both education and social betterment.

As an educational psychologist, Dewey found himself at odds with many of his contemporaries. He understood the human mind to be in need of cultivation. He believed that one's mind is constantly striving to make connections from lived and learned experiences to new encounters and information. Of utmost importance to one's ability to learn, thus, was the relevance of new information or concepts. In believing that we learn in order to live, Dewey believed that the child's interest or impulses must be the starting point for the school curriculum. If the child perceives no importance or purpose in the activity undertaken, the child will not only be less willing but less capable of learning from the activity. Relevance, purpose, and connection of the curriculum to the student's immediate daily life, Dewey felt, was crucial to a democratic and psychologically sound approach to school. In opposition to such an approach were the likes of G. Stanley Hall and David Snedden who saw school as serving the purpose of creating a unified, monocultural, socially efficient school and society. He also stood in opposition to the ideas of the famous educational psychologist of the day, Edward L. Thorndike.

It could be said that the scientific approach to education, conceived and developed by Edward L. Thorndike, has had the most profound and lasting impact on educational psychology and the urban school. In contrast to Dewey's understanding that one makes connections from one experience to another, and his view of the need for an individual to internalize and construct understanding, Thorndike held that students learned through response to stimuli. His "laws of learning" assumed children would learn only in response to punishment and reward. He also believed that what was learned in one context was not transferable to another. The need, therefore, for subjects such as Latin and the mental discipline that it nurtured, no longer existed. The notion of mental discipline as a concept was seen as mythical. Thorndike went on to create IQ tests and aptitude tests and many more mental tests to separate and track the intelligent from the unintelligent and the academic from the worker.

In *Left Back* Diane Ravitch, notes that this "mental testing was the linchpin of the scientific movement in education." The standardized test that remains with us today came from this period, the first created by Thorndike himself and his colleagues at Teacher's College. While most schools across the country used the tests as a convenient and easy method of sorting students, many critics at the time saw the danger of their misuse. According to Ravitch these critics warned that "the 'norm' on the new tests might be mistaken for a standard, when it was only a statistical average of those who had taken the test." Today we see the legacy of mental testing. It is a legacy that has left many believing one's intelligence is fixed and measurable. Thorndike's many textbooks and the administrative Progressives' desire for vocational schooling and a centralized school system all helped engrain such a notion in the generations of teachers and university professors that followed. Psychologists turned to the simplicity of testing to track students in the service of society, rather than engage, as would Dewey, a deeper and more complex psychology that recognized the cognitive process as a whole.

These views would lead Dewey to make highly significant contributions to the fields of philosophy, psychology, and educational theory, as we shall see. No less important was their challenge to widely accepted psychological beliefs of the day and their implications for theory and practice of education. Of particular interest here is the manner in which Dewey sought to democratize the notion of intelligence itself by challenging these beliefs and the way in which they shaped schooling to perpetuate existing social and economic inequalities. This he would do by emphasizing the importance of lived experience as the basis for future learning and attempting to give to all students the opportunity to bring their particular experience to bear upon the social, economic, and political issues of their own day. There is no better way to come to an appreciation of the persistent optimism of Dewey's thought and his constructivist stance on these matters than by understanding his early career and his social activism.

FORMATIVE INFLUENCES

Born in Burlington Vermont in 1859, John Dewey began his professional career as a rather shy young schoolteacher after completing his graduation from the University of Vermont in 1879. Having spent some 3 years teaching, in 1882 he entered graduate studies in philosophy at the Johns Hopkins University in Baltimore. Following the completion of his PhD in 1884 he accepted a teaching position in the philosophy department at the University of Michigan. In 1894 he moved to the University of Chicago as a professor of philosophy and head of the Department of Philosophy, Psychology and Pedagogy. Dewey founded the Laboratory School at the University of Chicago where he worked closely with his wife. After a disagreement with the university authorities related to the running of the Laboratory School, in 1904, Dewey moved to the New

York City and the Department of Philosophy at Columbia University, where he remained until his retirement in 1929.

Though known to many in education as the "father of progressivism," it was as a philosopher and psychologist that Dewey first gained widespread recognition. At Chicago and Columbia, and even following his retirement, however, he was deeply involved in a variety of social, educational, and political undertakings, becoming in many ways as much a social activist as a philosopher. While still in Chicago, alongside his innovative work with the Laboratory School at the University of Chicago, he was also active in a number of social causes. Perhaps most notable among these was his work with Jane Addams in conducting the affairs of Hull House. Hull House was a settlement house for those, including immigrants, dislocated by the rapid social, industrial, and technological changes of the era.

Following his move to New York, Dewey became a founder member and the first President of the American Association of University Professors in 1915. In addition, he was a charter member of the Teachers Union (TU) in New York City and later the New York Teachers Guild. Dewey was also active in the "outlawry of war" movement after the World War I. He held office in a number of civic organizations such as the American Civil Liberties Union, and he helped found the New School for Social Research. During the 1920s he lectured in countries around the world including China, Japan, Mexico, Russia, and Turkey. In 1937 he traveled to Mexico City while serving as the chairman of the commission of inquiry into the charges brought against Leon Trotsky.

To know of these varied practical involvements by Dewey aids in understanding a fundamental feature of his thought in philosophy, psychology, and education, namely, the interplay of thought and action, of experience and reflection, of science and philosophy, of education and psychology. It also explains why Dewey's thought has come to be seen today as contributing to a serious critique of contemporary psychological theory in education. In educational terms these aspects of his approach were exemplified in the Laboratory School at Chicago. The teachers in the Laboratory School were charged with the continuous search for more effective ways of teaching. Here ideas and theories from psychology and philosophy were put into action to assess their effectiveness and reliability in improving schooling. Following observation and further reflection, refinements could be made and educational reform placed on a more scientific footing. This interplay between the scientific method and human cognition as Dewey perceived it is the central focus of his book, *How We Think*. In this book he is concerned with coming to understand the complete act of thought and he envisions the book as a sort of guide to understanding how we come to know. By contrast with the educational psychology of his time, Dewey strongly believed that individuals come to understand the world they encounter in a unique way. As Joe Kincheloe notes in *Rethinking Intelligence*, Dewey realized that only in relation to "lived context can individuals aspire to cognitive growth because higher thinking always references some lived context." As a basic philosophical stance, he believed that to remove context was to remove relevance. School, therefore, must be of relevance to the child's present day life, and school activities should connect to the everyday needs and actions of the students. For school to disconnect prior experience and daily life from the classroom, he believed, was to render school in many ways useless. His characterization of how we think also reveals how Dewey placed great faith in the capacity of human beings to think and reason.

Of all his practical involvements, however, Dewey's interest in and association with the progressive education movement is the one that most impacted his work as an educational theorist. Although he was never an official spokesman for the movement, and on occasion felt compelled to point out the errors of its ways—most notably in the publication of *Experience and Education* in 1937—he was often associated in the public's mind with many of the movement's weaknesses and excesses. Interestingly, in the judgment of historians he is generally held in high esteem.

Indeed, the ideas and ideals of Dewey have been claimed by traditionalists and progressives alike, a testament, no doubt, to his insight into the educational, psychological process. This being so, it may be helpful to introduce Dewey's thoughts on education by way of an organizational framework that identifies a number of the key concepts that may be said to characterize progressive educational theorizing in general. In doing so it will assist in highlighting the distinguishing features his educational thought while drawing on his philosophical ideas to elaborate where necessary.

ORGANIZING PRINCIPLES OF PROGRESSIVE EDUCATION

In his book, *Issues and Alternatives in Educational Philosophy*, George R. Knight has identified the following six principles that can be used to characterize progressive educational thought: (1) The process of education finds its genesis and purpose in the child; (2) pupils are active rather than passive; (3) the teacher's role is that of advisor, guide, and fellow traveler rather than that of authoritarian classroom director; (4) the school is a microcosm of the larger society; (5) classroom activity should focus on problem solving rather than on artificial methods of teaching subject matter; (6) the social atmosphere of the school should be cooperative and democratic.

The process of education finds its genesis and purpose in the child. Although Dewey would never approve of efficiency models in education either in his own time or today, he did express the need for a social vision in schooling. Above all, he believed most clearly in the centering of the curriculum around the child. Where proponents of social efficiency like Philbrick said school was about the imposition of tasks whether or not the child liked it, Dewey argued that tasks without a known purpose reduce one's desire to complete that task successfully, and to fight a child's nature is counterproductive. He says, in *The School and Society*, that one should "begin with the child's ideas, impulses, and interests" and use those to direct the child's education.

For Dewey, the starting point in learning and in teaching is a problem felt by the child, as distinct from a need or desire felt by the teacher or the community to pass on information about a topic considered important to any particular body of knowledge. Knowledge, he wrote, was of no educational value in itself but only insofar as the child could benefit from interacting with it. This, of course, is in stark contrast to the view of educational psychologists such as Thorndike who believed knowledge transfer from one experience to another was not possible. As Dewey colorfully put it, the fact that we do not feed beefsteak to infants does not mean it has no nutritional value. It simply has none for infants who are not ready to consume it. Similarly with knowledge and the psychology of the student: in and of itself information is of no educational value until the child is ready to benefit from interacting with it. At the same time, he was keen to emphasize that responding to problems of inquiry encountered by the child could be the very means of bringing him or her into contact with important bodies of knowledge. Rejecting what he considered the faulty either/or dichotomy between child and subject matter, in *Experience and Education*, Dewey argues that a continuum could be constructed from the incomplete and unorganized experience of the child to the highly organized and abstract knowledge of the adult world represented by the teacher and housed in the academic disciplines. The teacher's job was to introduce this knowledge to the child in accordance with his or her interests and level of prior experience or knowledge—just as a child's diet is gradually strengthened as it grows and is capable of digesting more adult foods. This would be done through the "progressive organization of subject matter." Hence Dewey emphasizes on method.

Pupils are active rather than passive. Central to method in Dewey's view is the recognition that children are naturally active rather than passive. Writing of the nature of method in *My Pedagogic Creed*, according to Ronald F. Reed and Tony W. Johnson, Dewey said, "the active side precedes the passive in the development of the child-nature . . . the neglect of this principle is the cause of a large part of the waste of time in school work. The child is thrown into a passive, receptive, or absorbing attitude. The conditions are such that he is not permitted to follow the law of his nature; the result is friction and waste." The admonitions of Rousseau notwithstanding, when Dewey began his work in education, the 3 Rs and the classical liberal arts subjects dominated the curriculum, and both schooling in general and teaching in particular were highly regimented and authoritarian. Teachers were believed to possess knowledge and it was their job to ensure the child received that knowledge. As populations exploded in cities across the United States and schools were overwhelmed with new students, authoritarian and socially efficient schooling assumed its role as problem solver. In Dewey's opinion, however, this approach ran counter to the learning process and the psychology of the child. Dewey searched for a new, alternative approach. He sought a curriculum that would put the primary focus on the child's needs, and the natural dispositions, and ways of learning of the child rather than on predetermined sets of information that were disconnected from the everyday life of the child. Understanding that the educational psychology of his day was in support of the authoritative, behaviorist approach to school, he spoke out in opposition pointing out that such an approach did not encourage what he called "cognitive inventiveness" but rather worked to shut down the mind of the child.

Drawing on how he envisions a young child's learning taking place naturally in the home—the natural psychology of the child—Dewey suggests that just as participation in household tasks becomes an occasion of learning in the home so also in the school setting can activities lead to learning. In the school, moreover, it could be done more systematically. In *The School and Society* Dewey points out that, once again, the starting point for learning would be the activities of the child: "The child is already intensely active, and the question of education is the question of taking hold of his activities, of giving them direction. Through direction, through organized use, they tend toward valuable results." It then becomes the role of the teacher to guide such activities toward valuable ends.

The teacher's role is that of advisor, guide, and fellow traveler rather than that of authoritarian classroom director. For Dewey, the teacher is a facilitator rather than an instructor. He or she must start with the child's impulse and, as described in the excerpt above, guide the child through its own discovery and learning. Here he is careful to point out that engaging in mindless or merely indulgent activity by the child does not lead to worthwhile learning. He says that we must not "simply humor" a child's interest. Rather, when confronted with "the world of hard conditions," that interest or impulse must accommodate itself, "and there again come in the factors of discipline and knowledge." With organization of equipment and materials the teacher can be a true guide and fellow traveler toward knowledge. This Dewey explains with reference to an example drawn from the Laboratory School where the teacher led children to explore and discover based on a lesson centered on the cooking of eggs. When one boy asked to follow a recipe the teacher responded by saying that doing so would not enable them to "understand the reasons for what they were doing." Instead the class reviewed the constituents of the egg, how eggs compared to vegetables and meat, and then experimented with cooking the egg in different water temperatures. The point being, for a child simply follow directions—drop the egg in boiling water and take it out after three minutes—"is not educative." To "recognize his own impulse" and come to understanding, is indeed educative.

While the teacher may be a guide, and must be responsive to the progressive organization of subject matter, the teacher must also be a follower: a follower of the child and, importantly, a follower of how the interests and concerns of the child are related to how he or she learns to become an independent learner and knower. For Dewey, this process followed a logically discernible course and was considered so important for the teacher that he presented the idea in a form specially written for teachers in *How We Think*. It is an aspect of Dewey's educational psychology that is closely linked to his general philosophy of pragmatism, and to its epistemology in particular. It also has implications for both the methodological and for the curricular aspects of education.

As was said earlier, in *How We Think* Dewey explains the process in which we come to know with reference to what he termed the complete act of thought (CAT). It is a psychological process that reflects the influence of scientific method and Dewey's view that living precedes knowing. That is to say, we do not live in order to know but rather know in order to live. This understanding again points up the importance of school activities being relevant to the child's present life for if new information does not relate to it, the child's mind perceives it as being of no use. The complete act of thought is set out by him as a five-stage process. In stage one a person encounters a problem in living that appears as an obstacle to be dealt with if progress is to be made. In the second stage, one moves beyond initial bafflement, identifies the particular obstacle or problem to be dealt with, and engages in an initial reflection upon the problem. Steps are taken to ascertain the circumstance in which the problem arose, its likely causes, and how it should be dealt with. In the third stage, there is reflection on the most likely answer or solution to the problem during which time the individual ponders a possible range of solutions and frames some tentative hypotheses. This leads to a fourth stage in which a hypothesis is chosen—following more prolonged and systematic reflection on the likely consequences of a given action. Stage five consists of putting to the test the chosen hypothesis in order to see if it holds up by solving the problem that has been encountered. If the hypothesis holds up—if it works—it is deemed to be true, or as Dewey preferred to put it in *How We Think*, the hypothesis is treated as "a warranted assertion." If it does not work, it is not deemed to be true and another hypothesis must be chosen.

Classroom activity should focus on problem solving rather than on artificial methods of teaching subject matter. If the complete act of thought represents the way we think and come to know, it is important that teaching and learning in the classroom should follow a similar sequence and begin with problems encountered by the child. Drawing from Kilpatrick, Dewey developed the idea that problem solving was an integral part of a child-centered curriculum. Such an approach works with the natural psychology of the child. It develops social skills, cooperation, and discovery, and problems can be generated by the students to ensure relevance and purpose. It is for this reason that, for Dewey, teaching and learning should follow from the interests of the child and not be forced upon him or her. But even when knowledge is arrived upon in this way, he was careful to emphasize that knowledge or truth is not to be seen as fixed and permanent. He used the term warranted assertion to signify that something may be considered knowledge in so far as it works to solve a particular problem. But in different circumstances the same "knowledge" or "truth" may not be borne out. In keeping with this, and in opposition to the trend of educational psychology of the time, Dewey spoke not of education or learning as a preparation for life—as in something down the road—because he believed that children had lives to live in the here and now. Given that he recognized the unfixed nature of "knowledge," the fixed nature of the school curriculum presented a second reason for not viewing education as a preparation for life. It follows that Dewey believed that learning how to learn was the more fundamental educational acquisition.

The school is a microcosm of the larger society; the social atmosphere of the school should be cooperative and democratic. "What nutrition and reproduction are to physiological life," Dewey wrote in *Democracy and Education*, "education is to social life." Up to this point the methodological aspects of Dewey's thought and their philosophical underpinnings have been dealt with. But for Dewey education and schooling were inextricably interwoven with the immediate community and the broader society. Education is the lifeblood of society, its source of sustenance and continuance; society, including its values, institutions, and practices, are to be the shapers of the young and hence of their education and learning. In advanced societies there are attendant dangers in the latter. In particular, there is "the standing danger that the material of formal instruction will be merely the subject matter of the schools, isolated from the subject matter of life-experience. The permanent social interests are likely to be lost from view." In *Rethinking Intelligence*, Kincheloe notes that Dewey maintained the educational psychology of his day was "antithetical to preparation for life in a democratic society." He goes on to stress that Dewey was "especially critical of those psychologists and educators who argued that many students . . . were incapable of working with their minds." Dewey believed that IQ testing, along with noninterpretive psychology in general, ran counter to the ideals of a democratic society. He saw its implementation as a means of maintaining the status quo.

Just as importantly for Dewey, as Perkinson points out in *Since Socrates*, "the emerging democratic society required more than simply taking the traditional education previously given to the few and extending it to the many. . . . A democratic social order stood in need of a new kind of education, a democratic education." It was such an education that Dewey envisioned for the Laboratory School in Chicago, one where children learned from living and working with and for one another in daily tasks. In this way they learned not only subject matter but also what it meant to share and to come together to form community.

FIFTY YEARS LATER

In contemporary discussion, John Dewey could most obviously be associated with educational psychologists in the constructivist camp and even with critical pedagogy. As constructivists believe in the ongoing assimilation of new information into one's being, Dewey makes clear, in *My Pedagogic Creed*, that he too believed that education was "a continuing reconstruction of experience." The constructivist psychology teaches that the process of learning is an internal process unique to the individual. This belief runs counter to the behaviorist belief that persisted in schools of Dewey's time and persists in schools today. Just as he recognized that viewing knowledge as existing outside the individual and applicable outside of context is folly, constructivists today resist the notion that testing knowledge void of context is somehow relevant. He assumed each child came with understandings and knowledge based on their lived experiences. These experiences, "the child's own social activities," as Dewey put it according to Diane Ravitch in her book *Left Back*, should be understood as the basis for how the child will receive and assimilate new information. In keeping with this belief in the individual construction of understanding and knowledge, and in the efficacy of "hands-on" discovery learning, Dewey promoted projects and experiments over a preset curriculum.

Critical pedagogy also draws on Dewey's educational psychology. Dewey believed, for example, as do those in critical pedagogy, that relevance to the child's life is of vital importance. He said in *My Pedagogic Creed* that school "must represent present life." In addition, the belief that knowledge is not unchanging is common to both Dewey and critical pedagogy. Just as critical pedagogy speaks of the inseparability of the knower and the known, of how knowledge is not existent in space but only exists as a part of one's psyche, he sees knowledge as always changing and only valid in relation to the individual and how it relates to his or her life experience. Furthermore, as does the critical pedagogue, Dewey believes that school is responsible for producing socially aware, democratic citizens. In *The School and Society*, he makes clear that school needs to provide a socially guided experience that prepares individuals for changing times and so should be "an active community . . . an embryonic society, instead of a place set apart in which to learn lessons."

In the same way that Dewey rejected the notion that some students were unable to work their minds and recognized the use of tracking as a tool to suppress the economically deprived and otherwise marginalized citizens, critical pedagogy also rejects blind adherence to so-called scientific truth. In moving beyond the positivistic belief that meeting certain criteria (especially when decontextualized and overlooking social and economic factors) is a valid form of assessment, critical pedagogy recognizes that social, political, and economic contexts, one's life experience, and an infinite number of other factors that influence our unique perspective, cannot be overlooked. Dewey's educational psychology took account of the impact such factors have on the child's mind and predisposition to learning. When Dewey spoke of the need to develop social intelligence, it was the need to account for this variety of contexts and conditions that he was emphasizing. These are contexts and conditions largely overlooked in the standardized testing movement heralded by the behaviorist psychology of Thorndike and others.

FURTHER READINGS

Cremin, Lawrence A. (1957). "The Progressive Movement in American Education: A Perspective." *Harvard Educational Review XXVII*, 4: 251–270.

Dewey, John (1956). *The School and Society*. Chicago: The University of Chicago Press.

Dewey, John (1937/1963). *Experience and Education*. New York: Collier.

Dewey, John (1996). *Democracy and Education*. New York: The Free Press.

Dewey, John (1933). *How We Think*. Boston: D.C. Heath.

Garrison, Jim (1999). John Dewey. In *Encyclopedia of Philosophy of Education*, http://www.vusst.hr/ENCYCLOPAEDIA/john_dewey.htm.

Knight, George R. (1989). *Issues and Alternatives in Educational Philosophy*. Berrien Springs, MI: Andrews University Press.

Perkinson, Henry J. (1980). *Since Socrates*. New York: Longman.

Ravitch, Diane (2001). *Left Back: A Century of Battles Over School Reform*. New York: Touchstone.

Reed, Ronald F. (2000). Tony W. Johnson. In *Philosophical Documents in Education*. New York: Longman.

Tyack, David B. (1974). *The One Best System: A History of American Urban Education*. Cambridge, MA: Harvard University Press.

CHAPTER 7

Erik Erikson

JAMES MOONEY

INTRODUCTION

Erik Erikson was one of the most influential minds of the twentieth century. Philosophically rooted in the psychoanalytic theories of Sigmund Freud, who he knew and with whom he worked, Erikson's work in the field of psychology, particularly the areas of identity development, psychohistory, and psychosocial development, were groundbreaking and continue to have relevance in the study of human psychological development. This chapter will give a biographical account of Erikson's life, as well as describe the important intellectual contributions he made to his field and to educational psychology.

BIOGRAPHICAL INFORMATION

Erik Erikson was born in Frankfurt, Germany on June 15, 1902. He was raised as Erik Homburger, having been given his stepfather's surname. Erikson completed school at the age of 18 and spent a year traveling throughout Europe, reading, writing, and sketching. He briefly attended two art schools, the Badische Landeskunstschule in Karlruhe and the Kunst-Akademie in Munich. His artistic works included huge woodcuts that were displayed in an exhibition in Munich's Glaspalast (Coles, 1970).

After two years in Munich, Erikson moved to Florence, where he befriended an American writer (and later child psychoanalyst) named Peter Blos. In 1927, Blos opened a school in Vienna for the children of Dorothy Burlingame and other Americans living in Vienna. He invited Erikson to join him at the school as an art and history teacher. This move would first usher Erikson into the fields of education and psychology. Mrs. Burlingame was very close friends with Anna Freud, child analyst and daughter of Sigmund Freud, and it was through this association that Erikson began to work with Sigmund and Anna Freud in the field of psychoanalysis (Coles, 1970).

From 1927 to 1933, Erikson lived in Vienna, teaching art at his friend Peter Blos's school, working with Anna Freud and himself being analyzed by her, and studying clinical psychoanalysis with August Aichhorn, Edward Bibring, Helene Deutsche, Heinz Hartmann, and Ernest Kris at the Vienna Psychoanalytic Society. He also studied the Montessori philosophy of education and graduated from the Lehrerinnenverein, the Montessori teachers' association (Coles, 1970).

Blos and Erikson's school in Vienna balanced a traditional teacher-centered model with a more progressive form of education that could later be described in the field of educational psychology as Constructivism. The students were given a greater degree of freedom to determine what and how they wanted to learn. Hands-on activities and projects were encouraged, and the students selected what aspects of history, geography, mythology, and the arts that they were to learn, and how to explore these concepts and demonstrate their mastery of the material (Coles, 1970).

Upon the completion of his studies at the Vienna Psychoanalytical Society in 1933, Erikson was granted the title of full member of the Society. He and his wife, concerned about the rising political turmoil in Germany, Russia, and Italy, decided to leave Vienna and eventually settled in Cambridge, Massachusetts. Despite the fact that Erikson was not a doctor and had no degree, his uncommon and much sought-after training as an adult and child psychoanalyst landed him positions at the Harvard Medical School and Massachusetts General Hospital. His studies at Harvard included a study on the role of play in human development and self-expression (Coles, 1970).

In 1936 Erikson left Harvard to become an instructor and shortly thereafter an assistant professor in the Yale Medical School. There, he continued his analysis of troubled children. In 1939, Erikson moved his family once again—this time to California, where he resumed analyzing children and taught at the University of California at Berkeley. His research and work in California, including his study of the Yurok Indians, culminated in the 1950 publication of *Childhood and Society*, one of his most important and well-known works. It was also during this time that Erik Homberger became an American citizen and officially changed his name to Erik Erikson (Coles, 1970).

Erikson resigned from Berkeley on June 1, 1950, and returned to Massachusetts to work at the Austen Riggs Center in Stockbridge. It was here that Erikson developed his theories of adult ego and identity development. Erikson also became interested in the relationship between the studies of history and psychology, and in 1958 he published another major work, *Young Man Luther*. In this book, Erikson studied the childhood of the fifteenth-century Christian Reformer and how his upbringing effected his adulthood (Coles, 1970).

Erikson's other major works include *Dimensions of a New Identity*, *Life History and the Historical Moment*, *Toys and Reasons*, *Identity and the Life Cycle*, *The Life Cycle Completed*, *Vital Involvement in Old Age* (with Joan M. Erikson and Helen Q. Kivnick), and *A Way of Looking at Things: Selected Papers from 1930 to 1980* (edited by Stephen Schlein). Erikson died in 1994.

ERIKSON'S CONTRIBUTIONS TO THE FIELD OF PSYCHOANALYSIS AND HIS INFLUENCE ON EDUCATIONAL PSYCHOLOGY

Issues of Identity

Erik Erikson contributed significantly to the field of psychoanalysis and was considered one of the great intellectuals of his time. He unwittingly brought the terms "identity" and "identity crisis" into common use. Because of the enormous impact that education has on each child's life, educators must be aware of the ongoing struggle that children face to develop a strong and positive sense of "identity." Erikson described "identity" as something that is developed in a person from the time of the person's birth, and that reaches its "crisis" point during adolescence. Identity provides a connection between one's past and one's future. The "identity crisis" of adolescence is crucial for a complete identity development because it is during that time that the individual establishes not only a personal identity (or self-knowledge), but also determines the individual's place within culture and society (Evans, 1967).

It is important to note that in the context of the concept of "identity crisis," Erikson described the word "crisis" not as an impending disaster, but rather as a critical developmental turning point. It is during an "identity crisis" that an individual's development can and must turn in one direction or another, to determine who that person is to become. Educators must recognize that being violent and angry or depressed and withdrawn during an "identity crisis" is not necessarily a sign that an adolescent is mentally or emotionally disturbed; rather, these behaviors may be a normal part of the developmental process (Erikson, 1968, pp. 16–17).

Psychohistory

Erikson also broke new ground in the field of psychohistory with his analyses of the lives of political and spiritual leaders Martin Luther and Mahatma Gandhi. "The main object of psycho-historical investigations," said Erikson, "is to try to relate the particular identity-needs of a given leader to the 'typical' identity needs of his historical times" (Evans, 1967, p. 66). In other words, Erikson's psycho-historical works, in combining the fields of history and psychology, examined how the childhood and young adulthood experiences of Luther and Gandhi and their own senses of identity matched the overall identities of the groups of people they led in their respective times and places.

During his investigations in psychohistory, Erikson developed the notion of "moratorium." He noticed that many men who later in life would become great historical figures took a kind of break from life during their adolescent or young adult years. Erikson described the moratorium as delay, a gap between the end of identification as a child and the beginning of identification as an adult. Erikson himself took a moratorium of sorts starting at the age of 18, wandering Europe as an itinerant artist.

In today's society, the college years are meant to serve as the bridge between childhood and adulthood. However, for many college-age people, the pressures and demands of traditional schooling fail to provide a break or "moratorium" that allows for positive identity development. Perhaps that is why so many young adults during this time drop out of school, enter therapy, or commit suicide. In relation to Erikson's work, depending upon each person's individual needs, a one or two year "moratorium" between high school and college may be a healthy and beneficial step for ensuring later success and happiness.

Erikson's work in the area of psychohistory makes clear that educators must recognize that the identity-needs of any individual child are greatly influenced by the social and historical context in which the child is living. Erikson (1968) pointed out that for today's children, technology is playing a greater and greater role in their lives. All children must negotiate positive relationships with the technology surrounding them, because part of a sense of competence that is so crucial to positive identity formation is technological competence.

Also it is critical for educators to acknowledge and understand how race or culture impacts a child's sense of identity within the larger society. Erikson (1968)wrote, "Where he finds out immediately, however, that the color of his skin or the background of his parents rather than his wish and will to learn are the factors that decide his worth as a pupil or apprentice, the human propensity for feeling unworthy may be fatefully aggravated as a determinant of character development" (p. 124).

Psychosocial Identity Theory

Perhaps the most notable and well known of Erikson's contributions to the field of psychoanalysis is his adaptation and expansion of Freud's five psychosexual stages of human development into his eight psychosocial stages of human development. Erikson differed from Freud in that he looked at human development from a broader cultural and societal viewpoint, and he proposed that human development does not end with physical maturation, that is, at the end of puberty.

Rather, adults also develop and go through stages, with each stage having its own crisis that must be resolved.

The crisis Erikson identified in each stage is a conflict between the development of a positive characteristic and its opposing negative characteristic, such as trust versus mistrust. While the more positive trait is certainly desirable, Erikson warned that a balance must be struck. While autonomy is certainly preferable to shame and doubt, children must learn about their own limitations, and they must develop a realistic understanding of the world and their place in it. The successful negotiation of each stage leads to the acquisition of what Erikson calls a virtue or strength, such as hope or willpower (Evans, 1967).

Erikson's stages are epigenetic in nature, meaning that each stage builds upon the previous. For example, a child must develop trust in the first stage in order to be successful in becoming self-willed in the second. Identity formation begins during the first stage, builds and climaxes in the "identity crisis" of adolescence, and continues throughout adulthood. Erikson noted that not only are the stages sequential, but hierarchical as well. He also noted that the ages associated with the stages are rough estimates and that the stages of each individual will vary in duration and intensity (Evans, 1967, pp. 21–22).

Table 7.1 shows the eight stages of human development as defined by Erikson. The quotes were taken from an interview with Erik Erikson while he was a professor at Harvard (Evans, 1967).

In 1997, 3 years after Erik Erikson's death, Erikson's wife Joan Erikson published an extended version of his book *The Life Cycle Completed*. Joan Erikson proposed a ninth stage that occurs when people reach their 80s and 90s. While she did not offer one particular crisis or set of conflicting characteristics for this ninth stage, she did address each of the conflicts of each of the first eight stages and the related characteristics and how each of these are relevant and recurring in the ninth stage.

Particularly relevant to the field of educational psychology are Erikson's theories regarding the latent, or school-age, stage of psychosocial development. It is during this stage that teachers and school take on a central role in a child's life and the child's development of a sense of identity. Depending upon the child's success in navigating the crisis of this stage, the child can enter adolescence with a strong sense of competence, or feelings of ineffectualness and inferiority that can plague the child for the rest of the child's life. In order for a child to achieve a sense of competence, he or she must learn to be industrious. It is a strong psychological urge of children in the school-age stage to develop a sense of industry, of being able to create and to carry a project through to a successful conclusion (Erikson, 1968).

Erikson (1968) examined two models of American education, traditional and constructivist, and explored the advantages and pitfalls of each. A more traditional model of education offers students a needed structure, a sense of direction, and a purpose; however, Erikson noted "an unnecessary and costly self-restraint" can arise from this form of education and can inhibit a child's natural desire to learn, as well as the child's own creativity, imagination, and playfulness (Erikson, 1968, p. 126). A more unstructured approach to education, on the other hand, can cause children to lack basic skills and knowledge necessary for successful participation in society, and can create uncertainty and a lack of confidence in children's learning experiences (Erikson, 1968).

SELECTED MAJOR WORKS

Childhood and Society (1950)

Erikson's first book, *Childhood and Society* is also one of his most well known and highly respected. It is divided into four parts: Part One describes and illustrates his case study

Table 7.1
Erikson's Eight Stages of Human Development

Stage	Ages	Virtue/Strength to be Acquired	In Erikson's Words
Sensory-Oral Stage: Basic trust vs. Basic mistrust	0–1 year	Hope	"A certain ratio of trust and mistrust in our basic social attitude is the critical factor. When we enter a situation, we must be able to differentiate how much we can trust and how much we must mistrust" (Evans, 1967, p. 15).
Muscular-Anal Stage: Autonomy vs. Shame and doubt	2–3 years	Willpower	"Just when a child has learned to trust his mother and to trust the world, he must become self-willed and must take chances with his trust in order to see what he . . . can will" (Evans, 1967, p. 19).
Locomotor-Genital Stage: Initiative vs. Guilt	3–6 years	Purpose	"It is during this period that it becomes incumbent upon the child to repress or redirect many fantasies which developed earlier in life. He begins to learn that he must work for things . . ." (Evans, 1967, p. 25).
Latency Stage: Industry vs. Inferiority	7–12 years or so	Competence	"Every culture at this stage offers training. . . . [T]he word "industry" . . . means industriousness, being busy with something, learning to complete something, doing a job" (Evans, 1967, pp. 27–28).
Adolescent Stage: Identity vs. Role diffusion	adolescence, 12–18 years or so	Fidelity	"We have almost an instinct for fidelity—meaning that when you reach a certain age you can and must learn to be faithful to some ideological view" (Evans, 1967, p. 30).
Young Adulthood Stage: Intimacy vs. Isolation	20–30 years or so	Love	"Intimacy is really the ability to fuse your identity with somebody else's without fear that you're going to lose something yourself" (Evans, 1967, p. 48).
Adulthood Stage: Generativity vs. Stagnation	30–50 years or so	Care	"At this stage one begins to take one's place in society, and to help in the development and perfection of whatever it produces" (Evans, 1967, p. 50).
Old Age and Maturity Stage: Ego integrity vs. Despair	50s and beyond	Wisdom	"Only in old age can true wisdom develop . . . some wisdom must mature, if only in the sense that the old person comes to appreciate and to represent something of the 'wisdom of the ages' or plain folk 'wit'" (Evans, 1967, p. 54).

methodology; Part Two describes his work done with the Sioux and Yurok Indian tribes; Part Three describes his theories on ego development and introduces his eight stages of human development; and Part Four describes how a person's sense of identity evolves during youth.

Young Man Luther (1958)

The first of Erikson's two psycho-historical books, *Young Man Luther* examined the youth of Protestant Reformer Martin Luther. This book broke new ground by fully engaging the methodologies of psychoanalysis and historical biography.

Identity: Youth and Crisis (1968)

Identity: Youth and Crisis is a collection of essays that Erikson wrote in the 1950s and 1960s. Essay (chapter) titles include "The Life Cycle: Epigenesis of Identity," "Identity Confusion in Life History and Case History," and "Race and the Wider Identity." In this book, Erikson addressed the connections between psychosocial development and education.

Gandhi's Truth (1969)

Erik Erikson won a Pulitzer Prize and a National Book Award for his work on *Gandhi's Truth*, a psycho-historical look at the life and struggles of Mahatma Gandhi. It is "an account of a search for 'the historical presence of Mahatma Gandhi and for the meaning of what he called Truth'; a search by a Western man for the enduring side of a great Indian leader's character; [and] a search by a psychoanalyst for a particular person's ethical spirit" (Coles, 1970, p. 293).

CONCLUSION

Erik Erikson's long life was filled with rigorous scholarly research. He spent his life reading, writing, teaching, and examining the psychological development of human beings. Not least among Erikson's achievements was the development of his epigenetic stages of human psychosocial development. Erikson's theories on identity-formation and psychosocial development, as well as his work in the field of psychohistory, offer insights for educators and students of educational psychology. Through attempting to understand the natural psychological development of human beings as outlined in Erikson's theories, practitioners can develop philosophies and strategies to meet the needs of their students and aid in helping them develop competence and positive senses of identity.

REFERENCES

Coles, R. (1970). *Erik H. Erikson: The Growth of His Work*. Boston: Little, Brown and Company.
Erikson, E. (1968). *Identity: Youth and Crisis*. New York: W. W. Norton & Company.
Evans, R. I. (1967). *Dialogue with Erik Erikson*. New York: Harper & Row.

CHAPTER 8

Howard Gardner

JOE L. KINCHELOE AND TODD FELTMAN

Howard Gardner has been a key figure in educational psychology over the last three decades. Gardner was born on July 11, 1943, in Scranton, Pennsylvania, to Jewish parents who escaped Nuremberg in 1938. Gardener's parents wanted him to attend high school at Phillips Academy in Andover, Massachusetts, but Gardner chose the Wyoming Seminary, a preparatory school in Kingston, Pennsylvania. After a successful stint at Wyoming, Gardner was admitted to Harvard University prepared to study history and eventually go into law. As fate would have it, Gardner worked at Harvard with well-known psychologists Erik Erikson and Jerome Bruner. In 1965, Gardner graduated *summa cum laude* and the next year began work in the university's doctoral program in psychology.

While pursuing his doctoral work Gardner became involved with the Project Zero research team on art education—an affiliation that continues into the twenty-first century. Project Zero gave Gardner an opportunity to expand his interest in cognitive, developmental, and neuropsychology. After completing his doctorate Gardner continued to work at Harvard. Currently, he is the Hobbs Professor of Cognition and Education at the Harvard Graduate School in Education and an adjunct professor of neurology at the Boston University School of Medicine. He now codirects Project Zero.

Gardner's theory of multiple intelligences (MI)—made popular by his 1983 book *Frames of Mind*—has exerted a profound influence on cognitive studies, educational practice, and the field of educational psychology in general. Rejecting the notion of a single manifestation of intelligence long promoted by psychometrians, Gardner maintained that people possessed MI. In *Frames of Mind*, he posited seven different intelligences—in the 1990s he added an eighth one. The following is a delineation of Gardner's eight intelligences:

- Linguistic intelligence involves a facility with the use of spoken and written language. Individuals who possess this particular intelligence, Gardner argues, are able to learn foreign language(s) more easily. Such individuals use language as a way to enhance their memory of information. In this linguistic context Gardner maintains that writers, poets, lawyers, and public speakers as those people who possess linguistic intelligence. This particular intelligence, of course, is prized in the classroom environment.

- Logical-mathematical intelligence deals with the ability to analyze problems using logic, perform operations in mathematics and science. According to Gardner, people with this particular intelligence possess the capacity to reason using deduction, think sequentially and linearly, and discern patterns in data. Engineers, architects, scientists, and mathematicians, Gardner posits, tend to possess this mode of intelligence—a form of cognition, like linguistic intelligence, that is highly valued in the traditional classroom.

- Musical intelligence involves the ability to perform, write, and appreciate music. According to Gardner one who possesses musical intelligence is able to identify and create musical pitches, tones, and rhythms. Obviously, musicians and composers would generally be the people who possess this type of intelligence.

- Bodily kinesthetic intelligence involves the capacity to use the body to perform physical feats that often involve solving problems. In this context individuals are able to coordinate mind with bodily movement. Gardner sees great athletes, artists, and artisans as individuals often endowed with bodily kinesthetic intelligence.

- Visual-spatial intelligence, according to Gardner, involves the ability to fashion a mental representation of the spatial realm and to employ that construct to execute valuable endeavors. Gardner contends that artists, architects, engineers, and surgeons typically possess high levels of visual-spatial intelligence. Gardner's construction of this intelligence involves the capacity to discern the visual world in an "accurate" manner, to interpret such perceptions according to one's experience in the world, and to reconstruct various dimensions of such perceptions far away from the original object of perception.

- Interpersonal intelligence—one of Gardner's two personal intelligences—involves the ability to understand and act in response to the motives of other people. Individuals who possess this intelligence, Gardner believes, are able to work successfully with diverse people. Educators need a highly developed interpersonal intelligence, as well as do businesspeople, counselors, and leaders in religion and politics.

- Intrapersonal intelligence—Gardner's second personal intelligence—is focused on self-knowledge and self-understanding. An individual with great intrapersonal intelligence is aware of and constantly monitors how one's emotions affect his or her well-being and his or her relations with the world. According to Gardner intrapersonal intelligence is a central dimension in the effort to regulate one's life.

- Naturalistic intelligence is the ability of individuals to situate themselves in the natural environment. Such "situating," Gardner argues, involves the ability to recognize and classify the flora and fauna of a region, to recognize a species. The central manifestation of naturalist intelligence from Gardner's perspective involves this ability to categorize and classify. Individuals who possess naturalist intelligence often move into the fields of biology, ornithology, and agriculture. Also, Gardner adds, those who hunt and cook often exhibit this form of intelligence.

In addition to these eight intelligences, Gardner and his colleagues have proposed two other possible intelligences. These include spiritual intelligence and existential intelligence. In the last half of the first decade of the twenty-first century Gardner feels that spiritual and existential intelligence should not be added to the list because innate complexities of these domains. Of course, many would argue that all of the intelligences fall into the same complex matrix. Numerous educational psychologists and scholars from other fields believe that Gardner made a critical categorical error in his original research when he decided to call these domains "intelligences" and not another, less historically inscribed term.

Ever confident, Gardner boldly asserts that all these eight intelligences are essential for living a fulfilling life. Therefore, in MI theory it is important, especially in the elementary school years, that teachers teach to all these intelligences. Gardner insists that his theory of teaching with the application of various intelligences is connected to the child-centered learning philosophy of John Dewey. In this context he maintains that everyone is capable of seeing the world through the lens of the eight intelligences. Via his cognitive research Gardner reports that he empirically proved that students have different types of minds and as a result they learn, remember, act, and comprehend in diverse ways. Thus, the Deweyan connection emerges, as Gardner pushes schools to move away from exclusive reliance on linguistic and logical intelligences. There is no question that this linguistic-logical combination is important for mastering the agenda of school, he contends, but educators have gone too far in ignoring the other intelligences.

As teachers de-emphasize the other six intelligences, Gardner argues that we relegate numerous students to the domain of "low ability." A multiple-intelligence grounded curriculum, he promises, would preclude such relegation and help all students succeed. Thus, Gardner's educational psychology insists that educational leaders should examine the eight MI and make sure they are implemented in the general curriculum and the everyday life of the classroom. Students could benefit from an awareness of the intelligences they possess, how they operate in their learning, and how such an awareness might inform career choices.

When many of us concerned with the postformal issues of cultivating the intellect while concurrently working for social, educational, and economic justice first read Gardner's theory of MI in 1983, we were profoundly impressed by the challenge he issued to traditional educational psychology, psychometrics in particular. We believed that Gardner stood with us in our efforts to develop psychological and educational approaches that facilitated the inclusion of students from marginalized groups whose talents and capabilities had been mismeasured by traditional psychological instruments. Gardner's theory appeared to assume a wider spectrum of human abilities that were for various reasons excluded from the domain of educational psychology and the definition of intelligence. We taught MI theory to our students in hopes of exposing and overcoming some of the ways particular students were hurt by these exclusionary disciplinary practices. As Gardner has continued to develop his theory over the last twenty years, those of us associated with postformalism and critical pedagogy grew increasingly uncomfortable with many of his assertions and many of the dimensions he excluded from his work. Simply put, we did not believe that MI theory was succeeding at what it claimed as its cardinal goal: helping students from diverse backgrounds and cognitive orientations succeed in school.

Gardner's *Frames of Mind* was enthusiastically received by sectors of a public intuitively unhappy with psychometrics' technocratic and rationalistic perspective on human ability. Within the narrow boundaries of the American culture of scholarship, Gardner became a celebrity. Teachers emerging from a humanistic culture of caring and helping were particularly taken with the young (forty is young in the world of academia!) scholar, many traveling all over the country to hear him speak. Multiple intelligences, such teachers maintained, provided them with a theoretical grounding to justify a pedagogy sensitive to individual differences and committed to equity. Though Gardner consistently denied the political dimension of MI, liberal teachers and teacher educators viewed it as a force to democratize intelligence. Living in a Eurocentric world, many interpreted Gardner to be arguing that cognitive gifts are more equally dispersed throughout diverse cultural populations than mainstream psychology believed. They took MI as a challenge to an inequitable system.

Frames of Mind struck all the right chords:

- Learning is culturally situated.
- Different communities value different forms of intelligence.
- Cognitive development is complex, not simply a linear cause–effect process.
- Creativity is an important dimension of intelligence.
- Psychometrics does not measure all aspects of human ability.
- Teaching grounded on psychometrically inspired standardized testing is often deemed irrelevant and trivial by students.

Numerous teachers, students, parents, everyday citizens, and some educational psychologists deemed these ideas important. And, we agree, they are—especially in light of the positivist reductionism and standardization of the twenty-first-century educational standards movement, No Child Left Behind, and its cousins proliferating throughout numerous Western and Western-influenced societies. As with most popular theories, the time was right for Gardner's unveiling of MI theory. Multiple intelligences resonated with numerous progressive impulses that had yet to retreat in the face of the right-wing educational onslaught coalescing in the early 1980s.

Initially, most of the critiques of MI emerged from more conservative analysts, who argued that theory shifted educational priorities away from development of logic in the process producing a trivialized, touchy-feely mode of education. In *Multiple Intelligences Reconsidered* (2004) Joe Kincheloe and a group of well-respected critical researchers provided a progressive/postformal critique of the theory, maintaining that despite all its democratic promise Gardner's theory has not met the expectations of its devotees. The reasons for this failure are multidimensional and complex but often involve many of the basic postformal concerns with educational psychology in general. One aspect of its failure comes from Gardner's inability to grasp the social, cultural, and political forces that helped shape the initial reception of MI. Even when he has addressed what he describes as a "dis-ease" in American society, Gardner fails to historicize the concept in a way that provides him a broader perspective on the fascinating relationship between American sociocultural, political, and epistemological dynamics of the last two decades and MI theory.

Postformalists argue that Gardner is entangled in this sociocultural, political, and epistemological web whether he wants to be or not. Not so, he maintains, contending that his is a psychological and pedagogical position—not a social, cultural, political, or epistemological one. In what critical analysts view as naïve, decontextualized, and psychologized modus operandi, Gardner asserts that the psychological and pedagogical domains are separate from all these other denominators. Grounded in cultural psychological ways of seeing and social theoretical lenses, postformalists maintain that such an assertion constitutes a profound analytical error on Gardner's part. The epistemology (ways of knowing) traditionally employed by Gardner's psychometric predecessors and contemporaries is the epistemology of MI. As Richard Cary puts it in his chapter on visual-spatial intelligence in *Multiple Intelligences Reconsidered*: "Although MI theory is more appealing and democratic at first glance, it remains a stepchild of positivism's exclusively quantitative methodologies and of grand narrative psychology." Indeed, there is less difference between Gardner and the psychological/educational psychological establishment than we first believed. As in so many similar domains, Gardner has been unwilling to criticize the power wielders, the gatekeepers of the psychological castle.

In her important chapter in *Multiple Intelligences Reconsidered*, Kathleen Berry extends this point:

[Gardner's] works, as scholarly and beguilingly penned as they are, have seduced the field of education into yet another Western logo-centric, psychological categorization. Under the guise of educational/school reform, his theory of MI has spawned a host of other supportive theories, practices, disciples, and critics. . . . Once labeled, however, whether in the singular or the plural, intelligence acts as an economic, social, political, and cultural passport for some and for others, a cage. . . .

Obviously, many scholars within the postformal universe are especially concerned with the democratic and justice-related dimensions portended in Gardner's early articulation of MI. Taking our cue from the concerns of many people of color, the poor, colonized individuals, and proponents of feminist theory, we raise questions about the tacit assumptions of MI and its implications for both education and the social domain. In the spirit of postformalism we raise questions about knowledge production and power in the psychological domain in general and in MI. Postformalism is especially interested in modes of cognition that recognize the complicity of various academic discourses, psychology in particular, in the justification and maintenance of an inequitable status quo and an ecological and cosmological alienation from the planet and universe in which we reside. As Marla Morris puts it in her chapter in *Multiple Intelligences Reconsidered*:

If we are to talk about a naturalistic intelligence, we need to understand that intelligence does not mean anything goes, just because a scientist works with or in nature. Further, one need not be a farmer or a biologist to develop a naturalistic intelligence. On this point, I think Gardner is too literal. I argue that an ecological sensibility springs from a sensitive, ethical, and holistic understanding of the complexities of human situatedness in the ecosphere.

Gardner seems either unable or unwilling to trace the relationship of MI to these issues.

Indeed, what postformalists and any other cognitive theorists designate as intelligence and aptitude produces specific consequences. The important difference between postformalism and Gardner's educational psychology involves postformalists' admission to such ramifications and their subsequent efforts to shape them as democratically, inclusively, and self-consciously as possible. Gardner, concurrently, dismisses the existence of such political and moral consequences and clings to the claim of scientific neutrality.

Despite all of these concerns we still believe there is value in Gardner's work. Postformalists call on their colleagues to seek the kinetic potential of Gardner's ideas in the sociopsychological and educational domain. In this context we seek to retain the original democratic optimism of Gardner's theories, confront him and his many sympathizers with powerful paradigmatic insights refined over the last 25 years, and move the conversation about MI forward with a vision of a complex, rigorous, and transformative pedagogy. In particular postformalists want to engage Gardner in a conversation about power, cognition, schooling, and the future of educational psychology. We hope he will work with us in a synergistic, mutually respectful conversation.

Power is omnipresent in both its oppressive and productive forms. In its oppressive articulation postformalists trace its effects in educational psychology. In a world where information produced for schools and media-constructed knowledge for public consumption are misleading, ideologically refracted, edited for right-wing political effect, and often outright lies, the notion of learning to become a scholar takes on profound political meanings—whether we like it or not. Do we merely "adjust" students to the misrepresentations of dominant power or do we help them develop a "power literacy" that moves them to become courageous democratic citizens? While the stakes were already high, dominant power wielders have upped the ideological ante in the twenty-first century.

In raising these concerns we are not arguing that Gardner has supported this type of ideological management. We are contending that Gardner has fallen prey to false dichotomies in his work separating the political from the psychological and educational. Indeed, he has been unwilling to address the relationships connecting dominant power, psychological theory, and teaching and learning. In this era of U.S. empire building and the effects of transnational capital and the knowledges they produce, such political decontextualization can be dangerous. This fragmentation has exerted a profound influence on the character and value of Gardner's work. Like other educational psychological theories Gardner's MI fail (or refuse) to consider such dynamics in the course of their development and application.

The power concerns emphasized here played little role in Gardner's previously mentioned educational experiences in developmental and neuropsychology at Harvard.

Such an educational and research background protected Gardner from the emerging concerns with the relationship between psychological knowledge production and power. In writing about motivation and learning in *Frames of Mind*, for example, he addresses the development of a general, universal theory of motivation. Such theorizing takes place outside the consideration of motivation's contextual, cultural, and power-related specificity. A student, for example, from a poor home in the southern Appalachian mountains in the United States whose parents and extended family possess little formal education will be situated very differently in relation to educational motivation than an upper-middle-class child of parents with advanced degrees. The poor child will find it harder to discern the relationship between educational efforts expended and concrete rewards attained than will the upper-middle-class child. Such perceptions will lead to different levels of performance shaped by relationship to dominant power in its everyday, lived world manifestations. Such motivational and performance levels have little to do with innate intelligence whether of a linguistic, visual-spatial, or mathematical variety. Gardner has not made these types of discernments in his MI theorizing.

Thus, power theory has not been important to Gardner's work. Sociopolitical reflection is not an activity commonly found in the history of developmental and neuropsychology. Indeed, such concerns have been consistently excluded as part of a larger positivistic discomfort with the ethical and ideological. Such political dynamics reveal themselves in Gardner's *Intelligence Reframed* (1999), as he writes of Western civilization as a story of progress toward both democracy and respect for the individual. Democracy has been achieved in the United States and the civilized West, Gardner assumes, as he cautiously avoids confronting democratic failures in these domains outside the tragedy of the Third Reich. He explores business involvement with education in *The Disciplined Mind* (1999) but expresses little concern with corporate power's capacity to shape the ideological purposes of schools.

Although Gardner writes about MI producing "masters of change," it seems to postformalists that he describes such individuals as mere technicians to be fed into the new corporate order of the globalized economy. They are not empowered scholars who understand the larger historical and social forces shaping the macro-structures that interact with the complexities of the quest for democracy and the production of self. There is no mention here, for example, of the

- impact of 500 years of European colonialism;
- continuing anticolonial movements of the post-1945 world;
- Western neoliberal/neoconservative efforts to "reclaim" cultural, political, and intellectual supremacy over the last 25 years;
- education for the new American Empire being promoted by George W. Bush and his corporate and political cronies around the world.

Such macro-forces exert profound influences on how we view the roles of Western psychology and education or where we stand or are placed in relation to them. MI and its masters of change stand outside history. They are passive observers of the great issues of our time.

Studying Gardner's work, we perceive no indication that he has ever imagined a critique of his work in light of the issues of power. In *Frames of Mind* he asserted that he could envisage two types of modifications of MI: he could be convinced to drop one or two of the intelligences or he could be persuaded to add some new ones. In this power vacuum Gardner is not unlike many other upper-middle-class North Americans and Western Europeans in that he cannot imagine how dominant-power inscribed psychologies and educational practices can harm individuals—especially those marginalized in some way by the dynamics of, say, race, class, colonialism, or gender. Gardner's naïve acceptance of the benefits of school for all came across clearly in *Frames of Mind*:

... the overall impact of a schooled society (as against one without formal education) is rarely a matter of dispute. It seems evident to nearly all observers that attendance at school for more than a few years produces an individual—and, eventually a collectivity—who differs in important (if not always easy to articulate) ways from members of a society that lacks formal schooling (1983, p. 356).

Gardner would be well served to familiarize himself with literature that documents the way school often serves to convince many individuals from marginalized backgrounds that they are unintelligent and incompetent. The most important curricular lesson many of these students learn is that they are not "academic material." The individuals we are talking about here are young people who are profoundly talented but because of their relationship to the values and symbol systems of schooling are evaluated as incapable of dealing with the higher cognitive processes of academia. Was it not some of these individuals that MI theory was supposed to help? Weren't we supposed to see valuable talents in individuals that were overlooked by a monolithic mode of defining intelligence?

In conclusion, MI is a child of a Cartesian psychology that fails to recognize its own genealogy. Gardner uses the intelligences to pass along the proven verities, the perennial truths of Western music, art, history, literature, language, math, and science. The notion of constructing a meta-analysis of the ways cultural familiarity occludes our ability to see the plethora of assumptions driving work in these domains does not trouble Gardner's psychic equilibrium. If Gardner were interested in performing a cultural meta-analysis of his theories, he would begin to see them as technologies of power that reproduce Western and typically male ways of making meaning. Gardner seems oblivious to the epistemological, cultural, and political coordinates of his work. We don't understand why he doesn't sense that the classification systems and cognitive frameworks of MI routinely exclude "the knowledge and values of women, nonwhite races, non-Christians, and local and premodern ways of knowing. How can a man so erudite who proclaims a progressive ideological stance miss these omissions?

In the descriptions of what counts as intelligence and curricular knowledge in Gardner's eight domains resides a battle over cultural politics. Whose science, literature, music, history, art, ad infinitum gains the imprimatur of the labels classical and canonical? When patterns of racial, cultural, gender, and class exclusion consistently reveal themselves in Gardner's work, why would nonwhite and non-European individuals and groups not be suspicious of it? Again, Gardner's reading of expressions of such concerns is inexplicable. In *Intelligence Reframed*, for example, he states that MI has been disparaged "as racist and elite . . . because it uses the word intelligence and because I, as its original proponent, happen to be affiliated with Harvard University . . ." (1999, p. 149). We can assure Gardner that if he were a professor at Brooklyn College's School of Education who developed the "theory of multiple talents" and had exerted comparable levels of influence on the fields of psychology and education, postformalists would still criticize his exclusionary scholarship. Gardner the progressive is trapped on a terrain littered with cultural political and epistemological landmines. His work with all of its possibilities and limitations serves as an excellent example to educational psychologists of the need for a postformal critique of the discipline.

CHAPTER 9

Carol Gilligan

KATHRYN PEGLER

> From Erik Erikson, I learned that you cannot take a life out of history, that life-history and
> history, psychology and politics, are deeply entwined. Listening to women, I heard a difference
> and discovered that bringing in women's lives changes both psychology and history. It literally
> changes the voice: how the human story is told, and also who tells it.
> —Gilligan, 1993, p. xi

Gaining this postformal perspective from Erik Erikson was like the planting of a seed inside of Carol Gilligan leading her to a gradual awakening on the journey to a powerful discovery. For centuries, a critical part of the population was missing from theories of moral and intellectual development. Until Gilligan published her findings in an article that led to the publication of her book, *In a Different Voice: Psychological Theory and Women's Development* (1982), women's voices had not been present in human or moral development theories. This revolutionary and controversial book demonstrated how the inclusion of women's voices challenges the existing theories of psychological development that are based solely on the studies of boys and men. In addition, Gilligan's postformal ideas challenge the notion that there is only one single and absolute path to moral or philosophical truth. Gilligan's theory has had a tremendous impact on a multiplicity of fields including psychology, education, gender studies, and law.

Matters of moral significance have been an intricate part of Gilligan's life since childhood. She was born in New York City on November 28, 1936, and grew up during the Holocaust. Her parents' examples influenced her greatly as they were involved with aiding refugees from Europe. William Friedman, Gilligan's father, was a child of Hungarian immigrants. He became a lawyer, and during the Holocaust, he accepted other lawyers into his firm who were escaping Hitler. Mabel Caminez Friedman, Gilligan's mother, was the daughter of German and Ukrainian immigrants who helped refugees by getting them settled in New York. In addition, Gilligan was a student at the Walden School in New York City. Walden was a progressive school widely known for calling attention to and discussing issues of moral relevance.

As an English Literature student at Swarthmore College in the 1950s, Gilligan was at ease participating in the small coed classes where they studied the human experience as they read the works of many celebrated male and female writers. Later on as a student attending Harvard and studying psychology, she did not feel that same comfort. Something was amiss. At Harvard, the focus of study was on male psychologists researching mainly male subjects in the long-established and unquestioned patriarchal practice. Gilligan could not yet identify the discord; however, she felt there was a discrepancy in the way professors spoke. These discussions lacked the intricacy and the aliveness of the authentic human experience that she learned through her study of Euripides, Shakespeare, George Eliot, and Virginia Woolf.

During the sixties and early seventies, Gilligan was a social activist involved in issues of moral importance. As a lecturer at the University of Chicago, she refused to present grades because they were being used as basis for the Vietnam draft. Gilligan also took part in sit-ins and became involved in the civil rights movement, the antinuclear movement, and the women's strike for peace. In addition, she went knocking on doors in order to get people to register to vote.

Initially Gilligan had no plans of entering the field of psychology. As the mother of three small sons and a member of a modern dance group, she taught part-time to make money in order to have some help in the house. At this time, she had the opportunity to teach with Erik Erikson at Harvard in his course on the human life cycle. She then taught with Lawrence Kohlberg in his course on moral and political choice (Wylie and Simon, 2003). Gilligan was drawn to Erikson and Kohlberg, as they had similar interests concerning the connection of psychology and political choice and philosophy and literature. Furthermore, like Gilligan, both men were dedicated to the civil rights and antiwar movements. Gilligan worked closely with Kohlberg and even coauthored the article "The Adolescent as a Philosopher: The Discovery of the Self in a Postconventional World" (1971) with him. However, during this time, Gilligan began to feel uneasy using Kohlberg's criteria to judge moral development because of the way women were categorized. Under Kohlberg's model, the average female scores were a full stage lower than the male average scores, implying that women were less morally developed than men. Concurrently, while teaching Kohlberg's course, Gilligan also became fascinated in how people respond to real-life situations of conflict and choice. She was interested in people's real-life moral struggles where people had the power to choose and have to live with the consequences of their decisions. It was the height of the Vietnam War, and male students were faced with the draft. Gilligan wanted to know how these young men would act when they had to make a choice about serving in a war that many believed was neither justifiable nor moral; hence, she began a study related to their choices. However, in 1973, President Nixon ended the draft, and that ended Gilligan's study. During this time, the Supreme Court had ruled that state antiabortion legislation was not legal in the case of *Roe v. Wade*. Realizing that *Roe v. Wade* would give "women the decisive voice in a real moment of choice with real consequences for their personal lives and for society" (Goldberg, 2000, p. 702), Gilligan shifted her study to women making this moral decision.

While sitting in her kitchen reviewing the transcripts of pregnant women considering abortion, Gilligan made a dramatic discovery. She recognized the emergence of a different pattern. There were differences between the public abortion debates over right to life or right to choice and the women's unease about acting responsibly in relationships because for many women their problems concerning abortion involved issues relating to relationships. For example, Gilligan noted that the women felt apprehensive, "If I bring my voice into my relationships, will I become a bad, selfish woman, and will I end my relationships" (Goldberg, 2000, p. 702)? Listening to these women, Gilligan heard a perception of self that differed from the theories of Freud, Piaget, Erikson, and Kohlberg. Moreover, she became conscious that the theories used to judge emotional health and typical experiences were embedded almost exclusively in studies of white male behavior. Subsequently, these theories were then applied to women. Gilligan shared this discovery with her friend Dora. Dora found this to be intriguing and suggested that Gilligan write about it (Wylie and Simon, 2003). Consequently, Gilligan wrote an essay published in the *Harvard Educational Review* in 1977 titled "In a Different Voice: Women's Conceptions of

Self and of Morality." That article was the genesis of her book *In a Different Voice* (Gilligan, 1982).

In this book Gilligan presents a theory of moral development that maintains that women are more likely to think and speak in a way that is different from men when faced with ethical dilemmas. Gilligan draws a distinction between a feminine ethic of *care* and a masculine ethic of *justice*. Under an ethic of justice, men judge themselves guilty if they do something wrong. Accordingly, men tend to think in terms of rules, individual rights, and fair play. All of these goals can be pursued without personal ties to others; therefore, justice is impersonal. Under an ethic of care, women, who allow others to feel pain, hold themselves responsible for not doing something to prevent or allay the hurt. Hence, women are more inclined to think in terms of sensitivity to others, loyalty, responsibility, peacemaking, and self-sacrifice. Thus an ethic of care comes from connection, and necessitates interpersonal involvement. In addition, Gilligan believes that these differences of moral perspectives are the result of contrasting images of self. These identities are shaped during early childhood and adolescence by the primary people who provide physical and emotional care. Gilligan observes that both sexes have the capacity to develop either perspective. Hence, there are women who view moral dilemmas in terms of justice, and there are men who make moral decisions based on an ethic of care. Gilligan views it as two separate and noncompeting ways of thinking about moral problems.

Gilligan describes her stages of moral development, and like Kohlberg, Gilligan's theory has three major divisions of moral maturity: preconventional, conventional, and postconventional. A major difference is that Gilligan's stages happen due to changes in the sense of self whereas Kohlberg's stages occur due to changes in cognitive capacity. In the first stage of preconventional morality, there is a selfish orientation to individual survival. Women lack a sense of connectedness. They are unable to see beyond their own self-interest as they look out for themselves. In the second stage of conventional morality, goodness is self-sacrifice, and morality is selfless. Women define their moral worth on the basis of their ability to care about others. They search for solutions where no one will get hurt, but realize they often face the hopeless task of choosing the injured party, that injured party is usually themselves. They feel a responsibility to give others what they need or want, especially when these others are considered defenseless or dependent. Finally, in the third stage, postconventional morality reflects the responsibility for consequences of choice. At the heart of moral decision making is the exercise of choice and the willingness to take responsibility for that choice. Women in this stage realize that there are no easy answers, and so they make an effort to take control of their lives by admitting the seriousness of the choice and consider the whole range of their conflicting responsibilities. Gilligan (1993) explains, there is a shift "from goodness to truth when the morality of action is assessed not on the basis of its appearance in the eyes of others, but in terms of the realities of its intention and consequence" (p. 83). Therefore, unlike conventional goodness, this view of truth requires that a woman extend nonviolence and care to herself as well as others.

For Gilligan, the different voice indicates a paradigm shift because it exposes a disconnection at the core of a patriarchal racist social order that is so deep and so critical. This disconnection obscures the experiences, thoughts, and feelings of

all people who are considered to be lesser, less developed, less human, and we all know who these people are women, people of colour, gays and lesbians, the poor and the disabled. It [is] everyone who [is] "different" and the only way you [can] be different within a hierarchical scheme [is], you [can] be higher or you [can] be lower, and all the people who [have] been lower turn out—surprise, surprise—to be the people who did not create the scheme. (Gilligan, 1998)

In a Different Voice has been both innovative and influential. The book strikes emotional chords in both women and men. Its impact has been compared to Betty Friedan's *The Feminine Mystique*

(1963). Furthermore, Gilligan's *In a Different Voice* (1982) has enjoyed a worldwide audience. The book has been translated into seventeen different languages and has sold more than 750,000 copies, an amazing accomplishment for an academic book. Gilligan first realized that her book was going to make a statement when she picked up the retyped manuscript and the woman who typed it had given it to her cousin to read, and the cousin wanted to meet her. But initially, the book received a lukewarm response, so it was published in paperback fairly quickly at a low price allowing access early on to a wide audience. Unfamiliar people began talking to Gilligan about her book. One woman working in a local shop asked Gilligan if she was the woman who wrote that book and proceeded to tell her that she had explained her marriage. A *Globe* reporter said that Gilligan had described his divorce. After reading the book, many women felt heard and able to speak in a new way. The book also justified for men a voice that had been associated with what were seen as "women's weaknesses," but which Gilligan had acknowledged as human strengths (Wylie and Simon, 2003).

Just as many people connected with and praised Gilligan's book, others have strongly criticized it. Some people fear Gilligan's efforts to establish a different but equal voice merely reinforces the cultural stereotype that men act on reason while women respond to feeling. In addition, some social scientists attack the lean research used to support and validate her theory. They cite the small specialized sample in her abortion study, the fact that she used anecdotal evidence instead of providing empirical support, and that her data has not been published or peer-reviewed. However, Gilligan states that the "different voice I describe is identified not by gender but by theme" (Wylie and Simon, 2003, para. 13). Gilligan also claims that her data has been published in peer-reviewed journals, and that Freud, Piaget, and Erikson's theories were not rejected based on interpretive style of research (Vincent, 2000).

For the past 25 years, Gilligan has continued to engage in research in the areas of psychological theory and education including studies on women's, girls', and boys' developmental experiences. In addition, Gilligan has coauthored and edited a series of books on gender and development as well as initiating numerous programs and projects for advancing the healthful development of boys and girls. In 2002, following 35 years at Harvard, Gilligan moved back to New York to become a professor at New York University. She is associated with the law school, the graduate school of arts and sciences, and the school of education. Furthermore, that same year, Gilligan published her first book authored alone since *In a Different Voice* (1982).

In her book *The Birth of Pleasure*, Gilligan (2002) explains how the emotional truths and the ability to say what we see and say what we know is hidden in the interests of maintaining the long history of patriarchal order. For Gilligan, feminism is the movement to end the long-standing contradiction between democracy and patriarchy. This contradiction runs as deep and is as harmful as the contradiction between democracy and slavery. Patriarchy is not a battle between the sexes, but an arrangement that constrains both men and women. Patriarchy actually means a rule of fathers where men are separated from women, from other men, and from children; hence, Gilligan asserts that this system presents a hierarchy in the midst of our most intimate relationships between lovers and between parents and children. Furthermore, Gilligan stresses that the restrictions of patriarchy are passed on from generation to generation, and compromise our psychological development from early childhood, crippling love, making pleasure perilous, "and enforcing taboos against truth-telling" (Wylie and Simon, 2003).

Gilligan's *Birth of Pleasure* (2002) received hostile criticism for representing a type of feminism that lays all of society's ills at the feet of patriarchy. Her critics believe this is unnecessary because the patriarchal society has ended. Responding to her critics, Gilligan asks, if patriarchy has ended, then who is running the Fortune 500 companies and congress? She also observes that patriarchy is wreaking havoc citing Enron and WorldCom as examples as well as the scandal in the Catholic Church, the FBI, and the CIA (Wylie and Simon). However, Gilligan (2001) also believes that "the transformation from patriarchy toward a fuller realization of democracy will be one of the most important historical events of the next 50 years" (para. 3). She observes that there are already signs, for example, there are more women in the U.S. Congress than 20 years ago, women are marrying other women and having children, and gay men are marrying other men and adopting children. The educational system, Gilligan reasons, will be at the center of this "historic transformation," especially gender studies programs because these programs provide the knowledge that can foster human freedom and possibilities.

Carol Gilligan and her life work embody the essence of a postformal thinker. As Joe Kincheloe and Shirley Steinberg (1999) explain, postformal thinkers are metacognitively aware and understand the way that power affects their own lives and the lives of others; therefore, they apply postformal analysis to the deep structures in order to expose insidious assumptions. As Carol Gilligan's groundbreaking research clearly demonstrates, when postformal analysis is applied to education and psychology, the implications are boundless. Gilligan's research has had major repercussions, and it has inspired a wealth of research and scholarship not only in education and psychology but also in ethics and law. Her work has led to a wide range of educational and cultural projects designed to encourage girls' voices and build on their psychological strengths. Primary and secondary schools across America have developed girl-friendly curriculums and teaching methods in order to resist the principles of femininity that were psychologically and intellectually damaging to girls for reasons that required them to be nice, to be silent, and to suppress vital part of themselves. Furthermore, her work motivated colleges to incorporate women's studies programs, women's campus centers, and sexual harassment policies as well as speech codes of conduct. Many popular psychology books such as Naomi Wolf's *The Beauty Myth* (1991), Mary Pipher's *Reviving Ophelia* (1994), and John Gray's *Men Are from Mars, Women Are from Venus* (1998) resulted from Gilligan's studies. It also was the impetus for the 1991 American Association of University Women's report "Shortchanging Girls, Shortchanging America." Moreover, Gilligan's research was one of the driving forces behind the 1994 Gender Equity Act in Education (Wylie and Simon, 2003).

In addition, postformal theorists use feminist theory in order to unify logic and emotion, unlike formalists who insist upon a separation of logic and emotion. Postformal thinkers recognize that emotions develop into "powerful thinking mechanisms that, when combined with logic, create a cognitive process that extends our ability to make sense of the universe" (Kincheloe and Steinberg, 1999, p. 76). This idea is at the heart of Gilligan's research, and accurately describes Gilligan's theory of moral development. Finally, postformal scholars know that history is not complete and democracy cannot survive without the inclusion of all voices, specifically the voices of people who have been outside the mainstream of the conversation. Carol Gilligan actively opens the conversation to "different voices" because she knows that the inclusion of all voices is an act of social justice that adds to the richness and depth of the story and promotes creativity and understanding for all because the world looks and sounds very different after suddenly seeing and hearing something that you've never seen or heard before.

REFERENCES

Gilligan, C. (1982). *In a Different Voice: Psychological Theory and Women's Development.* 1st ed. Cambridge, MA: Harvard University Press.
———. (1993). *In a Different Voice: Psychological Theory and Women's Development*, 2nd ed. Cambridge, MA: Harvard University Press.
———. (1998, June 1). Remembering Larry. *Journal of Moral Education*, 27(2). Retrieved on December 12, 2005, from http://sas.epnet.com/citation.asp?
Gilligan, C. (2001, October 1). From White Rats to Robots the Future of Human Development. *Ed. The Magazine of the Harvard Graduate School of Education.* Retrieved on December 10, 2005, from http://www.gse.harvard.edu/news/features/gilligan10012001.html.

————. (2002). *The Birth of Pleasure*. New York: Alfred A. Knopf.

Goldberg, M. F. (2000, May 1). Restoring Lost Voices: An Interview with Carol Gilligan. *Phi Delta Kappan* [Electronic version], 81(9), 701–704.

Kincheloe, J. L. and Steinberg, S. R. (1999). A Tentative Description of Post-formal Thinking: The Critical Confrontation with Cognitive Theory. In J. L. Kincheloe and S. R. Steinberg (Eds.), *The Post-formal Reader: Cognition and Education*, pp. 55–90. New York: Falmer Press.

Vincent, N. (2000, June 7–13). Higher Ed Class War the Sommers–Gilligan Cat Fight. *The Village Voice.* Retrieved on December 11, 2005, from www.villagevoice.com/nyclife/0023,vincent,15447,15.html.

Wylie, M. S. and Simon R. (2003). Carol Gilligan on Recapturing the Lost Voice of Pleasure. Psychotherapy Networker Retrieved on December 4, 2005, from http://www.psychotherapynetworker.org/interviews.htm.

CHAPTER 10

Emma Goldman

DANIEL RHODES

EMMA GOLDMAN

Emma Goldman is probably one of the most controversial figures in United States history and an obscure but important contributor to the field of education and educational psychology. She was instrumental in developing and promoting what was called the Modern School in the United States, a somewhat obscure but very progressive and groundbreaking philosophical educational system. The Modern School had its roots and development in Spain and was founded by the educator Francisco Ferrer y Guardia, but it was Emma Goldman and her connection to Anarchism and political activism, not to mention her own personal background, that lead her to support and promote the ideas of the Modern School in this country.

Emma Goldman herself was a product of a very suppressive and oppressive background. Born in Russia in 1869 where she and her family struggled with poverty for most of her tenure in that country her parents shipped her off to the United States to live with her half-sister when Goldman was twenty. This move to the Untied States foisted on Goldman by her parents was mainly a result of the ongoing conflicts between Emma and her father, but it was also these conflicts that eventually led to her philosophical beliefs and eventual support of the ideas put forth with the Modern School movement, which were very libratory. Her home life in Russia was emotionally cold and aloof at best, with at times her father being extremely abusive, both physically and mentally. Goldman was very rebellious and defiant which lead her father to often beat her and rage at her with the intent of getting her to obey his authority. Her family attempted to marry her off at the age of 15, which she refused, and the conflicts between her and her father grew until the family finally decided to send her to the United States in 1889 at the age of 20.

Being a Jewish immigrant in the United States in the late nineteenth century Goldman had few employment opportunities afforded to her so she mainly toiled in sweatshops and as a seamstress. While she was working in these factories she started recognizing the abuses inflicted onto the working class and those in poverty around her by the owners of the factories and others in power, which she considered to be the capitalist class. Goldman herself struggled with the jobs where she worked, having to labor long hours in hot tortuous conditions. These were formative years for Emma Goldman, being in her twenties during the late nineteenth century, where she started to develop a concern for women and children, the poor and the labor class. It was through these firsthand abuses and her studies of how the labor class would be suppressed for attempting to stand up for their rights that she was prompted to become more politically active. During this same period several political and labor groups were directly involved in fighting against the abuses that the working classes were subjected to and these groups garnered the attention of the politically sensitive Goldman.

Some of these groups identified themselves as Anarchists and were very involved in the labor movement of the time. The Anarchists held to the belief that any centralized authoritative power, whether it would be the government or capitalist class, would be corrupt. What the Anarchists were seeing at this time in the nineteenth century was the government using the police and military to defend factory and mine owners and would use these troops to attack strikers who were crusading for better working conditions and livable wages. These abuses and the rejection of overt forms of authority was the foundation of the psychology of Anarchism, which were also very libratory, and encouraged self-determination in each individual. Since Emma Goldman had to work in these factories and under the same harsh conditions she understood firsthand the plight of these workers. It was her connection to these Anarchists and her rejection of overt forms of authority (including her past experiences with her abusive and oppressive father) that the groundwork for the psychology of the Modern School began to develop in Goldman's psyche.

Her popularity among Anarchist groups increased and over time she became more involved with these groups, touring the country giving speeches and eventually, along with fellow comrades in the Anarchist movement, she began publishing a magazine titled *Mother Earth*, where she wrote prolifically about the social issues that she spoke of during her lecture tours. It was in 1909, however, with the execution of the founder of the Modern School movement Francisco Ferrer y Guardia by the Spanish government that Emma Goldman became a staunch supporter and advocate of the Modern School philosophy. After Ferrer's execution Goldman helped to create the Modern School Movement in the United States and started the Modern School Association. She also promoted the Modern School movement through her speeches and writings in her journal *Mother Earth*. Emma Goldman's views of education can best be summarized in her autobiography *Living my Life*:

No one has yet fully realized the wealth of sympathy, kindness, and generosity hidden in the soul of the child. The effort of every true educator should be to unlock that treasure – to stimulate the child's impulses and call forth the best and noblest tendencies. What greater reward can there be for one whose life-work is to watch over the growth of the human plant than to see it unfold its petals and to observe it develop into a true individuality?

MODERN SCHOOL

Although Emma Goldman and Anarchists promoted the Modern School in this country, the philosophy and psychology of the school was actually founded by, as we mentioned earlier, a Spanish educator named Francisco Ferrer y Guardia and often his name is used synonymously with Modern School (i.e., Ferrer School) or specific schools would bear his name. Ferrer wanted to develop an educational environment that was to be more student centered and to take into account the rights and dignity of the child. Ferrer believed in a form of libratory education that would promote independence in children and encourage them to grow and learn emotionally, psychologically, and physically in a more open environment instead of one typically oppressive and rigid. Manual pursuits as well as intellectual ones were strongly supported in students and they were allowed and encouraged to seek out projects that they were interested in.

Unfortunately Ferrer was promoting his ideas of education in Spain during a very tumultuous time and both the government and the church in Spain did not view them very favorably. Eventually Ferrer was accused of conspiring against the government and encouraging an uprising and was arrested, charged, and given a mock trial where no solid evidence of these activities could be brought forward. Regardless of this lack of evidence he was found guilty and executed in 1909. This created an enormous outcry in the rest of the Western world among social activists and educators and in many regions schools bearing his name sprang up in honor of him, specifically supporting and attempting to emulate his educational philosophy. It was in this country that Emma Goldman became such a strong supporter of Francisco Ferrer and his Modern School movement. Several Modern Schools were organized in the United States and some stayed relatively active up to the early 1950s.

The Modern School was not seen as just a school, but a community of learners that included teachers as well as students. The students were the central important aspect of the educational process, not standardized tests that are mandated by governmental figures. The students' rights were valued and their growth was highly regarded, with emphasis placed on the dignity of the child. One main aspect of the Modern School, and one of the reasons that Emma Goldman was so supportive of its philosophy, is its rejection of overt and centralized authority. It is this rejection of overt and centralized authority that signifies the psychology of the Modern School philosophy. Individual psychological growth was greatly encouraged in the Modern School. Ones ability to learn was based on that individual's own personal developmental stage, not on a developmental stage that was mandated by the educational institution, teachers, or theories subscribed to by that institution. If a student was not doing well in a certain area or was not as interested in a certain subject, then emphasis was placed on the students learning ability and what they were ready to learn. Students were not coerced or forced into learning something they were not ready to learn or not interested in. They were also not evaluated or labeled if they were not ready to learn a certain topic or subject. Students were however encouraged to develop individually and independently within a community of learners.

With the philosophy of developing individuality within each child there is also this sense of communalism; this is where students learn to work together in the educational environment as opposed to being so competitive. Grades, tests, and class rankings were all abolished in the Modern School and learning became a spontaneous event where one could learn from other students, teachers, and learn together in groups. It was through this process that educators of the Modern School felt that allowing the student to learn and grow in an open and free environment brought out the true and unique character of each child. Another important aspect of the Modern school was that learning did not end at a certain point in a person's life, that learning was an ongoing and lifelong process. So you may have a class at one of the Modern Schools where students and teachers were learning a subject together. It was also the belief in the Modern School setting to provide as much material as possible for students, not to limit or restrict them to just certain subjects, and to show the connections of those subjects to each other. Through the Modern School, learning became more than just internal or external. It became both—learning became experiential.

POSTFORMAL EDUCATION

The Modern School attempted to break away from formal education and tap into the essence of who the student was and this mirrors the ideas that Joe Kincheloe and others would call *postformal education*, or education that goes beyond the formal framework. Postformal thinking attempts to break away from this notion of using a developmental model and behavioral psychology as a reference for the educational process. When education is so inextricably connected with scientific process, the most important aspect of what education should be about is completely lost, and that is the human element. Individuals learning in an educational environment are not test subjects that can be reduced to the most statistically appropriate teaching methods and evaluations. They are unique individuals who learn in different ways and have different experiences and aspects of themselves that they can bring to the educational environment. The postformal view of education is not so much focused on standardizations, evaluations, linear teaching methods, or rote memorizations, all of which place the educational process above education itself as the central point of learning. Postformal view focuses more on the student himself or herself, having the student as the center of the education and how each individual student learns and what their basic interests and ideas are.

Postformal educational setting becomes more democratic and focuses on probably one of the most important aspects of its value system, which is not seen in formal education at all, and that is the idea of critical thinking. In the postformal classroom emphasis is placed more on examining an issue or idea critically and it is through this critical process that students are encouraged to view things more holistically as opposed to the formal where learning is done in a more linear fashion. The formal view of education, with its strong developmental background, does not apply as much in the postformal setting where learning becomes more fluid and organic, which is what we are really dealing with in the school setting, unique and organic individuals. When students are encouraged to learn at their own pace and to pursue those ideas that are of interest to them, they become more mindful of themselves and those around them. The formal sense of hyper-individualism slowly begins to melt away and each student becomes a unique individual in relation to the community around him or her. Learning in the postformal setting is not rigid or heavily structured, the classroom and school becomes the students laboratory, and instead of the teacher being the head of the class, the students and teachers all become educators and learners and have something unique and different to bring to the class.

FORMAL EDUCATION

The Modern School greatly mirrored the ideas of the postformal thinking, and tried very specifically to break away from the formal ideas of education which were prevalent at the time and have been handed down since then. Formal education has a long history and tradition, especially in this country and is distinguished by what some would consider its rigidity. All one has to do is to look at the arrangement of the formal classroom even today to get an understanding of what the formal process of education is like. Classrooms are established on a very fixed pattern, with rows and isles arranged so that the students have to sit, in place, and face in one direction toward the educator. In the classroom itself interaction is discouraged among peers and all eyes must be forward, facing the authority figure that becomes the central focus of the class.

Desks and chairs in the formal classroom are not particularly comfortable but one is to maintain silence and stillness throughout the learning process. Students are allowed to speak, but only if specifically identified and authorized by the teacher. The educational process itself is performed in what the educator Paulo Freire called the "banking method." This banking method is where the students are basically repositories to be filled by the teacher's knowledge, much like a bank where the teacher deposits information into the suspected empty mind of the student. The student really does not have much to offer the class except what he or she can memorize from the lessons the teacher teaches them and from the textbook, and what they can regurgitate in a process known as testing. It is through testing that a student is evaluated on his or her ability to sit still, listen, take in information, memorize it, and repeat it back to the teacher. This testing becomes highly competitive and students are punished if they attempt to help each other or learn from each other during the testing process.

After testing, students are then ranked on their ability to acquire knowledge through rote memorization and recall this information in a standardized way by a process known as grading. Those students able to memorize large quantities of data, even if the information seems trivial to them, are rewarded by higher grades and higher rankings in class and those students that do not perform as well on these tests are given lower grades and lower rankings in class standing. Learning in this environment becomes very linear and concepts such as independence, creativity, being able to articulate and think in abstract ways or critically are strongly discouraged. The competitiveness of the testing, grading, and class ranking, coupled with the physical structure of the classroom itself, creates a hyper-individualized atmosphere where the thoughts and ideas of others are not valued. In this banking method the student really has nothing of value to offer to the teacher or the rest of the class, except obedience.

Formal education is also based on a more developmental psychological model, which was developed and tested by theorists that also looked at the behavioral aspects of learning. These ideas were greatly supported and promoted by two developmental psychologists, Erik Erickson and Jean Piaget. From the perspective of both of these theorists, they believed that individuals developed at certain stages and how they develop should closely mirror their age and at what stage they should be at that time, that learning is very linear and progresses on an upward pattern. Images such as a ladder or stairs are often invoked in demonstrating their theories. One would begin at the bottom of a ladder or steps, and as they grow and learn they should move upward and there is very little room for moving back and forth on this development model. Once one has "mastered" a certain skill, one should continue upward on their progress and should not go back or jump forward, but continue on the path, as one should behaviorally. The mind in this model is actually perceived of as a muscle and the best way that one can learn is in this formal educational setting by a process of rote memorization. One of the interesting aspects of this model is that little emphasis is placed on the learning process of adults, so once an individual has made it to a certain point in his or her life, one has mastered the basic skills needed to survive and not much more emphasis is placed on education.

One unfortunate but very important side effect of this style of learning in this formal educational environment is that it mainly establishes ones place in society, which is an obedient follower that does not question authority. Education today is based on the ideas of means and production, where one is to become a "productive" member of society, which basically means to produce and consume goods. Ideas such as individuality (being a unique self as opposed to the hyper-individuality of formal education which is to be competitive in the market economy), spirituality, concern for others and the environment are discouraged since these ideas pose a threat to the market economy. What tends to happen in the psychological aspect of this educational environment is that if one is unable to perform, accept, or adept appropriately to these standards then one has a tendency to be "labeled." These labels can range from something as simple as just having a "learning disability" to a more severe label as one having a "behavioral problem," but the main emphasis of the label is that the student is deficient in one way or another.

In the formal setting, students who have a tendency to reject forms of authority or attempt to express themselves individually are not meeting up to the standards and this in turn may require intervention by a professional or specialist. Very little emphasis is placed on the students learning ability, since standardized tests are considered the norm and the only appropriate way to evaluate ones progress in this formal setting. Interventions based on a psychological model that is to help students become more productive members of the educational process, or in other words are able to conform to the educational standards, are very valued in the formal educational setting. In too many cases alternatives such as medications that help students "focus" and stay still are utilized and these alternatives are on the increase even though there is very little research that has been conducted on the long-term effects of these medications on young developing minds. So the sense of individuality and creativity are strongly discouraged in the formal setting and the psychological educational model is to help students conform to these formal educational standards.

This, needless to say, is one of the reason that Emma Goldman and the Anarchists were so supportive of the Modern School values, philosophy, and psychology, and why Ferrer was so disliked and distrusted in Spain during the time of his execution. The philosophy and psychology of the Anarchists was one of rejection of these forms of overt authority put forth in formal educational settings. The Modern School was also heavily influenced by the understanding of oppression toward the working class, women, and the poor by centralized authoritarian and power figures and held true to the Anarchist influences of Emma Goldman and other Anarchists who founded and promoted the movement in the United States and other Western countries. Another aspect of understanding the philosophy and psychology behind the Modern School movement is to look at what Anarchism is and how it influences the ideas of the Modern School.

ANARCHISM

Although Anarchism itself has a long and rich history, the word "Anarchy" has been greatly misunderstood, especially in our contemporary society. Most people connect Anarchy with the punk movement of the late 1970s and early 1980s, especially with the punk band The Sex Pistols and their anthem *Anarchy in the U.K.* Although some punk movements and punk songs do have a connection to the philosophy, especially rejection to overt authoritarianism, the ideas of contemporary Anarchy predate this movement by close to 150 years. The word Anarchy itself comes from the Greek word *anarkhia*, which loosely translated means without rule, or to a society without government. A French political philosopher Pierre-Joseph Proudhon, in an effort to express his own personal and political ideas, adopted this term in the mid-1800s and many of his followers and ideological descendants continued to use the term Anarchy to describe their beliefs.

The ideas and philosophy of Anarchy were a reaction to poverty and oppression, especially enforced by both the government and capitalist class, which at the time used the military to protect them from the laborers themselves. The belief behind Anarchism, sometimes invoking indigenous cultures, was that society could govern itself without a strong, powerful, and centralized leadership. The overall belief was that any centralized power, whether capitalist, communist, or other, would eventually abuse that power and oppresses its citizens and the same would go for any centralized power that is educating its citizens. That power, when it becomes centralized, is narrowed down to the hands of the few and this minority in turn will start to think that they know what is best for the overall society and will use that belief to justify laws and rules that really do not protect society, but enslaves it.

For Anarchists, the purpose of formal education is to create good citizens who will not question the authority of the centralized power structure. Emma Goldman and the Anarchists supported the Modern School because it allowed an individual to grow and develop independently, and yet still be highly aware of those around him or her and the connection that he or she has with the planet as a whole. Where formal schools encourage and promote this sense of hyper-individualism, it is not an individualism that encourages independent thinking. It is more of a hyper-individualism that supports a materialistic and consumer lifestyle, where ideas of freedom and democracy are closely related to the free market and not to actual engagement in society as a whole where informed citizens have direct knowledge of social concerns.

Anarchism feels a spiritual connection to the democratic, communal, and emancipatory ideas that we have laid out because it sees all things on the planet as symbiotic, and the educational psychology of the Modern School reflected those ideas in its educational philosophy. Students were encouraged to be independent and articulate thinkers. The educational process attempted to move away from the formal process of education, where teaching and learning was very linear and rigid, to a more holistic form of education where students were not as much evaluated by grades and standards as they were encouraged to pursue those things that made them happy and encourage in them emotional growth. Teachers are not seen as authoritarian figures as they are more a part of the learning and growing experience and the distinction between authoritarian and having authority are very important in this setting.

Just because an educator is not seen as an authoritarian, does not mean they are not an authority in something; the difference is how they present themselves to the students. One can be an authority in something; such as a surgeon is an authority in the specific type of surgery they perform. This does not mean they are authoritarian in how they present themselves, this just means they have acquired certain skills and knowledge and have become an authority in their specific field. Authoritarian and authoritarianism comes when individuals abuse their skills, position, and power. An authoritarian educator is one who exerts his control over the students, feels that he or she knows what is best for the students, and punishes them for attempting to learn at their own pace or what is important to them. Rankings, tests, grades, psychological evaluations for students who don't perform up to standards, are all tools of an authoritarian system. Concepts related to evaluating a student's progress in relation to how others perform using such standard and formal tools as grades were concepts that were not allowed in the Modern School. Students were given the opportunity to grow and learn at their own pace and were not coerced or forced to memorize details in a rote manner that had no interest in a child's life. The basic foundation of the Modern school was libratory education and the freedom of the child's mind and spirit without the use of authoritarian methods.

A good way to present the differences between how a school operates in a formal educational framework and how the Modern School operated is to take a specific example of how both schools would approach the learning process. In this example we can see how the student's own learning process and connection to the material that they are attempting to learn come into play.

AN EXAMPLE OF FORMAL AND MODERN SCHOOL APPROACH

Given a standard text that is required in the formal setting, generally a novel, we use this as an example for both the formal setting and the Modern School. Both would read the book, the difference would be how both would approach it. In the formal setting the book would be assigned at a certain point in a person's educational process (e.g., eighth grade). All students in this grade would be close to the same age and academic level and the text would be assigned in a detailed and rigid manner where the students would read certain sections by a certain time. Specific questions may be posed to the students as they slog through the text with the pretense of having them look at the text "critically." But what they will actually be doing is not reflecting on the text critically, or looking at it holistically, but more than likely memorizing specific aspects of the text that they will be graded on and may eventually show up on a standardized, sanctioned test. The critical aspect of the text would be more in line of agreeing with the teacher about certain aspects of the book, which the teacher in turn is getting from a teachers guide.

In the Modern School setting the same book may be studied in a class that reflects on different types of literature. The class makeup would be more diverse (much like the characters in the book would probably be also). Students of different ages and academic levels may be in the class and bring in different skills, knowledge, and experiences. Instead of just reading the text verbatim over a period of time and then being tested on it, the teacher would work with the students on how to bring this particular book to life and one idea that may be considered would be to enact a play based on the book. With the concept of making this book into a performance, student's different levels and skills would come into play. Some students may have artistic talents and could help design and create a set. Those students who are more adept to working with tools could help build a set that would reflect the story of the text and the creativity of the students themselves. Those students who are creative writers could help develop the text into a script. The possibilities are endless and what ultimately happens is this book slowly comes to life for the students.

Since the book itself would be acted out as a theatrical production, the process of actually critically looking at the text becomes important. Characters in the play would have to have personalities developed so the students would have to attempt to get into the minds of the individual that he or she would be playing. The abstract story in the book becomes more and more real and students start to look at it more holistically instead of linearly with the hope of making a "good grade" at the end of the class. Of course approaching a text in this manner would take a longer period of time than just reading it and memorizing certain details of the book that will be forgotten as soon as a test is over. What one should question is which example would be more appropriate in educating students? Do we want to teach our students to memorize a great deal of abstract data that will be forgotten as soon as they are out of school, or would we rather our students be able to approach things with a critical mind and view them holistically, developing skills and techniques that they can apply to everyday tasks?

CONCLUSION

Emma Goldman dedicated her life to being a voice for those oppressed, to speaking out for the rights of workers, women, and for children and to standing up against any form of authoritarianism. She was also instrumental bringing the ideas of the Modern School and its philosophy to this country. Because of her beliefs and determination in advocating her views she became very unpopular with those in power and the government which resulted in her being jailed numerous times and several death threats were made against her. It was with her support for the Russian Revolution of 1917, when the Communists and Bolsheviks took over power in that country that she was perceived as more of a threat to the United States. She was also very outspoken about the First World War and finally, during one of many Red Scares in the United States, she was deported back to Russia in 1920, even though she was a legal citizen and resident of the United States. She spent only a few years in Russia before she escaped that region, once again railing against overt authoritarianism of the Soviet government. She eventually settled in Canada and in 1940 at the age of 70 she died of a stroke and was brought back to this country and buried in Chicago.

The last Modern School in the United States that Emma Goldman worked so tirelessly to start in this country closed in the early 1950s, although students and educators of these Modern Schools started meeting again in the 1970s to continue to promote its ideas and philosophy. Though it made it through several Red Scares in the early twentieth century in the United States, the Modern School could not survive McCarthyism of the 1950s and several leftist groups such as the Communists and Anarchists were attacked for their philosophical and ideological beliefs. Since the Modern School in the United States were founded and supported by the Anarchists, they eventually became an ideological victim of those dark times.

The question that we should be asking is not what the Modern School provided to the landscape of contemporary education, but what it should have provided if the contemporary formal educational setting had listened. At the time of the Modern Schools, formal schools were very rigid and structured in their classroom setting, and testing, grades, and competitiveness were valued over students' ability to learn and grow independently. What has happened now, however, is that the formal developmental and behavioral psychological model has become more and more pervasive in the contemporary school setting and standardized tests have become the only norm for evaluating a persons intelligence and ability to learn (even though research has demonstrated that these tests are heavily biased toward more affluent, Caucasian male students and are not an accurate reflections of a persons intelligence). If we don't follow the Modern School example of education and start moving toward the postformal teaching method, we will slowly begin to develop in students not an ability to think holistically, independently, critically, and in abstract ways, but students that have been taught in such linear fashions that they will only be able to operate within a standardized box.

CHAPTER 11

Jurgen Habermas

IAN STEINBERG

Jurgen Habermas, the German social theorist and last surviving member of the Frankfurt School, has a lot to offer to the theory and practice of education. Though his project was not specifically about pedagogical theory or education systems, his work informs the philosophy of education in several grounding ways. First is his contribution to our understanding of epistemology and the nature of knowledge through his critique of positivism. Second, he provides valuable pedagogical insight through his theory of communicative action and the role of learning and language in the reproduction of society. Finally, through his experience of the European student movements of the 1960s, Habermas provides insight into the roles of institutions of learning, especially universities, in society. Habermas does not present a unified theory or philosophy of education, it is the other way around. To Habermas knowledge, learning, and the means of conveying and utilizing knowledge *is* social theory.

Paulo Freire describes the traditional model of education as a "banking" method of education (Freire, 2000). The banking method is a positivist paradigm that embodies subject–object duality on two levels. On one level, knowledge, to a banking educator, consists of an arsenal of discrete facts. These facts are considered objective truths, meaning that the fact is based on phenomena that exist outside of human interpretation. On another level, the teacher is the acting subject who presents the world of fact to the student. The student is the object of the teacher's effort and passively receives the facts and stores them up, like a bank. The typical role of a teacher and educational system under the banking method is to bestow upon the student knowledge that will prepare the student for a vocation. Habermas's critique of positivism and his identification of the role interest plays in the pursuit of knowledge provide a point of departure from traditional banking education.

In *Knowledge and Human Interests* (1971) Habermas discusses the origins of "value-free" knowledge, that is, positivist epistemology. He argues that ancient Greek philosophers claimed that the philosopher needed to be free of material interests in order to perceive the transcendent truths of the cosmos. If the philosopher was more concerned with pursuing personal interests, then the philosopher would not be able to perceive truths that reached beyond those personal interests. In this sense, Habermas argues, that the interest-free knowledge of the Greeks was not at all "value-free" or "ethically neutral." Indeed, Greek philosophy was normative and very much concerned with uncovering those truths that would guide Greek civilization toward an idealized state (pp. 301–303). Positivist knowledge descended and departed from the Greek theoretical tradition. Under the regime of scientistic methodology the concept of "interest-free" knowledge that was normative truth became "value-free" objective truth. In other words, science took the notion of "pure theory" and ran with it (p. 315). The scientific process created a conceptual framework that hid the way knowledge and the interpretation of phenomena was not outside of human experience and in so doing, concealed the interests at play in the pursuit of knowledge. (pp. 304–306). Habermas's critique of positivism is not only geared toward the so-called "hard sciences." He also contends that historicism can fall into the positivist trap by claiming to be interest- or value-free (p. 309).

To demonstrate how interest and knowledge are inseparable, Habermas categorizes three broad methods of inquiry and their associative interests. These three "knowledge-constitutive interests" are: technical, practical, and emancipatory cognitive interests (p. 308). The technical cognitive interest refers to the knowledge of "empirical-analytical sciences." This type of knowledge is typically generated through hypothesis testing and experimentation. The method of empirical analysis is to learn or create knowledge by assessing the results of some sort of process under controlled environments. The results of hypothesis testing are observations that are considered to be a natural and objective state of nature, and are considered truthful, or at least reliable, because they preclude human subjectivity. The purpose of this knowledge is to expand the ability of humans to essentially transform nature for social needs; "[t]his is the cognitive interest in the technical control over objectified processes" (pp. 308–309). Habermas does not reject this type of science, nor does he claim that it can't create useful knowledge. Habermas rejects an epistemology that claims the correspondence of knowledge with truth that exists outside of human interpretation.

The "historical–hermeneutic sciences" create knowledge in a different manner than the empirical–analytical sciences. Historical–hermeneutic method is to create knowledge through the interpretation of texts. These sciences are concerned with understanding meaning, unlike the empirical–analytical sciences that are concerned with observation. This is the knowledge interest that Habermas designates as the "practical cognitive interest." Habermas criticizes the positivism of historicism in a similar vein as his critique of scientism. When a historian claims to have revealed historical fact by interpreting the meaning of texts, that is, writes history, this knowledge "is always mediated through [the interpreter's] pre-understanding, which is derived from the interpreter's initial situation" (p. 309). Habermas claims that any "practical" knowledge is only as good as the interpreter's ability to "expand the horizons of understanding" between the worlds of both the text and the interpreter in order to create an intersubjective understanding of the interpreter's own world *in relation* to that of text's world (pp. 309–310). The practical, intersubjective knowledge interest is important to an understanding of how separate individuals, with unique (but shared) experiences within a collectivity, can form a social reality (Pusey, 1987, p. 25).

Critical social sciences, certain philosophical traditions that seek normative social action, as well as psychotherapy, employ a method that is different from the previous two cognitive interests. The knowledge interest of these disciplines is the third cognitive interest: the emancipatory interest. This is a knowledge interest that emphasizes critical self-reflection. Habermas sees the role of the emancipatory interest as one that works in hand with the other two interests by helping to reveal the way in which the interests of the knower impacts the method and analysis of what is to be known. The purpose here is to transform the unreflective state of positivist thought to one of critical self-reflection through the articulation of the assumptions inherent to the method of analysis (Habermas, 1971, p. 310). The political point, to Habermas, is that ideological control (the rationalization accepted as common sense) is rooted in an empiricist way of understanding laws of nature. Unreflective thought and type of knowledge it produces accepts a priori worldviews as "natural" and law-like. The emancipatory-interest is the initiation of reflection on why and how "natural" laws exist as well as an initiation in the understanding of how ideology conceals arbitrary power relations in society (Habermas, 1971, p. 315; Pusey, 1987, p. 26). By describing these knowledge-constitutive interests, Habermas describes the fundamental ways people understand and relate to reality (Habermas, 1971, p. 311). He then goes on to link knowledge with the organization of social life:

The specific viewpoints from which, with transcendental necessity, we apprehend reality ground three categories of possible knowledge: information that expands our power of technical control; interpretations that make possible the orientation of action within common traditions; and analyses that free consciousness from its dependence on hypostatized powers. These viewpoints originate in the interest structure of a species that is linked in its root to definite means of social organization: work, language, and power. (p. 313)

His thesis that "knowledge-constitutive interests take form in the medium of work, language, and power" is of direct relevance to a discussion about education. Schooling is a social institution that vitally links all these components in daily practice. When Habermas makes the normative claim that grounds his social theory as belief in the collective pursuit of "the good life" he places an important burden on the educational system. Therefore, to take Habermas's lead, an educator and a student have a mutual responsibility to approach the task of gaining knowledge as a pursuit that goes beyond banking facts. Teachers and students need to incorporate a reflexive process that treats knowledge not objectively, but intersubjectively. How this is carried out in practice is difficult to conceive, but Habermas provides some clues through his theory of communicative rationality and communicative action.

Habermas details the theory of communicative action in 1,200 plus pages of a two-volume set published in 1984 and 1987. I will not go into specific details about the theory, since this will be beyond the scope of this essay, rather, I will discuss the theory of communicative action as a general concept that can inform pedagogical practice. The theory of communicative action posits an alternative type of rationality than instrumental, or purposive, rationality. Instrumental rationality is rationality toward a specific, technical end. Communicative rationality and communicative action are oriented toward a state of mutual understanding between communicating participants (Bernstein, 1985, pp. 18–20). This rationality is dialogical, that is, intersubjective. Instrumental rationality is object-oriented, the relationship between the acting subject and acted upon object is a one-way causal relationship. According to Habermas, the act of speaking inherently contains the intent of reaching understanding between the speaker and the hearer. Therefore, communicative rationality is an alternative rationality that builds upon this mutual relationship.

One of the primary concerns for Habermas, then, is the creation of the "ideal speech condition." The ideal speech condition has several components:

(1) freedom to enter a discourse, check questionable claims, evaluate explanations, modify given conceptual structures, assess justifications, alter norms, interrogate political will, and employ speech acts; (2) orientation to mutual understanding between participants in discourses, and respect of their rights as equal and autonomous partners; (3) a concern to achieve in discussion a consensus which is based on the force of the argument alone, rather than the positional power of the participants, in particular that of dominating participants; (4) adherence to the speech-act validity claims of truth, legitimacy, sincerity, and comprehensibility. Democracy and equality, for Habermas, are rooted less in the operation of power and domination and more in a search for rational behaviour and a consensus that is based on the rational search for truth, and which is achieved discursively. (Morrison, 2001, p. 220)

This is an idealized situation, a normative goal that educators can strive to achieve in their classrooms. In the classroom, the teacher has a "more than equal" role and the authority of greater knowledge about the subject. In which case it is doubly important for the teacher to beware of becoming a "dominating participant." Due to structural inequities in society, people will be able to engage in "critical rational discourse" at different levels and in different contexts. By striving for the ideal speech situation; the settlement of disagreements through communicative rationality; and a pedagogical practice informed by the goals, Habermas implicates all of society in a normative call to come up with solutions to structural inequity. This in turn reaffirms Habermas's fundamental belief in the democratic process. Indeed, Pusey (1987) characterizes Habermas's concept of democracy "as a process of shared learning" (p. 120).

What, then, is the role of a university, specifically, in a democracy? In *Toward a Rational Society* (1970) Habermas details the relationship of the university to democracy. The role of the university consists of four concurrent tasks that resonate with Habermas's earlier conception of knowledge interests. First, research at a university pursues the technical mastery of nature and the production of new generations of scientists. Second, the university is a place where students learn practical knowledge, cultural knowledge, which prepares them for life in modern society as well as provide the "extracurricular" but necessary knowledge for a profession (like quick decision making skills for a future doctor). Third is to produce, interpret, and pass on the "cultural tradition of society." And, finally, the university is a place of development of political consciousness (pp. 1–3).

Habermas claims that, in Germany during the 1960s, the university system faces a crisis. In his eyes, the university was pulled in different directions by the technical knowledge interest and emancipatory knowledge interests. On the one hand the university was increasingly stressing the importance of developing technical knowledge for industrial applications. On the other hand, the university was increasingly oriented to the politicization of students in the post-War era. However, the university, as an institution, remained unchanged in organization since the Middle Ages. Habermas presents this quandary as having two different solutions. The university could either retreat into depoliticized, factory-like knowledge production or else the university could "assert itself within the democratic tradition" (p. 6). Either way, the university has to change its structure. Habermas's belief in the democratic tradition leads him to "substantiate [his] vote for this second possibility by trying to demonstrate the affinity and inner relation of the enterprise of knowledge on the university level to the democratic form of decision-making" (p. 6).

Habermas reinforces what he considers democracy. It isn't the formal political apparatus of modern welfare states, instead he argues for political decision making that is in a "Kantian manner." This means that "only reason should have force" and that consensus is arrived in a discussion free of coercion (p. 7). Kantian and Habermasian reason is not purpose-driven; it is based on reflection in the tradition of Enlightenment philosophy. In the context of the university, across all disciplines, Habermas call for a "philosophical enlightenment" that "illustrate[s] a self-reflection of the sciences in which the latter become critically aware of their own presuppositions" (p. 8). This self-reflection within research traditions and the pedagogical process will yield more critical and complex ways of understanding the relation between different subjects and courses of inquiry. This also brings new "continuity" to the university campus: "critical argument serves in the end only to disclose the commingling of basic methodological assumptions and action-orienting self-understanding. If this is so, then no matter how much the self-reflection of the sciences and the rational discussion of political decisions differ and must be carefully distinguished, they are still connected by the common form or critical inquiry" (p. 10). Further, Habermas argues that only through this reflection process can the university system achieve the three goals that transcend the technical or instrumental goal of advancing the science of industry. A university in a democracy, then, becomes a site for the rigorous advancement of critical rationality based on self-reflection and democratic deliberation. There is a dialectical unity to the university and democracy in that the ability for the democratization of the university to take place is contingent on a greater pursuit of democracy in society. The democratic society will look to the university system for a source of critical rational debate about the important issues of the time, scientific and cultural changes, as well as the source of new generations of democratic deliberators in all professions, not just politics.

REFERENCES

Bernstein, Richard (Ed.) (1985). *Habermas and Modernity*. Cambridge: MIT Press.

Freire, Paulo (2000). *Pedagogy of the Oppressed* (30th Anniversary Edition). New York: Continuum.

Habermas, Jurgen (1970). *Toward a Rational Society*. Boston: Beacon Press.

Habermas, Jurgen (1971). *Knowledge and Human Interests*. Boston: Beacon Press.

Morrison, Keith (2001). Jurgen Habermas. In Joy A. Palmer (Ed.), *Fifty Modern Thinkers on Education*. London: Routledge.

Pusey, Michael (1987). *Jurgen Habermas*. London: Routledge.

CHAPTER 12

Granville Stanley Hall

LYNDA KENNEDY

Perhaps no one in the history of educational psychology embodies the phrase "he was a man of his time" more that Granville Stanley Hall. His life spanned a period of great change in the United States and the world. The economy was shifting from agriculture to manufacturing; slavery ended as the country rebuilt itself after the Civil War; women slowly forged their way toward full citizenship; the sciences and philosophies of the Enlightenment gained legitimacy as they established themselves in the academy and threatened the authority of religion; and immigrants poured in from non-Anglo Saxon countries, swelling the population and bringing new and alien languages and customs. This was Hall's world, and he was a product of it.

Born in rural Ashfield, Massachusetts to a religious family in 1844, Hall originally focused on becoming a minister, then followed his interests into philosophy, physiology, natural sciences, and beyond, finally becoming the first American to be granted a PhD in Psychology. Like many of his generation, Hall attempted to reconcile his faith in religion with his interest and belief in science and reason, not least by writing *Jesus, the Christ, in the Light of Psychology* in 1917. A teacher of John Dewey, and a strong opponent to the Committee of Ten's proposal for an academic curriculum for all, Hall advocated a child-centered approach to education, flying in the face of the then accepted notion of the universal benefits of academic subjects.

Though many credit Hall with facilitating the emergence of the field of educational psychology through his efforts to found the American Psychological Association, today Hall's approach to education remains controversial. Hall's advocacy of a completely child-centered, "natural" education and a focus on child study may be welcome in schools applying an approach to education which is still considered alternative, but is anathema to those who are proponents of State and national standards. His belief in the power of hereditary strengths and weaknesses—particularly those attributed to race and gender—should make us shudder, while the differentiated curricula that arose from this belief remain with us in career and technical and vocational education programs. Though the theory that ontogeny recapitulates phylogeny has long fallen out of fashion, Hall's contribution to the development of the child study movement and his pioneering exploration of adolescence continue to be major influences on American educational psychology. Understanding the influence of Hall's work on current psycho-educational practice and theory is essential for postformal students of the field, for, as Joe Kincheloe has pointed out in his

Getting Beyond the Facts: Teaching Social Studies/Social Sciences in the Twenty-First Century (2001), a postformal approach requires us to reach past the understandings that have come down to us as fact and examine their social construction.

BACKGROUND, INFLUENCES, AND ACHIEVEMENTS—A BRIEF SUMMARY

As mentioned above, Hall came of age during a time of great societal change, all which came to bear on his educational philosophies. Hall's first interest was the church. He attended Williston Seminary in Easthampton, Massachusetts, from 1862 to 1863, transferred to Williams College until 1867 (receiving his BA and MA), and then spent a year in New York at the Union Theological Seminary as a divinity student. While in New York he attended many of the meetings held at Cooper Union where he was exposed to radical thinkers of the day. He even went to a meeting at the house of the famous (some would say infamous) social reformer, Victoria Woodhull, and attended at least one séance. Hall was introduced to the well-known abolitionist and minister Henry Ward Beecher at Beecher's church in Brooklyn Heights. Beecher, on hearing that Hall wished to study philosophy in Europe but lacked the funds, in turn introduced him to lumber magnate, Henry Sage, who gave Hall a check for $1,000 to finance his study.

Traveling abroad in July of 1868, Hall's European studies began with philosophy then turned toward psychology. Hall returned from Europe in 1871 and worked as a tutor to the children of a well-to-do Jewish family in New York. Through this family he was introduced to more social reformers and progressives who were concerned with children and education such as Felix Adler, the son of a Rabbi, who went on to found the Society for Ethical Culture and the Ethical Culture School. After a short teaching stint at Antioch College and then at Harvard, Hall returned to Europe in 1876, studying in Leipzig under philosopher and psychologist, Wilhelm Wundt, and experimental physiologist, Carl Ludwig. Upon his return from Germany, Hall studied at Harvard under William James and Henry Bowditch, and was granted the first PhD in psychology earned in the United States. He went on to an appointment as a professor of pedagogy and psychology at the Johns Hopkins University then served as the first president of Clark University in Worcester, Massachusetts, from 1889 until his death in 1924. Hall founded many professional journals, including the *American Journal of Psychology* (1887), the *Pedagogical Seminary* (1891) and the *Journal of Applied Psychology* (1915). He also served as the first president of the American Psychological Association.

THEORY

Ontogeny Recapitulates Phylogeny

As the theories of Darwin and other evolutionists swept the world, Hall's focus began to center around child development and its relation to evolutionary theory. Hall applied German zoologist Ernst Haeckel's theory that ontogeny recapitulates phylogeny—that the development of embryos mirrors the evolutionary stages of a species—and expanded it to mean that the psycho-educational development of the child followed the evolutionary path of human society. This is sometimes referred to as the *culture-epochs* theory. One must remember that for Hall, as well for many of those living in Hall's time, evolutionary belief was heavily colored by the bias toward Western society as being the highest level achieved in the history of mankind. Therefore, in Hall's view, the young child experiences the "animal" stage until about six or seven years of age, then progresses to the "savage" stage and so on until becoming a "civilized" adult. Hall did not believe that the child in his "animal" stage should be unduly pressured. Nature, he felt, was the best teacher. With this understanding, Hall recommended that reading not be taught until at least the age of 8, if at all. He based his belief on the fact that great leaders in the past such as Charlemagne were illiterate, and other figures he considered important, such as the Virgin Mary, achieved great things without the need for literacy. In Hall's view, the true nature of the child—which owed itself completely to heredity—would lead the child to achieve as much as he or she would be able to, without the interference of education.

Hall's belief in the power of heredity over instruction greatly influenced those who became his students at Clark University, such as Henry Goddard, who was an advocate of eugenics, and Lewis Termin, who revised the Binet intelligence test into the Stanford-Binet test. Hall's work and recommendations in this area are at odds with those today who strive for a postformal understanding of cognition that allows for intelligences and knowledges that are not honored by such tests or that differ from knowledges legitimized by middle class, white culture.

Developmental Psychology and the Child Study Movement

Hall's developmentalist approach came out of the belief that the study of child development was the most *scientific* approach to determining instruction, and was directly influenced by his study of psychology. This perception of pedagogical theory emerging from "scientific" research appealed to the increasingly science-obsessed world of academia. When he became president of Clark University Hall he founded a pedagogical "seminary" for the scientific study of education, out of which came the journal *Pedagogical Seminary* that later became the *Journal of Genetic Psychology*. Even earlier in his career Hall encouraged his colleagues and students to collect "scientific" data about children, their innate knowledge, and their physical and psychological development. He felt it was of the utmost importance and the highest achievement of a scientific understanding of education to get to the point where the school system would be aligned with the child's "nature and needs" rather than trying to force the child into aligning with the needs of the school system. He advocated the use of questionnaires to find out everything from what children entered school knowing to their habits and their fears. By 1915 Hall and his colleagues had developed 194 questionnaires by his own count.

Many of the questions that Hall had about the knowledge of children in industrial cities stemmed from his own childhood which he describes in his 1927 autobiography, *Life and Confessions of a Psychologist*, as bucolic. He considered it his good fortune to be born on a farm removed from even the closest village by more than a mile and exposed to the influences of the natural world throughout his childhood. In his 1883 work, *The Contents of Children's Minds*, Hall showed that the children of Boston had no idea of the natural world due to their urban experience and he proposed that classroom teachers made too many assumptions about what the children arrived understanding. In response to the popularity of Hall's work—a popularity which he attributed in part to the increase in urbanization and the problems that were arising for children, families, and schools in that setting—the National Education Association founded a Department of Child Study in 1894.

Sexist Psychology, Hall and Women

Though in his written work Hall mentions with respect many woman colleagues and students, he held some of the typical beliefs of the nineteenth century regarding women. Hall, like many men of his era, believed that too much study interfered with a woman's reproductive system. He was also concerned about the potentially detrimental psychological effect of the overwhelming presence of women in schools both as teachers and students during a male's adolescent years and advocated separation of the sexes for the upper grades. He wrote of psychology identifying pathological traits in adolescent girls, such as a penchant for deceit, and declares the stereotypical belief that women are more full of intuition and intense emotion than men, in his 1904 work *Adolescence: Its Psychology and Its Relation to Physiology, Anthropology, Sociology, Sex, Crime, Religion and Education.* In the same work, Hall also recommended that courses in maternity and domesticity be given to most adolescent girls and suggests that too much interest in books bodes ill for a girl's development. However, he did allow that—for a few, exceptional girls—an education more like that given to boys could be considered.

Hall and the Committee of Ten

Hall vehemently criticized the 1893 report from the Committee of Ten which suggested that all students—whether likely to attend university or not—should be exposed to a high quality liberal academic education. Though two of the major figures on the Committee—Harvard President, Charles Eliot and then U.S. Commissioner of Education, W. T. Harris—were considered liberal and reformers in the field of education at one time due to their advocacy of "modern" subjects (such as the modern languages Italian and German), the Committee's findings were viewed by Hall as elitist and old fashioned. Hall was so offended by the recommendations of the Committee that he was still harshly criticizing them in his 1923 autobiography. Hall deeply believed that all students were not created equal in capability and that those who were not intended for college should not be exposed to learning that was overly academic. He advocated instead a differentiated curriculum that allowed each student to fully realize his or her ability to contribute to society based on his or her innate, hereditarily determined abilities and interests. Hall felt that there was a real danger of a sort of psychic burnout for those who had been made to go through higher academic institutions in spite of their true natures. He felt it was cruel to teach those whom he considered lacking in intellectual strength and went so far as to suggest that some students would be better off not going to school at all.

LEGACY OF HALL

Considering the influence of Hall's child study work and the fact that at one point over half of the Doctoral degrees given in psychology in the United States were given to those who had studied with Hall, it would be impossible to ignore the impact of his theories on the field of educational psychology. As stated above—major contributors to the fields of educational and general psychology such as Goddard, Terman, Gesell, and Dewey all studied with Hall. Certainly, the study of children within their day-to-day environment was pioneered by Hall, and, though losing favor to laboratory studies in the psycho-educational practice of the mid-twentieth century, it has now returned as a favored methodology. Those involved in educational psychology today are also taking a page from Hall's book when it comes to respecting teachers enough to allow them to add their observations and opinions to the conversation.

On the negative side, the either/or division that followed the report of the Committee of Ten is another legacy of Hall that plagues us today. Educators who have trained in a child-development-focused teacher education program may see nothing wrong with tailoring the school curriculum to the child or accepting the sentiment behind Hall's exhortation that a teacher should learn more from his or her students then he or she teaches them. But, under the current call for Standards and academic rigor there are those who would argue that this approach will ultimately damage certain children by denying them exposure to content knowledge valued by wider society. In her *Left Back: A Century of Battles of School Reform* (2000), Diane Ravitch attributes the diminishment of the status of the academic curriculum in large part to Hall's child study movement and suggests that tendencies to romanticize and mysticize childhood and learning stem from Hall's views. For those educators on both sides of the "child-centered" fence as well as those who are committed to finding a balance between academic rigor and the needs of the child, there is a shared concern of the legacy of Hall's plan for a differentiated curriculum—particularly how it has been applied on the basis of race or ethnicity, class or gender. The "scientific" tests so widely depended on by the psycho-educational community for so many years to determine the correct placement of the child in school are considered by many to be inherently biased. Unfortunately, in spite of criticisms in recent years which point out the disproportionate amount of children of color in special education classes or vocational schools, tracking according to perceived ability is still the norm and much of the criteria used by those involved in the study of children in education is still reliant on unexamined, tacit understandings of normal behavior, cognition, and psychological development.

CONCLUSION

We who are living and teaching in the early twenty-first century are facing many of the same issues that Hall and his colleagues faced a century ago. Once again we are faced with a changing economic base, causing a renewed discussion of the best way schools can contribute to student job readiness. Once again the increased volume of immigration is spawning discussions around citizenship education and the teaching of English and flooding schools with children who come with different knowledges and understandings. The field of educational psychology is perfectly placed to examine the new needs and developments that will arise under these conditions, but we must be vigilant against bias and uncritical assumptions. We must remember that Hall's ideas which today are viewed as misguided were taken by many as sound scientific approaches in Hall's time. Today, the science of genetics has replaced the "science" of eugenics, but questions of hereditary capabilities are reemerging in the psycho-educational discussion of performance gaps between students of different backgrounds. The fact that Hall's educational and psychological philosophies are so obviously influenced by his own background and the social and scientific beliefs of his time serves as a good reminder of the need to examine the epistemological and ontological underpinnings of any psycho-educational approach we adhere to, including ones of our own development.

REFERENCES

Hall, G. S. (1883). *The contents of children's minds*. In *Princeton review, May 1883, Vol. 11*. pp. 249–272.
Hall, G. S. (1994). Adolescence: *Its psychology, and its relations to physiology, anthropology, sociology, sex, crime, religion and education*. NY: D. Appleton and Co.
Hall, G. S. (1917). *Jesus, the Christ, in the light of psychology*. NY: D. Doubleday, Page.
Hall, G. S. (1927). *Life and confessions of a psychologist*. NY: D. Appleton and Co.
Kincheloe, J. (2001). Getting *beyond the facts: Teaching social studies/socialsciences in the twenty-first century*. NY: Peter Lang
Ravitch, D. (2000). *Left back: A century of battles over school reform*. NY: Touchstone-Simon and Schuster.

CHAPTER 13

Sandra Harding

FRANCES HELYAR

As should be obvious by examining the biographies of its leading theorists and practitioners for over a hundred years, the discourse of educational psychology is white, male, and European. This does not mean that in all that time, no one outside of the dominant discourse has had anything to say, but only that those voices have not been heard. Instead, ed psych has developed into one of the most monocultural and positivistic of all the sciences. The study of human beings in school has been reduced to a narrow range of questions within a closely guarded discipline. Differences have become deficiencies. Knowledges arising from indigenous cultures, women, working classes, homosexuals, nonwhites, and the Southern Hemisphere, among others, have not been permitted to impact research agendas. The research questions that are pursued tend to value particular ways of knowing while other epistemologies are marginalized and labeled as folk wisdom. The implications for marginalized groups is that their members become, by definition, "abnormal" and are then shut out of opportunities and privileges accorded to those who fit the definition of "normal." Knowledges that are valued are called "the truth"; those determined to be lacking value are "false." It does not have to be this way, however. Since World War II and more frequently since the 1970s, theorists have begun to identify the constructed nature of what is considered objective and rational in science, and the constructed nature of science itself. They are redefining "good" research methods and coming up with a new paradigm that allows previously silenced voices to be heard. They acknowledge the importance of complexity in arriving at an epistemology of ed psych that is useful and applicable to a broader range of populations than was previously possible under the old paradigm.

Sandra Harding is at the forefront of this redefinition of science. Harding is a professor of Social Sciences and Comparative Education at UCLA, and the director of the UCLA Center for the Study of Women. She received her PhD in philosophy from New York University, and specializes in feminist and postcolonial theory, epistemology, research methodology, and philosophy of science. Her work, in particular the book *Is Science Multicultural? Postcolonialisms, Feminisms and Epistemologies* (1998) offers a valuable example of a way to dismantle the assumptions and conventions of positivist science, a process that can be applied, by extension, to educational psychology. She examines the alterations in scientific method brought about by social change since the 1970s and the resulting redefinition of objectivity and rationality. The implications for scientific study are great, and Harding argues that since World War II, a kind of new scientific revolution has occurred. Because educational psychology is so entrenched as a discipline, the impact of the revolution has been slow to materialize, but the chapters in this volume clearly aim to speed the process.

Harding, with her particular focus on feminism and postcolonial theory, uses a number of tools to accomplish her reconceptualization of science. These include historiography, an examination of the gaps between dominant and marginalized epistemologies, an interrogation of the power structures inherent within a discipline, identification of the assumptions behind given episte-mologies, and identification of the structures and organizations of the original conceptualization. Harding's intention is to create a strategic map of the terrain of science and technology, but not *the* map, in order to encourage dialogue where formerly there was no room for discussion. This is the caveat Harding places on her work: "I do not claim truth for the narratives and claims that follow, but rather that they can prove useful in opening up conceptual spaces for reflections, encounters and dialogues for which many seem to yearn" (Harding, 1998, p. 1). This assertion alone places her outside of the realm of the positivists, providing an antidote to the "one truth" notion of science that tends to shut down rather than encourage discussion. The dialogue is what is important. If, as Harding writes, "Some knowledge claims are more powerful than others" (p. x), then the goal is to shift the balance to bring the marginalized knowledge claims closer to the center, not necessarily to usurp, but at the very least, to share the power.

It must be acknowledged that discussions about issues of race, class, gender, or postcolonialism cannot treat each as a discrete entity; class always impacts race, postcolonialism has a gendered aspect, and so on. This complexity is a hallmark of any epistemology, although the positivistic sciences would have it otherwise.

STANDPOINT THEORY AND BORDERLANDS EPISTEMOLOGY

A central feature of Harding's reconceptualization of science is her adaptation of standpoint theory, which she defines as "an objective position in social relations as articulated through one or another theory or discourse" (Harding, 1998, p. 150). She is careful to explain that she is not talk-ing about biases, and standpoint is not the same as viewpoint or perspective, because with these, the paradigms of science remain unchanged and the lens of difference is merely superimposed. Identifying the presence of women in the research laboratory, an emancipatory event does not represent a change if the research the women do follows the old paradigm. Rather, standpoint the-ory uses assumptions associated with particular ways of thinking as the point of origin for inquiry. Both science and political struggle are involved, because it is necessary to examine the structures of social life. Educational psychology assumes a Western structure. Its practices, definition of problems to be solved, identification of normal, abnormal, and acceptable tools and solutions, all fall within a strict paradigm. The question in moving beyond that paradigm, then, becomes not, for example, "What effect does adding a postcolonial feminist perspective have on ed psych?" but "What does ed psych look like if it begins within a postcolonial feminist epistemology?" An additional question is, "How has the dominance of the monocultural, positivistic standpoint impacted ed psych?" Research projects that have as their starting points issues in the lives of marginalized groups look very different from those springing from the standpoint of a dominant group, and definitions of knowledge and ignorance are similarly diverse. Standpoint theory is meant "to help move people toward liberatory standpoints, whether one is in a marginalized or dominant social location. It is an achievement, not a 'natural property,' of women to develop a feminist standpoint, or a standpoint of women, no less than it is for a man to do so" (Harding, 1998, p. 161).

The achievement of a standpoint, by Harding's definition, involves moving away from the center of traditional thought to the borderlands. Kincheloe (2001) describes the way Piagetian accommodation (the restructuring of one's cognitive maps to deal with an unanticipated event), when combined with the Frankfurt School's negation involving criticism and reorganizing of knowledge, creates a new epistemology. He uses the example of teachers who reach new definitions of intelligence by observing the sophisticated thinking displayed in other contexts by children who score low on intelligence tests. "Picking up on these concerns, teachers would critically accommodate nontraditional expressions of intelligence that would free them from the privileged, racially and class-biased definitions used to exclude cognitive styles that transcended the official codes" (Kincheloe, 2001, pp. 246–247). This represents a move toward the borderlands to which Harding refers.

HISTORIOGRAPHY

The origins of educational psychology as a discipline separate from the main branch of psychology can be traced back to the mid to late nineteenth century. Its development and fragmentation from the Herbartian model, through pragmatism, behaviorism, cognitivism, and a host of other "isms" reflects the dynamic nature of the study of teaching and learning. The dominance of a theory at any given time, however, can be directly traced to the societal preoccupations of that time, illustrating the constructed nature of the field. The Herbartians gained a foothold at a time in the nineteenth century when scientific study and the notion of objective, rational thinking was gaining ascendancy. Thorndike's ideas about intelligence and the possibility of its measurement nicely dovetailed with an increasingly industrialized society in which the early classification of workers would create smooth-running factories. Intelligence testing also eased the process of military recruitment during World War I, creating identifiable officer and militia corps. Behaviorism dominated ed psych for many years, and its impact is still felt in the twenty-first century in the continued reliance on testing and measurement to determine students' aptitude and achievement. The recessive branches of ed psych including pragmatism, constructivism, and humanism, while gaining some cachet during the twentieth century, suffered from being labeled unscientific, or subjective.

In her historiography, Harding cites cases where scientific research was clearly not intended to benefit the general population, but was instead a means of rewarding an elite. This is exemplified in ed psych where the purpose of study is to identify deficiencies instead of differences, creating normal and abnormal groups. Benefits then accrue to the normal, while the abnormal are problematized. For example, not everyone benefits from the notion of measurable IQ. Generally, those who benefit are those who are deemed by the test to be intelligent, and they don't need to think about the consequences of being judged deficient. The debate as to why this question and not that one is contained in the test, and questions as to how achievement and learning are defined, are not part of the discussion. Feminist and postcolonial discourse thus point to holes in this dominant strain of ed psych. Harding asks if social progress for humanity is social progress for women, or even for all men (Harding 1998). If the purpose of testing is to assign individuals to their "proper place" in society, how progressive is it to relegate them to a place where they cannot earn a living wage or afford decent housing?

GAPS BETWEEN DOMINANT AND MARGINALIZED EPISTEMOLOGIES

Harding refers to postcolonial feminisms, not feminism. The distinction is important, because use of the plural recognizes that gender, class, and race are all intertwined. The issues faced by a middle-class white girl in a North American suburb are different from those encountered by a poor lower-caste girl in an Indian city, and are different from those of a nomadic girl in sub-Saharan Africa. In addition, Harding describes the inherently masculine nature of eurocentric science. Her point is not that science failed to address women's issues, but that objectivity and rationality were inherently identified as positive and masculine, and then idealized as human, whereas women's ways of knowing were pathologized as subjective, irrational, negative, and subhuman. The antidote, according to Harding, is creative postcolonial feminisms that utilize a diverse set of approaches and tools, thus broadening scientific inquiry to include multiple cultures and practices. A postcolonial feminist ed psych also questions the universality of knowledge derived from narrowly structured investigations, preferring to address "the embodied knowledge that develops through daily activities" (Harding, 1998, p. 115).

It is important, Harding says, not to think of postcolonialism as monolithic. It is not one thing, but rather it is a way of opening up discursive space in which to examine the changes, both social and historical, in science and technology. The result is a "strong objectivity" that recognizes the historical and societal origins of knowledge claims, and recognizes that all claims are not equally valid. By examining knowledge claims for their usefulness to all peoples' lives, and not just those who benefit from the knowledge, a "robust reflexivity" offering plausible evidence for claims is possible.

ASSUMPTIONS

The assumptions of traditional educational psychology are closely connected to Cartesian–Newtonian–Baconian epistemology. Educational psychology is a grandchild of the Enlightenment, and the dominant stream of ed psych draws heavily on Cartesian, Newtonian, and Baconian thought. Réné Descartes separated the physical world from the internal world of the mind. Sir Isaac Newton upped the ante by further establishing the predictability of cause and effect, regardless of context. Completing the trio, Sir Francis Bacon identified the supremacy of reason over imagination. The influence of these three philosophers is evident throughout the development of ed psych. A child's physical hunger is presumed to have no impact on cognition. The study of phonetics is presented as the only way a child will learn to read, which is later replaced by whole language as the only way to go. Wait a few years and a new theory will dominate.

STRUCTURES AND ORGANIZATIONS

The structure of educational psychology is inherently Western. The "expert" psychologist identifies a "problem" to be solved, and uses a limited kit of tools to work this magic. The behaviorist and the cognitivist, for example, work within a narrow range of beliefs and assumptions that inform the methods used and the results anticipated. This compartmentalization precludes the recognition of complexity; in fact complexity is seen as an impediment to achieving valid results. These psychologists avoid the use of the classroom as a laboratory; the results are simply too messy, and not quantifiable.

The "cult of the expert" in ed psych is characterized by simple informational flows: once the problem is defined, the data is drawn from the student; the psychologist develops the interpretation, comes up with a possible solution, and this information is then fed back to the teacher and the parents. Clear distinctions are drawn between the researcher and the researched. The results of the research may be published in scholarly journals, shared with administrators and policy makers, or discussed between experts, but rarely are the teachers, the parents, or students themselves invited to respond to or question the findings in which they were so intimately and critically involved. The data assumes a sacred quality that is not to be questioned. Research in this paradigm is not a partnership, it is a one-way street, and the result is not necessarily improvement in the life of those studied, but only in the life of the psychologist whose career is advanced. In contrast, a postcolonial feminist approach develops out of questions identified not by the expert, but by the teacher, the parent, or the student. Thus in keeping with standpoint theory, the origin of the research is in the community, not with the researcher (Smith, 2004). The form that the research takes is negotiated, not imposed.

Harding delineates internalist and externalist scientific epistemologies, and others that represent a move beyond the first two. Internalism is the dominant epistemology, and it assumes that there is only one science, reflecting a nature that is "out there" and reproducible. Proponents of internalist science believe that attempting to achieve such a perfect reproduction, the pursuit of "one truth," is a valuable goal for scientific inquiry. Creators of tests who assume that they can identify an individual's intelligence and that this measurement is fixed for life represent an internalist epistemology. Externalism rejects this position as reductionist, particularly in its adherence to the notion that scientific method is the only method of obtaining knowledge. Social politics is what creates scientific claims, they say, and nature plays no part. Harding identifies reduction in externalism, however, and describes an even broader epistemology that includes science and culture continuously evolving together, with an emphasis on the way that "systematic knowledge-seeking is always just one element in any culture, society or social formation in its local environment, shifting and transforming other elements" (Harding, 1998, p. 4).

Related to this coevolution is Harding's assertion that it is too simplistic to identify European and non-European science as distinct from each other, or that in a colonial context, knowledge flowed only one way. The knowledge of each has informed the other, she says, since the time of first contact, and a postcolonial science should reject the association of rationality with Western thought, and bias and irrationality with the non-Western.

Harding outlines five types of eurocentrism saying, "good intentions and tolerant behaviors are not enough to guarantee that one is in fact supporting anti-eurocentric beliefs and practices" (Harding, 1998, p. 13). The overt eurocentric, for example, rejects outright as illogical a definition of intelligence that includes intuition. The covert eurocentric, in contrast, cites studies about intelligence in dismissing the inclusion of intuition. Harding also describes institutional, societal, and civilizational or philosophical eurocentrism. Institutional eurocentrism results, for instance, when departments of ed psych reject epistemologies outside of the traditional paradigm, and discourage students from investigating those epistemologies. Societal eurocentrism is the consequence when institutional practices become part of social assumptions. Civilizational or philosophical eurocentrism, according to Harding, is the most difficult to identify because "they structure and give meaning to such apparently seamless expanses of history, common sense, and daily life that it is hard for members of such 'civilizations' even to imagine taking a position that is outside them" (Harding, 1998, p. 14). Contrary positions, which may examine issues that are central to the lives of women or non-Europeans, are seen as irrelevant.

Different researchers have different questions about how children learn, but who gets funding and who gets published depends on the prevailing notion of what is interesting and what is important. The post-Sputnik scramble to improve American achievement in math and science as represented by the National Defense Education Act of 1957 is just one example of this tendency. The size of the educational testing industry is another. What are presented as the ways children learn will depend upon whatever theory of ed psych is prevalent at any given time, be it behavioral, cognitive, progressive, humanist, or other. Harding points out that while observations about the way social interests shape scientific questions are not controversial, what is controversial is "to claim that science, real science, includes the choice of scientific problems; to point out that the cognitive content of science is shaped by and has its characteristic patterns of knowledge and ignorance precisely because of problem choices" (Harding, 1998, p. 66). To the skeptic looking for one true science, Harding responds that science is not a jigsaw puzzle for which there is only one correct arrangement of pieces. Data or theories may have multiple explanations that are reasonable, and this is what provides science with its potential for growth. In conventional Cartesian epistemology, however, the possibility of multiple explanations is equated with error and relativism. The idea that truth is not absolute and may depend on context is anathema.

CONCLUSION

If we come, as always, to the dilemma of whether the baby should be thrown out with the bathwater, Harding responds with a no. The epistemology of modern science, she says, should be an important part of a new science.

The question should be not how to preserve as if carved in stone or else to completely reject the European legacy, but rather how to update it so that it, like many other 'local knowledge systems,' can be perceived to provide valuable resources for a world in important respects different from the one for which it was designed. (Harding, 1998, p. 125)

A "new 'objectivity question' " recognizes that whether the observer knows it or not, observations are always accompanied by the baggage of theory. Where in the past the question was "Objectivity or relativism? Which side are you on?" (Harding, 1998, p. 127), a new paradigm examines the epistemology in which that question is posed, and asks which definitions of objectivity among many are preferred. The choice is political because science, like education, is always political. There is no such stance as neutral. A scientific procedure that is identified as "normal" serves to define "the objections of its victims and any criticisms of its institutions, practices, or conceptual world as agitation by special interests that threatens to damage the neutrality of science and its promotion of social progress" (Harding, 1998, p. 133). New objectivity examines the assumptions and interpretive dimensions of research methods, recognizing that science is a socially, not individually constructed activity.

Educational psychology, like all of science, is a work in progress. For its practitioners to assume that it will not change is at best, naïve, and at worst, harmful. But it's not a question of all or nothing, the old paradigm or the new. As Harding makes clear, science does not and has never existed in a vacuum. It cannot help but be impacted by its contact with feminist, postcolonial thought; in fact the history and development of science shows its hybridity. The same is true of ed psych. As the discipline interacts with non-Western, non-Northern epistemologies, the resulting new paradigms represent a change for the better, a change that will benefit those who were previously merely labeled deficient.

REFERENCES

Harding, S. (1998). *Is Science Multicultural? Postcolonialism, Feminism, and Epistemologies.* Bloomington, IN: Indiana University Press.

Harding, S. (1991). *Whose Science? Whose knowledge? Thinking from Women's Lives.* Ithaca, N.Y.: Cornell University Press.

Kincheloe, J. L. (2001). *Getting Beyond the Facts: Teaching Social Studies/Social Sciences in the Twenty-first Century* (2nd ed.). New York: Peter Lang.

Kliebard, H. M. (1995). *The Struggle for the American Curriculum: 1893–1958* (2nd ed.). New York: Routledge.

Smith, L. T. (1999). *Decolonizing Methodologies: Research and Indigenous peoples.* London: Zed Books.

Spring, J. (2005). *The American School: 1642–2004* (6th ed.). New York: McGraw-Hill.

Webb, L. D. (2006). *The History of American Education.* Upper Saddle River, N. J.: Pearson.

CHAPTER 14

bell hooks

DANNY WALSH

My most passionate engagement with bell hooks came to light during a reading of *All About Love: New Visions* (hooks, 2001), a text not usually associated with schooling. In this work, hooks challenges what we are taught about love and how to love in a cultural milieu founded upon patriarchal, sexist, and racist ideologies. I read *All About Love* at a time when I doubted my ability to connect with others on any meaningful level, at a time when I recognized that I used silence and withdrawal as a weapon just as it had been used in the patriarchal, psychologically and physically violent home of my youth. hooks's alternative vision of love—a love rooted in a combination of care, commitment, knowledge, responsibility, respect, and trust—and her critique of a white, supremacist, capitalist patriarchy that creates and sustains lovelessness enabled me to see that although I was cared for in many ways and felt I would not be abandoned, I could neither offer nor receive authentic love. I wondered about my personal experiences with patriarchy and my subsequent inability to give and receive love and how such experiences reflected a society in which disconnection, domination, competition, and individualism ruled the day. Moreover, I questioned how such a history of domination reared its head in my teaching and learning. I associate this text with schooling and education because it is inextricably linked to the notion of cultural pedagogy—a recognition of the learning processes that occur in a myriad of locations, both in and outside of school buildings. Perhaps more important, hooks's alternative vision of love forces educators to confront the role of love in schooling, pedagogy, and our culture at large.

As a cultural critic and radical educator, hooks relentlessly challenges and presents alternative visions of a society grounded in white, supremacist, capitalistic patriarchy. I feel that my way of teaching and being in the world is profoundly connected to bell hooks and her role in the radicalization of my thinking. In essence, she has provided me with much of the intellectual sustenance needed to challenge the racist, classist, sexist, heterosexist, capitalistic, and patriarchal foundations of schools, classrooms, and society. I believe that she has done the same for many people and therefore the implications of her work for the reconceptualization of educational psychology are profound.

hooks often recounts her transition from segregated to integrated schools in the apartheid South to juxtapose two vastly different experiences with education. Born into a poor rural community in Kentucky in 1952, she remembers the segregated schools of her childhood as a place where black teachers taught black students through life in the black community—a practice that necessarily incorporated antiracist and liberation struggle pedagogy. However, with desegregation into white schools, "knowledge was suddenly about information only," teaching was disassociated from "respect and care for the souls of students," and learning was distanced from knowledge of "how to live in the world" (hooks, 1994). This disjunction between lived experiences and schooling and disjunctions among the mind, body, and soul would follow her, with exceptions, to her undergraduate days at Stanford and graduate school at the University of Wisconsin, Madison, and the University of California, Santa Cruz. Many of her transgressive acts—being "bad" in the academy by challenging dominant cultural constructions and conventionally approved ways of thinking and knowing—as both student and teacher emanate from her visions for democracy, equity, and justice. She has been "inspired by those teachers who have had the courage to transgress those boundaries that would confine each pupil to a rote, assembly-line approach to learning" (hooks, 1994). It is this courage that she carries into her own teaching, first as a graduate student, then as an assistant/associate professor at Yale University and Oberlin College, and finally to her resignation from the academy as a distinguished professor at The City College of the City University of New York. With the radical notions that teachers should care for their students' souls and that theoretical knowledge should be inextricably linked to knowledge of how to live in the world, hooks argues for a pedagogy and an educational psychology that is engaged, transformative, liberatory, and culturally responsive.

Reintegrating body, mind, and soul and reconnecting theory to practice in schooling are transgressive, counterhegemonic acts that deeply challenge formalistic thinking. "The erasure of the body encourages us to think that we are listening to neutral, objective facts, facts that are not particular to who is sharing the information" (hooks, 1994). The reverence of neutrality, objectivity, and rationalism upon which Western science rests demands that components be isolated from the systems that they comprise: the mind can therefore be separated from the body; social structures can be removed from schooling; and race, class, gender, language, and sexual orientation have nothing to do with how learners perceive the world. Knowledge is a stable, predictable, "out there" thing waiting to be discovered and teachers facilitate its discovery through information giving. In *The Stigma of Genius: Einstein, Consciousness, and Education*, Joe Kincheloe, Shirley Steinberg, and Deborah Tippins (1999) contend that reductionistic Western science asserts that all aspects of complex phenomena can best be understood through a process that essentially centrifuges constituent parts and then pieces them back together according to causal laws. Just as Newton separated time, space, matter, and motion, formalistic thinking in schooling separates the social, the political, and the economic from the mind, intelligence, and performance in school. Applying scientific, formalistic processes such as these to education results in nothing short of disengagement by teachers and students, reinforcement of the status quo, and subjecting all students to predetermined, ahistoricized, and purified (whitened) knowledge. Has this scientific approach to education—one that reduces knowledge to memorizable factoids, one that distances teachers and students from each other and the curriculum, one that isolates school from society—been maintained in order to prevent schooling from becoming dangerous, from becoming a place where transgressive and counterhegemonic acts are allowed to occur?

Classrooms and schools are always and already inscribed with power: they are politicized and contested spaces that reflect a struggle for culture production, which includes the production of knowledge. In these contested educational spaces, sanctioned ways of being and knowing (those that reflect the dominator) render some students more visible and more easily heard than others. hooks calls for a radical pedagogy grounded in presence through which classrooms become spaces that acknowledge teacher and student positionality, require shared personal experiences that are linked to theory, and demand inclusion. This is a particular type of multiculturalism, one that "compels educators to acknowledge the narrow boundaries that have shaped the way knowledge is shared in the classroom. It forces us all to recognize our complicity in accepting and perpetuating biases of any kind" (hooks, 1994). Through an exploration of the origins of knowledge, whose knowledge is shared, as well as the manner in which knowledge is presented, it becomes more possible and more probable that the voices of those who have historically been excluded and subjugated will emerge. However, "many teachers are disturbed by the political implications of a multicultural education because they fear losing control in a classroom where there is no one way to approach a subject—only multiple ways and multiple references" (hooks, 1994). It is not difficult to detect Western science's imprint on this desire for a certainty and predictability that create less contentious spaces.

A search for certainty necessarily eliminates diverse perspectives related to students' experiences. Often personal talk in the classroom, particularly in higher education, is viewed as distraction from the theoretical tasks at hand. Or, the theoretical is viewed as having no place in students' lived experiences. There is a disconnect. If from many teachers' perspectives, myself included, narrative and autobiography appear to have a powerful impact on academic and emotional growth, that is, they not only contribute to the cognitive complexity of a topic but also increase a sense of belonging and community that is so crucial to many students' success, why has the experiential been resisted so strongly? In the most simplistic term, I believe this returns us to the notion of fear—fear of knowing others and being known by others; fear of the passion that diverse, contradictory perspectives might incite; and fear of changing an entrenched way of teaching. While such fears cannot be completely eliminated (this may not even be desirable), they dissipate somewhat with an engaged pedagogical practice that encourages community building in the classroom as a way to recognize the value of individual voices. "Any radical pedagogy must insist that everyone's presence is acknowledged," yet "that insistence cannot be simply stated. It has to be demonstrated through pedagogical practices" (hooks, 1994). Another component of the fear of knowing and being known is that the sense of belonging that it can potentially create might lead teaching and learning to become pleasurable and loving acts. "Pleasure in the classroom is feared. If there is laughter, a reciprocal exchange may be taking place" (hooks, 1994) and such reciprocity, pleasure, and enjoyment might lead to an atmosphere of love, an avoided and somewhat dangerous topic in education because loving students and being loved by them is suspect.

hooks's engaged pedagogy "is rooted in the assumption that we all bring to the classroom experiential knowledge, that this knowledge can indeed enhance our learning experience" (hooks, 1994). It affirms presence, the right to a voice, and value of difference. "It's as though many people know that the focus on difference has the potential to revolutionize the classroom and they do not want the revolution to take place" (hooks, 1994). Difference entails the acknowledgment of the race, class, gender, sexual orientation, and ideological positions that we occupy because this positionality determines the consciousness that defines our experiences. Consciousness is a cultural, social, and political construct that cannot be separated from power. "The unwillingness to approach teaching from a standpoint that includes awareness of race, sex, and class is often rooted in fear that classrooms will be uncontrollable, that emotion will not be contained" (hooks, 1994). Again, we fear what we cannot control, what we cannot quantify, what requires us to engage in a true dialogue in which we are open to mutual change.

Willingness to engage with others in the difficult work of transforming a culture based upon white supremacy, domination, and patriarchy becomes more possible when we create a community dedicated to dialogue and change. "We need to generate greater cultural awareness of the way white-supremacist thinking operates in our daily lives. We need to hear from the individuals who know, because they have lived anti-racist lives, what everyone can do to decolonize their minds, to maintain awareness, change behavior, and create beloved community" (hooks, 2003). Classroom communities that reflect counterhegemonic content and processes have the potential to link body, mind, and soul as well as theory and practice, and to create a place "that is life-sustaining and mind-expanding, a place of liberating mutuality where teacher and student together work in partnership" (hooks, 2003). Such communities traverse the secure territory of what is to arrive at, what could be, a place of potentiality. Border crossing is possible because these classrooms challenge the status quo and create spaces of hope in which a culture of domination is not the norm.

"Teachers are often among that group most reluctant to acknowledge the extent to which white-supremacist thinking informs every aspect of our culture including the way we learn, the content of what we learn, and the manner in which we are taught" (hooks, 2003). We are entrenched in the hegemonic processes that discourage us from becoming radical educators and engaged pedagogues who see what could be over what is. Through our own experiences with schooling rooted in Western scientism and rationality, we see mind, body, and soul as separate entities and the theoretical disconnected from the practical. Often unbeknownst to us, we collude with the existing system, "even those among us who see ourselves as anti-racist radicals. This collusion happens simply because we are all products of the culture we live within and have all been subjected to the forms of socialization and acculturation that are deemed normal in our society. Through the cultivation of awareness, through the decolonization of our minds, we have the tools to break with the dominator model of human social engagement and the will to imagine new and different ways that people might come together" (hooks, 2003). Acknowledging the different ways of knowing and being in the world that result from the uniqueness of our racial, gendered, social, political, economic, linguistic, and sexual viewpoints allows for the creation of a radical type of community where "when we stop thinking and evaluating along the lines of hierarchy and can value rightly all members of a community we are breaking a culture of domination" (hooks, 2003). As alluded to above, redefining love also allows us to sever our ties with a dominator culture. hooks writes, "To be guided by love is to live in community with all life. However, a culture of domination, like ours, does not strive to teach us how to live in community" (hooks, 2003). Divisiveness and disconnection—students from each other, teachers from students, students and teachers from the curriculum and knowledge production, and *even from themselves*—better serve a capitalist patriarchy founded upon white supremacy, because such a disconnect removes contestation from schools and classrooms; teachers are simply presenting predetermined knowledge to be consumed unquestioningly, thereby rendering classrooms safe, secure, and whitewashed spaces.

Indeed our culture teaches us that disconnections such as those listed above are necessary for academic excellence. "Many of our students come to our classrooms believing that real brilliance is revealed by the will to disconnect and disassociate. They see this state as crucial to the maintenance of objectivism. They fear wholeness will lead them to be considered less 'brilliant.' ... The assumption seems to be that if the heart is closed, the mind will open even wider. In actuality, it is the failure to achieve harmony of mind, body and spirit that has furthered anti-intellectualism in our culture and made of our schools mere factories" (hooks, 2003). The factory metaphor conjures up images of repetitive, lifeless mass production in which workers are sorted, lined up, and do not deviate from their prescribed roles so that profit is maximized and resistant behavior minimized. Moreover, workers are separated from conceptual development and creativity as they perform isolated tasks devoid of the contextualization reserved for the managerial class. Once again we can decipher Western scientism's influence. The factory model as applied in both business and school sanctions the optimal amount of control and predictability so that the contestation and subsequent negotiation inherent in any community might be eliminated. Ultimately attempts at such control result in antidemocratic practices because true democracy requires recognition of power differentials that exist in a society enculturated with hierarchy and domination.

Despite such deep-rooted structures, many students and teachers defy the culture of domination through transgressive, hopeful acts that promote counterhegemonic ways of being and knowing that willingly surrender to complexity and diversity of a beloved community. hooks states, "To me the classroom continues to be a place where paradise can be realized, a place where all that we learn and know leads us into greater connection, into greater understanding of life lived in community" (hooks, 2003). Her prophetic imagination reminds us "that what we cannot imagine we cannot bring into being" and that "what must be takes priority over what is" (hooks, 2003). This imagination has the potential to reconnect what has long been severed and to force us to confront what we fear. "Dominator culture has tried to keep us all afraid, to make us choose safety instead of risk, sameness instead of diversity. Moving through that fear, finding out what connects us, reveling in our difference; this is the process that brings us closer, that gives us a world of shared values, of meaningful community" (hooks, 2003).

As Joe Kincheloe writes in the introduction to this text, "Cognitive activity, knowledge production, and the construction of reality are simply too complex to be accomplished by following prescribed formulae. The reductionistic, obvious, and safe answers produced by formalist ways of thinking and researching are unacceptable to postformalists." In this light, hooks's scholarly contributions to postformalist educational psychology are clear and profound. Her call for engaged and transformative pedagogy, new conceptions of love, and the creation of beloved, hopeful community demand connections between the knower and known and compel ways of knowing to change our ways of being in the world. Prescribed, formulaic approaches to teaching, learning, and knowledge have created chasms among all aspects of education and schooling and seek to disguise the impact of power on what has been sold as objectivity. Above all, I contend that it is hooks's delving into the critical ontological realm that has contributed to postformalism. Again, from the introduction to this text, "In a postformalist critical ontology we are concerned with understanding the sociopolitical construction of the self in order to conceptualize and enact new ways of being human." For hooks, new ways of being human are inextricably linked to transgressive, counterhegemonic, countercultural acts that offset white supremacy and patriarchy. Construction of the self occurs in a complex dance with others. "Living on the borderline between self and external system and self and other, learning never takes place outside of these relationships." hooks dares to imagine a psychological world in which relationships are crucial and in which challenge to the external system is critical for change. Without an excavation of the processes of knowledge production, knowledge loses its eroticism and passion, becoming sterile and fixed. Developing beloved community reintroduces the connectedness necessary for education psychology to become both life affirming and sustaining.

REFERENCES

hooks, b. (1994). *Teaching to Transgress: Education as the Practice of Freedom*. New York: Routledge.
———. (2001). *All About Love: New Visions*. New York: Harper Paperbacks.
———. (2003). *Teaching Community: A Pedagogy of Hope*. New York: Routledge.
Kincheloe, J., Steinberg, S., and Tippins, D. (1999). *The Stigma of Genius: Einstein, Consciousness, and Education*. New York: Peter Lang.

CHAPTER 15

William James

FRANCES HELYAR

William James's career may best be conceptualized as a bridge. His many biographers point out the way his work serves to link the nineteenth and the twentieth centuries, Europe and the United States, Darwin and Freud, the ancient realm of philosophy and the new world of psychology, and professional and popular audiences. There are a number of ways to gauge the importance of his work, including the "firsts" he accomplished, the dominance in the field of educational psychology of several of his students, and the influence he still exerts on his theoretical descendents. He lived in the company of the well-known and the yet-to-be famous thinkers of his lifetime: the novelist Henry James was one of his brothers; their father counted among his acquaintances Thomas Carlyle, Ralph Waldo Emerson, and Henry David Thoreau; among James's friends were Charles Peirce and Oliver Wendell Holmes; his sometime dinner companions included Carl Jung, Sigmund Freud, and John Dewey; and among his students were G. Stanley Hall, Edward Thorndike, and W.E.B. Dubois. William James's major works are still in print over a hundred years after their first publication and while in some ways his work represents a narrow view of the world, reflecting his privileged upbringing and professorial career, his writings are examined and interpreted to this day. It is a mark of the complexity of his contribution to educational psychology that direct lines may be drawn at the same time from James to the behaviorism of Thorndike, and the phenomenology of Husserl (Feinstein, 1984; Edie, 1987; Cotkin, 1990). In this way, James stands both in opposition to and as a precursor of postformalism.

THE LIFE

William James was born in 1842 to a wealthy New York family with recent roots in Ireland. James's father had strong views on education and mysticism (James's biographer Howard Feinstein calls the elder James a "renegade theologian" [p. 15]). The main result seems to have been that between 1855 and 1858, and again in 1859–1860, Henry Sr. removed the entire family of five children to Europe in order to give them an education in the senses. This trans-Atlantic journey was one William would take repeatedly during his lifetime. Family biographer F. O. Mathiessen says William resented his self-perceived "lack of exact discipline" (p. 73), a consequence of attending so many different schools as a child. James's first career choice was artist, with Eugene Delacroix his favorite painter. He suffered from depression for most of his life, and by the age of nineteen he had abandoned his artistic ambitions to enroll in the Lawrence Scientific School at Harvard. While Charles William Eliot was his chemistry teacher and mentor, the scientist Louis Agassiz made an even greater impression on the young man. After James enrolled in Harvard Medical School, he accompanied Agassiz on a research voyage to Brazil, and it was this experience that led to his decision to abandon natural science for the study of philosophy. James graduated with an MD in 1869; it was the only degree he ever earned (Matthiessen, 1961).

At the invitation of Eliot, by then the president of Harvard, James began a long career at that institution by becoming an instructor in anatomy and physiology in 1872. James's biographer Gerald Myers (1986) says the combination of those two streams of science served the young professor well in preparation for his future work, since in those early days, the field was known as "physiological psychology" (p. 5). Meanwhile, biographer Paul Woodring describes James's 1876 offering of a course by that name, the first of its kind in the United States and one of the first in the world (p. 10). In 1878, James was contracted to write his *Principles of Psychology*. The work was delivered in installments to the publishers, and finally published in 1890. It became a seminal text, with the full edition known to generations of students as "The James" and the shorter version as "The Jimmy." James gave a series of talks to a group of teachers in Cambridge, Massachusetts, in 1892, and the text of those lectures was published as *Talks to Teachers* (1899/1958), arguably the first educational psychology textbook. During his lifetime, James was elected president of both the American Philosophical Association and the American Psychological Association, and in addition to his professional presentations, he gave numerous public lectures. Toward the end of his life, he became increasingly interested in mysticism and spiritualism. William James married Alice Howe Gibbens in 1878, and biographer Daniel Bjork says the influence of Alice on James's career is underrated, while that of Henry James Sr. is overstated (1988, p. xv). Together, the couple had five children. William James resigned from Harvard in 1907 and died in 1910. The headline of his August 27th *New York Times* (1910) obituary reads "Virtual Founder of Modern American Psychology, and Exponent of Pragmatism and Dabbled in Spooks," the latter referring to James's enthusiasm for séances.

William James gained a wide audience during his lifetime, partly due to the fact that he spent his career at Harvard, and partly due to the illustrious company he kept. His broad reception may also be attributed in part to his travels, whether to Europe or across America (he experienced the San Francisco earthquake of 1906), as well as his fluency in many languages resulting from his youthful education. While his popular reputation today may be overshadowed by the greater fame of his brother Henry, and it is true that literary critics often identify Henry's presence in William's writing, psychologists just as often see the influence of William's thought in Henry's novels. The full texts of James's major works are available on the Internet, as are countless quotations and references to his ideas.

CONTRIBUTIONS TO EDUCATIONAL PSYCHOLOGY

William James's contributions to the field of educational psychology are numerous. Biographer Daniel Bjork calls James a critical link in a large sense between Darwin and Freud, bringing the ideas of the former into philosophy and psychology and anticipating the latter's depth psychology (1983, p. 2). In fact, it was William James who first introduced the writings of Freud to North America. At the same time, Bjork says, James also bridged the nineteenth-century transcendentalism of Emerson with the twentieth-century instrumentalism of Dewey (1983, p. 2). William James's publications alone are notable because they were central in creating a field of inquiry distinct within psychology. In particular, *Principles of Psychology* (1890) and *Talks to Teachers* (1899/1958) were pioneering works. Other writings that delineate James's thinking are *The Will to Believe* (1896/1967) and the later work *Pragmatism* (1907), and the posthumous *Essays in Radical Empiricism* (1912). In all, the combined legacy of James's writing is complex.

Principles of Psychology (1890) is a two-volume work that helped to establish psychology as a discipline apart from philosophy. In addition, it served to refute faculty psychology, which had been the dominant learning theory for much of the century and which divided the mind into discrete parts such as intelligence, creativity, and morality. At the same time, James is scathing in his reference to the brand of education advocated by Rousseau, whom he accuses of "inflaming all the mothers of France, by his eloquence, to follow Nature and nurse their babies themselves, while he sends his own children to the foundling hospital" (p. 125). Early in the first volume of *Principles*, James defines psychology, calling it "the Science of Mental Life, both of its phenomena and of their conditions. The phenomena are such things as we call feelings, desires, cognitions, reasonings, decisions, and the like" (p. 1). The two volumes also lay the groundwork on which James's student Edward Thorndike would later build behaviorism. This lineage is particularly clear in the passages in which James describes the function of habit, the origins of which he illustrates with the example of a young child who burns his hand with a candle and thus learns to avoid putting his hand in a flame. James calls habit "the enormous fly-wheel of society, its most precious conservative agent" (p. 121), and the foundation upon which society is set. James uses a series of class-based illustrations to promote the notion that everyone has a place in the social order, but those places are not the same, saying that habit "saves the children of fortune from the envious uprisings of the poor" (p. 121). He also describes a supposedly liberating aspect of habit saying, "The more of the details of our daily life we can hand over to the effortless custody of automatism, the more our higher powers of mind will be set free for their own proper work" (p. 122). In addition to presenting an essentially behaviorist theory of learning, James rejects the compartmentalization of the mind, describing the way an actor memorizes a part "by better *thinking*."

Similarly when schoolboys improve by practice in ease of learning by heart, the improvement will, I am sure, be always found to reside in the *mode of study of the particular piece* (due to the greater interest, the greater suggestiveness, the generic similarity with other pieces, the more sustained attention, etc., etc.), and not at all to any enhancement of the brute retentive power. [James's emphasis] (pp. 664–665)

In this passage, James also anticipates Dewey and progressivism, as he does when he urges teachers to capture children's attention: "Induct him therefore in such a way as to knit each new thing on to some acquisition already there; and if possible awaken curiosity, so that the new thing shall seem to come as an answer, or part of an answer, to a question pre-existing in his mind" (p. 424).

With *Talks to Teachers on Psychology: And to Students on Some of Life's Ideals* (1899/1958), James created the first psychology text addressed directly to teachers. In part, the book continues the emphasis on the role of habit in learning, defining education as "the organization of acquired habits of conduct and tendencies to behavior" [James's emphasis] (p. 37). Thus James reinforces the conceptualization of education as a means of social control. He stresses that an understanding of psychology is important to the classroom teacher in all grades, and his definition of education has clear deterministic qualities, for example, when he calls character "an organized set of habits of reaction" (p. 125). As with *Principles*, the book also presages some of the tenets of the progressive education movement, particularly in its emphasis on real-world applications. James warns that just because teachers are familiar with psychology, they are not necessarily good teachers, saying famously,

you make a great, a very great mistake, if you think that psychology, being the science of the mind's laws, is something from which you can deduce definite programmes and schemes and methods of instruction for immediate schoolroom use. Psychology is a science, and teaching is an art; and sciences never generate arts directly out of themselves. (pp. 23–24)

James recognizes the importance of the teachable moment, and recommends that the talented instructor, rather than simply lecturing, will seize the occasion and induce children "to think, to feel, and to do. The strokes of *behavior* are what give the new set to the character, and work the good habits into its organic tissue" (pp. 60–61).

   The Will to Believe (1896/1967) was a response to *The Ethics of Belief* by William Clifford. Here, James marks the beginning of a shift in his writing to the concerns that, because of his embrace of spiritualism, the *New York Times* at his death labels dabbling "in spooks." In this essay he introduces his topic as a justification of religious faith "in spite of the fact that our merely logical intellect may not have been coerced" (p. 717). The two great laws, according to James, are that we know truth and shun error. Greater emphasis should be on the former, he says, because the potential positive consequences of belief are greater than the potential negative consequences of error (pp. 726–727). In the same year *The Will to Believe* was published, according to Emory University's Web site chronology of his life, James gave a lecture in California titled "Philosophical Conceptions and Practical Results," and in it, he outlined for the first time the theory with which he would have his greatest association during his lifetime, pragmatism. Perhaps his most enduring legacy, however, is his later work, particularly in radical empiricism.

PRAGMATISM AND RADICAL EMPIRICISM

   Like his friend John Dewey, James believed in education that was rooted in the lived world. He adapted the ideas of another friend, Charles Peirce, and what he called pragmatism, in which theory and practice are intimately connected and combined with an ethical and moral sensibility. Simply put, as Joel Spring (2005) outlines in *The American School*, pragmatism in its conception rejects the divine origin of ideas, values, and social institutions, locating their origin instead in the situations of everyday life (p. 273). There is no final truth, because the truth of an idea is found in its consequences. In 1906 and 1907, James lectured at the Lowell Institute in Boston, and the transcript of those talks was published as *Pragmatism: A New Name for Some Old Ways of Thinking* (1907). The preface contains the warning that there is no connection between pragmatism and radical empiricism, saying that one may reject the latter and still be called a pragmatist (p. viii). In this work, James defines *pragmatism* as a method by which one determines whether it would make any practical difference if a notion were true; if the answer is no, then "all dispute is idle" (p. 18). He somewhat defensively explains that, in contrast to the social Darwinism of Herbert Spencer, his definition of pragmatism is not at odds with religion. He addresses truth by saying that it is not an inert, static relation; instead, he says, *"True ideas are those that we can assimilate, validate, corroborate and verify. False ideas are those that we cannot"* [James's emphasis] (p. 77).

   In a 1904 essay published in the *Journal of Philosophy, Psychology, and Scientific Methods* titled "A World of Pure Experience," James distinguishes between rationalism, which he says begins with the universal and then moves to the parts of the whole, and empiricism, which he says starts in an explanation of the parts. He continues,

To be radical, an empiricism must neither admit into its constructions any element that is not directly experienced, nor exclude from them any element that is directly experienced. For such a philosophy, *the relations that connect experiences must themselves be experienced relations, and any kind of relation experienced must be accounted as "real" as any thing else in the system.* [James's emphasis] (p. 533)

James's major explanation of his theory was published in *Essays in Radical Empiricism* (1912). In the editor's preface of this posthumous collection, Ralph Barton Perry says James valued radical empiricism more than pragmatism (pp. xvi–xvii). Perry adds that the term itself first appeared in print in *The Will to Believe* (1896/1967), and James defined it as a philosophic attitude (p. xix). James goes even further in *The Meaning of Truth* (1911), specifying that "Radical empiricism consists (1) first of a postulate, (2) next of a statement of fact, (3) and finally of a generalized conclusion" (p. xvi). Radical empiricism may also be defined as pure experience, or the inseparability of the knower and the known. He ends *Essays in Radical Empiricism* saying, "all philosophies are hypotheses, to which all our faculties, emotional as well as logical, help us . . ." (p. 279).

JAMES THE POSTFORMALIST

William James foreshadows twenty-first-century postformalism in three ways: in his conceptualization of truth, in his acknowledgement of complexity, and in his phenomenological, or as it may more properly be called, his proto-phenomenological writing, which in interpretations by theorists such as Husserl has been reduced to a positivist version bearing only partial similarity to the original. James alludes to the uneasy reception given to pragmatism when he writes in *The Meaning of Truth* (1911) about "warfare" (p. xv) between the pragmatists and the nonpragmatists. But he is firm in his notion that truth is ever-changing, saying,

"Truth" is thus in process of formation like all other things. It consists not in conformity or correspondence with an externally fixed archetype or model. Such a thing would be irrelevant even if we knew it to exist. (p. xv)

He is even less prosaic in *The Will to Believe* (1896/1967) when he writes, "Objective evidence and certitude are doubtless very fine ideals to play with, but where on this moonlit and dream-visited planet are they found?" (p. 725). James recognizes human beings for their complexity, writing in *Talks to Teachers* (1899/1958), "Man is too complex a being for light to be thrown on his real efficiency by measuring any one mental faculty taken apart from its consensus in the working whole" (p. 96). He continues by arguing that any attempt to quantify human understanding is reductive and suspect, saying, "There are as many types of apperception as there are possible ways in which an incoming experience may be reacted on by an individual mind" (p. 112). James is describing a truly human science. His intellectual descendent, Husserl, in contrast, takes the notion of lived world and attempts to make of it a phenomenology that is positivistic in its conceptualization. Philosopher G.B. Madison, in *The Hermeneutics of Postmodernity* (1988), describes Husserl's obsession with the idea of a unified science, and his construction of science as a hierarchy with phenomenology at the top (p. 43). Ironically, James's conceptualization is closer to the postformal model than is Husserl's, although James does not invoke issues of power and social justice. As Madison puts it in reference to James, "Pioneers, like Moses, do not always make it to the Promised Land" (p. 192, n27).

CONCLUSION

William James was a man both of his time and ahead of his time. He had the good fortune to be born into wealth and the equal good fortune during his life to come into contact with many of the major thinkers of his day. James was an insider, and at the same time the progression of his thinking toward the spiritual led him to the role of an outsider during his lifetime. His ideas have, since his death, been adapted, altered, and interpreted to support major positivists and postformalists alike. It is a mark of his importance that his intellectual and theoretical legacies are so complex and influential.

REFERENCES

Biography, Chronology and Photographs of William James. William James Web site. F. Pajares (Ed.). Emory University. Retrieved April 3, 2005, from http://www.emory.edu/EDUCATION/mfp/jphotos.html.

Bjork, D. W. (1983). *The Compromised Scientist: William James in the Development of American Psychology*. New York: Columbia University Press.

———. (1988). *William James: The Center of His Vision*. New York: Columbia University Press.

Cotkin, G. (1990). *William James, Public Philosopher*. Baltimore, MD: Johns Hopkins University Press.

Edie, J. M. (1987). *William James and Phenomenology*. Bloomington, IN: Indiana University Press.

Feinstein, H. M. (1984). *Becoming William James*. Ithaca, NY: Cornell University Press.

James, W. (1890). *Principles of Psychology* (2 vols). Retrieved April 3, 2005, from http://psychclassics.yorku.ca/James/Principles/index.htm.

———. (1896/1967). The Will to Believe. In J. McDermott (Ed.), *The Writings of William James: A Comprehensive Edition*. New York: Random House.

———. (1899/1958). *Talks to Teachers on Psychology: And to Students on Some of Life's Ideals*. Introduction by Paul Woodring. New York: W.W. Norton and Company Inc.

———. (1904). A World of Pure Experience. *Journal of Philosophy, Psychology, and Scientific Methods. 1*, 533–543, 561–570. Retrieved April 2, 2005, from http://psychclassics.yorku.ca/James/experience.htm.

———. (1907). *Pragmatism: A New Name for Some Old Ways of Thinking*. New York: Longmans, Green and Co. Retrieved April 3, 2005, from http://spartan.ac.brocku.ca/~lward/James/James_1907/James_1907_toc.html.

———. (1911). *The Meaning of Truth*. New York: Longmans, Green and Co. Retrieved April 2, 2005, from http://spartan.ac.brocku.ca/~lward/James/James_1911/James_1911_toc.html.

———. (1912). *Essays in Radical Empiricism*. New York: Longmans, Green and Co. Retrieved April 3, 2005, from http://spartan.ac.brocku.ca/~lward/James/James_1912/James_1912_toc.html.

Madison, G. B. (1988). *The Hermeneutics of Postmodernity: Figures and Themes*. Bloomington, IN: Indiana University Press.

Matthiessen, F. O. (1961). *The James Family: A Group Biography together with selections from the writings of Henry James, Senior, William, Henry, and Alice James*. New York: Alfred A. Knopf.

Myers, G. E. (1986). *William James: His Life and Thought*. New Haven, CT: Yale University Press.

Spring, J. (2005). *The American School: 1642–2004* (6th ed.). Boston, MA: McGraw-Hill.

William James Dies: Great Psychologist. *New York Times*, August 27, 1910. Retrieved April 3, 2005, from http://www.nytimes.com/learning/general/onthisday/bday/0111.html.

CHAPTER 16

Lawrence Kohlberg

ERIC D. TORRES

BIOGRAPHY

Kohlberg was born in 1927 into a wealthy family and grew up in Bronxville, New York. He attended Phillips Academy, where, as he recalled later, he was known more for his sense of mischief and forays to nearby girls' schools than for his interest in academic theories. He supported the Zionist cause as a young man, and participated in the smuggling of Jewish refugees past the British blockade of Palestine right after World War II.

In 1948 Kohlberg enrolled at the University of Chicago and earned his bachelor's degree in only one year owing to his high scores on admissions tests. Staying on to do graduate work in psychology, Kohlberg's plans were to become a clinical psychologist. But Jean Piaget's theories of moral development in children and adolescents fascinated him. Kohlberg shifted gears and found himself interviewing and analyzing interviews to children and adolescents on moral issues. The researcher was born, but it was not until his doctoral dissertation, published in 1958, that his reputation as the new psychology star began. In this dissertation he uncovered six stages of moral development—in contrast with Piaget's two stages—based upon the interviews of 72 white boys in Chicago about the dilemma of Heinz. Kohlberg's concept of "the child as a moral philosopher" broke radically with earlier psychological approaches to morality. He insisted on using empirical data and thus not only created a framework for looking for universal qualities of moral judgement, but managed to revive a field of inquiry.

In 1968 he went to Harvard. At that time he was married and had two children. The era's events—civil rights and the women's movement, Kent State and Vietnam—shaped Kohlberg in indelible ways. In 1969, conducting a study of the morality of adolescents living in an Israeli kibbutz, Kohlberg found that these poor, urban youths had achieved much higher stages of moral reasoning than similar youths who were not part of the kibbutz. Contrasting his new results with those obtained in the United States, soon he was convinced that he could never derive a model for moral education from psychological theory alone.

Meanwhile, in 1970, upon Harvard's request, he taught a course on moral and political choice. His energy in the following years was invested in bridging and he also became an advocate and activist. As of 1974, he began spending time building connections to high school faculties and students while implementing his ideas of "just communities": a democratic school where each person—whether student or staff member—had one vote in deciding school policies. Just communities differ from conventional American high schools and classrooms by providing students with a sense of belonging to a group that is responsive to individual concerns, while also having clearly defined group goals and commitments.

Scholars from around the country and the world converged around Kohlberg, and he was able to generate both great excitement and controversy. He strongly opposed the claim that psychology was a value-neutral social science and his determination to talk about moral values never ceased.

While doing cross-cultural work in Belize in 1971, Kohlberg contracted a parasitic infection, which made him live with increasing pain during the last 16 years of his life. While on a day pass from a local hospital on January 19, 1987, Kohlberg drove to Winthrop, parked his car on a dead-end street, and plunged into the cold winter sea. He was 59 years old.

HEINZ'S DILEMMA

Imagine the following situation as we begin to reflect on Kohlberg's contributions to psychology and how they relate to postformal thinking:

A woman was near death from a unique kind of cancer. There is a drug that might save her. The drug costs $4,000 per dosage. The sick woman's husband, Heinz, went to everyone he knew to borrow the money and tried every legal means, but he could only get together about $2,000. He asked the doctor-scientist who discovered the drug for a discount or let him pay later. But the doctor-scientist refused. Should Heinz break into the laboratory to steal the drug for his wife? Why or why not?

To steal or not to steal, what a dilemma! Let us approach to this fictitious scenario and try to articulate a line of thought. The first idea that might come to your mind is that Mr. Heinz should not steal because, if he is caught, he will be sent to prison. But, after some careful consideration, you may also arrive to the conclusions that if he doesn't, maybe his wife would die, and that that would really make him feel sad and guilty. So, maybe you want to reconsider your initial position and admit the possibility that, perhaps, he should steal.

Even more, let's assume that, as is natural, his wife really wants to live, so you are thinking that he should do something to get that medicine, that is, to steal it. But, again, doubt assaults you and makes you think that, perhaps, it is not what he should do. After all, stealing is against the law, and you and Mr. Heinz know that that is true regardless of what all of you might be feeling, needing, and wanting.

But, as you walk back and forth through the scenario, you have probably realized that what Mr. and Mrs. Heinz need and really want is not a drug, but to preserve Mrs. Heinz's right to live. So, now you might be backing up again and thinking that he should steal. Without doubt, her right to live should be considered the most important thing at this moment. Nevertheless, again, like a pendulum, you might be reconsidering your thoughts because you have also come to the realization that the scientist also has a right to be compensated. So you are again concluding that he should not steal.

In the back of your mind resounds the scientist-doctor's refusal to accept Mr. Heinz's partial payment and promise to pay the balance. So, you could be thinking that he should steal because saving a human life is more important than preserving the scientist's right to private property. But almost at the same time, you can already see that pendulum coming back and knocking down your thoughts because honesty, respect, and the dignity that comes with them are as important to you. So maybe your conclusion at this point is that he should not steal.

Table 16.1
Stages of Moral Development

Level III	Stage 6
Postconventional	*Morality of Individual Principles of Conscience*
Morality of Self-Accepted Principles	**Stage 5**
	Morality of Social Contract
Level II	**Stage 4**
Conventional	*Morality of "Law and Order"*
Morality of Conventional Role Conformity	**Stage 3**
	Morality of Good Relationships
Level I	**Stage 2**
Preconventional	*Instrumental and Hedonistic Orientation*
Premoral	**Stage 1**
	Punishment and Obedience Orientation

Finally, after quiet meditation, you may have reached more transcendental levels of thought and considered that he should not steal because you are accepting what Mr. Heinz and his wife apparently are denying, the fact that sickness and death are natural to the human condition, and maybe they just need to enjoy the time left together.

Or perhaps you have already come to the realization that this is not a dilemma but a paradox because one of the premises is false as it makes you think that the moral realm is the same as the legal realm. When the truth is that the former is only an imperfect effort to mirror the latter in an attempt to legitimize itself. So, at this point you are possibly thinking, "Go ahead Mr. Heinz, and steal. It might still be illegal, but surely is the right thing to do."

KOHLBERG'S MORAL STAGES

Using Piaget's concept of different stages of cognitive structures and applying them to the study of moral development, Kohlberg elaborated a theory of stages of moral development to explain the development of moral reasoning. He argued that human beings develop morally in stages as they mature, and the steps from stage 1 to stage 6 is learning. Persons at a more advanced stage reject the failed cognitive structures of the previous stage and reorganize their cognitive structure creatively in a new way.

A linearized interpretation of Kohlberg's Levels and Stages of Morality is shown in Table 16.1.

Stage 1. Punishment and Obedience Orientation

In this stage the reasoning is very elemental. The immediate consequences, especially on the negative side, and the consequent submission to authority are evaluated as constitutive of reasons of good and bad, without any reflection on what might justify the punishment, reward, or obedience to authority.

Stage 2. Instrumental and Hedonistic Orientation

In this stage the individual is still concerned with actions; however, these are justified by the goodwill of the subjects, providing the criteria for good and bad. Relations begin to appear in the formation of moral judgment, but in a pragmatic way, rather than as a matter of justice or loyalty.

Stage 3. Morality of Good Relations

The opinion of the group is important. This attitude is not just a matter of convenience or to avoid punishment, but one of identification and loyalty: one's intention is noted and valued.

Stage 4. Morality of "Law and Order"

Inclusion in the group is expanded to cover a broader society; moral judgments are based in the social order, which is based on ethical values.

Stage 5. Morality of Social Contract

The goodness of the actions is defined in terms of individual rights recognized by society through its laws. There is more emphasis on legal value, moral strength, and obedience to the laws.

Stage 6. Morality of Individual Principles of Conscience

Here the good is defined by one's conscience based upon ethical principles chosen by one. These are universal principles of justice, equality, human rights, and respect for the dignity of the person.

As you understand these stages better, you may also understand better why you have made certain moral decisions in the past. Also, you will realize that you and everyone else may operate on several levels at the same time. Recent thinking suggests a different image might be more appropriate to describe development, and one possibility is a cyclist moving over a varied terrain. Depending on the demands of the moment, the cyclist will shift gears. That is, as one moves through the complex world of experience, one develops a wider repertoire of strategies.

KOHLBERG'S LEGACY

Instead of seeing morality as a concept that adults impose on children (which is the psychoanalytic explanation), or as something based solely on avoiding bad feelings like anxiety and guilt (which is the behaviorist explanation), Kohlberg believed that children generate their own moral judgments. Moved by social relationships and by a variety of emotions—including love, respect, empathy, and attachment—Kohlberg saw children becoming moral agents. This new perspective constitutes his first great contribution.

Once the inquiry was done, regardless of the sense in which each participant morally responded to the fictitious case, Kohlberg explored the reasoning behind the answers. He tried to identify what different people had in common when they make a moral decision, rather than focusing in their differences. This was also new. His focus on the process of reasoning, rather than on the content, constitutes another great contribution.

Finally, although the just communities with which Kohlberg had been involved during his life did not endure long after his death, his intellectual ideas were instrumental in the design of a Risk and Prevention Program at the School of Education at Harvard, which deals with policies. Precisely the kind of policies he was so committed to develop and nurture in his just communities. In this sense, his greatest contribution would be his opening to the arena of policy, polity, and politics involved in promoting an educational environment nurtured by justice as supreme value.

As educational psychology is reconceptualized, it is important to look closely at these three contributions. Kohlberg's perspective of the child as a moral decision maker needs to be assumed in the context of the signs of our time: 90 percent of the Ritalin used on children in the world is used here in this country; the child suicide rate has gone up over the last decade with increasing acceleration, mainly among adolescent boys; our teen pregnancy rates are among the highest in the industrial world, and last but not the least, in the United States, more of our children per capita get arrested for crimes than in any other country, and the legislative trend toward criminalizing childhood is continuing at a fast pace, resulting in more children—with a high concentration of boys and young men—incarcerated in juvenile detention, prison, and psychiatric hospitals than in any other nation in the world.

Kohlberg's focus in the process of reasoning and his analysis of the language to identify a moral stage reveals an interesting psychological approach combined with linguistics, sociology, and anthropology. Nowadays, it is often asserted that perception is entirely determined by cultural circumstance. And language, in particular, is seen as selecting what is and what is not perceptible. In other words, the belief is that what is named can be noticed; what is not named is unlikely to be seen. In this sense, Kohlberg's approach offered concrete possibilities to discuss issues related to how we perceive what we perceive, how we learn to make distinctions, the relevance of what is being distinguished, and, most important, what is the morality behind formal education attempts that prompt their learners to notice certain aspects of their worlds and to interpret those elements in particular ways.

Finally, Kohlberg's practice of democracy and openness to the ideas of others in order to live justice as a pedagogical experience in the school setting not only represented a challenge to the academy concentrated in theoretical models, but the assumption into practice that teaching is an attempt to effect perception, in addition to involving a study of perspectives, positioning, and points of view.

KOHLBERG'S PARADOX

Some would argue that Kohlberg's attempt to go to practice weakened his academic work, but, without doubt, nobody could argue that he was not productive in his late years. Taking a look to the social context that supports moral development is a major endeavor; especially when there is a crisis of paradigms. From the perspective of postformal thinking then, it may be suggested that he was in a time of transition. Following this idea, there are at least five different ways in which his work can be related to it.

From a Critical Theory perspective, his praxis may reveal three important avenues to be explored: first, his belief that moral thought and power relations are linked; second, that justice is a necessary condition to counteract oppressive social arrangements; and third, that language is an important element in the formation of moral consciousness, identity, and subjectivity.

If Kohlberg resisted the idea of moral knowledge as a simple artifact to be transmitted uncritically, and linked democracy and politics to social ethics for the value of justice to reign supreme, then there is a postmodern perspective that needs to be acknowledged.

From a liberating perspective, something similar takes place. Kohlberg adopted a problem-posing concept in his research and practice where people were viewed as conscious beings in relation to the world. If he wanted to focus in the process of moral reasoning as an act of cognition, then there is a liberating educational approach that needs to be appreciated as a tool to develop a new awareness of the self.

From a postmodern point of view it is evident that his late day's practices were not context-free and value-neutral. On the contrary, they revealed more clearly than a written discourse, an emphasis in the need to understand the cultural, historical, political, and personal lives of those involved in the formal educational dynamics. Stated differently, there is clear evidence that he engaged in a broader conversation and expanded his framework, revealing a strong interest in creating an impact both in the human condition and the social structure.

Likewise, Kohlberg's just communities were based in a postcompetitive sense of relationship, where democracy played the most important role. And he also exhibited a postscientistic belief that moral and religious intuitions contain a truth that need to be considered to develop a sense of self and a worldview.

Nevertheless, from a feminist perspective, it is important to say that during a certain period, Kohlberg's theory was considered "fossilized" and out of touch with a reality that includes the voices of women and nonwhite people. Carol Gilligan, a former student of Kohlberg, developed a different model of female moral development. She used interviews with 29 women who were considering whether to have an abortion or not, as the basis for her moral classification system.

She concluded that women moved through three levels of moral development, on the basis of what she called the female responsibility orientation, which emphasizes sensitivity toward others and compassion. Years later, she would assert that her questioning of Kohlberg's theory was nothing more and nothing less than one aspect of a "major cultural shift" taking place in society.

Although recent research has generally not found any gender differences in moral development, and men and women may come to this point of convergence from different perspectives, the fact is that, as morally mature adults, they learn to synthesize the competing needs of the individual and the community as they formulate key decisions and make difficult choices.

Undoubtedly, Kohlberg's theory and his practice need to be seen through many different lenses to really understand the evolution of his ideas and the revolution of his praxis. A mechanical application of his moral stages theory will not reveal anything more than the shadows of the status quo. It is when the context is observed, considered, and questioned that those shadowed areas can turn into new sources of light that, carefully considered, will create contrasts, provide textures, and reveal images of morality not perceived before.

Owing to his illness, Kohlberg saw himself on a dead-end road. Ironically, it was on such a road that he left his car parked before taking his own life. But, as we reconceptualize educational psychology, we cannot see his praxis less than academically challenging and paradoxically promising.

CHAPTER 17

Jacques Lacan

DONYELL L. ROSEBORO

When Jacques Lacan died at the age of 80 in 1981, he left behind avid followers in the field of psychoanalysis and staunch critics. His writings and seminars attracted those who were genuinely drawn to his explanations of the human psyche, but others were simultaneously convinced that psychoanalysis was nonsense. Whatever your feelings toward psychoanalytical theory, Jacques Lacan undeniably influenced the way we conceive of identity as socially constructed through/within/across language. When he first introduced his theories, Lacan stimulated countless discussions about the connectedness of language to cognitive development. His work, therefore, has enormous potential for any reconceptualizations of identity. Indeed, his fascination with the human ability to *identify* led him to various explanations about cognitive development, all of which are rooted in his understanding of the theories of Sigmund Freud (1856–1939). To discuss Lacan as critical to future understandings of educational psychology, we must first situate him theoretically and historically. Not only the times he lived in but the social and political context as well shaped his thinking and writing.

Born in Paris in 1901 to an upper-class Catholic family, Lacan entered the world at a time when anti-Semitism was on the rise in France and Jewish people found themselves caught in the middle of a national debate between those who wanted the Catholic church involved in government and those who favored a more strict separation of church and state. Lacan would go on to attend a Jesuit (Catholic) school, where he studied Latin and philosophy (among other subjects). Later he would attend medical school and would begin studying psychoanalysis in the 1920s at the Faculté de Médecine in Paris. He was particularly interested in patients who suffered from "automatism," a condition that pushed the individual to feel they were being manipulated by a force outside of themselves, a force that was all-powerful and all-knowing. When he completed his clinical training in 1927, he worked at psychiatric institutions and, in 1932 (10 years after Benito Mussolini took over Italy and 1 year before Hitler's rise to power in Germany), he completed his doctoral thesis on paranoid psychosis. By the time of its completion, the nations of Europe were embroiled in a series of continental conflicts, which would eventually lead to the second World War.

Intellectually and theoretically, Lacan grounds his theory in the psychoanalytic work of Freud and the structural linguistics of Claude Levi-Strauss. As a Freudian, he elaborates on several basic principles of human development. He uses Freud's explanation of the id (the pleasure-seeking, instinctive drive), ego (the rational self), and superego (the moral/ethical drive) to construct a theory of the decentered subject—a subject that identifies itself as Other and in relation to that which it is not. This initial identification is what Lacan calls the "mirror stage" and is one that we will discuss in detail later. Equally important, Lacan grounds his work in structural linguistics. He believes that we *identify* our selves only as we come to accept and understand the rules of our primary language. In a basic sense, Lacan believes that language, as a structure that precedes our bodily existence, defines us; this is the crux of structural linguistics.

LACAN AND IDENTITY FORMATION

In 1936, Lacan published an article entitled, "On the Mirror Stage as Formative of the I." It received little attention until its re-publication in 1949, and since then it has become one of his most widely discussed theories. To explain this theory, we need to begin with a visual image. Picture an infant, between the ages of 6 and 18 months, sitting in front of a mirror. With the infant, there is a parental figure. At some point, the infant comes to realize that the baby in the mirror is herself or himself. The moment at which the infant identifies the image in the mirror as herself or himself is crucial, according to Lacan. But it is significant not only because the child recognizes herself or himself, but because it is at this point that the child "Others" or decenters herself or himself. In a sense, the child sees herself or himself as outside of its actual body.

At this moment, the child also understands herself or himself as a whole being, one that can then be called an "I." This "I" or ego, from the moment of identification in the mirror, is a projected identity—a reflected "I." Lacan argues that this projected identity is artificial because it gives the illusion of a unified subject or self. Where and how the child is positioned in relation to others in the mirror is also important. The child, upon recognition of herself or himself in the mirror, simultaneously perceives of herself or himself *in relation* to others. Whoever is in the mirror with the child becomes an immediate object of comparison. The child begins to determine how she or he is or is not like the other object in the mirror. The important point here is that very young children develop a concept of the self in relation to others and this category of "others" includes the child's image of itself in the mirror. And because this image is unified/whole, the child begins to think of herself or himself as a singular and coherent "I."

Perhaps what makes Lacan's mirror concept so intriguing is his implication that a child's learning to identify herself or himself as an "I" does not begin as an internal understanding. Instead, Lacan argues, the child must first recognize herself or himself externally (in the mirror) *before* she or he can construct an internal identity. In this way, the child's identity is decentered—it identifies first as an external observation. To put it more simply, the child is first an "Other" to herself or himself. Only when the child recognizes itself in the mirror can she or he internally claim to be an "I." If the child had been able to identify as an "I" without recognizing herself or himself in the mirror, then the child's identity would be centered. Lacan, however, believes such an internal identification is impossible without the mirror stage. Thus, the identity of the self *always* begins as decentered—as the child recognizing itself as an "I" only through a projected image.

When the child comes to understand that the image in the mirror is herself or himself *and* a reflection, identical to yet not the same as herself or himself, then the child becomes a subject. As a subject, the child is a social being and thus more than the sum of its biological parts. She or he creates the reflection in the mirror and constructs the self that is the reflection. How strange is that? My body creates the reflection of the object in the mirror, but *it is only when I understand that the reflection is me that I can identify as a self*. At the moment the child understands this paradox, she or he enters the world as a subject, one who affects the world as she or he is simultaneously defined by it. It is this question of subjectivity that compels Lacan to further investigate language and its effect on the construction of identity. Key here is the intersection of recognition and naming. When the child recognizes herself or himself as the object in the mirror and identifies as "I," the child has named itself in relation to the other objects in the mirror. With this initial naming, she or he enters the world of language, a world that Lacan believes defines the child.

LANGUAGE, SUBJECTIVITY, AND SELF-DEFINITION

Lacan begins his theory of language in what may seem like a strange place—the id or pleasure-seeking part of the unconscious. Like Freud, Lacan connected our unconscious desires to the sexual. The desires of the subject are tied to her or his sexual relationships (or perhaps a better way to phrase this is "relations between the sexes"). Lacan differs from Freud in that he does not think the unconscious is a container for repressed memories. Rather than say we discover or uncover memories, Lacan believes that we reconstruct them. The unconscious speaks and forces the "self" to interpret through language. So, the desires that we can identify are identified through words. There is no way to distinguish the desire as separate from language; it is defined within and by language.

So, how does the child come into language? In his explanation, Lacan returns to and builds upon Freud's explanation of the Oedipal complex that, in its most basic sense, is about our unconscious need to satisfy sexual desires. Lacan argues that all infants' early desires are structured in relationship to the primary parental figure (which, according to him, is usually the mother). From birth on, the child attempts to decipher what it is the mother wants. According to Lacan, the mother wants the father, and the symbol for the father is the phallus. The phallus is, ultimately, the object that the mother believes can satisfy her desires. When the child attempts to determine the mother's desires and fulfill them for her, she or he is engaged in the Oedipal complex. In a "normal" Oedipal cycle, the father permanently forestalls the child's sexual desire for the mother. Once the child accepts that she or he cannot serve as the phallus (sexually satisfying object) for the mother, the Oedipal cycle is resolved—Lacan terms this castration. Before the resolution of the Oedipal complex, the child (whether male or female) perceives the father figure as a threat and engages in a battle with the father that she or he will eventually lose.

How then is the Oedipal complex important to Lacan's theory of language? At the moment of resolution, the child understands herself or himself as bound by social law. For Lacan, the father is symbolic of a larger social order. As such, he represents the rules that the child must learn and obey in order to become a functioning and "normal" member of society. Thus, the child first recognizes that the father is the only fully satisfying object of desire for the mother. Because the father represents social law, the mother's desire for the father indicates her acceptance of social law/order. So, ultimately, the child equates the mother's desire for the father with her desire for social law/order. Equally important, the resolution of the Oedipal complex brings the child into language as a fully competent and participatory subject. She or he can thus begin to participate in the social order.

Once the Oedipal complex is resolved, the child (which has up until this point identified with the mother) has to find something else with which to identify. Lacan terms this *symbolic identification*—identification with a prescribed and intangible way of organizing the world. In simpler terms, the child learns to identify with cultural norms, practices that define the child's existence but that cannot be seen or eliminated by the child. When the child identifies with the symbolic (i.e., cultural norms), she or he enters the world of language. Once in this world, the child becomes a subject, one who speaks its existence in words that others can understand. Prior to this moment, the child has been in the process of becoming a subject. Thus from the mirror stage, when the child begins to see itself as an Other in relation to objects, to just before the resolution of the Oedipal complex, the child is not a speaking subject. Without having mastered the language of the dominant social order, she or he cannot communicate in the world as a fully capable and competent being.

When the child accepts the resolution of the Oedipal complex and becomes a speaking subject, she or he experiences life bound by language. Language mediates between the "I" and the rest of the world. When the child masters language, she or he can fully experience the world as a place of meaningful possibilities. In becoming a competent language speaker, the child comes to more fully understand the social rules of the society in which she or he lives. In this process, the child comes to believe that the world is definable in concrete terms. For Lacan, believing is a fundamental part of the child's transformation into a speaking subject. By accepting language as the way to identify the world, the child participates in and acknowledges an unseen social order.

Ultimately, the child's actions reflect unconscious desires. To explain, Lacan believes that we can compare the unconscious to language because "it speaks." Although it does not possess grammatical structure, the unconscious (as a language) connects the body to structured and patterned language. Physical symptoms are then enacted through and defined by language. The child may begin to act, speak, or behave in a way that reflects an unconscious desire. Here, Lacan brings in the concept of metonymy, using a part of an object to refer to the whole. In this instance, the unconscious uses any available language that is known by the subject. By doing so, the unconscious brings out the desires of the subject in various linguistic ways.

Language, as a system with rules and standards, thus serves as the road by which unconscious desires enter the world as a part of the established social order. Lacan speaks more specifically to how this entrance is accomplished when he discusses the signifier. Borrowing from the work of Ferdinand de Sausurre and other structural linguists, Lacan believes that language represents meaning and that this meaning comes out through the interplay of signs. Signs are interpretations, the combination of form and representation. Signs are created by signifiers and signifieds. A signifier is the form taken by a sign while the signified is the concept that is being introduced. Here, an example is necessary. Let's use the word *down*. The word *down* is a signifier. It is in the "form" of a word. If the word *down* were next to an escalator, it becomes a signified—a concept.

Together, we interpret the *signifier* (word) and the *signified* (concept). When the signifier and signified are interpreted together, they are called a *sign*. When we see the word *down* next to an escalator, we know what it means. All signs have a signifier and a signified (word + representation). And, the meaning of the sign can change if the context changes. For example, if we encounter the word *down* in a restaurant, the meaning may change slightly. It could mean that there is additional seating on a lower level. All of this is important to Lacan. He argues that the meaning of a signifier is never fixed until a sentence is completed. Until the sentence is completed, the signifiers are "floating." So, for Lacan, the sentence is the basic unit of meaning making; it is how we make sense of the world.

But why is all of this important to Lacan and cognitive development? It is critical because language, the speaking of it, is central to identity formation. If unconscious desires enter the world through language, we are faced with the daunting possibility of facing these desires in public space. As unconscious desires, they are feared by us in many ways. When they do come forward, they do so as we interact with others. Lacan's psychoanalytical foundation is important here. Because he is always interested in the mind and in how we engage with our unconscious desires, he sees language as a way to cope with the surfacing of the unconscious. Simply stated, his hypothesis is that the unconscious appears first as a symptom. When we experience the symptom, we go to an analyst (doctor, practitioner of some sort). Through the conversation with the analyst, the cause of the symptom is identified and the symptom vanishes. In short, we are able to identify the desire in conversation and, by doing so, satisfy the desire.

This hypothesis has profound implications for our understanding of identity. Lacan suggests that meaning (and, hence, identity) is formed through communication with others. As we engage with others in dialogue, we interpret our unconscious desires and then claim those interpretations. Once we claim those interpretations, they are embedded in our self-understanding; they become an integral part of what we identify as "I." For Lacan, this interpretive act is a psychoanalytic act, one which assumes that there is an analyst out there who can interpret the "truth" of symptoms or hidden desires. Equally important, Lacan claims that the emergence of our hidden desires into the spoken world/language is an attempt to integrate them into the social order. Once we integrate them in a way that corresponds to how we understand the world, they become part of our identity. Integrating our hidden desires into a conscious identity does not mean that we have constructed a new self; rather, it means that we can now reinterpret ourselves.

Finally, with regard to language, Lacan speaks to the importance of "master signifiers" and the construction of identity. Basically, these are the major categories we use to identify ourselves and give meaning to the world. When we claim a national, racial, or gender identity, we are using a master signifier. What makes these signifiers so important is our unwillingness to challenge their meaning. We are often afraid to do so because, if we did, we would have to completely reconstruct our identities. Master signifiers come laced with values and beliefs that ground our understanding of our selves and the world. The way we privilege some master signifiers over others also determines how we order the world. For example, if you were to identify as a Chicana woman, your life would center on this particular interpretation and all other signifiers will have meaning in relation to the primary one with which you identify.

Lacan believes that the psychoanalytic process enables subjects to question and rethink their master signifiers. In doing so, they reinterpret fundamental beliefs and perceptions of the self. If a person's master signifiers are leading to some type of neurosis or inability to function in the world, psychoanalysis can help the person reorder their master signifiers and reidentify in different ways. She or he can then engage with the world in ways that do not result in traumatic experiences. It is important to reemphasize that this reordering does not lead to a new identity. Instead, it brings to the forefront different master signifiers that allow the individual to navigate the world with different primary beliefs and/or values.

With his emphasis on language and identity, Lacan's theories are particularly relevant to any continued studies in educational psychology. His critics have challenged many nuances of his theory—the Oedipal complex and the symbolic phallus in particular—but the crux of his arguments pushes us to reconsider how each of us becomes a subject capable of daily existence within the dominant social order. Through his mirror image and language theories, Lacan stresses the subject as decentered and in relationship. In a basic sense, we develop our self-perceptions in relation to others and we use language to give meaning to experience. Lacan's theories serve as a starting point, one from which we can pose questions that will help us reconceptualize the importance of educational psychology today.

Some of these questions are as follows: How is a blind child's development of self different (if at all) from a seeing child? How do children learn the language of the dominant social order and then refute that language? Is it even possible for children to reconceive/rework/reenact language? Or are their base language patterns (even in the use of slang) always dependent on the language of the dominant group? How do children learn to enact different selves? And how are these selves protected, nurtured, subsumed, or contested by the dominant social order? Are we to assume that since language is so critical to the development of self, children who do not ever master language have no cohesive sense of self? And, finally, can we ever really reorder our master signifiers or are the ones we claim all held together by similar value systems? If so, are we not simply changing what we call our primary identity and maintaining the same key beliefs?

These questions are just a beginning, but they illuminate the continued relevance of Lacan to educational psychology. Any theory that generates more questions than answers gives a base from which to reconceptualize. If the theory failed to generate questions and, instead, provided all of the answers, how could it possibly help us rethink and re-create? Theoretically, Lacan's ideas remind us that identity building is interactive; it demands that we attune ourselves to the world around us. His claim that we are formed by and within language remains a persistent debate; to agree with him on this point challenges the notion that we create our selves, that we are the authors of our own identities. Perhaps the final question that begs discussion is, How do we author our lives *without* language? If we disagree with Lacan's structural linguistics, what is our answer to the question of authorship?

LACAN AND POSTFORMALISM

Postformal thinking requires that we discard the kind of rationality that limits us to linear ways of viewing the world. To think postformally, we must acknowledge multiple perspectives and concern ourselves with what is socially just. We cannot assume that there is some universal knowledge "out there" that will equally serve people across the globe. Instead, we must account for the various ways people construct identities in different contexts and we must consider how we are simultaneously constructed by context. In this regard, postformal thinking demands that we pay attention to identity and power relationships. Unlike formalists, who seek resolutions for all problems, postformalists recognize the importance of ambiguity and contradiction.

If we rethink Lacan using postformalism, we can connect his theories to more current research on identity politics and cognitive development. First, let's consider the implications of his language theory. Lacan says that we identify with and through language. Our unconscious desires come forward as symptoms that are then interpreted through language. If we are indeed defined by language, postformal thinking would force us to acknowledge the significance of the cultural context of language. What happens if a child's primary language is not the language of the dominant culture? How is his language, and by implication his identity, either affirmed or subsumed by the forced learning of the dominant language? How does the child come to understand the power relations of her or his community from the language experience? How does the child learn social responsibility through language? And how does she or he react if the social lessons of the dominant group are in contradiction to her or his racial, ethnic, or religious group?

We must further consider how the child manages to navigate multiple social orders simultaneously. How does she or he come to understand the rules of different groups and how does she or he learn when to switch languages (i.e., code switch)? Lacan claims that the child, in the mirror stage, learns to identify as an "I." If we rethink this statement postformally, we would need to ask, How does the child come to identify as multiple "I's"? And, how does she or he identify in multiple ways without being labeled schizophrenic? With Lacan, however, we do have a preliminary understanding of early childhood development, which, at the very least, does not deny the possibility of plural identity. His focus on the child's development as one that occurs in relation to others is important. Here, he allows for the possibility of children developing different self-perceptions in relation to the other objects of comparison. Equally as important, he contends that we learn to identify with master signifiers (i.e., race, gender, nationality). We can reorder these signifiers through reinterpretation and in conversation with what he calls an analyst. If we broaden his terminology, this means that we can re-create different identities as we engage with different people and in different social contexts. This is not to suggest that the changing of behavior from classroom setting to cocktail party is a re-creating of identity. But it does suggest that we have the potential to identify in different ways when we change social systems.

CONCLUSIONS

Critics of Lacan have argued that his theories are patriarchal, sexist, and narrow. But there is much to be learned from Lacan if we align his theories with different theoretical paradigms. In considering him within a postformal paradigm, we can stretch, deepen, and revisit his work in cognitive development. His emphasis on identity occurring in relationship has tremendous relevance to educational psychologists today who are attempting to unravel the notion that we create identities in isolation, that we are individuals divorced from the larger society. From his theories, we come to understand the contradictions inherent in identity building—we are creating and being created by language at the same time. Any reconceptualization of educational psychology must continue to grapple with this paradox and, by doing so, we may inject new possibilities into future theories.

FURTHER READING

The European Graduate School. *Jacques Lacan biography*. Retrieved June 28, 2005, from http://www.egs.edu/resources/lacan.html.

The Internet Encyclopedia of Philosophy. *Jacques Lacan*. Retrieved June 28, 2005, from http://www.iep.utm.edu/l/lacweb.htm.

Kincheloe, J. L., and Steinberg, S. R. (1993, Fall). A Tentative Description of Post-formal Thinking: The Critical Confrontation with Cognitive Theory. *Harvard Educational Review*, 63(3), 296–320.

Lacan, J. (1999). *ECRITS: A Major New Translation* (B. Fink, H. Fink, & R. Grigg, Trans.). New York: W. W. Norton & Company.

Pitt, A. (2001). The Dreamwork of Autobiography: Felman, Freud, and Lacan (pp. 89–107). In Weiler, K. (Ed.), *Feminist Engagements: Reading, Resisting, and Revisioning Male Theorists in Education and Cultural Studies*. New York: Routledge.

CHAPTER 18

Gloria Ladson-Billings

ROMY M. ALLEN

> A hallmark of the culturally relevant notion of knowledge is that it is something that each student brings to the classroom. Students are not seen as empty vessels to be filled by all-knowing teachers. What they know is acknowledged, valued, and incorporated into their classroom.
>
> —The Dreamkeepers, 1994, p. 84

This quote by Gloria Ladson-Billings is a signature to her decades of enriching work focused on addressing the pervasive achievement gaps between children of color, in particular African American children, and the mainstream Anglo children of the status quo. Many articles, books, and conferences have framed their research around multiculturalism, learning styles, school readiness, and teacher preparation in an effort to concentrate on the perplexity of diversity issues within school settings. However, Ladson-Billings went a step further and attached a name to all of the inter-tangling of the aforementioned topics. Hence, the emergence of a radical educational philosophy entitled culturally relevant pedagogy; an approach to teaching diverse learners that authorizes students to convey knowledge, skills, and abilities through and/or from their own cultural location and identity.

Gloria Ladson-Billings began her journey of defining culturally relevant pedagogy many years ago after receiving her PhD in 1984 from Stanford University in curriculum and teacher education. Her research interests have also investigated areas of racial identity, psychological testing and assessment, and racial/cultural counseling. Besides expertise in culturally relevant pedagogy, Dr. Ladson-Billings broadens her scholarship to include critical race theory and education, social studies, and multicultural education, in which she was a major contributor to the *Dictionary of Multicultural Education*.

Ladson-Billings has been the author of numerous publications. One of her most notable research studies, which spanned a course of several years in the early 1990s, profiled eight successful teachers of African American children. This research culminated into the "impactful" book *The Dreamkeepers* in 1994. The information specifically gleaned from this research prompted Dr. Ladson-Billings to author "Toward a Theory of Culturally Relevant Pedagogy," published in the *American Education Research Journal* the following year.

Along with her publications, Dr. Ladson-Billings is currently serving as a Professor in the Department of Curriculum and Instruction at the University of Wisconsin–Madison and has been the recipient of several teaching awards: the 1995 AERA (American Education Research Association) Committee on the Role of Minorities Early Career Award, the 1995 Division K Teaching and Teacher Education Outstanding Research Award, the 1995 National Association of Multicultural Education Multicultural Research Award, the 1996 Research Focus Black Education Outstanding Black Scholar Award, and the 1997 Society of Professors of Education Mary Ann Raywid Award, just to name a few. She has been invited to make presentations at national and international conferences and seminars, and has served on numerous boards. She has also been a reviewer of at least six educational journals, including the *American Education Research Journal*, one of the official journals of the American Education Research Association, of which Ladson-Billings is currently serving a term as president. These distinguished career accomplishments are only a few of the reasons she should be embraced as a viable contributor in the field of educational psychology.

According to the Division of Educational Psychology of the American Psychology Association, educational psychologists are concerned with conducting research to advance theory, developing educational materials and programs, and addressing issues related to how people learn, teach, and differ from one another. Ladson-Billings continues to refine her research and address components of educational psychology by turning her attention to the issue of the achievement gap between African American and other children of color from disenfranchised ethnic groups and their White counterparts from mainstream America. Her research has culminated into a body of respected works and publications that has promoted proactive teaching methods in diverse settings, or what she terms as culturally relevant pedagogy.

Culturally relevant pedagogy has been one of the most prolific topics of interest that Ladson-Billings has pursued in her research and writing over the years. By addressing her concerns of the growing achievement gap between African American students and their Caucasian counterparts, Ladson-Billings has developed a theory that focuses on the teaching practices of educators who teach African American children. The basis of her theory can also be applied to other disenfranchised, non-mainstream children.

Several tenets are connected to culturally relevant pedagogy that differentiates the theory from other models of teaching practices. In her research with eight teachers of African American students in the early 1990s, Ladson-Billings discovered one of the most powerful components that the "successful" teachers possessed. "Successful" meant those educators who provided instruction to African American children within the child's own cultural contexts, which allowed these children to process the prerequisite skills necessary to move to the next level of their educational career. Each educator embraced their student's diversity and celebrated those differences in a positive way, making success possible for a group of children who otherwise might have been dismissed away by institutional standards. Oftentimes, our society today adheres to preconceived attitudes about African American children. Perhaps these are latent leftovers from a country still reeling from slavery, racial hatred, and oppression of groups not from the mainstream status quo, but preconceptions nonetheless.

Although slavery is more than a century and a half behind us, the political and economical scars of elitism, born out of the post–Civil War era and Southern clout, still exist. Moving forward to the 1960s, approximately 100 years later, an era erupted of civil unrest and the Civil Rights Movement clashed violently with that Southern clout in the form of the "Good Ole Boy" system. Many white Southerners felt threatened by their own perception of insurgency by a group of people they felt should have been grateful just to be allowed to subsist—even though their sustenance was at the level of second-class citizenry. Segregation, Jim Crow Laws, and lynchings of African Americans by this country's Caucasian citizens have not been so far removed that latent memories of these lived experiences are still lingering into the consciousness of many groups today, including the oppressed and the oppressor. Fears and reprisals of past history are not easily forgotten and influence the practices, policies, and even governmental climates. These historical references have been imprinted upon the various cultural identities of our society.

As this country attempts to recover from these horrors of the past upon minority residents, the political and economic climate, traditionally established to benefit one group of residents, permeates through our laws, institutions, and society to favor a power base of affluent Caucasian men. This imbalance resulted in prejudicial ideas and misconceptions about children of color and their families. The educational institutions have evolved into setting expectations that assume each child learns in a uniform style. Teachers, specifically, have been trained to use a deficit approach when teaching African American children and other children of color. This approach came to the forefront of societal attitude after the Moynihan Report of the 1960s, requested by President Lyndon Johnson for justifying his War on Poverty Program. This controversial report highlighted a perceived pathology of African American families such as absent fathers, unstable family structure, households headed by poorly educated, single females, and joblessness. It emphasized the achievement of Anglo Middle America and implied that the "Negro" family needed assistance in the socialization of their children to attain an acceptable level of functional family structure. In sharp contrast, Ladson-Billings, in her research, found that successful teachers of African American children used the strengths approach. Teachers using this approach were observed as truly caring about the children they taught, they were dedicated to their students, they embraced their students' diversity positively, and, most important, they expected their students to strive to achieve at the highest level that their personal capabilities allowed.

A component of culturally relevant pedagogy is that it empowers students to achieve socially, intellectually, and emotionally by utilizing students' cultural contexts, or what Ladson-Billings calls "cultural referents," to make connections with the world around them. Ladson-Billings discovered that successful teachers of African American children extended their teaching beyond the classroom. These teachers designed learning activities that incorporated the community. Referencing the acquisition of knowledge to preexisting, relevant political and social issues made learning meaningful, exciting, and attainable. Engaging the students directly with issues of society, and then looping it back to their own cultural contexts or referents, made the lessons relevant to the students. Eventually, the students embraced their own knowledge, developed their own confidence to learn, and with the teacher's assistance began to understand the inherent power they possessed to conquer misguided expectations and make a difference in their lives and the lives of others.

Ladson-Billings has also been interested in preparing teachers to teach in a diverse society. Walking into a classroom unprepared to teach in a culturally explosive setting can be potentially devastating for the educator and potentially incomplete for the student. In her Teach for Diversity (TFD) project in the mid- to late 1990s, Ladson-Billings and her colleagues realized there was disparity between the way pre-teacher programs prepared novice teachers and the preconceived expectations of being placed in an urban setting of students with various racial, ethnic, and socioeconomic backgrounds blended together. The Teaching for Diversity program addressed these issues by guiding the pre-service teachers to understand three fundamental principles: (a) human diversity, (b) equity, and (c) social justice, and then applying these principles in settings during their field experiences, where the gap between theory and practice could be bridged. In a subsequent publication based on this 15-month project, *Crossing Over to Canaan* (2001), Ladson-Billings reflected on her own teaching experiences in her early years in Philadelphia to account for the necessity to prepare novice teachers for the challenges of teaching in diverse settings. She then offers practical models for teaching in these highly diverse environments by implementing those principles.

Bridging the gap between theory and practice and assisting educators in teaching diverse learners involve comprehending how to embrace the theoretical tenets of culturally relevant pedagogy based on several propositions: academic achievement, cultural competence, and sociopolitical consciousness. While most pre-service teachers may be thinking of assessing the academic achievement of their students, they typically do not give equal thought about which cultural context their students' learning might be attained. While most pre-service teachers may be able to categorize different cultures of their students, they do not typically and/or traditionally think of whether they themselves are competent in the nuances of various cultures to make relevant connections with their students. While most pre-service teachers may think about whether they will be assigned to a school of poverty or affluence, they do not usually think about how these socioeconomic factors specifically influence their students' ability to learn, or how the bias of the educational institution favors children from mainstream America. The theory of culturally relevant pedagogy addresses all these issues, and Ladson-Billings, by developing this theory, gives us a method of practice that transcends the traditional approach of teaching children. Successful learners are recipients in a culturally relevant learning environment, and are not quantified by culturally irrelevant standardized scores.

Culture is dynamic, and cannot be categorized neatly into formal operational stages such as Jean Piaget's four stages of cognitive development. Children are not static, nor do they necessarily fit into predesigned educational boundaries. Therefore, they need instructional practices that will allow and acknowledge their individual growth, and the array of components in their lives that influence or contribute to that growth, such as primary language/dialect, race, culture, ethnicity, and child-rearing practices. Postformal thinking pursues those influences as well as integrates other forms of knowing with caring, perceiving, reasoning/thinking, feeling, dialectical discourse, and transcendence. Ladson-Billings' theory of culturally relevant pedagogy aligns with the realm of postformal thinking because it approaches teaching as a dynamic process. Embracing children in their cultural context, involving them actively in their own learning process, providing meaningful learning experiences, and introducing them to community issues to help them become aware of their own power of agency—the ability to write their own script and create changes—are integral parts of postformal thinking. Unlike the stages of operations inherent in formal thinking, postformal thinking embraces forms or ways to elicit changes—changes that are necessary to keep abreast of the multiculturalism that is prevalent all around us. Furthermore, this cultural sensitivity assists each of us in developing the critical thinking skills that are necessary to create a difference.

To better understand postformal thought, a child's set of nesting cups might be an appropriate metaphor. When the child pulls out the nesting cups, there are several sizes of cups stacked within each other until they all fit together in harmony. If any one of the cups is placed out of order, or it is not understood how relevant that single or individual cup is to the whole piece (or total group), the cups cannot be properly arranged to complete the nesting order or the continuity of the nesting pattern. A child is part of a family, a community, a society, and ultimately a world. However, the child begins with the family unit and all the different components that make that family unique. Just like the nesting cups and all their parts needed to accomplish the whole product, families join together to create a community, a society, a country and intermingle together to create a world. Postformal consciousness recognizes that the influences upon each child affect their development within the context of their unique or specific cultural identity. In concert with culturally relevant pedagogy, the individual teacher and the individual child collaborate to construct a healthy, successful, nurturing learning environment that allows children from diverse backgrounds to thrive. If any part of that child's world is dismissed, the child will not be complete, just like the imagery of incomplete nesting cups implied. There will be part of that child absent in the learning process, creating an atmosphere of disconnection. Is it any wonder that children from diverse backgrounds are struggling so much in mainstream schools?

Gloria Ladson-Billings has been a contributor to the field of curriculum and instruction with her many rich research interests. Addressing the troublesome achievement gaps between black and white students has spurned her interest to develop a practical theory, a culturally relevant pedagogy, that can be implemented by instructors of pre-service teachers; as well as those teachers who have integrated alternatives in their instructional practices that embrace the whole child, a child with all of her or his culturally diverse components intact.

REFERENCES

Ladson-Billings, G. (1994). *The Dreamkeepers: Successful Teachers of African American Children.* San Francisco, CA: Jossey Bass.

———. (1995). Toward a Theory of Culturally Relevant Pedagogy. *American Education Research Journal,* 32(3), 465–491.

———. (2001). *Crossing Over to Canaan: The Journey of New Teachers in Diverse Classrooms.* San Francisco, CA: Jossey Bass.

CHAPTER 19

Jean Lave

VALERIE HILL-JACKSON

INTRODUCTION

Does knowledge occur in isolation—disconnected from the environment and social interactions? Can knowledge be stored away, in discrete packages, and retrieved later in life and applied to certain behaviors and practices? Jean Lave is a social anthropologist with a strong interest in social theory at the University of California, Berkeley, whose work seeks to address these questions. Much of her work has focused on the importance of culture and context and reimagining the study of learning, learners, and educational institutions in terms of social practice. In this way Lave pursues a social, rather than psychological, theory of learning. Lave argues that learning is a function of the activity, context (environment and world), and culture (ways of being) in which it occurs; in other words, it is situated.

This idea is remarkably different from nearly all classroom learning activities and knowledge that is abstract and out of context. *Situated learning*, or situated cognition, is a general theory of how knowledge is acquired. Situated learning has made a significant impact on educational psychology since it was first introduced by Lave, whose work has been instrumental in providing the research base for several related theories. In addition, *community of practice*, the belief that learning involves a deepening process of participation in a community, has also become an important focus within situated learning theory.

Lave is a formidable author with several books and articles to her credit. But three of them, *Cognition in Practice* (1988), *Situated Learning: Legitimate Peripheral Participation* (with Wenger, 1991), and *Understanding Practice* (with Chaiklin, 1993), stand out as her most influential texts that have helped develop a new direction in knowledge acquisition.

In this chapter I examine the impact of Lave's work on educational psychology by comparing it to other learning theories in education. To better understand Lave's work, it is best to review the competing theories in knowledge acquisition that it challenges. Next, I outline the phases of the sociocultural theory that helped to shape the broad and interdisciplinary situated learning theory. Third, I inspect Lave's situated learning theory more closely. And finally I briefly review the implications on organizational practice and instructional design.

BEHAVIORISM, CONSTRUCTIVISM, AND THE SOCIOCULTURAL LEARNING THEORIES

There are several perspectives on knowledge acquisition, or learning, in the discipline of educational psychology. Cognitive psychologists like B. F. Skinner represent the *associationist* perspective, in which skills and knowledge are acquired by way of associations and reinforcement. Such associations or "habits" become strengthened or weakened by the nature and frequency of the stimulus–response pairings. For example, if a learner is given increased opportunity to learn a math concept, then that concept will become learned over time through sheer trial and error. The hallmark of behaviorism is that learning could be adequately explained without referring to any observable internal states. The ideas of Edward Thorndike represent the original framework of behavioral psychology: learning is the result of associations forming between stimuli and responses. Likewise, contemporary psychologist John Anderson maintains that facts are stored and organized, then retrieved to produce intelligent behavior; learning goes from the abstract of facts or "what," to skills in which the learner knows "how." These educators believed that the mind could be trained with mental exercise, much like a muscle. The assumption being that if the mind were properly trained, knowledge and skills would automatically be applied when needed.

The constructivist philosophy maintains that learning is achieved by doing. The major theoretical framework of constructivism is provided by Jean Piaget and Jerome Bruner—in which learners construct new ideas or concepts based upon their current and past knowledge. Constructivism asserts that there can be an observable change in learning when the learner is involved in productive and meaningful activity. The learner selects and transforms information, formulates hypotheses, and draws conclusions, relying on cognitive structure, or mental models, to do so. Cognitive structure provides the meaning and organization to experiences and allows the learner to build knowledge for advanced forms of knowledge acquisition.

Lave's situated learning perspective comes out of the sociocultural theory on learning. It is a relatively new and emerging theory that takes its lead from Lev Vygotsky's notion that social interaction plays a fundamental role in the development of cognition and James Gibson's theory of information pickup in which perception requires an active organism. The problem with educational research in cognition, Lave suggests, is that it has two problems. First, the associationist or behaviorist theory has the tendency to see knowledge acquisition as an isolated, decontextualized phenomenon. In other words, it fails to consider the activity of learning in relation to the context (social environment of the world). Second, the constructivist theory restricts learning by "acting" or doing tasks in their environments. For Lave, contexts create and reflect different forms of mental functioning and problem solving. In addition, Lave proposes that learners do more than act in their environments; in fact, they help to create and maintain those task environments. Lave's work not only reinforces the sociocultural theory, but has provided a new way of perceiving cultural thinking in educational psychology.

THREE PHASES OF THE SOCIOCULTURAL THEORY

According to Rogoff and Chavajay (1995) there are three claims of the sociocultural approach to human cognition: (1) cognition is culturally mediated by material and semantic (meaning-making) artifacts such as tools and signs; (2) it is founded in purposeful activity; and (3) it develops historically as changes at the sociocultural level impact psychological organization. Lave concurs and suggests that learning is not independent of context, activity, and culture.

Rogoff and Chavajay (1995) distinguish three phases in the history of the sociocultural framework. The first, in the 1960s to 1970s, was one of cross-cultural research. Many researchers took up the task of translating cognitive tasks for populations in other cultures, and discovered that the tasks did not transfer well. It became apparent, to some at least, that the tasks were in some ways culture-bound, and also that the cognitive skills that researchers had presumed were universal in their form were actually linked to the practices and institutions of formal schooling in Western society. These tasks were artificial in nature, and examined skills like memory, logic, and classification within laboratory spaces. Lave broke tradition during this time and began to study cognition in everyday life.

The second phase was one of transition in the late seventies and into the eighties, as the theoretical underpinnings of cross-cultural research were rethought and researchers moved away from artificial tasks and into real-life contexts. The writing of Lev Vygotsky provided a new theoretical basis for this work. *Thought and Language* had been translated in 1962. *Mind in Society* was published in 1978, translated by Michael Cole and Sylvia Scribner. Vygotsky's work provided a language for talking about culture and cognition as dynamic processes that cannot be separated; of culture as localized in some sense; and of culture as no longer an independent variable. Blending the traditions of anthropology with Vygotskian sociocultural theory, the situative perspective focuses on the fundamentally social nature of learning that is intimately tied to the situation in which it occurs. It was during this time that Lave took learning from the psychological to the social—emphasizing the social nature of learning. Lave asserts that social interaction is a critical component of learning and that learning is dependent upon activity, context, and culture.

The 1990s welcomed a third phase of sociocultural theories of development in which this perspective has been stabilized. Rogoff and Chavajay identify a critical mass of scholars whose members include Michael Cole, Silvia Scribner, Jacqueline Goodnow, Urie Bronfenbrenner, Pierre Dasen, Robert Serpell, Patricia Greenfield, and, of course, Jean Lave. Lave's situated learning theory is broad and the characteristics have interdisciplinary appeal. The situated learning theory has set the stage for a new movement in the sociocultural perspective in educational psychology.

SITUATED LEARNING: AN EMERGING SOCIOCULTURAL PERSPECTIVE

To reiterate, Lave argues that learning is a product of the activity, context (environment and world), and culture (ways of being) in which it occurs; in other words it is situated. Most classroom activities involve learning that is abstract in nature and out of the context in which they might be used naturally. For many math educators of Algebra, for example, it is not uncommon to have students ask, "Why do I need to know this?" It is a credible question for learners because the concepts for learning Algebra occur out of the context (i.e., in the classroom), and out of its future use. In addition, early work in knowledge acquisition identified the essential elements as specific facts and skills that were unique across situations, and the specific condition was practice, lots of practice. These ideas of decontextualized learning and transfer of knowledge can still be found in current learning theories to a certain extent. These ideas make sense when discussing the transference of basic skills, but complex skills, such as problem solving, often do not transfer, even when the elements of the situations are similar.

Cognition in Practice makes the case that learning is not an individual enterprise, but a social activity in which the activity, culture, and context must be considered. Lave addresses and challenges the concept of "learning transfer"; how abstract learning is applied across contexts— from the formal to everyday life.

For Lave, social interaction is a critical component of situated learning and calls much of the foregoing cognitive theory into question. Lave's work also takes traditional learning theories out of formal (schools and organizations) to informal (everyday situations) settings. Lave's (1977) work with mathematics in everyday life spawned a new era in knowledge acquisition. Her work with tailors' apprentices and Japanese abacus experts found that there are no "general" skills. "The specifics of each practice (whether schooling, tailoring, or candy selling) are inseparable from the cognitive processes of the users of the system" (Lave, 1977, p. 865). Lave (1988) gave us new ideas of thinking about learning through her situated learning model because it provided a language for transfer that extends beyond the acquisition of basic skills in formal settings.

According to Lave and Wenger (1991), the two principles of situated learning maintain that (1) knowledge needs to be presented in an authentic context and (2) learning requires social interaction and collaboration. Since social interaction is a critical component of situated learning, learners become involved in a community of practice. Lave and Wenger (1991) illustrate their theory on community of practice by observations of different apprenticeships involving Yucatec midwives, U.S. Navy quartermasters, meat-cutters, nondrinking alcoholics in Alcoholics Anonymous, and tailors in an African community. At the beginning, people have to join communities and learn at the edge or periphery. As they become more experienced, they move from the periphery to the center of the particular community. Learning is therefore not seen as the gaining of knowledge by individuals so much as a process of *social* participation. The nature of the *situation* impacts significantly on the process.

Lave and Wenger propose that communities of practice are everywhere and that we are generally involved in a number of them at any given time—whether that is at school, home, place of employment, or in our personal and private lives. In some communities of practice we are key or central members, and in others we are more at the periphery. Over time, this collective learning results in practices that reflect both the goals of the group and the social relations of the group members. These practices are thus the property of a kind of community created over time by the sustained pursuit of a shared activity. It would follow, then, that these kinds of collaborating groups are called *communities of practice*. Members are brought together by joining in common activities and by what they have learned through their shared interactions in these activities. The concept of practice is a combination of the activity and the shared interactions as the learner is an apprentice to the practices of the group. Learning is therefore construed as an apprenticeship, or legitimate peripheral participation in communities of practice. In this respect, a community of practice, formal or informal, is different from a community of interest or a geographical community in that it involves a shared practice.

Lave and Chaiklin (1993) support both of Lave's earlier works and develop notions of practice by focusing on issues of context and, again, provide rich descriptions of everyday practices, including navigation, psychotherapy, artificial intelligence, and being a blacksmith. Cumulatively, these books have ushered in a new perspective in educational psychology, one that connects the fields of education and psychology to anthropology, with many connotations for teaching and learning.

SITUATED LEARNING AND IMPLICATIONS ON TEACHING

The implications on learning are many and growing due to situated learning's broad and interdisciplinary appeal. To begin, Lave and Wenger's work on learning as apprenticeship in communities of practice has been augmented by other researchers, and educators can now draw some conclusions about when the transfer of learning from context to context is most likely to occur. It appears that the main characteristics of transferable learning experiences occur in an environment characterized by meaningful learning experiences, expert guidance, and knowledge-building collaboration. These criteria for transfer are having huge impacts on instructional design and learning.

As practitioners, we all have seen the effects of communities of practice in our own classrooms. Research and textbooks are strongly pushing the concept of project-based learning, as the learning becomes an apprenticeship of the community of practice. In this way, project based learning is a learning model because learning is a part of active participation and satisfies the conditions of meaningful activity, expert guidance, and knowledge building. Project-based learning is an instructional technique that is heavily influenced by the situated learning theory.

In addition, ideas on community of practice have been adopted most strongly within organizational development circles. The apprenticeship model, explored in the research of situated cognition and communities of practice, was an attractive theory for those traditions of thinking whose work centered upon training and development within organizations. In the 1990s, there was an increasing interest in the learning organization for those concerned with organizational development. Lave's and Wenger's work around communities of practice offered a valuable complement to organizational thinking. It permitted supporters to argue that communities of practice needed to be recognized as important resources for the growth of organizations. The model gave those concerned with organizational development a way of thinking about how rewards could grow to the organization itself, and how worth did not necessarily lie primarily with the individual members of a community of practice.

Other theorists have also further developed the theory of situated learning and learning as apprenticeship. *Cognitive apprenticeship* is a term derived by Brown, Collins, and Duguid in their work *Situated Cognition and the Culture of Learning*. This research proposes cognitive apprenticeships with multimedia (videos, interactive computer programs, etc.), as opposed to Lave and Wenger's traditional apprenticeships for learning formal theories in a specific kind of community of practice. The computer enables learners to use a resource-intensive mode of education. Cognitive apprenticeships employ the characteristics of other traditional formal communities of practice, but with an emphasis on cognitive rather than physical skills.

CONCLUSION

In the introduction of this chapter I posed the question, Does knowledge occur in isolation—disconnected from the environment and social interactions? And, can knowledge be stored away, in discrete packages, and retrieved later in life and applied to certain behaviors and practices? Certainly the assumption underlying our educational system is that knowledge gained in school is decontextualized and focuses on the individual and will be available in the future to be applied to new problems as they arise both in school and in real-life situations. Lave's introduction of the situated learning theory disrupted these prevailing thoughts and took learning from the individual and psychological to the collective and social.

In this chapter, I explored the impact of Lave's work on educational psychology by comparing it to other learning theories in education. The associationist or behaviorist theory has the tendency to see knowledge acquisition as an isolated, decontextualized phenomenon. In other words, it fails to consider the activity of learning in relation to the context (social environment of the world). Second, the constructivist theory restricts learning by "acting" or doing tasks in their environments. Neither is aligned with what the sociocultural theory of learning asserts—that learning is essentially social in nature.

Next, I reviewed the three phases of the sociocultural theory: the first phase entailed cross-cultural research of the sixties and seventies; the second was the transition phase of translation and re-centering of the cultural work; and the third was one of consolidation of ideas and legitimacy of the theoretical perspective. Lave's work was extremely instrumental for building the foundations of the new sociocultural perspective—situated learning.

Upon closer review of Lave's *Cognition in Practice* (1988), *Situated Learning: Legitimate Peripheral Participation* (with Wenger, 1991), and *Understanding Practice* (with Chaiklin, 1993), situated learning emerges from the sociocultural learning theory as a new perspective that has provided a new direction to the field of educational psychology.

Recent learning models such as project-based learning, learning communities, and cognitive apprenticeships have adopted the techniques of communities of practice and apprenticeship in their research agendas as well. The situated learning perspective is quite broad and appeals to a variety of research and educational arenas.

To answer the questions posed in this chapter, Lave tells us that learning does not occur in isolation, but that it is social in nature. Lave would also assert that we cannot go back to our storehouses of knowledge to retrieve it across contexts, because knowledge is socially constructed and mediated in contextually specific ways.

REFERENCES

Lave, J. (1988). *Cognition in Practice: Mind, Mathematics, and Culture in Everyday Life*. Cambridge, UK: Cambridge University Press.

Lave, J., and Chaiklin, S. (Eds.). (1993). *Understanding Practice: Perspectives on Activity and Context*, Cambridge, UK: Cambridge University Press.

Lave, J., and Wenger, E. (1991). *Situated Learning: Legitimate Peripheral Participation*. Cambridge, UK: Cambridge University Press.

Rogoff, B., and Chavajay, P. (1995). What's Become of Research on the Cultural Basis of Cognitive Development. *American Psychologist*, 50(10), 859–877.

CHAPTER 20

Alexander R. Luria

WARREN SCHEIDEMAN

Alexander Luria contributes to the historical identification and understanding of new spaces for learning. To contextualize Luria one needs to locate his thinking in a biographic relationship to the ethnic, linguistic, and geographical complexity of Russia, and to relate him to the work of Lev Vygotsky, which centers on historical materialism. Historical materialism interprets history as the contextualizing agent, or determinant, for human thought and intellectual creation. Luria essentially focuses on the space inhabited by learners in time (across time, transhistorically) and how they can think, grow, and develop within that space, thus making it transformative, given the opportunity of language, values, cultural setting, and the intellectual capital available to their minds.

Alexander Luria's field was psychology. He was born in Kazan, Russia, near Moscow in 1902. Throughout his career he linked development and functioning of inner human mental process with outer environment, society, and culture. One way of phrasing this is that Luria's focus is on the activity transforming the inner and the outer self and the dynamic interactivity between mind and culture. He saw culture as mediating psychological processes. He viewed intelligence in relationship to historical and social environment. He regarded language as the "tool of tools." During the Second World War, Luria developed neuropsychology, the study of brain and thought.

To define Luria's significance, he connects intelligence and brain through activity with the social and cultural environment, context, particularly with mediation of language as a learning tool for making tools with which to learn. He puts an interesting metaphor to work, language as tooling up, to make tools to learn. An imaginary diagram is important: visualize the brain, which is inside the person, while the environment surrounds the person from the outside, and activity and language mediate back and forth. Luria's focus is on how the circuits are connected. Intellectual and cultural dynamics are at play in the dynamic process mediating brain and culture.

As an entry generalization to the study of Luria, with some oversimplification, Luria related the psychological process of thought with the linguistic and social, the historical context, the cultural milieu. He vividly connects, rather than separate, intelligence and environment. He extends instead of narrowing and dead-ending the human capacity for growth through intelligence interactive with sustaining social and cultural context. Much of his dynamic is cued by the phrase "at play." Luria focuses on cultural and social fostering that occurs inherently within cultures, which is part of the play, the life, of the culture. He elevates inherent learning, what only appear to be games, but are actually lessons in the sustaining culture of the community. And this has educational implications.

At a certain conference, a group of public school superintendents exploded in criticism of advocacy of individual attention for students. They wanted solutions to learning for large groups, not individuals, because of expense and complexity in implementation. The solution lay in Luria's approach of integrating social–cultural melding with individual self-efficacy. It indicates weaving seamless, but diverse, patterns of learning linking societies, groups, and cultures with individual growth. One might think of this interactivity as deep, complex intercultural transhistorical thinking, a globalization process, with links to postformalist thinking, that is based on human development and cognition, the way the human brain functions. It speaks to the concerns of the school superintendents, because Luria integrates large groups with individual learning. And it utilizes play, which means it can be fun.

Visualizing, however, the significance of his work requires, I believe, contextualizing A.R. Luria himself. To be well understood, he needs to be portrayed before a backdrop of the ethnic, linguistic, and geographical complexity of Russia. Imagine Luria in front of a map illustrating the hugeness of Russia, surging with a myriad of peoples and languages. This background needs to be then informed by the drama of Russian politics from the Revolution of 1917, through Stalinism, to the demise of the Soviet Union. Luria died in 1977. During his time, control of cultural politics and geography dominated twentieth-century Russian history. Luria's theories are far from abstract but relate to the historical and social realities of the development of modern Russian industrialization and political representation from conflicting minorities. To develop the trained minds needed to run a modern country, understanding had to be developed of the educational relationships between intelligence and culture, specifically about how people from traditional subcultures can be educated in advanced knowing.

Also, Luria is best understood relative to the work of Lev Vygotsky (1896–1934), which centers on historical materialism. Vygotsky, Luria, and A.N. Leontiev are seen as a troika of theorists in their use of prior work of Werner, Stern, the Buhlers, Kohler, Piaget, James, Thorndike. Luria was Vygotsky's student, colleague, and collaborator. Seen in a historic and political context, one can be aware of how understanding the manipulation of the historic and social environment can engineer and change social values and behaviors through socialization, conditioning, and as self-efficacy in learning. Transhistorical learning space can be productive of control—social engineering. However, this space can simultaneously be productive of self-efficacy, as in the case of Malcolm X, who uses his time in prison to transform and free himself as a thinker by raising his conscious understanding through practice and development in thought and language. Malcolm X intentionally uses language as the "tool of tools." In considerable detail, he describes how he copies from a dictionary in order to master words, to learn more words, to learn strategies to learn and grow, as his values change. He masters self-discovery, which facilitates his strategic rediscovery/reconstruction of the world. Mastery of language is his key to learning how to learn.

Polarized views of Luria's work as applied to learning can be shown in the example of Malcolm X. Interaction between brain and environment can be used to place bars around an individual or people (puts a person behind bars), or it can be used to facilitate freedom (freedom from bars that Malcolm X discovers). Luria's thinking is a two-way street. It can be used to manipulate, control, or foster self-efficacy—autonomous action that creatively uses environmental influence. Malcolm X goes behind bars at least partially because of negative educational opportunities. But paradoxically, he finds freedom because he gives himself the connections between culture and learning that society denied him. Malcolm X's autobiographical account of his self-transformation is also very similar as regards his ideas about thinking and self-empowerment, to the self-creation and self-invention within the dynamic personal space of intelligence, activity, culture, and language used by Benjamin Franklin. Malcolm X and Franklin each created zones for learning.

Positioning Luria in relationship to Vygotsky engages the latter's concept of Zones of Proximate Development, which deals with the relationship between where a learner is developmentally and his or her potential level of growth in problem solving through mature guidance or collaboration. Both Luria and Vygotsky see intelligence in a momentum between inner function and outer cultural environment and influence. And both see intervention in that momentum relative to historical, social forces. Quality of facilitating guidance in learning is important. Luria elevates coaching, particularly the quality of coaching inherent within the culture.

Nonexperts may be tempted to reduce Luria's connection of cognition and society. The inner processes of brain, mind, and behavior are daunting. But Luria can still engage nonexperts like us in the genesis process and signal the linkage between what we see and hear and what we create in mind and behavior. Becoming historically conscious, we can reroute (which is preferable to the mechanistic implications of "rewiring," but the notion is similar) the conduits for psychological creation of thoughts, ideas, skills, and abilities—changing activity. Or we can reroute through control. There is a tension in empowerment, which is signified by Luria's own background, the complexity of geography and language, and the milling, contesting social and political forces of modern Russia, including two World Wars and the Cold War.

Luria clarifies his position in *Language and Cognition* (1982, p. 27): "The basic difference between our approach and that of traditional psychology will be that we are not seeking the origins of human consciousness in the depths of the 'soul' or in the independently acting mechanism of the brain ... rather, we are operating in an entirely different sphere—in humans' actual relationship with reality, in their social history, which is closely tied to labor and language." Interplay of forces in *actual reality*, within historical time, then becomes very meaningful.

A benchmark of the implications of Luria's thinking can be found in his 1931 expeditions in Soviet Central Asia with the Uzbeki and Kazaki peoples. Theirs was a feudal society whose means of production and culture were being radically restructured through the socialistic revolution, economic changes, and the introduction of literacy. Here was a historic transition at which to test the hypothesis that thought processes are not fixed or immutable but can change in relationship to social and cultural life alterations and the introduction of mediating systems such as critical thinking and writing. Analyses were made of subpopulations such as women living in traditional Islamic isolation, male illiterates, and female activists who have had Western influences. Their critical thinking skills were analyzed. He inferred that "semiotic mediation systems act as determinants of higher level mental process."

Such cross-cultural analysis is fraught with problems. Luria essentially deals with metacognition. He finds that traditional peoples respond in different ways than schooled peoples. He finds "direct graphical thinking" replaced by "theoretical thinking." A movement in thinking occurs from the specifically concrete to the abstract. These changes demonstrate new reasoning forms, new self-assessment and imagination. Luria, with P. Tulviste, analyzed schooled and nonschooled use of experience contrasted with abstract reasoning.

One can view the platform of the 1931 Uzbeki research as introducing Luria's developmental interpretation of how children learn. This interpretation is an interplay between the environment and the brain, between the experiential and the increasingly abstract, as mediated through activity and coaching. Luria defines the development of self-regulation, that is voluntary action, as an evolution in gaining equilibrium with the social environment. As a child enters this world, it is at first overwhelmed by the environment. Coaching by caregivers, through speech, helps direct the child's activity. Activity at first is shared between adult speech, guidance, and the child's activity. Luria argues that the child then develops, "learns to speak and can begin to give spoken commands to himself/herself" (1982). Malcolm X and Franklin autobiographically model self-administered "spoken commands." A child's speech ultimately possesses the function of the adult and becomes internalized as its semantic properties are recognized. The child has internalized facilitating/coaching and learned to "talk to [itself]" through the steps of problem solving. The speech pattern emerges in response to a situation involving difficulties. Then it develops as a plan. There are, of course, individual differences in problem solving—in the internalization of reasoning skills.

Attention to the facilitating characteristics of coaching and the social environment become very important in education, particularly in education involving social change. This relates directly to concepts of scaffolding. Leontiev writes, "In society humans do not simply find external conditions to which they adapt their activity. Rather, these (external) social conditions convey within them the motives and goals of their activity, its means and needs. In a word, society produces the activity of the individuals that it forms" (1981). In a post-9/11 global society this relationship between society and the production of individuals becomes particularly poignant and intense.

Relatively little is known about cross-cultural transhistorical learning spaces. Emphasis was on differentiation between preliterate and industrialized people. Very important is to look for how different cultures organize learning experiences for their young people and how that organization facilitates or collides with schooling. This awareness would, for example, facilitate student, teacher, and parent collaboration in learning. The "play of culture" activity has a number of implications for educational psychology.

Historical changes in the social culture and environment influence what is important in the curriculum of schooling. Let us try some broad examples. There will be large differences of what one needs to sustain life in the "colonial household" as opposed to the "turn-of-the century 1900 household," on television historical reality shows. In these dramatized cameos of social reality, labor and culture seen historically, the nature of labor, and survival skills vary dramatically between "then" and "now." Thus the implications of language are quite different just as social culture continues to change. With an age of technology the educative function of popular culture increases. As social culture alters, attention needs to be directed to newer channels. The classroom then can become a cultural/psychological laboratory. Gender, class, and ethnic identity can be better understood within the spin of the historical dynamic of intelligence and social culture.

Examples of transhistoric learning space can be informative. For example 9/11 is transparently symptomatic of significant cultural collisions, which can be understood in terms of the past, present, and future. The status and role of women in Islamic countries can change the social configurations, the learning spaces, of numbers of people across the globe. China offers a similar example of global cultural collision and change. In a cartoon series in Hong Kong one of the most frequent subjects is the overorganization of education for very young children, giving them no time to be with their parents. At the time they are losing Chinese culture, they are struggling in Western culture and seeming to inherit loneliness and dislocation. Another example occurred in one of my film classes, where the outcomes of an African American woman were very higher in quality than in the other courses she was taking. The difference between her performance in my course and in the others was identifiable in the bantering ordinary-language conversations the two of us had. She was the first person from her family to attend college. She was from a very oral culture. She related to film, popular culture, in my course. But her performance also developed through casual coaching.

Our bantering conversation connected a somewhat familiar subject matter, film, with a new way of thinking, analytical criticism. Survival on the streets privileges "street smarts," a canny ability to quickly evaluate people and situations, to read character and action. These social skills draw upon the same intellectual skills used for critical humanities interpretation like analytic criticism, but humane facilitating can define the activity and make connections between intellect and environment, which otherwise might not be realized. Formal textbook approaches can intimidate and silence. Casual, ordinary-language conversation can mediate "new learning," and bridge the inner self and the outer world: home–school–work culture. This bridging can become a transformative learning space, and over time, developmentally, a transhisorical learning space as, for example, the historic transformation of African American culture with definable evolving learning spaces.

Luria supports theoretically the way for postformal thinking. People and culture have richer, deeper interactions than traditional methods of learning that are textbook-centered. Emphasis in both Luria and postformalism is creatively on portals of self-reflection, cultural interactions on deep levels, innovation beyond fabricated constructs like tests and curriculums, understanding as distinct from memorization. Luria makes "the origins of knowledge" important. "Thinking about thinking"—exploring imagination—are integral to both. Finding patterns and problems, exploring assumptions, achieve significance as does the discovery of new relationships for metaphors. Relationship of mind with ecosystems and patterns of life, and reading the world as a book, making connections between logic and emotion, and expanding consciousness—these characteristics of postformal thinking can be sustained by Luria's work and theory.

Complexities of neurophysiology aside, Luria creates pathways for teachers to make transformational connections between intellectual conduits for learning as they bridge minds, selves, and social and cultural environment in actual reality and create a larger, richer, ecological world consciousness and understanding.

REFERENCE

Luria, A. R. (1982). *Language and Cognition.* New York: Wiley.

CHAPTER 21

Herbert Marcuse

RICH TAPPER

Herbert Marcuse was a philosopher and teacher, an intellectual guru and "Father of the New Left," an American by force of circumstance, and a most important figure in the radical social and progressive political movements throughout the late 1960s and 1970s, a period in which he experienced popular attention rare for an American intellectual. Combining psychological, sociological, and political analysis in a German philosophical tradition, and practically linking the academy with an evolution and revolution in society, Marcuse espoused an alternative view of society grounded in a free and happy life for all individuals, a possibility for mankind in terms of revolution. The revolution, in this case, is liberation—one in which our material conditions *and* the consciousness of the individual transform, from the repressive, alienated, inauthentic, and *one-dimensional* to the vitally creative. As Marcuse understood, the world is not in crisis solely because of material events and circumstances, relations of power, and character of economy; crises grow because of the ways that people think, the ways that they think of themselves, and the ways that they think about the world around them. For these major themes in his work, his tireless critique of advanced industrial society, and his enthusiastic embrace of the New Left and youth movements, Marcuse belongs in the front ranks of theorists, researchers, and practitioners who have contributed and are contributing to the development of a new era for educational psychology.

Although Marcuse has insisted that his family history had little to do with his mature work, it is clear that his childhood in Germany, at the end of the nineteenth century, was auspiciously fertile ground for such a philosophical spirit. He was born on July 19, 1898, in Berlin, the son of Carl Marcuse and his wife Gertrude, upper-middle-class Jews. His first significant political (and philosophical) experience came in 1916, when Marcuse was summoned to duty in the German army. He was eventually assigned to a reserve Zeppelin unit because of poor eyesight and, consequently, had the opportunity to attend lectures rather than fight in the first World War. During this time, he had contact with some of the foremost thinkers and thoughts of his day, and was undoubtedly influenced by the political protests against the war by radical socialists.

In 1917, Marcuse joined the Social Democratic Party (SDP) in opposing the war, and involved himself with the worker strikes in Berlin during a time of historic upheaval in Germany. For a time during the November Revolution, Marcuse was part of a civilian security force organized upon the urging by what was known as the soldiers' councils as well as the communists, defending the socialist revolution in Germany against the counterrevolutionary forces of the former establishment under the Kaiser. Soon after, in 1918, Marcuse was discharged from the army and soon quit the SDP as well, disillusioned with their policies and activities. By 1919, the SDP, in Marcuse's view, had capitulated to "bourgeois" establishment. Trying to maneuver politically, the president of the SDP only betrayed the spirit of the movement; trying to ally itself to the old powers, the SDP only succeeded in becoming reactionary, destructive, and repressive itself.

Although he was to ultimately leave the ground activity of political revolution for a vocation in the academy, this entire period of direct political experience marks the central themes in Marcuse's work—his characteristic intolerance for compromise and his loyalty to the philosophy of Karl Marx. What might have begun as the unsurprising protest of a relatively privileged young man against the society that would provide a fertile base for such a horrible war became the foundation for a life's work. It was during this period of political activity that Marcuse began to seriously study Marxism and begin an inquiry into the question of why, if the conditions were so ripe for Marxist social revolution in the world and his country, did the revolution fail. Marcuse was to remain a Marxist throughout his life, perhaps the most radical and committed Marxist of the Frankfurt Institute, consistently arguing that the foundation of Marxism was its need and even demand for periodic revision, for a concrete response to changing concrete historical conditions.

After receiving his PhD in literature (with minors in philosophy and political economy) in 1922, and a short career as a bookseller in Berlin, in 1928 Marcuse returned to Freiburg and the formal study of philosophy with Martin Heidegger. At the time, Heidegger was one of the most influential thinkers in Germany (and Marcuse, throughout his life, considered him his greatest teacher), leading Marcuse both to Hegelian dialectics and to the existential phenomenology of thinkers like Husserl. During this time, Marcuse had crucial and fundamental insights into the trends in technological society that rob people of freedom and individuality, insights that were to find their fullest expression in his later, and most famous, work, *One-Dimensional Man* (1964).

To put this into a philosophical context, where Heidegger, and students of his philosophy, believed that they could "choose" authentic existence, and by implication leave repressive social conditions intact, Marcuse understood that "authentic" existence as such required a radical new way of being in the world that transformed existing conditions, accomplishing a radical social and cultural revolution. Marcuse experienced this lesson early, when after the November Revolution in Berlin, the soldiers of the army reelected their old officers to their same positions of authority (paralleling current political circumstance as well, both in America and notably in Iraq). Marcuse's entire philosophy was grounded here, in analyzing the forces of repression that exist because the conditions in society and consciousness make them possible and even inevitable. Our culture, in this regard, is held in place and re-created continually through the patterns of our language and relations, how we "think" about the reality of our world, and how we move within it. Perhaps this is why Marcuse can be most difficult to read, as if he wrote so that the revolution of the reader's mind ought (and can) only come through the reader's deliberate struggle with text. To make concepts too easily digestible is to ensure their assimilation, and their *repressive desublimation*—a notion that had a central place in Marcuse's work, particularly since the publication of *One-Dimensional Man* in 1964, in which he makes the term explicit.

In this, perhaps his major philosophical work (the themes to which I will necessarily return in this chapter), Marcuse explores the dominating forces of "technological culture," which create a society of such conformity that all genuinely radical critique is subsumed in the integration of opposites. Marcuse argues that the real forces of consumer society are subtle rather than grossly fascistic (those elements of more recognizable fascism: material and often violent repression of people and restriction of their behavior to serve the interests of a narrow group or person), as rare to acknowledge as the air that we breathe. They are "counterrevolutionary," alienating individuals from a genuine critical consciousness and significant discourse in their public sphere with their power to destroy anything truly subversive through absorption. The "radical act" is all but occluded by an increasingly hegemonic industrial society that inculcates "false" needs, which it then fills. Individuals are integrated into a cycle of production and consumption, laying consciousnesses flat—*one-dimensional*—and largely devoid of criticality or transcendent potentiality. People, in effect, are *domesticated* as needs are re-tooled according to the dictates of the technopoly and the market, refusals and negations rendered ideologically complicitous. Even sites of contention, such as authentic art, that might crack this *false consciousness* are only *allowed* to inhabit the margins of political (and psychological) discourse, and so help maintain the illusion of diversity of thought.

Key to this radically critical work is the notion that human beings are alienated, in industrial and (corporate) capitalist society, from their genuine and essential potential—so much so that genuine freedom is outside of our imagination, abstracted like most of the philosophies that deal with "freedom" and "existence."

Marcuse struck this theme even in his first published essays in the late 1920s and early 1930s. Throughout his life, he sought to bridge the gap between philosophies that dealt with the great issues of society and those that addressed the difficulties of the existing individual. Marcuse broke radically from abstractions and the myths of "objectivity," concerning himself instead with the concrete conditions of existing society. As a result, the emphases and ideas in his work have shifted considerably, but never veer far from his main themes except in terms of a progressive continuity. His work evolved, as his understanding developed through his life. If in his earlier work his writing sounds a number of existential themes (particularly in his first "Habilitations Dissertation" under the direction of Heidegger, on Hegel's ontology, for entry into the academy as professor), in his more mature work, Marcuse broke nearly completely with the existentialist—particularly Heideggerian—a historical assumptions about the nature of being human. In other words, throughout his life, Marcuse became increasingly concerned with the subjective conditions of revolutionary change and the barriers to them, and the individual's relation to the very real circumstances of existence. His fundamental question: How is authentic existence possible *today*? Marcuse confronted the problems in the real world; he sought the causes of suffering in the concrete, and tried to point a way beyond human misery, repression, and slavery. His life's work was to liberate the individual from alienation and revolutionize society.

In the 1930s, Marcuse, with the Institute for Social Research, laid the groundwork for many of his later projects with analyses of fascism and authoritarianism. In 1933, a day following Heidegger's public pronouncement of support for the National Socialist (Nazi) movement, Marcuse left Freiburg to join the Institute. Also known as the Frankfurt School of Critical Theory, the Institute was just in the process of shifting from Frankfurt owing to the political climate, the rise of Hitler and the National Socialists to power. Marcuse would never work in the Frankfurt offices, but instead in Geneva and then later at Columbia University after the exile of the Institute from Europe. Part of its "inner circle," Marcuse (with Adorno and Horkheimer, most notably) investigated the psychosocial conditions in which so many people are so easily manipulated by irrational, aggressive leaders. Throughout the 1930s and 40s, Marcuse worked with the Institute at Columbia University, which had granted them offices and academic affiliation.

In 1940, Marcuse became a naturalized U.S. citizen, and remained in the United States for the rest of his life aside from excursions and lectures in Great Britain and Europe in the 1960s and 1970s. His first major work in English, *Reason and Revolution* (1941), introduced many in the English-speaking world—particularly in America—to both Hegel and Marx. Significantly, Marcuse (who is often vilified as representing hopeless critical pessimism) meant the volume optimistically (again, most particularly for America), showing the relationship between Hegel and Marx and the possibilities inherent in the dialectical method. His philosophical point was to introduce and expand themes that would run throughout his work; his social intention was to catalyze a society against forces threatening to annihilate the possibility of freedom. He sought to free the masses of society from the slavery of totalitarianism, and restore an association of rational individuals in our modern world.

His commitment against fascism led to his work for the U.S. government from 1941 to the early 1950s, first in the OSS (Office of Secret Services) and then in the State Department. His particular duties included analyzing the German and Soviet cultures, to find the causes and weak links of fascism and communism. During this period, he wrote and published *Soviet Marxism*, a study quite critical of Soviet-style communism and the USSR. The study, like his *One-Dimensional Man* (Marcuse was never an uncontroversial thinker), understandably angered many on the left, unwilling or unable to see the distortions (and disruptions) of true Marxism in the Soviet Union, as well as reinforced the opinions of those on the right against the radical and Marxist Marcuse.

Most immediately relevant for educational psychology in this regard is Marcuse's related analysis in *Eros and Civilization* (1955) linking the seeming failure of the Marxist revolution to the psychological state of repressed people. While Freud theorized that man as a psychological being necessarily suffers in order to make civilization possible, Marcuse argued that so-called civilization has instead induced suffering to an unnecessary and extraordinary degree. In effect, Marcuse challenges Freud's basic assumptions about the nature of man and "civilization," even while accepting some of his central tenets (which also prompted a heated, and often polemical, series of arguments with his former colleague in the Institute, Erich Fromm).

Marcuse, in particular within the Institute, had explored the patriarchy of the family unit, which he understood (like other thinkers such as Wilhelm Reich) not as the natural order of things, but rather the unexamined basis of the existing social structure. Following his logic, the defense (like Freud's) of conservative family values is not a progressive and liberating tendency, nor even an objective and apolitical one, but a defense of the dominating capitalist economic structure. Family practices tend to legitimate authoritarian social ones.

In *Eros and Civilization*, he refutes Freud's basic argument that an unrepressive and unrepressed society is impossible. Happiness and pleasure, according to Marcuse, have *true* value in modern society—they must not be subordinated to the *false* value of the capitalist work ethic. In effect, and significant for his methods of *dialectic* and in particular the *negative dialectic*, Marcuse disagrees with Freud's basic dichotomization of "pleasure" and "reality" principles, and his emphasis on the latter as the principle of civilization. For Marcuse, the "reality" principle of modern capitalist society only enforces the totality of culture's demands on the alienated individual—and so Marcuse rather sets it in dialectical contrast to "pleasure."

In reconstructing Freud's theory (and particularly in critical contradistinction to *Civilization and Its Discontents*), Marcuse gives an account of how social forces condition our inner worlds. The forces of domination colonize the minds of people; Freud's "superego" is more properly the voice of repression, internalized. The superego as well as external authorities stand ready to punish those elements of society or individual judged to be perverse, or extraordinary; alienated labor has become a duty willingly performed as part of "reality." Domination in this sense applies whenever the individual's goals and purposes for his or her existence are prescribed, along with the means of striving for them. Domination is a process in which society comes to control both the inner and outer life of an individual: externalized, as organized wage-labor, exploitation, etc.; internalized, as the prohibitions, ideologies, ways of thinking, assumption of values and modes of being in the world. Domination takes the form of instrumental technical imperatives and mechanical behavior. It takes place through total administration (so important to note in an era in which "administrators" have unquestioned control of education)—its antidote is *true* education. Domination bounds our social and psychological dimensions, constituting our practical nature as human beings and "reality" as we know it. The specific "reality" principle that governs the behavior of contemporary society is the *performance principle*: the "pleasure" of the individual is subordinated to "reality."

One can see the far-ranging consequences of such a state in our concrete and common circumstances. Other than in exceptional circumstances, individuals are required (and require of themselves) to work long hours in unsatisfying occupations; "leisure" and "free" time have become rare quantities, to be privately hoarded; emotions repressed in private relationships cathect only through mass entertainment. *Human beings exist part-time*; "freedom" is had only in those intervals between being used as instruments on someone else's behalf. But in our society, even "free" time is determined in its character by the performance principle, either in our utter abandon to animal tendencies otherwise repressed in our economic duties, or in an obsession with private projects and concerns. What so-called civilization offers is repression marking both the "progress" of the human being in general (phylogenically) and the individual in particular (ontogenically). Marcuse shows in *Eros and Civilization* how the conditions of the greater culture are the conditions of the individual; the cure for the one necessarily the cure for the other, or it is no cure at all.

Marcuse also offers a new "reality" principle, again making a concerted effort to imagine an alternative to contemporary repressive conditions, an effort that was to be such a consistent theme throughout his work. Such a principle would rely on a radically different aim to reason in our culture, and on the existence of an instinctual human drive toward happiness and freedom. Rather than the repression of our instinctual drives as integral to progress and civilization, he imagines a perspective in which these drives are instead integrated into a liberated state of being. In the old "reality," human beings seldom (if ever) learn that our animal instincts are only the first part of a much greater story; that our innate drives are not meant to be burdens but sources of power.

Rather than positing a strict dichotomy between subject and object, individual and society, spirituality and animality, body and soul, the new rationality would instead encompass a subject transformed through reconciliation. The values inhered would be in practical opposition to the values of repression. The new values would include sensitivity and receptivity, nonviolence and compassion.

In effect, and turning back to Freud, Marcuse aims at reconciling the perceived opposition between the "pleasure" and "reality" principles in something like Freud's "Nirvana" principle, aiming at peace and harmony in existence. The Nirvana principle represents, as Marcuse shows (quite idiosyncratically, and not without its difficulties) through the myths of Orpheus and Narcissus, the ideal of unalienated Eros; the embrace of vitality and creativity rather than necrophilia (in Erich Fromm's term). Beauty, play, contemplation are the values Marcuse tries to incorporate in his imagination for a new "reality" principle. The conflict between reason and the senses would be overcome; new rationality is, in this way, prototypically postformal. Marcuse argues that liberated Eros would not only lead to greater, more complete sexual gratification, but to the transformation of human relations and creativity in general—here anticipating much of the counterculture of the 1960s, which would make him such an intellectual and political celebrity among the New Left, intolerant of the conservative (and repressive) social and political establishment.

Marcuse's distinction of *repressive tolerance* (from the 1965 essay of the same name, dedicated to his students at Brandeis University) makes this central point for our society in general and the education of individuals specifically. It is notable that the essay appeared just as Marcuse was being relieved of his post at the University (he'd received a tenured position in 1958) over a then-famous dispute with the University president. (His expired contract was not renewed, and he left for a position at the University of California at San Diego until his retirement in the 1970s.) In "Repressive Tolerance," Marcuse speaks from his experiences, which by then included not only the great, historical events of the German Revolution and the first World War, but also the Cold War and McCarthyism in the United States, and the vigorous and often ruthless "counterrevolutionary" activities of conservative social forces during the waxing of the struggle over civil rights in the United States. Here he argues that there are forms of behavior, of belief, of action in society that ought not be tolerated by progressively conscious individuals—and deserve to be met with concerted, deliberate, and perhaps violent, protest. "False" tolerance refers to the toleration (and so legitimization) of areas in our culture that in fact are repressive, even though they argue for themselves as progressive in the name of pluralism (and often God) and relativity of opinion; these areas offend the telos of true tolerance, which supports diversity, inclusion, progression, and evolution.

But who has the capacity, and is qualified, to make such distinctions? Here is a central point for educational psychology: everyone in the maturity of his or her faculties. The distinction between repression and progress appears to be a value judgment to the alienated mind, repressively tolerant, but in contrast is empirically rational and verifiable to the mature human being. The answer to the dictatorship, to the fascism of indoctrinating ideology and repressive superego, is the mature human consciousness, intolerant of repressive factors and contradictions masked by propaganda and Orwellian manipulation. The real crisis we face in the modern era is that of a closed society in which such maturity exists only as abstract possibility. If there were lasting human developments to issue from the Age of Enlightenment, they grow from the presumption that persons are rational, with access to universal truths and their own, direct experience of their conditions of existence. If society renders this presumption false, then "Enlightenment" is at best a lie.

Marcuse argued in "Repressive Tolerance" that we must be *intolerant* of the words, images, and processes that feed *false consciousness*. Education cannot be value-free, except through a repressive sleight of hand. Previously "neutral" aspects of learning must be understood as crucial and political in both style and substance. The liberating education is, again, empirically rational; it is radically critical. The student, Marcuse believes, must be able to think in the "opposite" direction of repressive forces; the student must be able to truly inquire into his or her concrete circumstances and the reality of his or her struggle. Education in general—and philosophy in particular—plays the progressive role in Marcuse's social theory by developing concepts that are subversive of prevailing ideologies, helping to develop imagination and the language of critique and possibility. Without such language, imagination, or critique, the real autonomous subject remains bound by abstractions, ideals, and representations, divorced from its true needs.

In his earlier work from the mid-1960s, *One-Dimensional Man*, Marcuse addressed most specifically (and what some criticize as pessimistically) the terms of this occlusion. Here he also addressed the two main historical predictions of inevitability in orthodox Marxism—that now seemed to be concrete improbabilities: the rise of the proletariat to power and the fatal crisis of capitalism. As he argues, explaining how Marxist thought must grow to include contemporary conditions: *one-dimensionally*, all thought conforms to the preexisting patterns of the dominant culture. "Bidimensional" thought, in contradistinction, represents "what could be"; it signifies human capacity and realization of critical subjecthood, the possibility for transcendence, subject as distinct from the dominating object. *One-dimensional* thought smoothes over differences and distinction, it quells radicalism and subversion through enclosing the possibilities for thought. History is relieved of its contentious concrete character, replaced by myths. *One-dimensional* persons have short and opaque memories, for both history and their own true needs. Both have been falsely administered by a totalizing society. Authentic individuality itself has become a myth, rather than a fact of existence. Human beings have largely lost touch with their capacities to look beyond current conditions and conditioned "reality," and to perceive alternative dimensions of possibility.

But rather than deeply pessimistic, *One-Dimensional Man* might instead (and has been) read as a critical manifesto. It set the stage for a series of Marcuse's articles and books—including

An Essay on Liberation (1969) and *Counterrevolution and Revolt* (1972)—helping to articulate a politics for the New Left emphasizing the power of the outcast and disenfranchised in general. His case is not for the working party per se to gain power, but that the decisive factor is the discontent, the *great refusal* of the nonintegrated individual. The radical intellectual is again key to the opening of the social imagination, just as the radical act is requisite for the liberation of the individual, the opening to true needs.

This concern with needs was to characterize Marcuse's later philosophy, particularly in *An Essay on Liberation*. In Marcuse's view, happiness is not ancillary, but central, to freedom. Freedom, in turn, necessarily involves the meeting of our *true* needs. Without such freedom, real happiness is impossible for human beings. Still, it is necessary to note, particularly for those who would like to see, and have seen, Marcuse as an apologist for "free" sexuality and the "me" generation, that Marcuse is arguing *against* a purely subjective and selfish happiness in his argument for the meeting of human needs. He argues that happiness is inherently connected to the transformation of social conditions and individual consciousness, that there is a clear distinction between "higher" and "lower" pleasures obscured (and inverted to a great extent) by contemporary culture: more and more, we recognize ourselves in our commodities; we define ourselves by what we own, what we have, and what we need to get. True needs are essential to human survival and development; false needs are superimposed on us and serve the interests of repressive social forces. Technology, in Marcuse's philosophy, plays a crucial role here: rather than being directed toward the maximization of profit (in all its forms), technology could (and perhaps ought) to be directed toward the satisfaction of true needs.

Like very few others thinkers, Marcuse was willing to embrace a notion of social transformation that includes the sensual, sensuous, and receptive as the foundation for our society, morality, rationality. It is again necessary to note as a response to vocal (though ultimately misinformed) critics that Marcuse's vision involves not the unbridled genital expression of our libido, but a *nonrepressive sublimation* of the sex instincts, the "eroticization of the entire personality," the freedom to truly *play*. Sexuality is, Marcuse argues (again similar to Wilhelm Reich in this), transformative and vital. Its free expression leads not to a progression of lewd, lascivious acts, but rather their minimization. Opening taboo to the light would incorporate these impulses (now only *allowed* "neurotic" expression in general society) into constructive society; it would transform so-called perversion into creativity. Marcuse did not advocate orgasmic expression (like Reich) as the key to liberation and social transformation, but rather the liberated Eros that would ultimately express across the levels of our human existence. In a rational world, sexuality, in Marcuse's terms, would cease to be a threat to culture and instead lead to culture-building; the human organism ought to exist not as an instrument of alienated labor, but as the subject of self-realization and social transformation together in the meeting of true needs.

What opens the space for this new imagination was a major focus in Marcuse's last book, *The Aesthetic Dimension: A Critique of Marxist Aesthetics* (1978). In a turn back to the beginnings of his writing and work (his 1922 dissertation on the German artist-novel), he argues for authentic art (as literature, primarily) as the authentic radical act. Similarly to the way he treats fantasy in *Eros and Civilization*, Marcuse argues for authentic art as integral to the Marxist social revolution; art (and again, literature especially) provides and catalyzes the imagination and consciousness for true revolution. True, authentic art breaks through *mystification,* through solidified reality. In effect, authentic art moves us in our hermeneutic experience *beyond*, opening spaces in the imagination for emancipation. This theme of emancipation, liberation, or revolution, of demystification, is part of the inner logic of authentic art, rather than its explicit style or content.

Marcuse's exploration in *Aesthetic Dimension* emphasizes his lifelong argument: the decisive fact of progression and evolution, over and against repression and fascism, is the liberated subjectivity of individuals, present to true needs, intelligence and passion, imagination and conscience.

To approach this subjectivity, to uncover it, is to be intimate with history, with our concrete personal histories in all their subtleties and dimensions. Marcuse's turn back to psychology as well as hermeneutics is most important for our purposes here in educational psychology: the remembrance of concrete personal history, the understanding of our own psychologies, of the nature of our internal laws, is decisive in demystifying our "reality"; reification is forgetting. Authentic art, in this sense, transcends social constrictions of language, thought, and form, even as it is overwhelmingly composed of their presence.

From authentic art emerges a new rationality, a new sensibility. Marcuse sounds these lifelong themes for the last time here, in *Aesthetic Dimension*: the need for liberatory imagination, for the subrogation of aggression and destruction to creativity, to life instincts; the place and necessity of the intellectual, and artist, in negating established "reality." In (once again) exploring the role of art and the artist, Marcuse underlines the need for true democratization, and generalization of creativity. Art so represents the ultimate goal of all revolutions: the freedom and happiness of the individual, in rational society.

It is difficult to imagine a more important figure in the development of the postformal movement than Herbert Marcuse. Not only did he, with the Institute for Social Research, provide the decisive critical strength for a final philosophical break with the repression of formal ways of thinking, but Marcuse in particular provided the imagination for an alternative rationality and "reality," based on reconciliation rather than domination and duality. Not only was his work decisive for philosophy and politics, Marcuse's project is most fundamentally a project about authentic and concrete human existence, beyond our contemporary logocentrism and habits of representation and reflection. No reification was exempt from his critical lens, except perhaps a deeply felt humanism, and faith in the power of the mind to break through obstruction and clear the ground for truth. Marcuse challenged every category of thought and culture dialectically, declaring quite early in his career his intention to carry out a negation of the present order. His was a philosophical approach, but not the approach of an abstracted intellect; Marcuse provided guidance throughout his career to the development of his individual students as well as to the growing youth movement and the social and political New Left. His was a project about the disenfranchised, the outcast, and the consciousness not yet integrated into the greater order as the keys and catalysts for a revolution in society.

Marcuse died on July 29, 1979, after having suffered a stroke while on a visit to Germany.

CHAPTER 22

Abraham Harold Maslow

RUTHANN CRAWFORD-FISHER

Abraham Maslow was the first of seven children born to uneducated Jewish immigrants on April 1, 1908. His parents came to the United States in an effort to provide opportunities for education and prosperity for their children. Because of their sacrifice, they expected a great deal academically from their first-born. It was assumed Abraham would excel and become a lawyer. He did enroll at City College of New York; however, after only three semesters he transferred to Cornell, only to eventually return to City College. Shortly after his return, he married his first cousin, Bertha Goodman. His parents were not happy with his choice of bride, nor were they happy about his seeming inability to focus on their goal of his becoming a lawyer. It was not until after he was married and he moved to Wisconsin that he would begin a path in psychology that earned him the place in history. Maslow's insights into the human condition allowed him to develop a hierarchy of needs that has guided modern-day philosophy of educational psychology.

Maslow's first venture into psychology came in the form of a basic psychology course while at City College in 1927. Interestingly, he earned a C in that course, but the beginning of his great thinking came after reading Graham Sumner's *Folkways* (Lowry, 1972, p. 1). This book allowed Maslow insight into society, how environment influences individuals, and how societies evolve. This ignited a passion within him that would sustain him for years to come.

When Maslow transferred to the University of Wisconsin in 1928, he came under the tutelage of behavioral psychologist John Watson. During the time Maslow was at the University, there were many notable psychologists in residence. The main focus of the evolving work of this group was in the ever-emerging field of behavioral psychology. While at the University, Maslow earned a BA in 1930, an MA in 1931, and his PhD in 1934. All his degrees were in the field of psychology. It was actually in 1932 that Maslow began examining primate psychology, which was the beginning of his work that would lead to his ultimate crowning achievement of the development of his hierarchy of needs. In 1934, Maslow presented a dissertation focusing on dominance and submission of primates. In 1935, he presented his body of work at the American Psychological Association's conference, where he garnered the attention of Edward Thorndike, noted psychologist at Cornell. Thorndike invited Maslow to return to New York and work at Cornell. After only two years, he left the side of his mentor and Cornell to accept a teaching position at Brooklyn College.

Figure 22.1
Maslow's Hierarchy of Needs

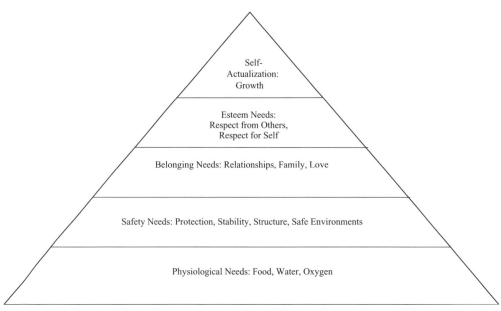

During his tenure at Brooklyn College, he had the opportunity to meet many European intellectuals such as Eric Fromm, Alfred Adler, and several Gestalt and Freudian psychologists (Boeree, 2005). Once on his own, Maslow began putting together the pieces of his life, his knowledge, and his insights into primate behavior into a concise methodology of psychology.

Maslow suffered from a low self-esteem. While he was successful in his own right as he grew up, he was less than his father had hoped for. This sense of never being enough, coupled with his father's frequent taunting about his appearance caused a lack of self-esteem to develop. His understanding of the need for emotional security came from his work with primate dominance studies during his years at the University of Wisconsin. Maslow did extensive work in the area of submissiveness and dominance within the primate community. He examined how these elements influenced relationships among the primates. He studied how impulses, needs, desires, sexual drive, and aggression factored into the relationships of the primates. His observations of behavior, motivation, and need coupled with his own personal understanding of environmental influence and primate behavior began the basis for his hierarchy of needs (Boeree, 2005).

Maslow's hierarchy of needs has huge implications not only to the world of psychology at large but to the field of education as well. Maslow used the term *hierarchy* to illustrate that in four of the five levels, the successful attainment of human needs is based on the fulfillment of needs at the lower level. The tiers of Maslow's hierarchy (Figure 22.1) are as follows: physiological, safety, belonging, esteem, and, self-actualization.

The base tier of the hierarchy addresses a person's physiological needs. The items that fall into this category are air, water, and food. When people are very hungry, they begin to focus only on the need to eat food. When hunger pangs escalate to the point where they can think of nothing else, thoughts focus on getting something to eat. If those needs go unmet, the thought of eating food becomes an obsession. All remaining thoughts dim as attention focuses on what food will be consumed. It is important to note, however, that if air intake of the starving individual were threatened, attention would instantly fade from hunger as a more primal human need of air came under attack. It is a fascinating phenomenon where one need that is so severe, that so dominates thought, is quickly replaced by an even more desperate human need. The implication of Maslow's understanding of the compelling nature of physiological needs is especially important to student performance in schools. If students come from homes where food is not readily available, they will not be able to focus on the activities happening around them. They will fixate on the need for food until that need is met. Many governmental programs have been integrated into the school day to address this very issue. Students who qualify for free and reduced-price meals are now offered breakfast and lunch at no cost so as to combat hunger and allow students to focus on learning.

The next tier of the hierarchy addresses the need for personal safety. Safety also encompasses the need for structure and stability. Once food, air, and water are secured for survival, finding a warm, dry place to sleep becomes of paramount importance. The safety and security of that place is important in the individual's effort to avoid pain or harm. Stability and protection are human needs most important in the formative years of children. These needs form the basis of their fight or flight response. The fight or flight response is an instinctive human response to environmental stimulus. When threatened with danger, humans will either flee the situation if they feel failure is imminent, or stand and fight if the situation does not pose imminent harm. Students who are provided stable, nurturing environments that have easy access to food, water, and security will develop with a fair degree of normalcy. Students who have intermittent access to food, water, and are uncertain about whether or not they will have a home to return to, whether or not a parent will be present, or whether or not the home they return to is in a safe environment can potentially develop many risk factors with regard to the fight or flight response. Students who live in unstable environments, which are not necessarily safe, develop with higher states of arousal. They are on constant edge trying to determine whether flight or fight is needed to secure personal safety, thus altering their brain chemistry. They operate in a portion of the brain closest to the brain stem, where the fight or flight response system exists. These students in unsafe environments have a difficult time processing higher-order operations because too many actions processed in the area of the brain stem affect their functioning. Students whose security needs are unmet and whose physiological needs are met on an intermittent basis are unable to function well in educational settings.

The next tier on Maslow's hierarchy is that of belonging. Belonging needs are those needs that involve connection to others. Love, community, and belonging to a group all form the basis of this level of function. Humans by nature are social beings. Since the dawn of time, humans have existed in colonies or social groups. Survival—then and now—depends on the ability to foster and sustain relationships. Especially critical to human development are the love bonds between parent and child. Children who grow up in homes devoid of healthy contact with adults will supplement that need with other individuals. Once into elementary age and beyond, positive peer relationships become a critical element to development. Individuals whose belonging needs go unmet may turn to less desirable groups in order to develop a sense of belonging. Gangs, cults, and negative peer groups supplement a human's need to feel part of a group. When students' needs in this level go unmet, they will be prone to developing a severe sense of loneliness, social anxiety disorders, maladaptive social disorders, and will have difficulty making and sustaining relationships needed to function in everyday society. Many of the students whose needs go unmet at this level can develop depression owing to a sense of inadequacy and inability to connect to the school community. Furthermore, students who develop maladaptive behaviors and whose needs are unmet or met intermittently at lower levels may develop aggression issues, violent tendencies, or delinquent behaviors. In relation to education, students such as these are likely to develop high-risk behaviors such as absenteeism, class cutting, violent behavior, and early withdrawal from school.

Esteem needs constitute the next tier on Maslow's hierarchy. Maslow designates two distinct categories within this tier. In the lower level of esteem, individuals seek respect from outside their self. They seek positive strokes via recognition, attention, status, and appreciation. Their esteem is based solely on how others see them. In the higher level of esteem the need focuses on self-respect. The needs at this level focus on feelings of independence, self-confidence, and personal accomplishment. Students whose needs go unmet at this level often may withdraw from communities and others. Their low self-esteem keeps them from the ability to make and sustain much needed healthy relationships with others. They may fail to achieve their potential because they feel a sense of inferiority. Because they have little or no respect for themselves, they may believe at some level that they are incapable of success. Teens whose needs are unmet at this level may engage in risky behaviors. They have little respect for themselves, so they essentially have a negative self-fulfilling prophecy. In seeing themselves as inferior, they will aspire to be inferior. These children will not often take risks or strive to attain goals they deem too lofty for someone like them. Risky sexual behaviors are common among teens with inferiority issues. When they have a negative self-image, they will seek and take attention in any form. Abusive and unhealthy relationships may develop as the negative self-fulfilling prophecy is fulfilled.

The four tiers of the hierarchy discussed thus far—physiological, safety, belonging, and esteem—all fall under the heading Maslow termed deficit needs or D needs. The reason he referred to these tiers in a deficit mode is because if humans do not have the needs met at these levels, they may have potential deficits in their functioning as healthy individuals. The concept of deficits states that if needs at all levels go unmet, then the needs at the physiological level will take precedence over all other needs. When needs at the lower level are met, then needs on the next level become predominant. Maslow refers to this system of checks and balances as homeostasis. In this sense, the body is a self-sufficient machine. When it lacks something, a switch goes on as an intense need develops for the element that is lacking. When the need is met, the switch goes off and stasis is restored until such a time as another need develops (Maslow, 1970).

The final tier of Maslow's hierarchy is that of self-actualization. Self-actualization is the most complex of all the levels of the hierarchy. These are not deficit needs; the needs here are defined as growth motivation or being needs (B needs). B needs may take many forms and focus on an individual's drive to become something better than the present form. These B needs include characteristics such as compassion, understanding, insights into the needs of others, goal setting, and a drive for excellence. To be self-actualized means becoming what you are to become in life. B needs focus on realizing the primary goals in life and on personal self-improvement, ways for the individuals to better themselves. Unlike D needs, B needs feed themselves. As people become successful and actualize goals, they feel a desire to feed that feeling of success. Typically at this level, success breeds more success. To quote a U.S. Army recruiting slogan, B needs challenge humans to "Be all that you can Be." The interesting phenomenon about this need level is that in order to operate on this level, lower-level needs must be met. Humans cannot focus on becoming something greater when they are worried about food, shelter, belonging, or esteem issues.

Self-actualized people have many common character traits. The people who become self-actualized tend to be well grounded in a sense of reality. These people have the requisite skills needed to step outside of situations and solve problems. They are able to give up their person-centered focus and see the situation in objective fashion. They have a sense of justice, independence, and accept others as they find them. Self-actualized beings have a true sense of humanness. They show respect to people of all walks of life, demonstrating compassion, care, and concern for others. Self-actualized people are comfortable with themselves and their place in the world. They look at the world and its people with awe and wonder. They are students of the world. Maslow feels these individuals show something called "human kinship or Gemeinschaftsgefuhl—social interest, compassion, humanity ... this is accompanied by a strong ethics, which was spiritual but seldom conventionally religious in nature" (Boeree, 2005, p. 5).

It is apparent, through Maslow's experiences, his insights into the human condition, and his research, that his approach to psychology during the time of his research was something new and emerging. The psychologies of Maslow's time were focused on psychoanalysis and behaviorism. The psychology emerging from the work of individuals like Maslow was known as humanism. Maslow refers to this new discipline as the third force, psychoanalysis and behaviorism being the other two. "Humanism deals with the state of a person's awareness or consciousness feelings in an understanding context" (Hillner, 1984, p. 235). This form of psychology looks at the whole person, focusing on adaptive behaviors of humans. Humanism seeks to look at individuals in their natural environment under everyday conditions. By understanding the human condition, psychologists can understand man's relationship to the world.

For education to achieve its greatest potential, it would benefit from a humanistic approach like Maslow's. By attempting to understand the needs of children and how those needs relate to their ability to achieve their full potential, we increase the likelihood of unlocking the hidden potential in all children. With regard to basic human needs, federal and state education programs fund free and reduced-price lunches. They do so to ensure a level playing field for students who are deficient in this need. In relation to safety needs, schools have zero tolerance policies to protect students' rights and to ensure student safety. In Maslow's philosophy of human development, school rules should be designed to provide stability, justice, and an ethic of care by meeting the needs of each child. Some elementary and middle school programs now focus on developmental esteem building. In some schools and classrooms, small group instruction, cooperative learning, and community service foster a healthy sense of belonging that provides the potential for the children to attain the higher level of needs.

Now with the advent of the Elementary and Secondary Education Act (The No Child Left Behind Act of 2001), schools are attempting to focus on what they believe is the final tier of Maslow's hierarchy. A great deal of investment has been put into achievement of standards in an effort to concentrate on improving the child's sense of self. The unfortunate part of this modern-day crusade for personal fulfillment is that the educational system drags all those whose needs are unmet at lower levels to this venue, and has the same expectation for all. According to Maslow's philosophy, students who are hungry, live in a car, succumb to severe feelings of loneliness, and have low self-esteem, will have little concern about standards, tests, homework, or even staying awake during a lecture. Maslow would assert that they cannot attain self-actualization because their D needs are not met. While many programs have been integrated into education to aide in the fulfillment of D needs, current educational funding levels create shortfalls in the ability of schools to meet the needs of all students. With regularity, students are asked to use higher-order thinking skills to process complex data. Many students have not developed these critical thinking skills because they are nowhere near the point of self-actualization. For students in deprived environments, the gap in skill development is paralyzing. Approaching education in a humanist view will require schools to value each individual child, seek to understand the worldview of the individual, and access needed resources so that the child may indeed realize the potential that lies within itself. Without looking beyond the test, the lecture, and the homework, we will fail to allow children to Be all that they can Be.

REFERENCES

Boeree, C. G. (2005). *Personality Theories: Abraham Maslow.* Retrieved December 6, 2005, from http://www.ship.edu/~cgboeree/maslow.html.

Hillner, K. P. (1984). *History and Systems of Modern Psychology.* New York: Gardner Press Inc.

Lowry, R. J. (1973). *A. H. Maslow: An Intellectual Portrait.* California: Wadsworth Publishing Co.

Maslow, A. H. (1987). *Motivation and Personality* (3rd ed.). New York: Harper & Row Publishers, Inc.

CHAPTER 23

Maria Montessori

KERRY FINE

Maria Montessori's (1870–1952) contributions to the field of educational psychology are represented in her groundbreaking theories of young children's natural cognitive and developmental abilities. Montessori's critical observations of her students led to the advance of novel understandings regarding human development and child psychology, hence bringing about revolutionary insights concerning how children learn and the best ways to teach them. Her work has informed the practice of educators and psychologists around the world to promote successful learning in schools.

Maria Montessori began her journey into the world of educational psychology by making history as the first female medical student at the University of Rome. There, she worked at a psychiatric clinic studying neuropathology, where she ultimately wrote her thesis on one of her patients. After graduating from medical school in 1896, and long after she finished her thesis, Montessori continued to work at the psychiatric clinic. While working at the clinic, she observed "idiot children" (the mentally retarded) who, unable to function at school or in their families, and with no other public provisions available to them, were locked in asylums, like prisoners. There, they were kept in bare, dark rooms, seeing no one but each other, and doing nothing but staring, sleeping, and eating the food brought to them by their caretakers.

Montessori's medical orientation was focused on the treatment of children as well as her passionate commitment to social reform. This background led her to be deeply concerned about the lives of children who were relegated to the Italian psychiatric hospitals. Montessori became convinced that the minds of these children were not as useless as society had determined them to be. She thus set about finding appropriate psychological and cognitive methods for developing the intellect of these special patients.

As a trained scientist, Montessori believed fervently in the power of observation. She spent many hours observing the children at the clinic and noted that they would play with, touch, and taste crumbs of bread on the floor for lack of any other objects of stimulation. She thus determined that sensory stimulation was a primary need of these children. Montessori, acting on what would later become one of the foundational principles of her method, concluded that their inherent sensorial needs should be harnessed as a method of developing these youngsters' minds.

She then began researching all previous methods of working with this child population. In doing so, she determined that the clinical environment in which her young patients were forced to live was contributing to their disabilities. Montessori came to believe that meaningful settings were critical to children's cognitive development. She was convinced that children's natural sensorial instincts would lead them to interact with the tools and materials around them, which they would then use to construct meaning of their world. Therefore, Montessori concluded that in order for her young patients to make progress, they needed to exist in more humane surroundings where they had appropriate materials to touch, feel, and manipulate. She decided that these children would never be cured in hospitals; instead they needed to be educated in special schools. This conclusion turned her attention from medicine to education and crystallized what was to become her life's work (see Kramer, 1988).

In searching for models, Montessori discovered two French doctors, Jean Itard and Edouard Seguin, who had developed educational materials based on sensorial and physiological stimulation that they had used successfully with "deficient children." Montessori was sure that these materials held the key to success with her child patients at the clinic. Having concluded that sensorial experiences were essential to the psychological and cognitive development of these children, she determined that if provided with an environment in which sensorial materials were present, her patients would naturally use these materials to engage in the learning process. Thus, Montessori's perspective suggested that children possessed an inherent desire to learn and that they would learn best through self-instigated actions in an appropriate environment. Before long, her novel ideas regarding the cognitive and psychological needs of children with disabilities became publicly acknowledged and she was soon lecturing widely about the imperative for a new kind of education for "problem children."

In 1900, Montessori was appointed director of the Orthophrenic School, an institution newly designed to serve "mentally incompetent children." This was the first school of its kind for such children in Rome. Montessori used the opportunity to experiment with the sensory materials developed by Itard and Seguin. Maintaining her belief that observation was critical to understanding children's needs, she studied her pupils carefully as she presented them with the materials. In this way, she gained important insights into their cognition and modified the materials and methods of presenting them as the pupils' developmental requirements became apparent to her. Montessori's practices contributed significantly to the field of educational psychology as they functioned to enhance understandings about the needs and characteristics of children's development at various stages (Standing, 1995).

On the basis of the information Montessori gained through her critical observations, she created a continuum of materials that captivated the children's natural interests while gradually bringing their understanding of concepts from the concrete and sensorial into increasing abstraction. For example, one of Montessori's designs was a three-dimensional wooden alphabet. The vowels were painted red and the consonants blue. The children instinctively held and touched the letters over and over again. Building on their natural curiosity, Montessori used the opportunity to repeat the sounds of the letters while the children felt them. Eventually, students began to internalize this letter–sound correspondence and over time, many of them learned to write and read. This form of education would later become known as the world-famous Montessori Method (Montessori, 1912).

Montessori's philosophies and practices worked so well that the children who had once been classified as unteachable, and assigned to live in asylums, became able to master a multiplicity of skills previously thought totally beyond their capabilities. By 1903, many of the students in her charge were even able to pass the standard sixth-grade tests given to "normal" children in the Italian public school system.

Never content with her initial successes, Montessori found her program's achievements troubling. She concluded that if her "deficient" students were able to meet the standards expected of "normal" students, then surely the expectations for "normal" students were not commensurate with their abilities. Eventually she became convinced that the pedagogical methods employed by traditional public schools prevented children from reaching their full potential because they were not responsive to the inherent cognitive and developmental needs of their pupils. She couldn't help but speculate that her materials and methods would help "normal" children to develop more quickly and progress much further (Lillard [2005] *Montessori: The Science behind the Genius*).

As Montessori's fascination with the learning process grew, she returned to the University of Rome to study education, anthropology, and psychology. She also visited traditional public elementary schools to observe teachers and students. In the schools she visited, Montessori noted that primary students were made to sit in neat rows, memorize discrete bits of information fed to them by their teachers, and recite these lessons back, word for word, in unison. The accepted understanding of the time was that academic learning was not a natural cognitive process for children, and therefore something that students had to be systematically "forced" to do. Montessori, however, had a radically different orientation to the psychology of children's minds. She believed that children were innately motivated to learn and that if schools provided the right materials and environment, students would *choose* to learn, often making tremendous progress in short periods of time.

This line of thinking prompted Montessori to attempt to gain approval for the application of her methods in the public schools. Unfortunately, the Italian Ministry of Education summarily denied her requests. Not one to be dissuaded, Montessori found an alternate opportunity to work with "normal" students. In 1907 she assumed a position coordinating a preschool in the poverty-stricken Rom's district of San Lorenzo.

At that time, the San Lorenzo district contained significant populations of economically disadvantaged children who were too young to attend the public schools and had no one to care for them during the day while their parents worked. These children were simply left home alone all day and, without anyone to supervise them, ran wild throughout the neighborhood defacing buildings and committing other petty acts of vandalism. The opportunity to work with these children was attractive to Montessori, as it spoke to her commitment to social responsibility as well as providing a suitable circumstance to experiment with some of her educational ideas on "normal" children. So, on January 6, 1907, in the San Lorenzo district of Rome, the first *Casa dei Bambini* (Children's House) was opened.

Montessori's success was almost instantaneous. With fifty students, ages three through six, her first step was to introduce the sensory materials that she had successfully used at the Orthophrenic School. Montessori was fascinated by the way in which the young children were intensely attracted to the materials, working spontaneously and repeatedly with them, and displaying long periods of total concentration. The multiage setting, now a hallmark of Montessori classrooms, fostered a cooperative learning environment through enabling the older children who had mastered the materials to help the younger ones. Another advantage of this multiage arrangement was that there was a wide range of materials available to serve the heterogeneous student population. This permitted children to learn at their own pace, unrestricted by "grade level" limitations (see Kramer).

Montessori, always the observer, drew conclusions about the developmental needs and learning patterns of these children through watching what they did naturally, unassisted by adults. She constantly refined her materials and methods based on these observations of the children's unprompted work. Among Montessori's most significant contributions to educational psychology was her establishment of particular stages of children's development, during which it was very easy for them to learn certain concepts because they had an overwhelming passion and dedication to command specific skills. Furthermore, Montessori determined that each of these stages only lasted for a certain amount of time and then disappeared when the related skills had been acquired. Perhaps most important, she concluded that the rate at which children would move through these stages was highly variable and could not be predetermined by an adult or arbitrary curriculum schedule, a discovery that reinforced her belief in flexible, multiage learning environments. Montessori called these stages children passed through, "sensitive periods."

Sensitive periods were essential for teachers and child psychologists to understand and recognize, argued Montessori, because as students were passing through these stages, educators needed to capitalize on their natural propensity to absorb important information by providing the appropriate learning experiences to support students' development.

Some of the sensitive periods for learning discovered by Montessori are outlined below:

*Birth to six years: **Language Development**—*Fascination with the use of sounds to communicate. This stage is marked by a progression from babble to words to phrases to sentences, with continuously expanding vocabulary and comprehension. Opportunities for language practice and improvement are essential.

*Birth to five years: **Coordination of Movement**—*Fixation on coordinating and controlling random movements. At this stage, children have a strong interest in practicing tasks that are challenging to the development of their fine and gross motor abilities.

*Three to six years: **Social Learning**—*Interest and admiration of the adult world and desire to copy and mimic adults, such as parents and teachers. Children at this stage are particularly captivated by how adults carry out social interactions.

*Four to six years: **Spatial Relationships**—*Developing understandings about relationships in space is all-consuming. Activities such as the ability to find one's way around familiar places and knowledge of how to work complex puzzles hold great appeal.

*Three-and-a-half to six years: **Reading, Writing, and Math Readiness**—*Spontaneous interest in the symbolic representations of the sounds of each letter and in the formation of words; fascination with the attempt to reproduce letters and numbers with pencil/pen and paper; and absorption with the mathematical concepts of quantity and operations. Activities and materials that take these interests from the concrete to the abstract are vital.

Montessori observed that students were intuitively drawn to specific materials and activities that developed the skills relevant to each sensitive period. Hence, she soon realized how important it was to give children the freedom to choose their own learning materials, as they seemed to have a natural instinct for their individual sensitive periods. This also reinforced the necessity for teachers to observe their students and prepare the classroom with suitable materials and activities for the pupils to choose from. Montessori called this "the prepared environment" and strongly believed that if the environment was not properly prepared, children would not be able to reach their full potential.

In order for students to have complete access to the materials, Montessori designed low, open shelves where the materials were stored when they weren't being used. In this way, children were able to select their own materials, work at their tasks for as long as they liked, and then put the materials back in the proper place on the shelf. Montessori also designed child-sized tables and chairs that the children could move themselves for ease of working. Her classroom was truly child-centered—fostering choice, autonomy, and independent activity, with the children's interests and needs guiding their learning, as well as promoting student responsibility for maintaining the order of the environment (Montessori [1912] "The Montessori Method"). This orientation to children's development was an extraordinary innovation to the field of educational psychology, as it departed radically from the behaviorist notion of teaching as a form of controlling human nature, positing instead that the best learning occurs in contexts of natural interest and active involvement (Lillard, 2005). Exactly three months after the opening of the first *Casa dei Bambini*, a second Children's House was opened in the San Lorenzo district. Using methods similar to those she had employed at the Orthophrenic School, Montessori soon taught the four- and five-year-old children in her schools to read and write. Before long, local newspapers began reporting that "miracles" were taking place in Montessori's schools. Visitors deluged her classrooms. In the fall of 1908, Montessori opened three more schools, two in Rome and one in Milan. Her materials and methods began attaining international recognition. Beginning in January 1909, the orphanages and kindergartens in the Italian sector of Switzerland were transformed into *Casa dei Bambinis*. Over the next several years, preschools based on the Montessori Method opened all over the world.

The widespread enthusiasm regarding Montessori's innovative approaches to the teaching and learning of young children represented a radical shift in the thinking of the psychological establishment of her time. Psychologists of Montessori's day still believed that intelligence was determined solely by hereditary factors. Early childhood education, focused on the cognitive development of preschool students, was considered a waste of time and money. The notion that enriched environments in the preschool years might serve to counteract the challenges represented by limitations in intellectual ability or socioeconomic background was a revolutionary concept. Montessori's methods, which illustrated the essential impact of early experiences on young children's cognitive potentials, dramatically changed the perspective held by psychologists toward child development.

As her philosophy and practice evolved, Montessori carried her passion for social issues directly into the classroom. She was a prominent public advocate of lasting world peace and felt that global harmony could only be achieved through teaching children, who were born without hatred and prejudice, to respect and honor all peoples of the world (see Standing). Montessori had developed world-renowned teaching practices based on her respect for the inherent needs of children, and so it was a natural transition for her to insert this theme of respect into her curriculum. She thus insisted that social consciousness, student responsibility, and multicultural/global awareness be an essential aspect of the independent activity, critical thought, and mental development cultivated among students in Montessori schools. This was translated into classroom practice through emphasizing peace education, community service, and investigation of diverse perspectives, alongside a strong commitment to a multicultural environment and curriculum. For her work in this area, Maria Montessori was nominated for the Nobel Peace Prize three times—in 1949, 1950, and 1951 (Kramer, 2005).

Maria Montessori died in Holland in 1952, but her vision lives on in the Montessori schools that still exist all over the world today. In many ways, her educational philosophy anticipates a postformal perspective. As Joe Kincheloe posits in the introduction to this volume, postformal thinkers look for alternatives to the rigid realities that are constructed by society's power holders. To do this, they often draw from the knowledge, perspectives, and abilities of marginalized peoples. Montessori's educational practices were developed in direct reaction to the dismal realities that had been carved out for society's disenfranchised. Her work with the mentally retarded and economically disadvantaged not only gave these children opportunities and skills they were formerly denied, but allowed their abilities to be granted respect and their needs to be met in ways that were both novel and profound. Furthermore, the insights Montessori gained through her work with these students proved to be legitimate for all types of learners. Educational psychologists of today must use Montessori's example and critically investigate the unique resources and capabilities of current communities that have been denied a voice in their educational process. In uncovering the psychological and cognitive perspectives of alternative groups, modern-day educational psychologists can work toward the creation of teaching and learning models that more appropriately meet the varied needs of today's diverse student populations.

Another area in which Montessori's work is representative of postformalism is that her philosophy reflects an understanding that there is not "one universal truth" which holds valid for all children. Montessori believed that students develop at varying, individual rates. Therefore, she argued, for education to be effective, both the classroom and the teacher must be prepared and able to work with children at their individual developmental levels, rather than where a decontextualized grade-level scope and sequence has determined they must be. In contemporary Montessori environments, students' progress is supported and measured in the context of their distinct developmental processes, rather than through the lens of irrelevant standards. Evaluation procedures, unless otherwise ordered by state or school district mandates, are authentic and may take the form of projects, performance assessments, student–teacher conferences, portfolios, logs, anecdotal records, or progress reports.

Furthermore, like postformalists, Montessori believed that if teachers were not thoroughly knowledgeable about their students, authentic learning would simply not occur. In Montessori's method of education, the teacher and student are engaged in a continuous relationship of mutual respect. The teacher, as observer, is constantly watching and learning from the children, determining their needs without passing judgment. When a child's needs become apparent to the teacher, he or she will present the appropriate materials to the student and the child's learning will therefore be supported. Thus, Montessori pedagogy reflects the postformalist belief that education is the result of human relationships, and does not occur in abstracted isolation.

Finally, like the postformalists, Montessori pondered questions of "what could be" in addition to questions of "what is." These questions changed the way education was conceptualized. In asking them, Montessori recognized the political implications of educational psychology and the act of teaching. Consequently, she insisted that students be educated to ask these kinds of critical questions as well. She understood the importance of educating children not just to be academically successful, but also to actively develop a critical consciousness and work toward social change. Montessori's emphasis on developing autonomy and choice in the classroom established a foundation for students to develop into adults who would be able to confidently act on informed choices and ultimately redefine societies and bring about social justice.

Educational and psychological reform movements of today still draw from Montessori's ground-breaking work of a previous century, which demonstrated that *all* children can become self-motivated, independent, critical learners. Today, Montessori's visionary ideas continue to inform our understandings of developmentally appropriate practice and the cognitive and psychological needs of children. There are currently thousands of Montessori schools in the United States, including hundreds of programs in public and charter schools, where Montessori's methods and materials have been extended for use in classrooms through high school. Her brilliant insights into human development and learning remain viable concepts that have profoundly influenced the modern landscape of educational psychology.

REFERENCES

Kramer, R. (1988). *Maria Montessori: A Biography.* New York: Addison Wesley.

Lillard, A. S. (2005). *Montessori: The Science Behind the Genius.* New York: Oxford University Press.

Montessori, M. (1912). *The Montessori Method: Scientific Pedagogy as Applied to Child Education in "The Children's Houses" With Additions and Revisions by the Author.* New York: Frederick A. Stokes Company.

Standing, E. M. (1995). *Maria Montessori; Her Life and Work.* New York: Plume Books.

CHAPTER 24

Nel Noddings

PATRICIA A. RIGBY

What do you teach? Inevitably when this question is asked of educators they will respond: reading, biology, world history, geometry, second-grade, high school, or some specific content area or grade level. It is the rare professional who will respond: "I teach children" and yet that is what teachers teach. It is not a curricula that is taught but rather a way of thinking or acting in the world in response to the standards, guidelines, or rubrics demanded by educational governance boards. The discipline of educational psychology is dedicated to the study of how children learn and hence by association how teachers teach so that children learn. Nel Noddings, a philosopher and former math teacher, demonstrates through her "ethic of care," which supplants traditional curriculum, that children learn the lessons for a life well lived through moral education steeped in caring relationships established between the carer and the cared-for. In Noddings philosophy of moral education, a four-stage process is invoked that facilitates the learning in the child of "traditional" feminine virtues of nurturing and caring. In this chapter, Noddings's contribution to the study of the learning process of children, including a review of her impact on care theory, as well as critique of character education will be explored.

Much of the foundation of Noddings's work can be found in her analysis and reflection on the writings of John Dewey. Dewey's insistence that education for each child should be determined by the interests and capabilities of each child, as well as the vital importance of building educational strategies on the purposes of the child (Noddings, 1984, 2002, 2003), not solely on the child's preparation for participation in a democratic society but also on the child's moral development, speaks to the essence of the ethic of care as set forth by Noddings. This is nowhere more clear than when Noddings addresses curricular issues that are useful only in the artificial settings of schools and not useful in the day-to-day life of the student outside of the educational facility (Noddings, 2002). It is her contention that the main aim of education should be a moral one, that of nurturing the growth of competent, caring, loving, and lovable persons. The curriculum should be organized around centers of care for oneself, others, the environment, and for ideas (Noddings, 1992). This holistic approach is revealed in an understanding "that the caring response is fundamental in moral life because the desire to be cared for is universal" (Noddings, 2002, pp. 148–149). Dewey directly addresses the psychology of how children learn by demonstrating how the various curricular interests of the study of science, history, geography, and other mandated subjects may be employed in the solutions of genuine problems. He further proposes that these interests must be progressively organized so that students who develop interests in specific fields may be invited to study them in greater depth as part of their own development. However, Noddings eschews what she sees as the liberal tradition in favor of more important and essential centers of care (Noddings, 1992). Noddings's argument, although more of a philosophical nature, addresses the nature of being human. She proposes that there are centers of care and concern in which all people share and in which the capacities of all children must be developed. Because of this, education should nurture the special cognitive capacities or "intelligences" of all children (using the schema suggested by Howard Gardner). The centers of care and the capacities to learn must be viewed in light of a consideration for difference between and among the children, and, most important, all must be done from a premise of attentive love and deep care for each and every child (Noddings, 1992).

Noddings asserts that many of the problems of society could be addressed if at the core of education there was a movement not to bring about equality in learning, but to recognize the multiplicity of human capabilities and interests—equity of learning. Education should be about instilling in students a respect for all forms of honest work done well (Noddings, 1992). It would instill a dedication for full human growth where people would live nonviolently with each other, sensitively in harmony with the natural environment, and reflectively and serenely with themselves (Noddings, 1992). In a system where human life and love are viewed holistically, the piecemeal approach to contemporary education would be reformed in the truest sense of the word. Noddings asserts that these existential questions become the curriculum: Who am I? What is my purpose? How am I in relation to others, self, and, the environment? Thus when there is a crisis in school or society that traditionally results in a new unit to be taught or program to be introduced, such as drug education, sex education, violence prevention and the like, in an ethic of care, there would already be a relational stance in place where the cared-for would understand the responsibility attendant to the relationship with the carer, and thus would result in the cared-for responding positively to the "other" as the situation, our capacities, and values allow (Noddings, 2002).

The ethic of care emerges from an understanding of feminine images and experiences in Noddings's perspective of the role of the maternal in society. A balance between the warrior model (maleness) and the maternal model (femaleness) must be established for a radical change in the current curricular practice. Students should learn from "the womanly and manly arts, and their learning must include both critical and appreciative analysis, as well as appropriate practical experience in living out these models" (Noddings, 2002, p. 113). She is direct in her analysis that while "warrior" stories may be used in teaching values they must be critically examined for the virtues they present and glorify. Are they in fact extolling a witness of a worthwhile attribute or are they examples of some evil embedded in the experience that will perpetuate a cycle of violence and tragedy (Noddings, 2002)? Her presumption that traditionally ascribed feminine characteristics are highly desirable is paramount in her work. Noddings places high valuation on the traditional occupations of women: care for children, the aged, and the ill.

There is no one curriculum or curricular approach that will provide for the adoption of the work of care ethicists; however, she offers a four-stage schema to assist in the transmission of the ethic itself: model, dialogue, practice, and confirmation. The key for the teacher in employing the ethic of care is a willing and committed entrance into a special relationship with the student. A teacher engaged in this dynamic thus receives not only a student's answers to specific curricular questions, but receives the student (Noddings, 1994).

In relation to the psychology of teaching, when modeling an ethic of care, the teacher shows how to care through the actions the teacher takes in her or his relations and care for others. An antiseptic treatment is not the aim, but rather a clear demonstration that one's own behavior will reveal at the deepest levels what it means to care for and to be cared for by another.

Open-ended conversation where there is no preconceived idea as to the outcome is the basis for dialogue in Noddings's view. It is an invitation to talk about what one tries to model. Dialogue is the premise that links the carer and cared-for in a search for engrossment, or an open nonselective receptivity to the "other." Engrossment is an active attentiveness to the other person in the relationship. When she speaks of dialogue as a "common search for understanding, empathy, or appreciation" (Nodding, 1992, p. 23), with neither party knowing as they begin their conversation what the outcome or decision will be, Noddings builds on the work of Simon Weil in that "the soul empties itself of all its own contents in order to receive into it the being it is looking at, just as he is, in all his truth" (Noddings, 1992, p. 16). It is at his level of engrossment that the maternal images of a mother receiving her child are most clearly articulated. The interaction at this juncture leads the carer to experience motivational displacement: the other's situation so totally encompasses the consciousness of the carer that, at least temporarily, the carer joins with the cared-for in trying to respond to the expressed and/or perceived need of the other.

Experience in and the repetition of caring actions is foundational to the practice of caring. Students, who have been received in a caring manner, should have opportunities to imitate that same behavior, not only in formalized school settings, but also in service work outside of the academic encounter. In working with and caring for others the student participates in actions of caring, along with their adult models, and dialogues with the adults about the rewards and challenges of the work (Noddings, 2002).

Within the field of educational psychology, application and understanding of confirmation in light of care ethics holds transformative possibilities. It is an "act of affirming and encouraging the best in others" (Noddings, 1992, p. 25). It is holding an "other" in such a way as to know them so thoroughly in and through the relationship that a vision to what the person is becoming is made manifest and when identified to the cared-for they recognize it as an epiphany moment: "That is what I was trying to do" (Noddings, 2002, p. 21).

The movement toward adoption of an ethic of care transcends traditional curriculum as is prescribed in standards movements and *No Child Left Behind* politics. Noddings is seeking a new way of teaching children so that children can learn not only skills for occupations, but also more importantly skills for life. An example frequently cited in her work is the topic of homemaking, and while at times in her earlier work it seems to be an idealized version of the nature of home, refined in later discourse, there is much room for discussion about the attributes she ascribes to the task of making a home. Her approach is very much an integrated curricular approach in the model of James Beane, who allows for student and teacher creation of the topic to be studied. Homemaking for Noddings can include many disciplines such as economics, geography, and literature, as well as be multicultural. It can be also be philosophical. What does it mean to "make a home" (Noddings, 2003)? In a society where most students will be homemakers, why not teach them to learn the skills associated with this experience. By extension, she believes that this exploration would also foray into discussion of those who are homeless and what the implications are for those who make the decision that allow for this condition to exist.

Noddings's philosophy informs the field of educational psychology through addressing issues of how to teach and what to teach so that students learn. A large component of the teaching–learning dynamic for Noddings involves the asking of existential questions. How do I live? Is there meaning to life? This approach attempts to reach essential or core desires within the human heart. While oftentimes these questions are presented in theological discourse, Noddings clearly speaks of spiritual encounters, rather than religious ones. In presenting her caring pedagogy, she makes the distinction between specific religious traditions and of an awareness that might be considered spiritual. However, it is interesting that she does see a need to inform students of the various religious traditions as part of their educational process. Oftentimes she speaks of the ability of a math teacher to bring the ideas of some of the great philosophers and mathematicians to the practice of teaching, yet she is adamant that the presentation of religion in the classroom should be from a disinterested point of view, not "I think" but "here are some things people have said about religion" (Halford, 1998, p. 30).

While emphasis on the ethic of care seems not to have made a significant impact on the transformation of the educational milieu, character education has been often presented as a desirable approach to healing the ills of this democratic society, yet who determines the content and the values to be inculcated and transmitted to the students? While oftentimes it is left to the school and/or the governing body of the educational institution, the reality is that many voices are left out of the discussion in even the most homogeneous groupings. The ethic of care as Noddings develops it, is fundamentally relational and is not individual-agent based in the way that character education is conducted in many schools; thus all voices are included when care is the guiding principle of teaching. Care ethicists rely on establishing the conditions and relations that support moral ways of life, not on the inculcation of values in individuals. Character education tends to favor inspirational accounts of individuals achieving some monumental task, while care ethicists utilize multidisciplinary works to present ethical decisions and the sympathies that these arouse (Noddings, 2002).

What are the aims of education? How do schools serve the society? As Noddings continues to develop and refine the ethic of care and her response to character education, she has advanced the consideration that happiness is the aim of education. She acknowledges that happiness is a common goal of the members of this society; hence, it should be an aim of education. While this objective cannot be measured in a strict sense in a society burdened with standards and measurement, happiness, also historically defined as human flourishing, is revealed when children learn to exercise virtues in ways that help to maintain positive relations with others, especially those others who share the aim of caring relationships (Noddings, 2003). Once again then, it is in the caring relationship—carer and cared-for—where the roots of happiness are found.

Relationships with self, the inner circle of friends, distant others, animals, plants, the earth, human-made world, and ideas grounded in an ethic of care (Noddings, 1992), as in the maternal care of a mother for her child, are essential for Noddings in her principles for moral development. Various examples of how this caring relationship reveals holistic appreciation for all aspects of life, including the respect for not only tangible realities but also the principles and ideas that humans hold, are pervasive throughout her work. There is a sense of a refinement over the years for her ethic; however, the essence remains firm and immutable: caring relationships are necessary for the well-being of the members of this postmodern world. While her work appears directed to the teacher and student in the American classroom, following strongly in Deweyian rhetoric, there is an appreciation for holistic concern toward all creation—local and global.

The discipline of educational psychology is dedicated to the study of how children learn and hence by association how teachers teach so that children learn. If Noddings were asked how do children learn, it seems clear that she would state unabashedly, "They learn by the modeling of competent, caring adults who demonstrate that the student is lovable and capable of loving." She would then assert that with dialogue and practice this message would become integral to the cared-for student, so as to be able to wholeheartedly answer in the affirmative, "Yes, I am good, that is exactly what I know about me," to the carer who confirms the goodness of the cared-for. Noddings's work presents many opportunities for an opening of the dialogue as to how students best learn and how to facilitate a movement toward student achievement, which at the core is concerned with an innate respect for the individual, and how they live in society.

REFERENCES

Halford, J. (December 1998–January 1999). Longing for the Sacred in Schools: A Conversation with Nel Noddings. *Educational Leadership*, 56. Retrieved December 7, 2005, from http://www.ascd.org/ed_topics/el199812_halford.html.

Noddings, N. (1984). *Caring: A Feminine Approach to Ethicist Moral Education*. Berkeley, CA: University of California Press.

———. (1992). *The Challenge to Care in Schools: An Alternative Approach to Education*. New York: Teachers College Press.

———. (2002). *Educating Moral People: A Caring Alternative to Character Education*. New York: Teachers College Press.

———. (2003). *Happiness and Education*. New York: Cambridge University Press.

CHAPTER 25

Ivan Petrovich Pavlov

DANIEL E. CHAPMAN

As we study the formalist institution of schools through a postformal lens, it is important to revisit the thinkers who created the theories and influenced changes. One such thinker was a physiologist named Ivan Petrovich Pavlov. Pavlov is famous for his theories on conditioning and, even today, references to "Pavlov's dogs" are common. He was an intriguing scientist because of the paradoxes in his thought and in his work. He won a Nobel Prize for research few people remember and his most famous work he was hesitant to begin. He always identified himself as a physiologist and despised psychologists, yet his legacy has been embraced and carried forth as a part of psychology (at least outside of Russia). Although it would make him turn in his grave, his theory of conditioning may be one of the many influences that helped shift our understanding of the world from formal to postformal.

Ivan Pavlov was born in 1849 to a poor priest in a small Russian town called Ryazan. After high school he enrolled in the local seminary. At that time, under Czar Alexander II, senior students could read progressive magazines and expose themselves to the latest intellectual ideas and scientific discoveries. This was quite liberal under the Czarist social structure. When he left the seminary for St. Petersburg University he was determined to have a career in science.

Pavlov valued empirical research and experimentation for his inquiry into the universe. He did not value reflection, introspection, or interpretation. Like many other formalists, he believed that the human body and brain could be fully understood by breaking the systems down into their parts and observing how they interact. A common metaphor is that of a clock. All the parts interact together to create the functions that make a clock. To Pavlov the human body and brain were nothing more than that and empirical scientific inquiries into these matters were the only inquiries that produced any form of truth.

While Pavlov won a Nobel Prize for his research that went into the book *The Work of Digestive Glands* (1897), it is not as well remembered as his work on conditioning (except by scientists in gastroenterology). Nonetheless, it deserves a few words here. For this research he was looking at the nervous system and how it influenced gastric juices in the stomach. He claimed that the nervous system determined the chemical makeup and the amount of secretion of gastric juices. This was revolutionary because it implied that outside forces could affect these gastric juices, while for the previous two millennia physiologists assumed that "bodily humors" influenced most of the bodily functions.

This research idea entered physiology from an American physician, who had a patient that was shot in the stomach. The physician took this opportunity to observe the internal processes of the stomach under different situations. Influenced by this work, two European scientists attached a tube to a dog's stomach that led gastric juices to a container for closer study. However, if the dog was not eating there were not enough juices produced to study and if the dog was eating the juices and the food were all mixed up making it difficult to study. Pavlov solved this problem by surgically isolating a part of a dog's stomach so no food could enter, while keeping the nerves intact. Attaching a tube to this part of the stomach allowed Pavlov to study the juices without being mixed up with food. Sometimes good science is simply good method and technique.

He noticed during this research, that the dogs would secrete more by just the taste of food in its mouth, before the nervous system, as he understood it, would be involved. This made him theorize that there was a "psychic" element to the secretion of gastric juices. Somehow, the "psyche" was influencing a chemical reaction. He first used the term *conditioned reflex* during this research. (Actually conditional, but this will be explained later.) He found himself drawn to this part of the study, but he was concerned about crossing the physiological–psychological divide. Psychologists of the day were mostly interested in studying consciousness and their methodology was introspection. This appalled Pavlov and he did not want to be associated with this kind of research. After talking with psychologists about how to cross the divide he became frustrated with them. He declared that psychology should really be handled by physiologists and placed within the realm of physiology.

In 1902, a pair of English scientists first discovered hormones and declared that the hormone secretin actually influenced gastric juices. To Pavlov, this brought physiology backwards, back to the days of bodily humors. After watching a friend do an experiment that proved to him secretin influenced gastric juices, he locked himself in his study. An observer recalls that he came out half an hour later and said, "Of course, they are right. It is clear that we did not take out an exclusive patent on the discovery of truth." Later research showed that secretin and the nervous system influence gastric juices, but at the time he felt defeated. This sense of defeat may have been enough to push him away from the nervous system and toward the "psychic" element he observed earlier.

There are four terms that one must become familiar to talk about Pavlov's experiments: conditioned stimulus, unconditioned stimulus, conditioned reflex, and unconditioned reflex. The unconditioned stimulus is a change in the environment that one reacts to predictably without being taught. The reaction is the unconditioned reflex. For instance, one pulls their hand away from a hot stove automatically. The extreme heat on one's hand would be the unconditioned stimulus and pulling one's hand from the hot stove would be the unconditioned reflex. A conditioned stimulus is a change in the environment that one notices, but one does not respond in the same way one responds to the unconditioned stimulus. However, one can be taught to associate the conditioned stimulus with the unconditioned stimulus, and respond in the same way. For instance, one does not pull their hand away just when a light flashes. However, if every time a light flashes one's hand is placed on a hot stove, one would start pulling their hand away as soon as the light flashes. The conditioned reflex would be pulling the hand away when the light flashes. The flashing light would be the conditioned stimulus. Originally, Pavlov used the term *conditional*, not *conditioned*. However, a mistranslation in English has made *conditioned* stick. The word *conditional* makes the point that the reflex is conditional on the appropriate stimulus's being present. Using the term *conditioned* loses this point. But, *conditioned* infers training, teaching, and learning, as in, the reflex has been conditioned in the subject.

Pavlov continued to work with dogs as he did in the digestive gland study. Food was used as the unconditioned stimulus and the salivation was the unconditioned reflex that he studied. He believed that his work applied more generally to many living organisms, including humans, and to other conditioned and unconditioned stimuli. Further research has shown this assumption to be true. It was important to him to control the atmosphere of the laboratory as much as possible. Any distraction could potentially influence the results. The lab had no windows and it was as sound proof as he could achieve. He built a large contraption that would hold the dogs in relatively the same position each time, looking at the same thing each test. Pavlov surgically attached a tube to the dogs' salivary glands, which dripped into a container. With this arrangement he could accurately count the drops of saliva.

To begin his experiments he would first introduce the conditioned stimulus, that is, the ringing of a bell. Then he would introduce the food, the unconditioned stimulus. At first, the dogs would salivate only at the food; however, eventually the dogs would connect the ringing of the bell with the serving of food. They would begin to salivate at the ringing of the bell. The longer they repeated this the more the dog would salivate at the ringing of the bell. Therefore, Pavlov hypothesized, they *learned* that the ringing of the bell meant food. Pavlov was able to empirically show that they *learned* something they had not known before.

After the conditioned reflex was established Pavlov did further experiments. When he took away the unconditioned stimulus, the food, out of the equation, the conditioned reflex would disappear. He called this extinction. The ringing of the bell would produce less and less and eventually no salivation in the dogs. The unconditioned stimulus must be repeated in order to reinforce the connection. The connections established are always temporary and conditional. Repetition was key to maintaining the conditioned state.

Pavlov also studied how timing affects the conditioning process. He showed that the conditioned stimulus must occur before the unconditioned stimulus for the learning process to take place. If the conditioned stimulus is presented after the unconditioned stimulus no conditioning will take place. This is called backward conditioning. For example, if one presents food and then a flash of light, the flash of light will not produce salivation. He also showed that simultaneous presentation of the conditioned stimulus and the unconditioned stimulus will not produce a conditioned reflex. The question of how long beforehand one can present the conditioned stimulus before the unconditioned stimulus is more complex. One can present the conditioned stimulus minutes before the unconditioned and establish a connection, provided that the conditioned stimulus is continuous. For instance, one can ring a bell continuously for five minutes and then serve the food, and the ringing of the bell will produce salivation. If the conditioned stimulus stops minutes before the unconditioned stimulus, it is harder to establish a connection and the connection is weaker. More recently, researchers did a test where they fed a dog and several hours later treated it to make it feel sick. It became difficult to feed the dog the same thing. This showed, at least in certain circumstances, that delayed conditioning does work.

Pavlov also researched how general is the connection between the conditioned stimulus and the unconditioned stimulus and how do these dogs discriminate among different stimuli. So, for instance, if a tone was used as the conditioned stimulus, would a different key, pitch, or volume produce a conditioned reflex? His findings showed that the conditioning was generalized, but the conditioned reflex was not as strong. The more different the stimulus, the less strong was the conditioned reflex. However, the dogs could learn to discriminate between different stimuli. If the tone with a different pitch was not reinforced with the food, the dog would not salivate at that tone, but would still salivate at the original tone. Pavlov's research also showed that the longer the training took place with the original conditioned stimulus, the more the dogs discriminated between different stimuli.

While much of psychology focuses on how subjects respond to present conditions or how they interpret past conditions, Pavlov's research explores how subjects anticipate the future. I would not claim that Pavlov anticipated the future, but as I will explore in the next section, the theory of conditioned learning had profound influences for the rest of the twentieth and into the twenty-first century.

POSTFORMAL REINTERPRETATION

How did the theory of conditioning become attributed to Pavlov? Like most science, his ideas were not new. Materialist philosophers, such as David Hume and John Stuart Mill, speculated about learning theories similar to conditioning well before Pavlov's research. Not to mention that many animal trainers and parents knew about conditioning through their own practice. The idea has been around for millennia, so why has it been firmly attached to Pavlov? What is special or different about the knowledge he produced? I put this question out there as a way into reinterpreting Pavlov through a postformal lens. We will return to it later, but for now speculate on your own about the answers to these questions.

As mentioned earlier, Pavlov privileged empirical observation as a way to produce knowledge; he did not appreciate introspection or interpretation. However, he produced a learning theory that is strictly associative. In other words, he deliberately researched a learning theory that is not deliberate or deliberative at all. He did not study how organisms learn through logic; rather he studied how organisms learn through associations. There are no logical conclusions to be drawn while being conditioned. Rather, temporary connections are made that need continual reinforcement in order to maintain.

Looking at the history of the twentieth century an argument can be made that Pavlovian conditioning has been the most influential teaching and learning tool in America during this time. In this case, I am not referring to what occurs inside the schools of America. Education occurs inside and outside of the school building. Learning includes what we take away from all of our experiences. One experience that most Americans shared, beginning in the early to mid–twentieth century, is an unprecedented amount of exposure to advertising. Modern-day advertising uses conditioning to create associations between products and deep needs most humans have. For instance, beer may be associated to a healthy social life. If we accept that learning happens no matter where we are then we can see that advertising may be the most influential teaching method of the twentieth century. Certainly more money goes to educating people through advertising than on educating people through academic methods.

In the nineteenth century, advertisements addressed people as though they were logical creatures. They introduced the product, explained what it did, and how one could use it. The citizen could read the ad and make a rational decision as to whether they need or want the product advertised. During the 1920s a shift occurred in how companies presented their products through advertisements. Rather than an explanation of the product and what it does, the representations showed the lifestyle of the people who used the products. Sex, wealth, happiness, and success were attached to the products. No longer were people addressed as rational creatures, but they were addressed on an irrational level. They were addressed as creatures that could be conditioned, using deep social needs—acceptance, power, satisfaction—as the unconditioned stimuli. If one thought about it rationally, a certain kind of lipstick, cream, or beverage will not make one wealthy, but conditioning does not require this kind of thought. Knowing that these kinds of connections are temporary, companies follow Pavlov's ideas of repetition, and continually advertise to keep these associations in people's minds. To this day, many Americans are addressed as conditioned creatures more times in our lives than as rational creatures.

Postformal thinking, to some extent, has followed the path of Pavlov's research, but not Pavlov's methodology. Postformal thought values introspection, anecdotes, and reflections as a way to discover knowledge. While postformal thought rejects the privilege of empirical research, it purports to place it equally on the continuum of all ways of knowing. This has led to listening to many voices in many positions, not just those in positions of authority. Being informed by feminists, minorities, homosexuals, immigrants, hunter-gatherers, etc. have led postformal thinkers to believe that people from different positions can use reason and come to different conclusions. What accounts for the difference, in many instances, are the symbolic associations one makes with the world. For instance, the Confederate Flag from one world experience is a symbol of heritage and from another world experience a symbol of hatred. Empirically the Confederate Flag is neither; it is a piece of fabric with specific color patterns. However, people believe it symbolizes deep emotional conflicts and/or needs. Postformal thought asserts that we cannot dismiss symbolic knowledge that has been influenced, perhaps conditioned, by our position, community, and language. If we only pay attention to reason, we run the risk of valuing certain people's reason over others.

In Pavlov's time, the industrial revolution was occurring. Factories and large machines were at the cutting edge of technology, and like computers today, were supposed to be the answer to many of the world's problems. This must have influenced Pavlov's perceptions of the world. The large contraption he built to hold the dogs reflects the value he placed on machines. It certainly influenced Pavlov's perception of humans, he believed them to be like machines. Even his term *reflex* reflects this perception, as in, apply a particular stimulus and a predictable result follows.

However, in some ways, Pavlov's own experiments and conclusions turned against what he valued most. He described learning as an associative, not a logical, process. However, he valued logic and reason and the scientific method. It was only a matter of time after Pavlov's conclusions that someone asked, have we been conditioned to believe in the authority of science? What associations are bound up with science and logic and reason? Playing with those questions can lead one to see that science and reason and logic have many associations that lend it its authority. If a scientist makes a claim, many laypeople assume it to be true. Many politicians make policy according to these claims. Many media outlets report these claims. Words like *statistics*, *logical conclusion*, *reasonable*, or *scientific* are given an authority over words like *fiction* and *feelings* and *anecdotes*.

Thoughtful scrutiny of scientists' claims is often trumped by these associative powers. There are many horrible examples of this in the twentieth century. In America, the eugenics movement asserted that some people should not be allowed to procreate. Many poor and many African American women were sterilized. Some scientists claimed genetic superiority of some people over others, which justified the sterilizations. German scientists produced ideas of racial superiority that justified the Holocaust. European scientists embraced Social Darwinism, which states that certain societies are more evolved than others. This justified rampant European imperialism across the globe. In these cases, feelings and sympathy were a sign of weakness and a distraction from the "empirical truths" of certain superiorities. These ideas were accepted as true, not because they were carefully evaluated, but because the authority figures said they were true. If you were a member of the privileged groups, family members and neighbors repeated these ideas as true. By stating they were true one was praised; by denying their truth one was suspect. All of the loving, caring, trustworthy people in the community said it was true. It appeared as precisely, actually, empirically true. But, it was merely conditioned. It was merely learned.

Let's return to the question that opened up this section, why has Pavlov been given credit for the theory of conditioning when the idea has been around for a long, long time? What was different about Pavlov and the way he displayed the claim to the world? The difference was that he brought it into a scientific laboratory. Rather than relying on observation of animal behavior in context, he took the subjects out of context and tried to isolate and observe the phenomenon within a laboratory. This type of observation had, and still has, a great amount of privilege over other kinds of observation.

As discussed earlier, during Pavlov's life, building large contraptions and performing surgery not only isolated the phenomena under study, but it added symbolic validity to the research. Not only did his contraption have a functional effect of trying to isolate the dog from its surroundings, and not only did surgically attaching the tube isolate the dog's saliva, but there were also associative effects. These associative effects granted his research authority.

This authority does not come from any scrutiny over his truth-claims, but rather because we have been conditioned to accept it as valid. White men with big, bushy beards that don lab coats and have the ability to engineer big contraptions are the only ones we trust to have access to the truth. What Pavlov observed may or may not be true; however, the idea that he, and only he, should be credited with the theory of conditioning is highly suspect. The laboratory, the large contraption, the surgery, the white skin, the male scientist all came together under the right circumstances to grant Pavlov credit with the theory of conditioning.

CHAPTER 26

Jean Piaget

RUPAM SARAN

Jean Piaget, the Swiss biologist and psychologist, was also an educator who inspired the world with his concept of "Piagetian education"—an educational phenomenon that is grounded in developmental psychology and constructivism. The educational implications of his scientific theories have inspired educators and education reformists throughout the civilized world to bring reform in the traditional mode of education. Although he was not an education reformer, he was one of the pioneering scholars whose conception of children's cognitive development influenced education reforms profoundly, in the United States as well as many European nations.

The constructivist tenets in education came to be known after Piaget's work on the cognitive development and knowledge construction of young children. Piaget believed children constructed knowledge by interacting with their environment and learned by "doing," rather than storing knowledge as passive learners. Piaget pressed for an active education for an inquiring mind. He declared that children learn best by trial and error. Thus, the concept of constructivism is attributed to Piaget. He was not an educationist and had never taught in a school setting, but he perceived teaching as an art. It was his belief that "the art of teaching" shaped students' minds, and therefore practitioners of this art must acquire knowledge of their students' minds (Piaget, 1948, 1953). Piaget argued that educators should have a good understanding of developmental psychology.

Until the early 1950s, Piaget's contributions were not fully recognized in the United States. Although in the 1920s and 1930s, his research of children's behavior and child development attracted American scholars, it failed to capture their full attention because his informal work was not considered scientific experimental study. However, in the early 1950s, American psychologists began to take interest in his research and his developmental theories.

Educators were the first ones to embrace Piaget's theories to construct developmentally appropriate curricula and to reform the old ones. Piaget's research set the stage for education reform and child-centered teaching practices in the American education system. His theories about human learning and cognition, children's inner thought process, and children's logic behind their action are the building blocks for those American progressive educational and pedagogical practices that advocate for developmentally appropriate curricula in schools. Piaget's theories of one's learning practices argued for children's active involvement in their own learning. Thus, he initiated those teaching and learning practices that encouraged children's active participation in their acquisition of knowledge and learning.

Jean Piaget's research into the reasoning of elementary school children was a milestone in education research. His theories of learning and knowing influenced the traditional education model that fostered the "banking concept of education" (Freire, 1921–1997), minimized student's creativity, and undermined teacher–student partnership (which perpetuated teacher–student distance in the classroom). The traditional model of education is grounded in passive learning and "storing knowledge" ideology, which prescribes a teacher's role as knowledge giver and a student as a receiver of knowledge. The teacher-centered traditional classroom discourses follow norms of obedience and constraints. In this environment children are treated as objects not capable of constructing knowledge on their own. In such a context, a teacher is the only person respected in the classroom. In the traditional education model, learning takes place in an environment of constraint and in the absence of mutual respect. In the context of learning, teaching, schooling, and adult–child relationships, Piaget advocated for mutual respect and a constraint-free learning environment. Piaget (1932) studied adult–child relationships that were based on constraints in which adults exercised their power and children played a subordinate role. According to Piaget, children did not attain higher levels of understanding of concepts in an adult- or teacher-centered classroom. Consequently, children do not learn in an oppressive learning situation.

BIOGRAPHY

Jean Piaget was born on August 9, 1896, in Neuchatel, Switzerland, in an educated family. Although, as a child, Piaget was interested in biology, later in his life he became interested in philosophy and the application of logic. In 1918, he received his PhD in science. After receiving the PhD he renewed his interest in psychology and studied techniques of psychoanalysis. He worked for a year in psychology laboratories and psychiatric clinics. In 1919 he became interested in intelligence testing and became involved in developing intelligence tests with Binet and Simon. During the 1920s, intelligence testing was a new field. The goal of intelligence testing was to set performance standards for young children by testing them and comparing their test results. Piaget was employed by Binet and Simon to administer tests. During this intelligence testing work, Piaget developed an interest in children's reasoning and thinking strategies. While administering tests he observed children's behavior and concentrated on their logic of thinking, their reasoning abilities rather than their test scores. Piaget regarded intelligence as biological adaptation that occurred at different stages of a child's life by assimilation of objects in children's thought processes. Children used their reasoning power to adapt objects and situations in their environment. In 1921 he published his first article about the psychology of intelligence. His interest in children's thinking strategies led him to work with elementary school children.

To study children's ways of reasoning and ways of knowing, Piaget developed a clinical method that is a fluid way of interviewing children. Piaget investigated the development of children's reasoning power by interacting with them and asking questions. His interview questions were not rigid or structured. The answer to each question determined the nature of the next question. His research method involved both observations and interactions. While studying children he interacted with them, pushing them to his desired interest direction. Thus, Piaget developed the ethnographic qualitative research methodology, which is currently the most popular research method among education researchers.

After his marriage to Valentine in 1923, and the birth of three children, his children became the subject of his research. He wrote three books on the observation of his own children. Before Piaget's study with children, there was not much known about children's thinking. The common belief was that children were not capable of thinking strategies and could not make a connection between action and imagination. In other words, children did things without thinking about the outcomes of their actions.

The year 1940 was very important for his work in experimental psychology. That year he became the chair of the Department of Experimental Psychology. He worked on psychological theories as the director of the Psychology Laboratory and the president of the Swiss Society of Psychology. As a biologist and psychologist, Piaget interconnected his work to both disciplines. By using both disciplines to analyze young children's behavior, Piaget produced the most significant work in the area of child study. By the age of 84, when he died, he had added three major fields to the domain of child psychology. His major theories are developmental psychology, cognitive theory, and genetic epistemology (the study of the development of knowledge).

PIAGET'S THEORY

In the context of children's physical and mental development, Jean Piaget's theory of cognitive development has been enormously influential. Piaget argued that human being's mental or intellectual growth involved major developmental stages and at each stage it went through major changes. The mental development implies the intellectual growth of a child from infancy to adulthood. Although his theory of cognitive development received criticism from many scholars, any given study of children's cognitive growth cannot be completed without considering his ideas about the systematic development of human intellect. Before the emergence of cognitive development theory, the eighteenth-century empiricists did not differentiate between a child's mind and an adult's mind. Nativist scholars of that time also believed that a child's mind and an adult's mind worked alike and differences between the two were insignificant. Piaget was the first scholar who believed that children's way of seeing the world and their reasoning strategies were different from an adult's. He was the first one to study the cognitive development of children's minds, and his theory was the first to suggest that infants and children perceived the world in their own unique ways.

As a biologist, Piaget knew that all organisms survived by adapting to their environment. The adaptation and survival theory of biology influenced his theory of cognitive development. He examined the development of human cognition or intelligences through the lenses of adaptation and survival. To Piaget, the human cognitive development is an organism's constant struggle for survival in an extremely complex environment. His interest in children's thought processes and their way of knowing or acquiring knowledge led him to explore children's minds by observing their adaptation strategies and interacting with them.

Piaget's theory of genetic epistemology is the study of the development of knowledge in human beings. Piaget studied how children stored knowledge, how did they come to know something, how their prior knowledge affected their newly acquired knowledge, and how their way of knowing was different from adults'. Piaget was interested in the epistemology of cognitive development and therefore he explored the epistemological dimension of intelligence progression. He was interested in the process of knowledge development rather than knowledge itself. He defined *genetic epistemology* as the study of the characteristic of knowledge in young children. He investigated how the nature of knowledge acquisition changed as children grew older. He studied children's cognitive development from earliest infancy to the age when they could perform formal operations. As a biologist, he was influenced by the discipline of embryology, which provides an account of the sequential development of a fetus in its mother's womb. Thus the theory of genetic epistemology is a "parallelism" between the development of an embryo and intelligence, and a sequence of construction of individual knowledge and the process of constructing knowledge.

Piaget defined *cognitive development* as a biological and psychological process that involved functions, cognitive structure, and schemes of an individual's mind. Piaget explained *functions* as inborn tendencies that guided individuals to *organize* knowledge in a cognitive structure and to adapt to the challenging environment. The term *organization* implies that all components of a cognitive structure are systematically interconnected and an individual accommodated new knowledge within the existing structure.

Piaget used the term *scheme* to describe the flexible cognitive structure of an infant's mind. As children grow older, their schemes become more individualized, because they learn more skills and gain abilities to differentiate between various activities. An infant uses his sensory skills or schemes to gain more knowledge of the world and accommodates it to the existing knowledge. The term *accommodation* implies fitting new knowledge to existing old knowledge. In other words, *accommodation* means using prior knowledge to learn new things.

Piaget explained cognitive structure as a flexible and interrelated system of knowledge that directs cognition or intelligence. He believed that intelligence is a process of *adaptation* and *assimilation*. As a biologist, Piaget viewed adaptation as a fundamental biological process of survival and believed that all organisms adapted to their environment for survival. In general terms, Piaget used adaptation for learning process. He implied the term *assimilation* to explain the complex process of learning that occurred with the help of prior knowledge. Thus, as new knowledge is added to prior knowledge, the cognitive structure changes. The constant construction of new knowledge activates constant changes in children's cognitive structure. Piaget argued that a stage of *equilibrium* or balance occurred between the cognitive structure of the mind and the new knowledge gained from the environment.

PIAGET'S EQUILIBRATION THEORY AND LEARNING

Piaget's theory of equilibration is about the cognitive balance that a child develops during the learning process. Piaget described four factors that contribute to changes in cognitive development of a child: *maturation*, *physical experiences*, *social experiences*, and *equilibration*. According to Piaget, among all factors that contribute to changes in cognitive development, equilibration is the most important one because it is the balancing factor. Equilibration is the act of self-regulation of cognition in which individuals try to understand environmental challenges physically or mentally and maintain a balance between assimilation and accommodation. According to Piaget, the self-regulating process of equilibration is the motivation to learn. For example, if a student encounters a challenge that he cannot understand or solve immediately, then cognitive conflict arises and disequilibrium appears. The effort to solve the problem with assimilation and accommodation until the problem is understood is the act of equilibration. Equilibration provides students a better level of understanding and enables them to acquire upward mobility. If a child encounters a challenge that he cannot relate to, the challenge is ignored and equilibration does not occur. Thus, the theory of equilibration provides educators insight into the learning process and motivates them to create challenging curriculum and make schooling experiences more interesting for students.

IMPACT OF PIAGETIAN CONSTRUCTIVISM ON EDUCATIONAL PRACTICES

According to the constructivist theory, knowledge is not an object to pass on nor is knowledge something that is separate from the learner. Learners do not receive knowledge passively. They are active participants in meaning making and actively creating their individual knowledge. In the last three decades, emergence of constructivism in education has led those in the educational practices to realize that behaviorist pedagogy had a negative effect on children's learning because it promoted a teacher-centered educational practice and treated children as passive learners. Behaviorism focused on outcome-based teaching, in which teachers provided input and children produced outcome according to what they received. Proponents of behaviorism believed that individuals' cognition developed with conditioning and learning. In contrast, constructivism argued that human beings learned by constructing knowledge.

Piagetian *constructivism* describes the process of learning as knowledge construction rather than knowledge accumulation. According to Piaget, children construct knowledge and transform them to fit to their cognitive structure. For example, in a classroom setting all children may learn the same content but they accommodate it according to their individualistic cognition and prior knowledge. Piaget claimed that children did not reproduce knowledge they received, but rather they constructed knowledge with the help of their prior knowledge. Thus, learning is not merely an act of receiving and reproducing information; it is a complex act of construction and reconstruction of knowledge. It is through the developmental processes of adaptation, assimilation, and accommodation that a child constructs knowledge.

Piaget created the foundation for a constructivist approach of teaching and learning. He claimed that human beings gain knowledge through their experiences and the mechanism of construction and reconstruction of knowledge. Although sociocultural constructivists criticize Piaget for focusing on developmental cognition and neglecting the sociocultural aspect of learning, the importance of Piaget's concept of the individual's vital role in their own learning is undeniable. According to Piaget, all knowledge is rooted in one's prior knowledge and preconceptions. Consequently, learning is assimilation and accommodation of new knowledge into the existing prior knowledge and preconceptions. In the process of constructing knowledge, children interpret new experiences by filtering through old experiences and make meaning of their experiences. In a classroom setting, teachers should create a learning environment that would allow children to construct knowledge. Piaget stressed on activity-based learning.

RELEVANCE OF PIAGETIAN STAGE THEORY OF INTELLIGENCE DEVELOPMENT IN EDUCATION

A biologist, Piaget's concept of cognitive development was influenced by stage theory, which argues that all children reach adulthood by crossing the same stages of cognitive development. According to Piaget, human intelligence develops in four distinct stages: *sensorimotor intelligence*, *preoperational*, *concrete operation*, and *formal operation*. Piaget's stage theory guides educators to create an age-appropriate curriculum to help children learn and gain desired achievement. Although there had been criticism of his stage theory of intelligence development, it has been a very useful framework for educators to construct meaningful pedagogy. Piaget's theory of distinct stages of intelligence growth is one of the major contributions to psychology and education.

The *sensorimotor* stage is the period from birth to two years of one's life. In this period an infant learns about his world through simple interactions with adults and objects. During this period an infant exercises reflexes, develops schemes, discovers procedures for actions, becomes aware of advantages of intentional behavior, benefits of exploration, and gains abilities for mental representation.

The period from two to six years is the *preoperational* stage, in which children learn to investigate their world symbolically and physically. Although during this stage children can do simple problem solving, they cannot perform complex problem solving. Their physical abilities are limited.

During the *concrete operational* period, from age 6 to 11, children gain the abilities to perform mental and logical operations. By this stage, children are able to perform mathematical problems such as adding, subtracting, placing objects in order, and many other operations with concrete objects.

The period of *formal operation* is the final stage of cognitive growth that extends from age 11 to adulthood. This is the higher level of intelligence growth. During this period children can do mental operations, understand abstract concepts, and engage in problem solving using various operations.

Although the stage theory focuses on biological development and does not highlight the social–cultural aspect of learning, it provides a very detailed account of children's competence and limitations at each stage. The understanding of different stages of children's cognitive growth enables educators to gain insight into children's capabilities at each stage of intelligence growth and its effect on learning. At the early childhood level, insights into children's abilities and limits enable a teacher to understand the importance of children's age-appropriate behavior, their symbolic play, and many symbolic functions in the classroom. Piaget described symbolic function as representational behavior or the ability to use an object to represent something. For example, in a classroom if a child uses a plate to represent a boat, his or her action is age-appropriate and the teacher should take it as a normal behavior and view it as a learning process.

Piaget's work on developmental stages of intelligence had a major impact on educational practices. He suggested that development of children's numerical understanding was influenced by their biological development. Much later research supported his argument of mathematical understanding. It made teachers aware of different stages of intelligence and motivated them to embrace teaching methods well suited for children's level of intelligence, their limitations, their cognitive difficulties, and their unique way of learning. Piaget's child makes major progress from the sensorimotor to the preoperational stage. A preoperational egocentric child resists listening to others and tries to cling to his or her perspectives. According to Piaget, egocentrism is not selfishness. It means difficulty understanding other perspectives. According to Piaget, the most common example of egocentrism is children's speech. Very often, young children act as if they know everything and do not listen to adults. A three- or four-year-old egocentric child will get into a fight or act stubborn because he or she cannot understand the other perspective. Thus, Piaget viewed egocentrism as a biological limitation of the preoperational stage. In a classroom situation, understanding the egocentric behavior of a preoperational child as a biological limitation may enable teachers to eliminate frustrations for both teacher and children by handling egocentric perspectives tactfully.

Piaget's stage theory maintains that learning is sequential and each stage of learning occurs with the mastery of the previous stage, and the cognitive structure of each stage determines children's behavior and their performance. Children at the concrete and formal operational stages can perform complex academic tasks, and they need a challenging curriculum to provide problem-solving opportunities.

EDUCATIONAL IMPLICATIONS OF PIAGET'S THEORIES

Piaget's theory has profound implications for educational practices. He argued that children did not learn by listening to their teachers or watching their teachers doing things; rather they learned by exploring themselves. Piaget as a biologist, as a psychologist, as a philosopher, and as an epistemologist contributed to every aspect of education. He emphasized on readiness or age-appropriateness. Children assimilated experiences in their cognitive structure only when experiences could fit into existing schemes. If the teaching method curriculum is not age-appropriate and children are not ready for the content or teaching strategies they will not learn in the absence of equilibration.

If the content matter presented to students is too complicated or too simple, there will be no cognitive balance. The content matter should be challenging but accessible, so that students can be motivated to assimilate new knowledge and challenged to solve disequilibrium. Piaget stressed different levels of cognitive development and provided information on children's competence and limitation at different levels of development. This enables teachers to understand the intelligence level of their students and to create learning environments suited to each stage and level of development. Piaget disapproved of passive learning and stressed that children should invent knowledge by being involved in their own learning. According to him, the role of a teacher should be that of an encourager and facilitator of learning. Teachers and educators should create an environment for active participation and learning.

REFERENCE

Piaget, J. (1953). *The Origins of Intelligence in Children*. London: Routledge and Kegan Paul.

CHAPTER 27

Carl Rogers

ANGELINA VOLPE SCHALK

Carl Rogers (1902–1987) made significant contributions to the fields of psychotherapy and educational psychology. At one point during his career, as a university professor, published scholar, and clinical psychologist, Rogers was considered to be the Psychologist of America. He was consulted on myriad issues and his concepts were so widely accepted that some are now thought to be commonplace. The main hypothesis postulated by Rogers, as stated by Peter Kramer (1995) in *On Becoming a Person*, is summarized in a single sentence, "If I can provide a certain type of relationship, the other will discover within himself the capacity to use that relationship for growth, and change and personal development will occur." The implications of his hypothesis are widespread and still relevant today.

Rogers believed that human beings possess an innate goodness that is only altered when traumatized in some way; therefore, counseling was presented as beneficial for routine self-maintenance and as-needed repair. While scholars within and outside of his field have criticized Rogers for a naïve and oversimplified view of both human nature and the role of therapy, numerous others hold him in high regard for his simple, strong contributions to the field. Clearly, whether one is pro-Rogers or not, he made a great impact on the field, given the volume of discussion surrounding his theories. Rogers himself questioned whether he had been hurt more by his enemies or well-meaning friends who have misrepresented his work (Rogers, 1961).

Rogers wrote for a small, selective audience, for those who view individuals as human beings, not objects to be observed or repaired. He wrote for wives, neighbors, friends, and professionals; that is, he wrote for common people and educated people alike, because he believed that all people could benefit from his thoughts. His works are clear and articulate, with a far-reaching appeal. The basis for his theories stemmed from his personal experiences and upbringing, which helped shape the man and his outlook on life.

Carl Rogers was the fourth of six children in a very close-knit and religious family. Rogers's parents instilled strict religious, ethical, and moral values in their children and stressed personal discipline while demonstrating their love and concern. His mother was a housewife and his father was a very successful engineer. His father was so successful that he was able to move his family to a farm away from the undesirable distractions of city life when Rogers was twelve. While on the farm, Rogers developed his love of science and blossomed as an observer of nature and people.

Rogers credits his parents' respect for knowledge and learning, as well as his own love of reading, for his early introduction to and deep involvement with Morison's *Feeds and Feedings*. This book exposed Rogers to experimentation, control groups, hypotheses, and scientific observation and laid the foundation for his adulthood academic passions.

Rogers initially studied agriculture at college in Wisconsin, due in part to his adolescence on the farm. During his junior year, however, he had an opportunity to travel abroad. This experience turned out to be life altering for Rogers. While in China for the international World Student Christian Federation Conference, Rogers was exposed to new ideas and a variety of people, without the stifling thoughts of his parents to limit him. Rogers claimed that he felt emancipated and finally felt free to let his imagination run wild, which enabled him to become a fuller, more independent person. His newfound independence did have a price, as his parents, especially his father, was disappointed and distant for quite some time after his return to America. During this period of his life, Rogers met and married his wife, so that they could attend graduate school together.

Carl Rogers credits his wife for much of his personal and professional growth, as she served as an unwavering and nonjudgmental sounding board and support throughout his life. Rogers began his graduate work at the Union Theological Seminary, where he realized that he did not want to work in a field that required him to settle on his ideas and maintain them, stagnantly, throughout his lifetime, in order to excel professionally. He then started to take courses at the nearby Teachers' College, Columbia University, and began to study and work in the field of child psychology. Around this time, Rogers and his wife began a family, which required that Rogers begin to look for a job; therefore, on completion of his graduate work, Rogers worked as a psychologist in Rochester, New York, for the Child Study Department of the Society for the Prevention of Cruelty to Children. During his twelve years at Rochester, Rogers had three significant experiences that influenced and reshaped his view of psychology and therapy. First, Rogers worked with a client who was not cured, even after they discovered the root cause of his disturbance. This realization led Rogers to recognize that authoritative teachings might not be absolute and that new knowledge was still ripe for the picking, even by him. Second, Rogers revisited an interview that he had conducted and held up as an exemplar early in his career only to realize that his methods of questioning had steered the interviewee's answers. This realization led Rogers to move away from coercive approaches in clinical relationships. Lastly, Rogers worked with a client's mother individually, after an unsuccessful run at working with the initial client, the son, and discovered that the therapist should not guide the sessions. Specifically, Rogers realized that therapeutically there was no need for him to shine; given that people inherently know what they need, he simply needed to listen and allow the client to guide the processes' movement. All of these insights, especially the last, helped Carl Rogers form his view of client-centered therapy.

Client-centered, or nondirective, therapy as espoused by Carl Rogers is an intensive, extensive, safe, and deep relationship between a therapist and a client, based on mutual trust, openness, and a willingness to not judge, but simply to listen and be guided by the client's revelations and growing humanity. He wrote *Clinical Treatment of the Problem Child* at this time, which was based on his ideas and his work with problem children in Rochester. Rogers started the initial development of client-centered therapy when he was in Rochester. While in Ohio, he began to recognize and to fully own the notion that he was capable of his own thoughts and theories and had, in fact, the credibility to share his knowledge with others. During this time, he wrote another book, *Counseling and Psychotherapy*, and continued to write seminal works for the field of psychotherapy when he moved to the University of Chicago and then the University of Wisconsin.

Carl Rogers's greatest contribution to the field of psychotherapy, and by association the field of educational psychology, was client-centered therapy. A therapist must have three qualities deemed by Rogers to be essential: congruence, empathic understanding, and unconditional positive regard. Congruence occurs when the therapist exists openly and availably to herself and the client, without façade, and responds honestly without playing a role. Unconditional positive regard requires the therapist to care for the client in a total, nonpossessive, and nonjudgmental way. Lastly, empathic understanding occurs when the therapist perceives the client's thoughts and feelings as if they were her own and accurately communicates all or part of this awareness to the client. Furthermore, this understanding occurs in light of the two previous elements, so the understanding is total and without judgment.

Rogers outlined conditions for learning, based on client-centered therapy, in several of his writings. Client-centered therapy calls for a nonjudgmental relationship between the therapist and the client and, when the aforementioned elements necessary for therapy to occur are present, both the client and the therapist grow. Rogers claims that in particular the client develops and changes in constructive ways. Similarly, Rogers posits that teachers and students should have an open, safe, and responsive relationship in order to foster greater individual and collective growth. Rogers uses the term changiness, meaning "a reliance on process rather than static knowledge," which supports his goal of education, that is, "the facilitation of change and learning" (Kirschenbaum and Henderson, 1989, p. 304).

In relation to educational psychology, educators should keep it real, according to Carl Rogers, and not don masks when interacting with students. Just as clients respond to therapists' true humanity, students will respond to their teachers' honesty and transparency. Students recognize their teachers' human self and respond in kind by exposing their true human selves and blossoming in the process. Rogers recognizes the difficulty in being real and trying to facilitate learning, especially in an academic environment that prefers obedience, distance, and knowledge transmission. Teachers who facilitate learning in their students through their authenticity also display another attitude expressed by Rogers as *prizing*, *accepting*, and *trusting* students in a nonpossessive caring fashion that avoids judgment (Kirschenbaum and Henderson, 1989). As clients communicate better with therapists when nonjudgmental support is evident, students relate to teachers who accept the good, the bad, and the difficult without casting judgment. Empathic understanding is another element that establishes clearer communication, facilitates self-initiated learning, and supports experimentation and growth. There is a profound difference between expressing oneself and doing so honestly. In order to keep it real, the teacher, similar to the therapist, must first accept herself unconditionally, as she will come to accept her students.

Essentially, Carl Rogers recommends that students are viewed as human beings in need of assistance and support to develop fully. As outlined previously, Rogers recommends that the following elements be in place to support the full development of students: prizing, accepting, and trusting. As Rogers (1989) states,

The "facilitative conditions" studied make a profound change in the power relationships of the educational setting. To respect and prize the student, to understand what the student's school experience means to her and to be a real human being in relation to the pupil is to move the school a long way from its authoritative stance. These conditions make of the classroom a human, interactive situation, with much more emphasis upon the student as the important figure who is responsible for the evaluation of her own experience. (p. 330)

Carl Rogers's focus for education models his focus for therapy and his approach to fostering general human development. Rogers calls upon therapists and educators to examine and know themselves in order to know others better. And, when therapists and educators truly engage with others, then change will occur and both parties have a greater chance of reaching their innate potential.

Carl Rogers wanted the field of education to move beyond its stagnant beliefs concerning the transfer of knowledge, and to transform itself from an institution that views educators as teachers who teach at an institution that supports facilitators of learning. Rogers spent a great deal of time in his later years writing on and peaking about the politics involved with education and the need to change. Top-down authority and control are the norm in education to this day, which is exactly what Rogers was fighting against. Rogers promoted shared decision making and student-directed learning. Through facilitated learning, Rogers believed that real knowledge and the skills necessary to grow fully as a human being could develop. The ideas postulated by Carl Rogers are similar in spirit to the ideas promoted by John Dewey, Lev Vygotsky, and other constructivists. In fact, if Carl Rogers's principles of congruence, empathic understanding, and unconditional positive regard were applied today, then society might see a greater realization of *Brown v. Board of Education* and the Individuals with Disabilities Education Act.

Carl Rogers made a significant contribution to the fields of psychotherapy and educational psychology. Through his beliefs and his works, Rogers developed clear and applicable guidelines for open, responsive communication. His simple, strong contributions to the field of education stemmed directly from his client-centered therapy approach. Rogers called upon educators to view themselves as facilitators of learning and to consider their students as other human beings on the same journey: to become more fully human.

REFERENCES

Kirschenbaum, H., and Henderson, V. L. (Eds.). (1989). *The Carl Rogers Reader*. New York: Houghton Mifflin.

———. (1989). *Carl Rogers Dialogues*. New York: Houghton Mifflin.

Kramer, P. (1995). Introduction. In C. Rogers (Ed.), *On Becoming a Person; A Therapist's View of Psychotherapy* (pp. ix–xvi). New York: Houghton Mifflin.

Rogers, C. (1961). *On Becoming a Person; A Therapist's View of Psychotherapy*. Boston: Houghton Mifflin.

———. (1989). *On Becoming a Person* (Rev. ed.). Boston: Houghton Mifflin.

SUGGESTED READING

Rogers, C. (1994). *Freedom to Learn* (Rev. ed.). Upper Saddle River: Prentice Hall.

CHAPTER 28

B. F. Skinner

KEVIN CLAPANO

B.F. Skinner's (1904–1990) operant conditioning theory and his approaches to the study of behavior have made significant contributions to a broad range of applied settings and disciplines. However, the contributions that operant conditioning has had on educational psychology through the development of teaching machines, programmed learning material, and the application of reinforcement stimulus concepts in classroom management is the most extensive.

Burrhus Frederic Skinner was born on March 20, 1904, in Susquehanna, Pennsylvania. Skinner's home setting is often described as a warm and stable environment. His father was a small-town lawyer and his mother a housewife. Skinner's childhood is characterized as spent on building and inventing things and actually enjoying school. Skinner built steerable wagons, sleds, and rafts. He made seesaws, slides, and merry-go-rounds. He made model airplanes powered by twisted rubber bands, tin propellers, and box kites that could be sent high into the air with a spool-and-string spinner. Skinner also invented things. Most college students are now familiar with the flotation system that Skinner built for separating ripe from green berries that helped him and his friend sell elderberries. For years, Skinner also worked on designing a perpetual motion machine that never worked. This truly provides a good insight into the childhood of the subsequent inventor of the cumulative recorder, the *air crib*, and the man who began the teaching machine and programmed instructions movement (Vargas, n.d.).

B. F. Skinner attended Hamilton College as an undergraduate where he majored in English. After receiving his bachelor of arts degree from Hamilton College, Skinner decided to become a writer. Encouraged by a letter from Robert Frost appraising his work, Skinner dedicated a year of his life to pursuing a career in creative writing. Skinner moved back to Susquehanna, Pennsylvania, but wrote very little. After a brief amount of time spent in New York's Greenwich Village and in Europe he gave up writing. While working in New York City as a bookstore clerk, Skinner happened upon books by Pavlov and Watson. Reading these works eventually left Skinner wanting to learn more.

B. F. Skinner enrolled in the Psychology Department of Harvard University at the age of twenty-four. Although Skinner considered his ideas to be mostly uninteresting, the stimulating and informal environment of Harvard gave Skinner the opportunity to grow and the freedom to not follow the path of any particular faculty member. Skinner received his PhD in 1931 and spent five postdoctoral years working in William J. Crozier's laboratory. Crozier, who was an experimental biologist, had a major influence on Skinner's philosophy and behavioristic position. Crozier, in contrast to psychologists who focused on studying the processes going on inside an organism, passionately believed in studying the behavior of an organism as a whole. This was the philosophy that paralleled Skinner's goal of relating an organism's behavior to experimental conditions.

In 1936, Skinner joined the faculty of the University of Minnesota. Skinner's tenure at the University of Minnesota can be characterized as remarkably productive wherein he was heavily engaged in scientific inquiry yet found the time to write a novel entitled *Walden Two*. Skinner stayed at the University of Minnesota for nine years, had a two-year stay at Indiana University as Chair of Psychology, and eventually returned to Harvard, where he remained for the rest of his life.

SKINNER'S DEVELOPMENT OF OPERANT CONDITIONING

Skinner remained consistent in his philosophy that the organism must literally operate upon its environment. This is in total contrast to Pavlovian conditioning, where the organism plays a very passive role. Furthermore, Skinner believed that antecedent events need to be considered when studying an organism's behavior and that an organism's behavior can be controlled by systematically manipulating the environment in which the organism is operating. These comprise the foundation of B.F. Skinner's operant conditioning theory.

As the organism operates in its environment, it encounters a unique type of stimulus that increases the organism's response. In operant conditioning theory, a stimulus that increases the likelihood of the organism's response is called a reinforcement or a reinforcer. Hulse et al. (1980) formally defined a reinforcer as a "stimulus event which, if it occurs in the proper temporal relation with a response, tends to maintain or to increase the strength of a response or of a stimulus-response connection" (p. 18). In contrast to a reinforcing stimulus or a reinforcer, an organism operating in its environment can also be exposed to unique types of stimuli that decrease the organism's response. A stimulus that decreases the likelihood of the organism's response is referred to as aversive stimuli.

It is worth noting that operant conditioning is also called instrumental conditioning because the organism plays an instrumental role in developing the stimulus–response connection. This can be best explained by thinking of an experiment involving a rat in a box. In the box, known as a Skinner box, is a lever that when depressed delivers a food pellet into the box. The rat is operating in its environment and accidentally depresses the lever. A food pellet is then delivered into the box. In time, the rat will vigorously depress the lever to get more food pellets. Let us now examine the experiment through the operant conditioning theory. The rat (the organism) is operating in the box (the environment) and accidentally depresses the lever (operant response) and receives a food pellet (reinforcing stimulus). The rat then depresses the lever vigorously (increase in response) to receive more food pellets (reinforcing stimulus). This stimulus–response connection is established over time and this series of stimulus–response connections is considered as behavior. One can then ask, what if the reinforcing stimulus (i.e., the food pellet) is no longer delivered? Over time, the rat will stop the lever-pressing response because the reinforcing stimulus is no longer available. It could be said that the behavior has been extinguished. In the operant conditioning theory, this phenomenon is called extinction.

While engaged in heavy operant conditioning experimentation, Skinner ran low on food pellets so he had to reduce the number of food pellets that were given to the rats as reinforcement. Interestingly, even though the rats received less reinforcement, the operant behavior continued to be exhibited over a period of time. This led Skinner to the discovery of the schedule of reinforcement.

There are primarily four types of reinforcement schedules: (a) fixed-interval (FI), (b) fixed-ratio (FR), (c) variable-interval (VI), and (d) variable-ratio (VR). In FI reinforcement, organisms are given or exposed to reinforcement stimulus on a fixed time schedule. When an organism becomes conditioned to an FI schedule of reinforcement, its behavior becomes stable. The general rule with FI reinforcement is that an organism's rate of responding is inversely proportional to the interval between reinforcements. In this type of reinforcement schedule, organisms learn that responses early in the interval are never reinforced immediately and organisms will tend to pace the responses and "pile up" its responses toward the end of the interval. In an FR schedule, the reinforcement stimulus is provided after a fixed number of responses have been exhibited by the organism. With this schedule, the organism learns that rapid responding is important. There is a direct correlation between the rate of responding and the rate of reinforcement, that is, the higher the rate of responding the higher the rate of reinforcement. In a VI reinforcement schedule, time is a critical factor. After an organism has learned a particular response, the amount of time it takes for the next reinforcement stimulus to be presented keeps changing. It will not be possible for an organism to learn the time interval accurately. Organisms tend to respond at an extremely stable rate under the VI schedule. In a VR reinforcement schedule, an organism is given the reinforcement stimulus after a different number of responses have been exhibited. In short, variable number of responses is required to produce successive reinforcers. Reinforcing well-learned behaviors on a VR schedule generate extraordinarily high rates of performance.

An overview of operant conditioning has been presented. Behavior, which is a series of stimulus–response connections, is followed by a consequence, and the nature of the consequence (e.g., presence or absence of reinforcing stimulus) modifies the organism's tendency to exhibit or inhibit the behavior in the future.

OPERANT CONDITIONING APPLIED TO EDUCATIONAL PSYCHOLOGY

Most biographical accounts of B.F. Skinner suggest that Skinner's interest in educational psychology began on that fateful day of November 11, 1953, Father's Day, when Skinner visited his daughter's fourth-grade arithmetic class. While sitting at the back of his daughter's classroom, Skinner observed that the students were not receiving prompt feedback or reinforcement from their teacher and were all moving at the same pace despite differences in ability and preparation. Skinner had researched delay of reinforcement and knew how it hampered performance. If mathematical-problem-solving behavior is perceived as a complex series of stimulus–response connections that had to be effectively established, then the teacher in Skinner's daughter's fourth-grade arithmetic class definitely needed help. It was simply impossible for the teacher with twenty or thirty children to shape mathematical-problem-solving behavior in each student. In operant conditioning theory, the concept of shaping requires that the best response of the organism be immediately reinforced. In the math class, however, some of the students had no idea of how to solve the problems, while other students breezed through the exercise and learned nothing new. Furthermore, the children did not find out if one problem was correct before doing the next problem. They had to answer a whole page before getting any feedback, and then probably not until the next day.

That afternoon, Skinner constructed his first teaching machine. The first teaching machine that was developed by Skinner was a device that presented problems to learners in random order. This machine simply practiced and rehearsed skills or behaviors already learned. Learners did not learn any new responses or new behaviors. A few years later Skinner developed and incorporated programmed instruction into the learning machines. Learners would respond to content to be learned that were broken down into small steps. The first responses of each content sequence were prompted but as the learner's performance improved less help was provided. In the end, a learner would have acquired new behavior.

Skinner's concept of reinforcement stimulus paved the way for the development of programmed instruction and outcome-oriented instruction in today's institutions of learning. The influence of programmed instruction is still affecting the teaching technologies used in today's society. Today's instructional designers are still using Skinner's operant conditioning concepts to create courses that contain measurable behavioral objectives. In addition, traditional instructor-led, computer-based, and online courses are being built based on the concepts of small frames of instruction, immediate feedback regardless of correctness of the response, self-pacing, and learner's response to knowledge checks. In addition, instructional designers are also designing knowledge checks so learners compose their answers rather than selecting answers from a set of choices. Instructional designers creating online courses are also starting to realize that course lessons, modules, and topics must do more than present blocks of content with quizzes or tests at the end of the instruction sequence. Depending on operant conditioning, the sequencing of steps is also very critical and is an important factor to consider in designing online courses. Furthermore, if instruction is to be effective, learners should be required to respond to what each screen of information presents and to get feedback on their performance before advancing to the next level of the course. Skinner strongly cautioned against technology that merely presents information to the learner. Teachers must be aware of their teaching strategies so that the learner or the student is not merely a passive receiver of instruction but an active participant in the instructional process. This concept helped in shifting education's focus to the outcome behavior of the learner.

Aside from the influence of programmed instructions, Skinner's operant conditioning concepts have been applied in classroom management. Hall and Lindzey (1978) have referred to token economies that have been used extensively in classroom settings with such populations as normal children, delinquents, and severely retarded children. When students exhibit proper classroom behaviors like completing assignments, paying attention, and not being late for class, tokens can be awarded. These tokens can be later exchanged for whatever reinforcement stimulus a particular student happens to value, whether they are in the form of food, movies, or periods of free play. In the classroom setting, the systematic and skillful use of reinforcement stimulus can produce beneficial and dramatic behavioral changes in students.

Skinner (1968), in his book *The Technology of Teaching*, described the modern classroom as particularly averse to learning and discussed behaviors in school administration and organization that were not conducive to learning. These behaviors that Skinner referred to were (a) the infrequency of reinforcement, (b) the lapse between response and reinforcement, (c) the aversive stimulation, and (d) the lack of a long series of contingencies for desired behaviors. To offset these behaviors, teachers must learn to use multiple stimulus control techniques. The other concepts that Skinner believed could aid teachers in helping students learn were the use of modeling, shaping, priming, and prompting. Skinner opined that if teachers already had a broad range of teaching strategies and tactics, then they would always look for additional elements and tools to add to the intellectual and practical repertory. Teachers can be trained to view teaching as a process that can be broken down into progressive stages with reinforcements following each stage. However, the classroom setting provides numerous variables and contingencies that teachers cannot realistically arrange. Despite this limitation, Skinner believed that operant conditioning could still provide the means necessary to effectively control human learning by building complex responses out of many simple responses and associating reinforcement closely in time with the response to be learned.

Skinner saw the world through the lens of operant reinforcement theory and through the eyes of a behaviorist. Skinner was a modernist and a believer in the value of a molecular approach to the study of behavior. He searched for simple elements of behavior to study, and he was certain that the whole is no more than the sum of its parts. Skinner's approach, as with most modernists, was both scientific and reductionistic. What distinguished Skinner from the average experimental psychologist was his ability to study behavior in its complex natural settings and to devise and build technological equipment. Skinner almost immediately saw the relevance and interaction of major concepts and principles using his theoretical position. In addition, Skinner was a master at being able to combine elegant laboratory techniques and precise experimental control with the study of individual subjects. This truly represents a unique achievement. In a discipline where generalization of findings to a group is highly valued, Skinner's results were often reported in terms of individual records. Skinner emphasized the importance of studying individuals in detail and stating laws that apply fully to single subjects instead of only to group data. Furthermore, Skinner's findings were reported with a degree of lawfulness and precise regularity that is unequaled among behaviorists. Through the lens of an action researcher, B.F. Skinner can be viewed as a creative teacher who tried to improve his students' learning through the use of a systematic process while avoiding the use of aversive stimuli and punishment.

Burrhus Frederic Skinner is the most important American psychologist of the twentieth century. His theoretical influence is arguably one of the most important since Sigmund Freud. B.F. Skinner passed away on August 18, 1990. Teaching and instructional methods based on the basic elements of Skinner's operant conditioning theory and approaches to learning are still commonplace in educational systems ranging from preschool settings to institutions of higher learning.

REFERENCES

Hall, C. S., and Lindzey, G. (1978). *Theories of Personality* (3rd ed.). New York: John Wiley and Sons.
Hulse, S. H., Deese, J., and Egeth, H. (1958). *The Psychology of Learning* (4th ed.). New York: McGraw-Hill.
Skinner, B. F. (1968). *Technology of Teaching*. New York: Appleton Century Crofts.
Vargas, J. S. (n.d.). *Brief Biography of B. F. Skinner*. Retrieved December 11, 2005, from http://www.bfskinner.org/bio.asp.

CHAPTER 29

Robert J. Sternberg

KECIA HAYES

In 1949 in Newark, New Jersey, Robert J. Sternberg was born into a working-class family. The contemporary educational experiences of many urban students is reminiscent of Sternberg's elementary and middle school years in that he consistently performed poorly on IQ tests that were widely used by the educational establishment during that era. Influenced by the results of his IQ tests, most of Sternberg's teachers held low academic expectations of him. While pedagogically problematic, this situation spurred Sternberg to immerse himself in the study of human intelligence. As early as the seventh grade, he created his own mental abilities test, Sternberg Test of Mental Abilities (STOMA), as a science project. Upon entering Yale University for his undergraduate studies, Sternberg was committed to declaring psychology as his major field of study. He graduated from Yale with honors, with exceptional distinction in psychology as well as summa cum laude and Phi Beta Kappa. After Yale, Sternberg headed to Stanford University, where he obtained his PhD under the tutelage of Gordon Bower, and began to develop his ideas for componential analysis. Sternberg joined the faculty of Yale University in 1975 and still remains there now. He is a prolific researcher and scholar, having written more than 500 articles, books, and book chapters to date.

Throughout the 1980s, there was a rise in Multiple Intelligence research that focused on the mental processing that undergirds an individual's abilities and talents, which represented a shift from a focus on the identification of specific skill sets and intelligences. Sternberg emerged as one of the main theorists advocating this approach. He fundamentally changes the discourse on Multiple Intelligences with his conceptualization of a Triarchic Theory of Human Intelligence which centralizes the idea that intelligence is contextualized within individuals' relationships to their internal worlds, external worlds, and experiences. Sternberg defines intelligence as "the mental capability of emitting contextually appropriate behavior at those regions in the experiential continuum that involve response to novelty or automatization of information processing as a function of metacomponents, performance components, and knowledge-acquisition components" (Sternberg, 1985). In addition, unlike some other theorists of intelligence, Sternberg acknowledges that there is an interaction between people's social environment and their development of intelligence: "Intelligence is in part a production of socialization – the way a person is brought up" (Sternberg, 1988). Within the framework of this definition, Sternberg conceptualizes intelligence through three fundamental subtheories, including the contextual, componential, and experiential, as he structures his Triarchic Theory of Intelligence. The componential focuses on the relation of intelligence to the internal world, the experiential addresses the varying levels of experience in task performance, and the contextual suggests that information processing is applied to experience in order to achieve one of the three broad goals of environmental adaptation, change, or selection.

Within each subtheory, there are specific mental-processing components. For the componential subtheory, there are metacomponents, performance components, and knowledge acquisition components. Metacomponents relate to recognizing the existence of a problem, assessing the nature of the problem, selecting and organizing the lower-order mental processes to solve the problem, implementing and monitoring the problem-solving mental strategy, judiciously soliciting external feedback, and evaluating the problem-solving process. The performance components refer to the lower-order mental processes that are activated to fulfill the instructions of the metacomponents. The knowledge acquisition components learn what is needed for the metacomponents and performance components to eventually fulfill their tasks. It engages the mental processes of selective encoding, which involves determining relevant from irrelevant information; selective combination, which requires that seemingly isolated pieces of information are merged into a useful whole that may or may not resemble the original parts; and selective comparison, which entails the connection of newly acquired information to previously acquired information. According to Sternberg, the problem-solving approach related to the componential framework is analytical, which reflects those skills used to analyze, judge, evaluate, compare, or contrast. This paradigm is most consistent with the traditional psychometric conceptualizations and measures of intelligence.

The experiential subtheory addresses intelligence from the perspective of whether a task or situation is relatively novel or in the process of automatization or habituation. Assessing intelligence as a function of task novelty is an essential element of Sternberg's theory because he believes that intelligence is not only demonstrated in the ability to learn and reason with new ideas but to do so within new conceptual models. It is not sufficient to grow within a particular conceptual system with which one is familiar but to expand one's learning and reasoning across conceptual systems that may be somewhat or completely unfamiliar. For Sternberg, the intelligent person is the one who can not only apply existing knowledge to new situations in order to achieve a particular goal but also more readily move from conscious efforts to learn a new task to an automatization of the new learning. The problem-solving approach associated with this subtheory is the creative, which includes skills used to create, invent, discover, imagine, or suppose.

The contextual subtheory conceptualizes intelligence as mental activity to achieve one or more of three particular goals, including environmental adaptation, shaping of environment, or environment selection. The focus of this subtheory is not with the specific behavior or the external forces that facilitate or impede the contextualized activity but rather with the specific mental activities utilized to select and attain a particular goal. Within this paradigm, Sternberg concentrates on assessing intelligence as a function of how individuals engage their real-world everyday external environments. Sternberg seeks to recognize that socialization has an impact on how individuals determine which goal is appropriate and how they then work to achieve the particular goal. In terms of a problem-solving approach, practical abilities, represented by skills used to apply, put into practice, implement, or use, are characteristic of the contextual subtheory. While this framework is often considered in terms of possessing "street smartness," it is more significantly about an individual's purposive adaptation to her real-world environment in order to achieve particular goals.

Sternberg's Triarchic Theory of Intelligence has been described as the model that synthesizes the paradigms of intelligence that preceded it. While this is a fair assessment, it falls short of indicating the extent to which Sternberg expanded our conceptualizations of not only how to define and measure intelligence but also how to educate for intelligence. Through its recognition of a pluralistic configuration of intelligence, Sternberg's framework allows for multiple points of entry to develop intelligence because it centralizes the idea that individuals deploy various abilities to navigate through their worlds. Consequently, people need to be educated to strengthen their abilities across the three different problem-solving domains so that they can leverage the full range of their intelligence. Unfortunately, our systems of education have not been structured to utilize this approach. Students "are being taught by methods that fit poorly with their pattern of abilities. As a result, they are not learning or they learn at minimal levels. At the same time, they and their teachers are concluding that they lack vital learning abilities. In fact, many of them have impressive learning abilities but not the kind that are used in the methods of teaching to which they are exposed. As a result, they never reach the high levels of learning that are possible for them" (Sternberg and Williams, 1998).

Our educational approaches tend to be imbued with a unilateral focus on the development of students' analytical abilities. "By the time students reach adolescence, their experiences with reading materials and practices in school have taught them to dislike schooled literacy activities. Bean cites studies that point to how adolescents dichotomize reading in school, which they often view as boring and irrelevant, and reading outside of school, which they often view as useful and enjoyable" (Alvermann et al., 1998). Rose makes the point that the ways in which we currently and predominantly teach literacy dissects language from its daily usage, which can be problematic for some students (Rose, 1989). Within this context, individuals are presented with problem-solving scenarios that are structured by others, and with informational parameters, which have one specifically appropriate methodology that will yield the only correct solution. Such problems tend to be devoid of a connectivity to the real world of the student, which only helps to minimize the student's intrinsic interest in engaging in the process of solving the problem. "The abilities emphasized in formal schooling have limited value if they cannot be used to address practical, everyday problems" (Sternberg et al., 2000).

Sternberg's model of intelligence dictates that we need not only teach to develop the analytical but to also develop the creative and practical abilities. In doing so, we would present students with practical problem-solving scenarios that are not fully structured and predefined by an external source, lack the necessary information to achieve resolution, and have multiple possible methodologies to achieve a variety of appropriate solutions. The process of problem solving and learning would force the learner to utilize a larger range of their abilities that exist outside of the realm of the analytical. Using practical abilities to solve a practical problem presented within the academic sphere will be more meaningful for students.

In addition, through its rejection of a compartmentalization of knowledges and skills, focus on the development of practical abilities, and acknowledgement that intelligence has a sociocultural context, the Triachic Theory of Intelligence provides educators with a landscape to integrate students' indigenous knowledges into the learning process. As they facilitate an educational approach that connects the learning process and the lived real-world experiences of their students, educators can further expand the work of Sternberg. Because practical problem-solving scenarios tend to be related to everyday experiences as well as involve the need for students to reformulate problems and acquire information to achieve resolution, there is an opportunity for students to begin to incorporate the indigenous knowledge that inform their real-world experiences into their problem-solving process. Furthermore, this paradigm also provides for an occasion for students to juxtapose the reality of their experiences against the constructed realities of society as they work toward a variety of solutions, including the evaluation of those solutions, for practical problem scenarios. While the paradigm articulated by Sternberg does not specifically delineate this condition, it does open the door for educators to create it.

Herein rests the possibility to move students toward the development of a critical literacy where they begin to deconstruct information and use their indigenous knowledge to construct and question the meanings, power differentials, and perspectives of the information that they encounter. Movement toward critical literacy is essential if we are to embrace the idea that the demonstration of successful intelligence necessarily involves the extent to which individuals leverage all of their abilities, by utilizing their strengths and correcting or compensating for their weaknesses, to achieve particular goals within the contexts of their everyday real worlds. To successfully utilize their intelligence for purposive navigation through everyday life, individuals need to be able to critically read the world in which they live. Within the context applying Sternberg's model to pedagogy, the goal should not only be to maximize the cognitive skills of students through a recognition of the plurality of their intelligence but to also give them new opportunities to think critically about the society in which they exist so that their education empowers them to transform the structures rather than conform to it. Interestingly, Sternberg's own early educational experiences can be understood within this context. He was a student academically condemned by traditional models of intelligence testing that labeled him as an underperformer or unintelligent. However, rather than conform to the circumstance of the stigmatizing label, he challenged it by engaging in efforts to acquire the knowledge to deconstruct the theoretical models that were foundational to the creation of the circumstance, and constructing an alternative theoretical model. Sternberg's work was informed by information and knowledge generated from his childhood experiences with intelligence.

Another important element of the Triarchic Theory of Intelligence is the way in which it focuses not only on the deficiencies, but also on the assets, of skills and abilities of successful intelligence. As we consider the extent to which many American youth, who have not fared well under our current pedagogical models that privilege an analytical approach, are demotivated and alienated from the learning process, Sternberg's paradigm can be incredibly helpful in constructing new and more effective models of schooling to alter this circumstance. Through his theoretical framework, there is an acknowledgement that students have a wide range of intellectual assets, even if they coexist with deficiencies that need to be addressed. This asset-based approach can be an important motivator for students who have historically experienced overwhelming failure in the traditional modalities of schooling. A deliberately active recognition and embrace of students' analytical, creative, and practical abilities can be incredibly empowering, particularly when their creative and practical abilities have been overlooked by our traditional approaches to pedagogy.

In addition to the motivational benefits that can be gained by students who are pedagogically engaged in a learning process imbued with a Triarchic approach, there are also opportunities to enhance academic performance. Learning triarchically allows students encode material in three different frameworks, which consequently strengthens and increases the ways in which students are able to retrieve and utilize such information. In his research studies of the model, Sternberg has documented performance gains across all three domains for students who previously had been recording poor academic performance. "Students who have studied triarchically excel in their performance not only on tests measuring analytical, creative, and practical achievement, but also on multiple-choice tests that require little more than memorizing the material. Moreover, students who formerly were not achieving at high levels start achieving at high levels when they are taught triarchically" (Sternberg et al., 2001). Sternberg and his colleagues also found that the Triarchic model gave teachers an opportunity to employ a greater variety of pedagogical approaches to deliver particular academic content, which is an important motivator for them as well. Just as students can be moved toward a critical literacy, perhaps teachers simultaneously can be moved toward critical pedagogy as they are empowered to engage their own knowledge and skills, outside of those dictated by prescribed and scripted curricula, in the facilitation of learning within their school spaces.

In thinking about the field of Multiple Intelligences and how its various theorists have articulated particular conceptual frameworks, Sternberg's Triarchic Theory is a model that can be used as an important point of entry to progressively advance the discourse on intelligences. The promise of Sternberg's theory to move the discourse primarily rests in its ability to socioculturally contextualize successful intelligence, its focus on the pluralistic domains of cognitive processing rather than talent or skill identifications, its acknowledgement of assets as well as deficiencies, as well as its recognition that successful intelligence can be taught. The promise of Sternberg's theoretical paradigm can only be realized if educators actively engage the framework and critically shape its application to pedagogical and curricular practices. This means that educators must be equipped and empowered to transform their approaches to teaching and learning such that their strategies include not only the more traditional didactic and fact-based inquiries of academic materials but also a more dialogic and thinking-based questioning as they help their students consider alternative explanations and evaluations of the phenomena and knowledges that they encounter throughout a lifelong learning process. In light of the educational experiences and outcomes of our youth, we need to embrace, exploit, and expand the potential that Sternberg's Triarchic Theory of Intelligence offers to educate individuals to develop a web of intelligence that they can successfully leverage within the real world of their everyday lives, and simultaneously affirms and builds upon those skills that they bring to the learning process.

REFERENCES

Alvermann, D. E., Hinchman, K. A., Moore, D. W., and Phelps, S. F. (Eds.). (1998). *Reconceptualizing the Literacies in Adolescents' Lives* (p. 29). New Jersey: Lawrence Erlbaum Associates.

Rose, M. (1989). *Lives on the Boundary.* New York: Penguin Books.

Sternberg, R. J. (1985). *Beyond IQ: A Triarchic Theory of Human Intelligence* (p. 128). New York: Cambridge University Press.

———. (1988). *The Triarchic Mind* (p. 250). New York: Penguin Books.

Sternberg, R., and Williams, W. (Eds.). (1998). *Intelligence, Instruction, and Assessment: Theory into Practice* (p. 2). New Jersey: Lawrence Erlbaum Associates.

Sternberg, R. J., Forsythe, G. B., Hedlund, J., and Horvath, A. J. (2000). *Practical Intelligence in Everyday Life.* New York: Cambridge University Press.

Sternberg, R., Grigorenko, E., and Jarvin, L. (2001). Improving reading instruction: The Triarchic Model. *Educational Leadership*, 58, 48.

CHAPTER 30

Beverly Daniel Tatum

PAM JOYCE

Beverly Daniel Tatum has been working in the field of educational psychology for more than twenty-five years. In this domain she has managed to bring a new perspective on race and racism from a postformalist and critical constructivist point of view, incorporating a nontraditional stance on these topics. Her fresh perspective injects much needed insight into the role of race and racism into the discourse of educational psychology. She is a scholar, teacher, author, administrator, and race relations expert who has extensive background in both psychology and education. Her detailed vita can be accessed at http:www.spelman.edu/president. Her central research interests include black families in white communities, racial identity in teens, and the role of race in the classroom and its implications for our students, schools, communities, and society.

Tatum is the author of *Why Are All the Black Kids Sitting Together in the Cafeteria? And Other Conversations about Race* (2000, 2003), and *Assimilation Blues: Black Families in a White Community: Who Succeeds and Why?* In addition, she has been published frequently in social science and education journals. In 1997 Tatum participated in President Clinton's "Dialogue on Race" and in 2002, she appeared as a guest on the Oprah Winfrey Show as part of a broadcast concerning American youth and race. Presently, Tatum is the president of Spelman College. Prior to her appointment at Spelman, she was acting president and dean, as well as professor of Psychology and Education, at Mount Holyoke College.

Tatum's written and oral contributions, in addition to her career accomplishments, span a continuum of hope. This underlying hope unfolds in her books, beginning with the exploration of the psychology of internalized racism, gradually traversing to an honest look at a specific school setting that implicitly holds a powerful message for all, and finally expanding from the nuclear geographic setting of a school cafeteria to the wider geographic area of a predominately white community. Developing an understanding of these geographic contexts is essentially acknowledging that the consequences generated from these situations first spill into the larger society and then sadly gush out even further over the globe for both conscious and unconscious mass consumption. It is when this occurs that the populous is exposed to the ugliness of racism in disproportionate doses. Tatum's goal is to expose the ugliness as it appears to be and thus break the silence and tacit underpinnings of racism that have always been omnipresent in society. In addition, she dramatically alters racism's lethal grip on the world in a more natural fashion through her works as well as through conversation rather than the use of other blatantly obtrusive options that have been used in the past to achieve the same goal. In other words, conversation as a natural path is being pursued in contrast to past accusatory and culpable methods of change involving racism. In this way, her work is a source of hope as well as possibility, and subsequently becomes an audible call for human agency.

Another natural approach to learning about racism involves the ability to be insightful, and Tatum certainly manages to capitalize on her insights. She utilizes them as she reverts historical shortsightedness about race with its limited boundaries into multidimensional peripheral vision. As a result, multidimensionality develops from a three-pronged micro, meso, and macro perspective on race. This broad perspective incorporates the individual's internalized unrest on the micro level, the school/community's perpetuation of black invisibility on the meso level, and the larger society's blatant installation of the trickle-down effects of racism on the macro level. These three levels combined are represented under the auspices of the cycle of oppression. However slowly, the salient points enveloping racism materialize through these micro, meso, and macro representations and, therefore, heighten the awareness level of people everywhere.

Tatum's own heightened awareness alters the approach to racial boundaries and exemplifies enhanced vision for possibilities, ultimately allowing space for change and the foresight to act against the odds. Her awareness captures, in a nuclear school setting, racial dynamics in a traditionally "inclusive" democratic environment and demonstrates the pervasiveness of racism from self to society, from within to without. The irony of the pervasiveness of racism is that the so-called inclusive American school environment and the American neighborhood community are traditionally seen as places where the objectives of democracy can be fulfilled. Racism is in fact present within the school walls and continues to manifest itself like a version of distorted surround sound within the imaginary speakers of a massive educational music system. That is to say, racism and the denial thereof are omnipresent in education, the construction of identity, and cognitive activity.

According to Tatum's research, the subsequent dynamics of racism have no choice but to ooze into American institutions. For example, the turbulent micro world of black kids translates into the meso lived world of the school community and becomes identifiable by negative labels, as seen in subjugated student positioning in lower-level classes and unequal academic opportunities. Eventually, the macro world is influenced through subjugated work placements of these kids in the larger society. Tatum's exposure of the negative does not imply that she comes solely from a deficit point of view, but rather that she is brave enough to represent the racial inscription of "what is." The dim reality of racism under these circumstances thus becomes the transference of the dominant mindset to an inept socialization process, which eventually frames the structure of adulthood. The end results of the circular process of racism correlate directly with the ability, or inability as it may be, to cope with the overload of racist stimuli coming from internalized prompters and societal as well as global negative forces. This overload includes dynamics that are generated in physical spaces as well as in the psyche of society, which are interrelated and connected and which contribute to the phenomenon of silenced black voices.

In *Why Are All the Black Kids Sitting Together in the Cafeteria? And Other Conversations about Race*, mixed feelings about "same race" grouping emerge from a supposedly "neutral" school setting, the cafeteria, and questions the validity of the ideals of democracy and equality. The word "conversation" used in the title actually paves the focus of the book and provides a new direction for those in search of promoting understanding among people. On one hand, close interactions with people of the same race are interpreted sometimes in a favorable light as a private support group. On the other hand, the exclusivity of black groups specifically can be interpreted as self-segregation and carry a negative onus that undoubtedly cements a connection to the negative past with slavery and segregation laws. Either way, whether the conversations sparked are positive and/or negative, this book evokes thought to at least engage in talk about race and the situation of racism in America. This kind of "talk" has quelled the overwhelming silence about race over the years and sanctioned the need for race discourse. It provides on one hand a social context for race and on the other hand rejects the idea of "racelessness," which mechanistic educational psychology has perpetuated for a long time.

Openings originating from race conversations foster change as well as awareness. In conversations, movement begins to stir beyond talk and, in fact, evolves from discourse moving forward as an agenda of agency that promotes emancipation from the age-old debilitating conditions of racism. Some changes also emerge from intrinsic and/or extrinsic origins, thereby representing dual perspectives of the cafeteria phenomena as well as highlighting powerful hegemonic groups. Intrinsically, racism is the inner turmoil that stings and sometimes blisters the black child's lived world experiences and, as an internalized experience, it has the unfortunate ability to fester and penetrate the human core. Extrinsically, racism operates from outside of the "self" and finds reinforcement in schools, communities, and the larger society. Coupling and sorting out the intrinsic and extrinsic aspects first on an individual level and then from a collective standpoint can assist in the possibility of constructive change. Tatum starts with dissecting intrinsic upsets of the black individual, aptly exploring the psychological dynamics, and then continues to transfer and intermix that information to the language of the educational and social arenas. Thus, through the intermingling of psychological, educational, historical, and social dynamics, educational psychology becomes enmeshed in the process.

Tatum draws on intrinsic information from an etymological sensibility, which emerges when she examines racial identity and unearths the origins of racism as it aligns with the development of identity. Although the point of origin is "self," the end result always encompasses the whole. In actuality, the nuclear "self" simply mushrooms into intricate connections of life like an amazing geometric diagram developing slowly but surely, all pieces fitting together and forming a complete circle of humanity rolling along as every one affects the other. In *Why Are All the Black Kids Sitting Together in the Cafeteria? And Other Conversations about Race*, she refers to the psychologist William Cross to clarify the theory of racial identity that involves five stages: preencounter, encounter, immersion, internalization, and internalization/commitment. In a nutshell, Cross discusses how a person from a racial minority begins life by thinking he or she is like everyone else, then an awareness sets in that he or she is different, next this awareness seems to surround the individual from various points of the lived world, and with a gradual overstimulation of the senses, the individual begins to internalize the "what is." Finally, in many cases, the individual accepts the "what is," which eventually becomes his or her reality. The critical postformal reconceptualization of educational psychology, in accordance with Tatum's works on race and racism, call for rigorous engagement with the psychological origin of "self" as well as exploration of group dynamics and its relation to the "self."

Group dynamics and the relationship of "self" join together to create the cafeteria phenomenon. Why should it be an issue of concern that black kids are sitting together in the cafeteria, whereas, on the contrary, the idea of white kids sitting together in the cafeteria is not an issue? Regrettably, black kids sitting together and eating in a specific space usually solicits a shock-wave response to what should otherwise be considered a normal everyday social event. When a group of same-race black kids sits together, it often elicits a reaction that prompts questions and, at times, creates in the public mind the formation of a threatening environment. In fact, cause for concern usually ignites when any minorities gather together in one specific location.

Under these extenuating circumstances when everyday activities of a specific group of people are questioned and/or frowned upon, one might be inclined to pose a poignant question such as, "How does democratic practice apply in this situation?" In sum, the same-race grouping phenomenon can either be seen as a positive action, whereby it can be interpreted as kids simply involved in supporting each other, or it can be seen as something negative, that is, as a situation that needs to be fixed. Consequently, the unsettling incidents that are revealed through Tatum's cafeteria-like self-segregation phenomenon shed light on yet another complex race situation and often result in critical enlightenment concerning issues of power and dominance at work in a democratic society. Although these views about racism, whether positive or negative, originate from natural spaces, they are not necessarily experienced in totally isolated contexts. Furthermore, Tatum's research introduces various coping mechanisms dealing with racism used by blacks in specific environments and also exposes examples of trickle-down negative consequences, from childhood to adulthood, that are connected to black lived world experiences.

Tatum's introduction of coping mechanisms for racist acts emerges from a new critical consciousness and a rigorous form of criticality that aligns with postformalist thinking. She is able to launch the criticality necessary to pursue the discomfort that is usually associated with discussions on race and in addition, embrace the subsequent life changing revelations that generally follow these experiences. This innovative way of thinking critically about race sheds new light on the power and influence of the web of reality for black kids as well as black adults and demonstrates how this intricate interconnected web affects others. Tatum's research about race in *Why Are All the Black Kids Sitting Together in the Cafeteria? And Other Conversations about Race* and in *Assimilation Blues - Black Families in White Communities: Who Succeeds and Why?* provides the resources needed to transfer pertinent coping mechanisms to the minority population and begins to plan for change. Operating in a manner similar to Joe Kincheloe's postformalist framework, Tatum proceeds to go deeper into the "what is" and then questions the norm with her willingness to do the rigorous work by addressing the "what could be." She is able, from a postformalist viewpoint, to exercise the criticality necessary to pursue the stages of discomfort usually equated with discussions on race and also acknowledge the subsequent life-changing revelations that follow the conversations.

Tatum's work on race relations gives educational psychologists, lay people, and educators the nudge to seek out the larger, more intrusive issues surrounding black kids and, consequently, in doing so buy into a more challenging, rather than accepted and predetermined, existence. What tends to be missed, sometimes blatantly ignored or even callously disregarded, is the kaleidoscopic world black kids are expected to face on a daily basis. In this particular world filled with mixed stimuli and an array of contextually based mixed messages, there is an endless variety of racist patterns configuring themselves in blinding displays of bright converging and confusing colors. These messages are presented from multiple lenses which intensify human existence and cause, on one hand, a constant need for blacks to search for survival skills and, on the other hand, enables the powers of the hegemonic groups to be nurtured and simultaneously enhanced. Therefore, context needs to be examined with a critical eye, and that is where Tatum's particularly perceptive peripheral vision again becomes apparent and necessary. With this vision, she emphasizes the power of and need for hermeneutics in the field of educational psychology.

In the context of the school cafeteria, a place customarily deemed as a "neutral" space where people can be free to choose whom they wish to socialize with, Tatum's critical eye is needed to interpret the reality of the situation. In a sense, the cafeteria appears to assume the idea of claiming territorial rights whereas students stake out areas in specific spaces mainly for reasons of bonding, comfort, and support. Thus, it is territorial only because black kids feel as if they have to protect a space for themselves in which they are allowed to say anything they want, to interact with people who look like them and possibly have similar life experiences as well. Tatum acknowledges as well as supports the need for black kids to secure sacred bonding spaces. In taking this stand, she gives credence to the black voice and encourages reaching out to one another within the confines of select spaces to satisfy growing life needs and become visible by means of action as well as speech. The action of racial solidarity demonstrates that power exists in numbers, if only in the united front of a simple school lunch table, and speaks volumes through the silence of unity.

Tatum reiterates the micro, meso, and macro aspects of racism in *Assimilation Blues: Black Families in White Communities: Who Succeeds and Why?* In this publication, she assumes a dual perspective, emic as well as etic. She assumes on one hand the emic perspective as a resident in a predominately white community, called Sun Beach, coupled with the points of view of twenty other black families from an insider's perspective aligned with the situation. On the other hand she assumes an etic perspective in the role of researcher as well as scientific observer and in doing so presents the outsider's side to the situation. The dual perspective, from the inside emic and outside etic perspectives, imparts a comprehensive picture to the research information of the myriad dimensions of being black in the specific setting of the suburbs and the consequences of adjustment that must be endured for the "privilege" of remaining in the community and earning acceptance. The impact of the conceptual and social framework of a predominately white community on black people and the deep social structures surrounding them is visible from many angles. The impact can be visible from a psychological viewpoint, through the mind; from a sociological viewpoint, through interpersonal relationships; as well as from an anthropological viewpoint, through the treatment of blacks in the context of a specific community where hegemonic forces are most prevalent.

The impact of being black in a predominately white community can also result in a bicultural experience. Exposure to biculturality, or in this case, the merging of the values of white and black culture, often becomes a necessity in order to survive in the home community while simultaneously counteracting inner racist turmoil. The duality of this bicultural existence is reminiscent of the concept of "double consciousness" penned by Du Bois. The basic premise of "double consciousness," as summarized by Joe Kincheloe in *Critical Pedagogy: A Primer*, is having the ability to see oneself through the perception of others. This heightened level of consciousness is an acquired skill, and often a necessary tool for survival. In Tatum's predominately white town, blacks can survive by learning two ways of doing things, the white way or the correct mixture of the white way and the black way in order for desirable coexistence. Double consciousness is a part of the black world in multiple contexts and, unfortunately, a concept that has not been explored in mainstream educational psychology.

In addition to biculturality as a response to efforts of fitting into the dominant context, Tatum proposes blacks can exist by assuming a position of racelessness, where they systematically void their culture. In essence, racelessness is when an individual basically neutralizes his or her being and erases racial identity in order to blend into the hegemonic culture for purposes of survival. Under these circumstances, white culture usually takes precedence over black culture. Comparatively, the notion of racelessness carries a burden similar to the one created by assuming the role of emissary, which is that of imposing an aspect of invisibility of the inner "self." The emissary role, which refers to someone who sees all of his or her achievements as advancing the cause of his or her specific racial group, is another viable option for survival for some people of color. Of course, within this definition, the individual essentially carries the overwhelming burden of being the savior of the race. According to Tatum, however, the emissary role used for black survival in hegemonic settings as well as biculturality and the idea of racelessness all have the capability of robbing the black individual of some aspect of the "self." Tatum's acknowledgement of pertinent variables interconnected with black existence brings educational psychology into a more realistic perspective compatible with the changing times.

Another survival technique used by blacks living in a predominately white community, which is more self-assuring, is to import a relationship into the home by rallying the black extended family together for purposes of establishing a better sense of black "self." Although pursuing familial ties by reaching out beyond the lived community might be a strain on the family, yet it might also have rewarding results, especially under the often-extreme existing circumstances that tend to void black human existence. Weighing the potential positive impact the family can have, Tatum sees the support of the black community, familial and/or otherwise, especially in the mixed-race community, as a protective buffer zone for the child. Thus, support from black family members is one way of counteracting the effects of invisibility.

Invisibility is just one of the possible consequences of operating in an alienating environment that often lists the definition of black people as synonymous with the word "intruder." As Tatum points out, the "intruder" is seen simultaneously as visible and invisible, and in light of this dichotomous relationship the community assumes conflicting views. Blacks are seen visibly from the outside, from a surface perspective as cloaked in a skin of shaded brown hues. In contrast, however, they are not truly seen in the sense that they are essentially invisible and ignored, from an inner, core perspective as a human being. Owing to this fractured view of conflict and gross mislabeling as "intruder," black people not only have limited power, but limited access to power as well. The "intruders" then remain in limbo under these conditions, teetering between visibility and invisibility.

Historically, blacks struggled for visibility and access to power through the possibility of acquiring land and/or education. Today, as emphasized by Tatum in her research, geographic location and education are linked to black families in school situations as well as in community-living situations. The nefarious connections between race and power loom in the context of situatedness, for example, as Tatum suggests in school or community, often lurking in the shadows of lived experiences as a constant reminder of past injustices. Subtle and sometimes overt indications of racism often rise up, which are rooted in history, thereby giving credence to the fact that racially charged occurrences are not isolated or mythical incidents but actually are embedded in society. These social dynamics affect every dimension of educational psychology and need to be included in this domain in order to get a broader picture of the "what is."

Tatum, like Donaldo Macedo in *Literacies of Power: What Americans Are Not Allowed to Know*, addresses embedded societal myths. Overall, it seems the myth that society promotes is that there are no connections among the inner self, the school, and the larger society and this is heard in a resounding manner throughout Tatum's research findings on race. The myth that racism no longer exists in the schools is also creating cacophony in the educational arena owing to the perpetuating literacy issues in the school system involving black kids and the inability of research to provide a solid reason or viable solution for these issues. Through the exposure of these myths, Tatum establishes a place for the reality of internalized racism and, therefore, builds credence about the roots of the turmoil that so often rages within the consciousness of black people. She illuminates the "what is" into future possibilities of the "what could be" by expanding awareness of the web of reality, across multiple individual and collective life-time encounters, and among diverse web prongs jutting out into the world clutching onto all that it comes in contact with in the lived world. Alignment with this level of agency can only be possible if one's eyes are open, senses are piqued, and the need for involvement is understood.

In actuality, a microcosmic as well as positivistic representation of society which strives to distinguish and separate lived experiences by race ultimately represents the macro version of society in the "what is" present experience. The idea of using the cafeteria as a medium to accentuate the existence of racial problems in America in everyday normal situations is profound. Her innovation clearly portrays, especially in its nuclear setting, that the problem of racism is not isolated, fragmented, or housed in one area at all but, in contrast, is quite prevalent in many different areas of the world. In addition, the cafeteria scenario geographically transcends America because students in the cafeteria are engaged in a day-to-day experience shared by many other people around the globe in different ways based on varying cultural practices. Hence, the macro experience comes to fruition.

Therefore, same-race students who gravitate and cling to each other are simply duplicating what the hegemonic society has unconsciously as well as consciously set up as an accepted comfort zone. Minorities who are thus encapsulated by various overt and covert acts of racism on a daily basis, for example in the movies, the media, their communities, and their school environments, are prone to gravitate toward each other in specific contextual circumstances. With a barrage of negative information, black youth are all but commandeered to make inappropriate assumptions about their worth and identity. The possibility to exceed seemingly predetermined boundaries and customized zones of learning in this limited claustrophobic space is thus threatened by these overwhelming factors. Again, the social dynamics of race profoundly shape the concerns of educational psychology.

Lev Vygotsky espouses that it is possible to create our own Zones of Proximal Development (ZPDs). ZPDs are zones or spaces that scaffold learners to higher-knowledge plateaus with the capacity to be custom designed to suit the needs of the individual. They can be orchestrated to address individual needs, with the possibility of extrapolating a variety of existing useful items and incorporating new items for the purpose of reconstructing the existing "what is." In a school environment as well as in a predominately white community, blacks can customize their space in some cases, as Tatum suggests, with bringing family members into the experience, in order to expedite the possibility of transformative change. But if we are, in fact, to make this change happen, we must not look at racism as a type of cancer that is incurable and prevalent throughout the land or we might not recognize a glimmer of hope when we see it. Instead, it seems we might have to redefine racism as a society in order to move toward change as well as encourage the field of educational psychology to expand its racial empathy and insight and deal with issues of race and racism.

Tatum herself defines racism as a system of advantage based on race. She uses the world like an artist's palate to paint a picture of this definition by discussing the advantages of race for one group as compared to the disadvantages of another and, in doing so, she expounds on the ever-present societal racist overtones. In addition, she erases fragmented thoughts and jargon and concentrates on the interconnected nature of the world and how racism fits into the schemata. The results of seeing the connected nature of little incidents is the realization that life's patterns and relationships are intertwined and at some point enmesh together to form a bigger picture. Thus, insights gained from merged relationships can be the catalyst for future possibilities, and Tatum's work inspires this level of emergent possibilities.

In keeping with Tatum's emergent possibilities, one might consider Kincheloe, Steinberg, and Tippins (1998) term *critical constructivism*, introduced in their book *The Stigma of Genius*, which involves critical consciousness of the social construction of self and society. Critical constructivism involves taking a critical stance that is open to acknowledging the existence of power in relation to and corresponding to the "real" world that is enveloped in the web of reality. It equates the major conflicts and recurring issues of race as due to the lack of self-reflection and exploration of origin as well as to the presence of the hegemonic societal umbrella that pervades all parameters of space. In short, critical constructivism embodies principles to explore in order to move from the "what is" and ultimately get to the "what could be" in relation to the multifaceted aspects of race relations and racism in today's world. I argue that tacit aspects of school culture and damaging societal myths can find an avenue for exploration and open expression with an alignment of critical constructivism and educational psychology.

The ability to question representatives of and sources of power is a basic tenet of critical constructivism. In this sense, Tatum as a critical constructivist, in Kincheloe's words, approaches "world making" from a united, cohesive standpoint by connecting the micro, meso, and macro world representations and thereby acknowledging the multidimensional sources of power and their effects on selfhood. Essentially, she abandons traditional reductionistic methods of fragmenting bits of information from the past and present, and manages instead to keep all of the information together. Needless to say, as Maxine Greene (1995) implies in *Releasing the Imagination*, critical consciousness propels the race discussion to "open up lived worlds to reflection and transformation" (p. 59).

Further relating to critical constructivism, Maturana and Varela's (1980) cognitive theory of enactivism involves a critical change as well. Enactivism proposes that individuals have the ability to transport select schema or inner knowledges to different spontaneous situations in order to construct or create individual experiences. The power to do so, Maturana and Varela argue, lies within, stemming from multiple relationships. Tatum exemplifies how the use of schema aids in the construction of race identity as she projects the possibility that black kids might be able to mobilize themselves for change if they would begin to see themselves as complete and not fragmented by life's varied experiences. This thought process, however, demands a critical mind that knows, or has the ability to distinguish, myth from reality as well as the ability to appropriately use that knowledge under varying circumstances at any given time. Therefore, it is our social responsibility to nurture and stimulate more critical minds so that in turn, schema may be implemented differently from the past and eventually used as a tool for change.

The possibility of black kids using critical schema to carve out a new existence from the "what is" lived world, incorporating an enactivist psychological perspective, would ultimately be up to the individual. Therefore, how they internalize their collective past and present life relationships, and the responses and interactions engendered by the larger society would be a consideration in the change process. In this manner, the individual would then see his or her self as capable of taking control of spontaneous as well as long-standing situations with the "self" as the main component. According to Varela's autopoiesis, self-organization or self-production, individuals are allowed to be in a lifelong marathon with self-(re)construction. Tatum proposes multiple ways, which were previously mentioned to engage in that reality. In other words, the essence of this theory gives individuals power to create a world, which then affords, as Kincheloe espouses, a new era of immanence, or "what could be" in our web of reality. Ultimately, in our ZPDs, in our relationship with others, the web of reality is open to what we can conceive and then construct and/or reconstruct.

Critical immanence helps us to see possibilities buried deep within our minds that we lost access to or misinterpreted because of lack of perspective or insight, social positioning, or inability to change the "what is." Regrettably, it seems that individuals often struggle and sometimes respond without challenge to life's moment-by-moment encounters in inappropriate or self-damaging ways. Through Tatum, we discover that problems with race might have internal origins but they ultimately go beyond the "self." Consequently, the "self" is a good starting place, but by far not the only stop on the continuum of hope. If one can digest reality and possibly feel the frightening fury that exists in racist acts and through this process, recognize how racism has spiraled out of control over time, then it might be possible to get its damaging presence into perspective.

It might be possible to imagine the "real" meaning of the fluidity of change and the existence of limitless possibilities by extricating ourselves from the devaluing and demeaning stories, both past and present, of racism and realigning our lived order by first, critically deconstructing the negative and, then, critically reconstructing something new. It is the use of criticality that seeks to change this perspective. Tatum's honest and revealing conversations, which encourage awareness of the interconnected nature of life, along with the understanding and awareness of the psychological roots of racial identity and its formation, provide a working format for the beginning of transformative change about race relations and the long-standing effects of racism.

As stated in Kincheloe's introduction to this encyclopedia, knowledge can never stand alone or be complete in and of itself and, thus, the context of meaning in Tatum's scholarly works comes from the heated conversations about race, the socialization process, embedded implicit and/or explicit societal messages, and the situatedness of people in general. She captures a well-rounded profile of blacks in specific societal situations and, consequently, manages to successfully eke out an honest account of what it means and feels like to be black in a white-dominated society. The social networks that surround black people have been an especially significant consideration of Tatum's research from a reconstructive and emancipatory standpoint and are very important avenues of exploration in educational psychology.

In addition to context, Tatum builds and synthesizes knowledge by using what Joe Kincheloe has described as a bricolage approach to research. She starts with the topic of race and expertly weaves in the far-extending and disguised tentacles of racism. The multiple lenses that she engages to approach this research serve to enhance her work as well as her agency, which assist overall in increasing human possibilities. The circular nature of the data collected from the cafeteria, the community, and the larger society unfolds, and connections ultimately emerge from the ever-expanding and fluid perspectives of lived world experiences. Her research is a textured web penetrating the inner and outer worlds of people everywhere. It goes deeply into the black psyche starting with identity development, introduces the school community as a part of the development, and finally establishes the interconnections of the larger society in the development process. As Berry and Kincheloe (2004) argues in *Rigour and Complexity in Educational Research: Constructing the Bricolage*, these multiple lenses make for a *clearer* understanding of the relationship between race and educational psychology.

Tatum layers the psychological, educational, sociological, anthropological, ontological, and historical domains generated through research and ultimately harnesses a bricolage of information. Each layer of research connects to more information and subsequently, loops back to itself even more enriched and enlightened in a true cyclical sense. The layered information exemplifies the micro, meso, and macro levels of human existence and, as a result, multiple insights emerge from these varied perspectives. In sum, viewing the research in its complexity and visualizing the process as nonlinear, as Kincheloe proposes in his work on postformalism, collectively adds comprehensive dimension to Tatum's work and allows for increased comprehension of the work we must do in and for the world concerning matters of race. In this "era of immanence," possibilities remain present in Tatum's promotion of a more positive arena for the recognition and development of black voices and, finally, an opening for a true understanding of the sources of pain endured by black people for so long. Mechanistic educational psychology cannot remain stranded on its deracialized island once it takes these insights into account.

REFERENCES

Berry, K. S., and Kincheloe, J. L. (2004). *Rigour and Complexity in Educational Research*. London: Open University Press.

Greene, M. (1995). *Releasing the Imagination: Essays on Education, the Arts, and Social Change*. San Francisco: Jossey-Bass Publishers.

Kincheloe, J. L. (2004). *Critical Pedagogy Primer*. New York: Peter Lang.

Kincheloe, J. L., Steinberg, S. R., and Tippins, D. (1998). *The Stigma of Genius: Einstein and Beyond Education*. New York: Peter Lang.

Macedo, D. (1994). *Literacies of Power: What Americans Are Not Allowed to Know*. Boulder, CO: Westview Press.

Maturana, H. R., and Varele, F. J. (1980). *Autopoiesis and cognition*. London: D. Reidel.

Tatum, B. D. (2000). *Assimilation Blues: Black Families in a White Community*. New York: Basic Books.

———. (2003). *"Why Are All the Black Kids Sitting Together in the Cafeteria?" And Other Conversations about Race*. New York: Basic Books.

CHAPTER 31

Lewis Madison Terman

BENJAMIN ENOMA

Lewis M. Terman was a renowned psychologist situated in the pantheon and generation of eminent American psychologists influenced by "the Great Schools." In this era, the number of theoretical and empirical investigations of "intelligence" increased considerably. Terman was the twelfth of fourteen children born on a farm in Johnson County, Indiana, on January 15, 1877. As a teenager, he left home for College at Danville, Illinois. He made a living oscillating between the pursuit of higher education and school teaching. In 1905, he received his PhD from Clark University, Worcester, Massachusetts, six years after Henry Herbert Goddard, who also graduated from Clark.

Terman's dissertation was on individual differences in intelligence. He employed a variety of tests to measure and differentiate between the cognitive abilities of "gifted" and "stupid" preadolescent boys. Although this work preceded Goddard's translation in 1908 of the 1905 "Binet–Simon Scale," the approaches to measuring human intelligence bore some similarities. Terman spent thirty-three years on the faculty of Stanford University, Stanford, California, twenty of them as head of the Department of Psychology.

The works of Francis Galton (1822–1911), eminent British psychologist who coined the term "eugenics" and the phrase "nature versus nurture" largely influenced Terman. Galton was Charles Darwin's cousin. His theory of intelligence, part science and part sociology, held that intelligence was the most valuable human attribute and that if people who possessed high levels of it could be identified and placed in positions of leadership, all of society would benefit. Terman was also influenced by French psychologists Alfred Binet (1857–1911) and Theodore Simon (1873–1961), who codesigned the Binet–Simon scale, which comprised of a variety of tasks they thought were representative of children's aptitudes based on chronological age.

STANDARDIZATION AND TRACKING

As mentioned earlier, Terman's era was replete with theoretical and empirical investigations on human intelligence. On the one hand some foregoing scholars like French Psychologists: Alfred Binet and Theodore Simon approached this subject with the focus on ascertaining the level of intelligence that requires special education. In other words the goal was to identify the "least endowed" children so as to give the extra support needed for them to cope. In the United States other psychologists such as Henry Goddard, Robert Yerkes, and Lewis Terman were fixated on the higher echelon, the "highly gifted." These positions used similar techniques and shared the same basic assumption that intelligence in humans was a natural endowment that varied from individual to individual. While it is fair to say that both approaches were aimed at the ultimate good of the society, it is pertinent to note that the focus on the least endowed individual has a social justice slant, that is to say, provide special education for those who need it and level the gaps in achievement. While the quest for the highly gifted possessed an elitist slant, its proponents, Terman included, sought to control or eradicate the existence and reproduction of the least endowed. Furthermore, the former used the IQ tests to determine what a child needed to learn while the latter used the IQ tests as a tool to predict the child's ability to learn.

If individual intelligence levels could be clearly ascertained then the population can be sorted on the basis of their IQ test scores and assigned to different levels within the school system, which would lead to corresponding socioeconomic destinations in adulthood. The explanation of these variances on the part of the gifted school was dependent on bloodline, racial or gene superiority as espoused in "Eugenics," a popular and emergent theory at the time. As stated by Charles Davenport (Galton's U.S. disciple), Eugenics is the science of the improvement of the human race by better breeding. Terman was very open about his position that the etiology of intelligence is largely hereditary. Terman more than any other individual in recent history raised the bar on standardized tests and its uses in schooling to track and differentiate the college bound from the vocational or life adjustment education of children.

The use of IQ tests gained more grounds as a result of two notable events. First, the Congressional bill or Immigration Act of 1924: Henry H. Goddard discovered that more than 80 percent of the Jewish, Hungarian, Polish, Italian, and Russian immigrants were mentally defective, or feeble-minded. He believed that such a defect was a condition of the mind or brain, which is simply transmitted as a genetic trait. He paid no attention to other factors that may have had a significant effect on the test scores. Tests were administered in English and under an arduous environment to immigrants after traveling great distances. "It would be impossible to rate real intelligence by using a test that is based on only verbal skills to someone in a language they are illiterate in." (Judge, 2002)

Secondly, the U.S. Supreme Court ruling in 1927 upholding Virginia State's involuntary sterilization of Ms. Carrie Buck, where Justice Oliver Wendell Holmes penned, "Three generations of imbeciles are enough. . . . He had decided that it was constitutionally legal for states to sterilize anyone they decided was eugenically undesirable. The principle that sustains compulsory vaccination, he elaborated, is broad enough to cover cutting the fallopian tubes." In other words, the general health of society could be protected at the expense of the rights of individuals. This ruling gave further legitimacy to the claims of the advocates of mental testing.

Terman, in his seminal work "Giftedness," on human intelligence and achievement, would go a step further and combine the Binet–Simon Scale with Wilhelm Stern's numerical index to explain the *ratio* between mental and chronological ages. The result of this effort is the development of the Intelligence Quotient (IQ) test, employing among other kinds of tests the Stanford–Binet Scale.

U.S. ARMY ALPHA BETA TEST

In 1917 at the onset of the First World War, then APA president Robert M. Yerkes, assumed chairmanship of a committee comprising 40 psychologists to develop and administer a group intelligence test, the U.S. Army Alpha Beta tests. Notable members included Henry Goddard, Walter Bingham, Lewis Terman, Carl Brigham, Edward L. Thorndike, and William Dill Scott, the first American professor of psychology, who soon resigned from the committee on account of differences with Yerkes. The significance of the Alpha Beta tests is that it is the pivotal exercise that moved intelligence testing beyond the individual toward the group. Thanks to the contributions of Lewis Terman, more than 1.7 million U.S. inductees were tested. The success of the sorting of men into ranks of officers and foot soldiers by the use of these tests lent credence to the belief that testing and tracking was the most efficient way to position the most talented to achieve their fullest potentials while identifying and curtailing the proliferation of those with low levels of native endowments. The Alpha test was designed for literate inductees while the Beta test was designed for illiterate or English-as-second-language inductees.

LARGE-SCALE ACCEPTANCE/LEGITIMIZATION

Lewis Terman conducted the best-known longitudinal study on human intelligence. In 1921 Terman and his colleagues began a longitudinal study of 1,528 gifted youth with IQs greater than 140 who were approximately twelve years old. Over a period of approximately forty years, the researchers laid the groundwork for our understanding of giftedness and paved the way for efforts to identify and nurture giftedness in school. Terman died in 1956 but the study will continue until 2020, to encompass the entire lives of his original 1,528 gifted youths. Results of the study have been published in several volumes. Prominent amongst his many findings was the fact that highly gifted children with 140+ IQ, contrary to popular beliefs about their looks and physical attributes, were well developed physically and often athletically inclined.

In 1922 Terman called for a formal multiple-track plan made up of five *psychometrically defined groups*: gifted, bright, average, slow, and special. While the possibility for transfer between tracks must be maintained, the abilities measured by the tests were considered for the most part constant and determined by heredity. Test scores could also tell us whether a child's native ability corresponds approximately to the median for the professional class, semiprofessional pursuits, skilled workers, semiskilled workers, and unskilled labor. "When his Stanford Achievement Test was published in 1923, the evaluative fate of school children for the next few decades was sealed" (Ballantyne, 2002).

Ellwood P. Cubberley, Education Chair at Stanford, a prominent advocate for professional school administrators, collaborated with Terman on many fronts. Terman himself having served as school teacher and school principal was able to influence school administration to adopt segregated curricula as the most efficient way of educating school children, hoping to eventually build a cluster of law-abiding, industrious men and women while by proxy ridding the society of potential criminals, prostitutes, and delinquent citizens all in the cost-efficient and scientific manner of aptitude testing.

MERITOCRATIC NORMS AND STATUS QUO

The field of applied psychology, like other disciplines that deal with human cognition, has a rupture in its approaches to theory. There is the formal, mechanistic, and positivistic approach and the postformal relativistic, constructivist, and critical approach. In the former, knowledge is objective and universal, determined by technical rationality, based on "science" and devoid of contextual or sociocultural variances. The assessment and evaluation of this formal body of knowledge is also inscribed with reductionist prescriptions. Formal knowledge is thus a finished product, absolute, finite, monological, and, I might add, reactionary. It possesses the ability to morph into new forms when debunked or discredited, for example, eugenics became genetics. Lastly, formal approach to theory is laced with power politics, mainstream ideology, and a hegemonic agenda. Eugenics is a good example of the formal approach to human intelligence based on heredity.

Postformal thought on the contrary features comprehension of the relativistic nature of knowledge, the acceptance of contradictions, and the integration of contradictions into existing canons, its methods and assumptions can be analyzed critically, questioned, and reexamined ad infinitum. Knowledge is ephemeral and subject to anachronism. Postformal approach comprises evolving and dynamic constructions that take into account contextual subjectivity, individuation, and marginal or subjugated stances. In the postformal viewpoint was Terman's view of intelligence as a gift or natural endowment valid? Is his definition of intelligence consistent or questionable? Terman, in line with most mental testers and advocates of eugenics, saw human intelligence as a hereditary possession handed down from parents to offspring via the genome. This position to some degree asserts defeatism around the fates of the least endowed. If intelligence is a genetic transfer absent any individual effort or cultivation then it follows that schooling, indeed education, could serve no ameliorative purpose or hope to raise human intelligence levels; in sum, education is impotent vis-à-vis heredity.

This viewpoint incited disapproval from Walter Lippmann, who claimed that to isolate intelligence unalloyed by training or knowledge, and to predict the sum total of what a child is capable of learning after an hour or so of IQ testing ensconced in the name of science was a contemptible claim. William C. Bagley opined that IQ testing was undemocratic because of the fatalistic inferences and deterministic nature of the tracking that follow its findings. Alfred Binet, whose 1905 intelligence scale is at the origin of the IQ testing movement, denounced the American use and customization of his scale and the link of intelligence solely to heredity, tagging it as "brutal pessimism and deplorable verdicts."

In the name of science, Terman's colleague Goddard asserted in his day that he could determine the mental ability of individuals by a cursory examination of their physiognomies, which is right up there with Gall's phrenology. He put this pseudo-scientific ability to "infamous" use at Ellis Island, New York.

Despite staunch opposition to mental testing, its opponents were quickly labeled conservatives, unscientific, and emotional liberals. The argument of administrative efficiency with its ease of sorting and tracking large numbers of students by "legitimate" means in this progressive era in education won over the school system and governing policies. They also appealed to the fundamental American ideal of meritocracy, where rewards are based on individual intelligence plus effort.

Is Terman's view of intelligence as a hereditary gift valid? In the light of critical and constructivist discourses, Terman was off by a mile. Intelligence is not an innate possession, whose appropriation and development is absent other critical factors such as social milieu and cultural capital, environmental and artifactual influences. While one cannot argue against the existence of special-needs or at-risk students, grouping them along racial and social economic lines and assigning them a life adjustment or vocational curriculum is megalomanic. This usurpation of power and exercise of social control is a vitiation of the democratic order.

REFERENCES

Ballantyne, P. F. (2002). *Psychology, Society, and Ability Testing (1859–2002): Transformative Alternatives to Mental Darwinism and Interactionism.* Retrieved August 4, 2006, from http://www.comnet. ca/~pbllan/Index.html.

Cross, T. L. (2003). Examining Priorities in Gifted Education: Leaving No Gifted Child Behind: Breaking Our Educational System of Privilege. *Roeper Review*, Spring, 101.

Judge, L. (2002). *Eugenics* (Semester Research Project) - ENGL 328.004/HIST 1302.106. Retrieved March 24, 2005, from http://www.accd.edu/sac/honors/main/papers02/Judge.htm.

Owen, D. (1985). Inventing the SAT. *Alicia Paterson Foundation Reporter*, 8, Index 1.

Ravitch, D. (2001). *Left Back a Century of Battles over School Reform*. New York: Touchstone.

Seagoe, M. V. (1976). *Terman and the Gifted*. Los Altos, CA: Kaufmann.

Shurkin, J. N. (1992). *Terman's Kids: The Groundbreaking Study of How the Gifted Grow Up*. Boston: Little, Brown and Company.

CHAPTER 32

Edward L. Thorndike

RAYMOND A. HORN JR.

Currently, education is dominated by a standards and accountability movement. A full understanding of the nature and consequences of this standards and accountability movement requires an exploration of the movement's origins. A central figure in the origins of this movement is the comparative psychologist Edward L. Thorndike. Thorndike's ideas so dominated the early years of the field of educational psychology that educational historians recognize him as one of the significant individuals who transformed American education in the early twentieth century. Thorndike's work in educational psychology is still a formidable presence in contemporary education. His influence on contemporary education will be explored through a discussion of his work in psychology and the application of that work in education.

THORNDIKE AND PSYCHOLOGY

While pursuing his bachelor's degree at Wesleyan University, Thorndike became acquainted with the work of William James, an acquaintance that would lead Thorndike into the field of psychology. After graduating from Wesleyan in 1895, Thorndike continued his studies at Harvard University where he studied under James and began his animal studies, which would lead to the discovery of behavioral principles that formed the foundation of his forty-year career in psychology and education. Thorndike graduated from Harvard in 1897 and completed his PhD at Columbia University in 1898. After working one year as an instructor at the Women's College of Western Reserve University, he began his forty-year tenure at Teachers College, Columbia University.

Thorndike's early studies focused on learning in animals with chicks and cats. His now-famous cat experiments uncovered principles about learning that became part of the original theoretical foundation for behavioral psychology and, specifically, operant conditioning. In his cat experiments, Thorndike put a hungry cat inside a locked puzzle box with food outside the box. As a cat randomly struggled to get out of the box, it would at some point accidentally release the lock and thus acquire the food, which would reinforce the cat's successful behavior. After successive occurrences of this kind, the cat learned how to manipulate the lock and escape from the box at will. From experiments like these that involved trial-and-error learning, Thorndike formulated the Law of Effect and the Law of Exercise.

The Law of Effect simply states that when an animal's behavior is followed by a rewarding experience, the probability that the animal will repeat the behavior when faced with the same context will increase. In this realization, Thorndike theorized that there was a connection between a stimulus and a response in that when an animal acted within its environment the response from the environment would affect what the animal learned. Thorndike followed the Law of Effect with the Law of Exercise, which stated that repetition strengthens the connection between a stimulus and a response. These connections, which Thorndike characterized as connectionism, between an animal's behavior, the environmental response, and the effects of that response on the animal would be developed to a more complex and sophisticated degree by B. F. Skinner in his development of operant conditioning. In 1911, Thorndike published his findings in his seminal work *Animal Intelligence*. Through the work of Thorndike and other behavioral psychologists, the field of behavioral psychology would influence all aspects of the field of education.

Through his use of scientific experimentation and statistical analysis, Thorndike also contributed to the development of empirical measurement in psychology and education. In the early 1900s, Thorndike and his colleagues began to develop objective measurement instruments that could be applied to educational contexts, especially in the measurement of human intelligence. For instance, in 1904, Thorndike published *An Introduction to the Theory of Mental and Social Measurements*. Through efforts such as this, Thorndike was able to promote the quantitative measurement of educational phenomenon and linked the field of statistics to the field of education (Lagemann, 2000, p. 65). Thorndike's use of statistical analysis and large-scale quantitative testing was especially evident in his contribution to the development of the understanding of intelligence as a multifaceted entity rather than a single, general intelligence as theorized by Charles Spearman. Thorndike theorized that there were three categories of intelligence, abstract, mechanical, and social, rather than the single "g" that Spearman proposed. One of his significant publications in the area of intelligence was *The Measurement of Intelligence* in 1927.

THORNDIKE AND EDUCATION

Thorndike's application of his psychological principles and methods in the field of education is still a powerful influence on the field today. Thorndike applied his theory to education in publications such as his 1901 *Notes on Child Study*, the 1912 *Education: A First Book*, his three-volume *Educational Psychology* that was published in 1913, and later works such as *The Teacher's Word Book* in 1921 and *The Fundamentals of Learning* in 1932. Today in the field of educational psychology, Thorndike's influence on education through behavioral psychology, standardized testing, and the statistical analysis of educational data is evident in the behavioral and analytical techniques that are available for educators to employ in their teaching and learning, classroom management, motivation, and assessment practices. The knowledge, skills, and dispositions of many school administrators also reflect Thorndike's behavioral and quantitative ideas and perspectives. In fact, in 1913 Thorndike and George D. Strayer published one of the first books for school administrators, *Educational Administration: Quantitative Studies*. However, Thorndike's influence also extends to curriculum, the acquisition of knowledge, and the role of educators.

Thorndike's Influence on Curriculum

In contemporary education, organization of curriculum is predominately disciplinary, not interdisciplinary, in nature. Curriculum that is organized around disciplines (i.e., math, science, social studies, language arts, fine arts) is one in which students study each discipline as a separate body of knowledge with little or no connection to another discipline. In other words, in a math class students only focus on math knowledge and skills, and they are not expected to study other disciplines such as language arts or social studies in the math class. An interdisciplinary curriculum is one in which the different disciplines are combined to foster an authentic real-life encounter with the knowledge from all of the disciplines included in the interdisciplinary curriculum. An example would be a project that would require students to use math, social studies, science, and language arts knowledge and skills in a setting that would allow the interconnected knowledge to unfold in a natural manner similar to how it would unfold in real life. Curriculum that is organized in a disciplinary manner reduces knowledge from its naturally occurring interconnected whole to discrete parts that are disconnected from how the knowledge actually exists in real-world contexts.

In the early 1900s, the idea of disciplinary curriculum became entrenched in education through the efforts of individuals such as Frederick Winslow Taylor, who promoted the scientific management of education, John Franklin Bobbitt, who was a major contributor to the social efficiency movement, and Edward L. Thorndike, who was an advocate of differentiated curriculum. Thorndike argued for the differentiation of curriculum, especially in the secondary schools. A differentiated curriculum was organized in such a way that it would meet the anticipated future vocational needs of the students. The educational historian Herbert Kliebard (1995) provides a detailed discussion on this period in curriculum development, especially Thorndike's promotion of a differentiated curriculum. Concerning Thorndike's position, Kliebard writes,

He [Thorndike] went on to estimate that not more than a third of the secondary student population should study algebra and geometry since, in the first place, they were not suited for those subjects and, in the second, they could occupy their time much more efficiently by studying those subjects that would fit them more directly for what their lives had in store. (p. 94)

Those individuals who agreed with this position on curriculum maintained that an integral way to determine who studies what would be through the results gained from extensive intelligence testing. In this way, once it was determined which students would study a different level of knowledge in a discipline (e.g., basic math versus algebra and other higher-order forms of math), psychological principles such as Thorndike's connectionism (i.e., the use of stimulus–response sequences) could be applied to the step-by-step organization of the curriculum and instructional strategies.

Kliebard (1995) and Cremin (1964), another scholar who studied this time period, both situate Thorndike within the Progressive Movement in education. However, both indicate that Thorndike's social philosophy, like those who promoted scientific management and social efficiency, was conservative. Unlike liberal progressives such as John Dewey, Thorndike's conservative views aligned with the conservative position that education should be tailored for each student in that some would pursue intellectual knowledge and skill, while others would pursue the knowledge and skill necessary for their intended occupation. Thomas S. Popkewitz (1991) explains that differentiated curriculum and vocationalism actually promoted class differences between the wealthy and the poor. Popkewitz proposes that the field of educational psychology as envisioned by individuals like Thorndike became a central dynamic in the production of power relations through education in the twentieth century (p. 102). Through this organization of education, the power arrangements within American society were reproduced, thus continuing the dominance of certain social classes over others.

In relation to the reproduction of one class's power over another, differentiated curriculum, as envisioned by Thorndike, decontextualized the knowledge that students were to acquire. For instance, this means that the learning of math, science, or any other discipline was done within a tightly controlled context that was devoid of any moral, social, economic, or political factors and conditions that mediated and informed the knowledge in real life. A decontextualized curriculum places the emphasis for a student's educational needs, knowledge, and achievement solely on the individual, thus denying all of the other factors that contribute to the student's social status, intelligence testing results, and educational achievement.

Thorndike's Influence on the Acquisition of Knowledge

How knowledge is acquired affects the nature of knowledge. For instance, if what is considered true knowledge can be acquired only through one view on knowledge and the methods of its acquisition, then all other knowledge about a phenomenon acquired through other methods of inquiry is considered less valuable knowledge, or even false knowledge. Currently in education, there is a sharp divide between those who view quantitative inquiry and qualitative inquiry as exclusive methods of knowledge acquisition. A recent movement towards a mixed methodology, or the use of multiple inquiry methods (i.e., both quantitative and qualitative in all of their diverse forms) is attempting to bridge this divide in order to gain a more holistic and realistic understanding of educational phenomena. Until the last decade or two, quantitative methods of inquiry dominated education's attempt to develop effective curriculum, instruction, and assessment. Despite the ascendance of qualitative methodologies in the late 1980s and 1990s, with the No Child Left Behind Act of 2001 (NCLB) quantitative methods are regaining their former position of dominance. In essence, the reductionist and empirical research that characterizes quantitative inquiry is representative of the formal philosophy of inquiry that only accepts empirical knowledge as valid knowledge. In contrast, postformal methods of inquiry attempt to capture the full and often hidden contexts of an educational phenomenon through their use of diverse and multiple forms of inquiry. Postformal methods value all forms of knowledge as valid in relation to their contribution to the holistic understanding of a phenomenon.

The work of Thorndike was instrumental in ensuring the dominance of quantitative inquiry. Through his early preeminence in educational psychology, Thorndike's precise scientific experimental processes, which relied upon statistical measurement, became the accepted academic process for knowledge acquisition. As the father of the measurement movement (Lagemann, 2000), Thorndike's influence has been greatly seen in the consistent use of standardized tests to determine student ability, achievement, and position in education. Large-scale assessment of students continues to be used not only as indicators of student success in all levels of education but also as indicators of the effectiveness of teachers and school administrators. The empirical assessments that Thorndike helped to initiate and promote have proven very effective in the ranking and sorting of students within educational contexts, in the construction of curriculum and assessment, and in the management of schools.

Many individuals have contested the equity of these assessments in making decisions about students, curriculum and instruction, and schools. One of their arguments is that despite their functional effectiveness, standardized assessments do not take into account all of the factors that determine student success, effective curriculum and instruction, and the ability of schools to meet the diverse needs of their students. As previously mentioned, standardized assessments decontextualize the act of assessment. What this means is that when students are assessed through SAT, GRE, MAT, or state standardized tests, they are assessed in a narrowly defined representation of the tested knowledge. Through the statistical procedures developed by individuals such as Thorndike, attempts are made to statistically control for other variables such as socioeconomic status, test bias, test anxiety, and a plethora of other variables that do affect a student's performance. This debate over decontextualized assessments versus holistic assessments that seek out the additional contexts that affect student performance has been greatly renewed with the implementation of NCLB.

With the advent of NCLB, the kind of large-scale empirical measurement and analysis originally promoted by Thorndike has become the exclusive definition of what constitutes scientific research by the U.S. government (National Research Council, 2002). The U.S. government, to ensure the dominance of this view, has constructed a new educational research infrastructure. Through organizations such as the Institute for Education Sciences and the What Works Clearinghouse, large-scale quantitative research in the form of experimental randomized trials has become the accepted process that is used to guide decisions about educational practice and the federal funding of educational research. Interestingly, the antecedents of this resurgence of the exclusive use of empirical research include the behavior and measurement work of Thorndike that occurred in the early 1900s.

Thorndike's Influence on the Role of Educators

A significant influence on education of Thorndike's work relates to the professional roles of educators. One immediate outcome of Thorndike's use of empirical scientific procedures is the ascendancy in importance of the expert. Since the employment of this type of research involves strenuous study, skill development, and time, only a few experts can generate this type of theory. Therefore, these experts have generated educational theory involving curriculum, instruction, assessment, and school management. Of course, teachers and school administrators rely on their own experiential knowledge, knowledge of the local context, and intuition to generate their own theory that guides their practice. However, in an empirical environment, this very different type of professional research and knowledge is not considered valid knowledge.

In addition, just as Thorndike's differentiated curriculum is the norm, so is a related organizational strategy called differentiated staffing. Differentiated staffing involves the development of an organizational hierarchy in which each individual performs specifically defined tasks within a well-defined role. School administrators administrate, teachers teach, and students learn. Traditionally, as has been the case, this is only one way to organize and utilize human resources in education. However, due in a large part to Thorndike's work, differentiated staffing is the entrenched norm. One outcome of this expert-driven differentiated structure is the deskilling of teachers. Deskilling refers to the narrow roles that teachers are to perform in this type of system. When deskilled, a teacher becomes a technician whose responsibility is to deliver the prescribed curriculum in a prescribed instructional manner. This type of role is often reinforced through scripted lessons and teacher-proof materials that restrict the autonomy of the teacher in adapting curriculum and instruction to better meet the needs of the students.

Another outcome deals with the issue of authority. In educational systems that are organized in this manner, different degrees of authority are allowed for each person's position in the hierarchy. Generally, the experts have the greatest authority in determining what is considered to be best practice, with the school administrators having the authority to mandate the proper delivery of the assumed best practice by the teachers. In turn, teachers are authorized only to make sure that the assumed best practice is effectively delivered. Those with the least authority are the students, whose function is to receive the mandated curriculum and comply with the mandated instruction. In essence, this is a system of control with the purpose of the differentiated delegation of authority to solely ensue compliance.

CONCLUSION

In conclusion, Thorndike's work, which began in the late 1800s with the scientific experimentation with chicks and cats, has led to a science of pedagogy that still influences education in the beginning of the twenty-first century. According to Lagemann (2000), "Thorndike was pivotal in grounding educational psychology in a narrowly behaviorist conception of learning that involved little more than stimuli, responses, and the connections between them" (p. 235). Thorndike's work has freed educational theory and practice from many questionable assumptions, and continues to influence all aspects of education. In her book, Ellen Lagemann has eloquently described the debate between Thorndike's view of education and that of John Dewey. Lagemann's conclusion is that Thorndike won that debate and because of his victory, education is very different than it would be if Dewey had won.

REFERENCES

Cremin, L. A. (1964). *The Transformation of the School: Progressivism in American Education 1876–1957.* New York: Vintage Books.

Kliebard, H. M. (1995). *The Struggle for the American Curriculum: 1893–1958* (2nd ed.). New York: Routledge.

Lagemann, E. C. (2000). *An Elusive Science: The Troubling History of Education Research.* Chicago: The University of Chicago Press.

National Research Council, Committee on Scientific Principles in Education Research. (2002). *Scientific Research in Education* (R. J. Shavelson and L. Towne, Eds.). Washington, DC: National Academy Press.

Popkewitz, T. S. (1991). *A Political Sociology of Educational Reform.* New York: Teachers College Press.

CHAPTER 33

Rudolph von Laban

ADRIENNE SANSOM

Many of us have marveled at the way very young children begin to find their footing as they totter to take their first steps, but have you ever given thought to the intricacies involved in that process? Have you ever given thought about the way we move and perform our daily tasks? Have you ever given thought about the way we describe human movement? If you have been involved in dance education, human development, or in some other aspects of physical education or physical therapy, there would, no doubt, be times when you have used certain terminology to instruct, or used specific vocabulary to describe the concept of movement you are observing or wish to explore. But have you ever wondered where that language or terminology came from and why certain descriptors are used to describe movement?

For the purpose of this chapter I am concerned, in particular, with the terminology used to describe human movement especially as it is applied in dance education. This concern or interest arises because, from the perspective of dance education within a Western or Eurocentric paradigm, one man developed much of the discourse we use in dance education today. This man was Rudolph von Laban.

WHO IS RUDOLPH VON LABAN?

Rudolph von Laban (1879–1958), an Austrian, was born in Czechoslovakia. He was an artist, dancer, choreographer, and movement theorist. He has also been described as a visionary, and there is no question that he was certainly a great and creative thinker. To this day, he is well known for his contributions to the field of dance, especially dance education and for the development of movement/dance notation (Labanotation), which is a system of notating movement that can be used for the purpose of recording and, thus, replicating historical and choreographed dances. In a sense, it could be said that Laban brought a form of literacy to the art of dance and, consequently, helped elevate the status of dance as an art form during his time.

Laban (1988) developed his interest in the study of human movement in Paris when there was the emergence of a new form of dance, which was called modern dance in most English-speaking countries but was referred to as "free dance" or "la danse libre" in France for reasons that will become apparent. At a time when there was a rising interest in machines and technology during the development of the industrial age, artists such as Laban found that urbanization increasingly separated the artist and, thus, society and people, from life. Laban, like many other artists during that time, wanted to reconnect to nature so as to counterbalance the fragmentation and separation that was occurring between being governed by machines and being more fully human and in touch with nature. This was part of a counterattack against the urbanization of society that was seen to be separating the artist from life. There was a desperate need for artists to reconnect to nature and, therefore, being human. For this reason Laban focused on the human body as a counterdiscourse to the industrialization that occurred in the eighteenth and nineteenth centuries.

There was very much a move during this time toward seeking an inner awareness of life and self, through tapping into one's emotions or feelings and, thus, seeing the world in a more spiritual and connected way as opposed to just being aware of the outside world without connecting to that world. During this time of seeking a new way to live in the world, dance was often exhibited as a commune with nature, where the objective was to feel the environment or space, not only through a commitment to engaging fully from a physical point of view, but also to enveloping the emotional dedication such a commitment would bring. Laban wanted to focus on the movement of the body as a means of discovering and exploring the capabilities of the human body for the purposes of promoting creativity, imagination, insight, and knowledge.

It was his belief that the body reflected the world one lived in, such as the formation of muscles and patterns of the body, which very much influenced dance at that time. It was these body patterns that, from Laban's perspective, required systematic study so as to offer another way of being in this world, physically, mentally, and emotionally. This was the visionary nature of Laban's theory and, thus, fuelled his desire to create a system that could be utilized in education and life in general for the purpose of "turning the tide" of human decay or despiritualization. Ultimately, Laban's development of the study of movement was a way of connecting the body, mind, and spirit, individually and collectively, so that what affected the self also affected society.

In the process of developing his study of human movement in the early 1900s, Laban worked closely with, among others, Mary Wigman (one of Germany's early modern dancers and a student of Laban) to explore his ideas of weight, space, and time. Laban's approach to observing, analyzing, and describing human movement was very exacting and it has been noted that Wigman often found Laban's precise and systematic approach to observing and eliciting movement somewhat restrictive. As a dancer, Wigman wanted to create or apply more emotion to the movement theories of Laban, so as to gain a far more sensuous approach to what was otherwise outwardly devoid of expression.

Despite this seemingly clinical approach to the observation and analysis of human movement, Laban was very much a man of passion and artistic and aesthetic sensibility. In a rare glimpse of Laban recorded on film, I had the fortunate opportunity to witness Laban playing a flute while promoting a bevy of dancers around him to gain freedom while they danced. Indeed, such words as liberation and excitement are used salubriously throughout modern educational dance texts written by Laban when describing the outcome of exploring particular movements for the purpose of promoting creativity and expressiveness using the language of dance. This promotion of "finding freedom" or flow was part of Laban's ideology of connecting with nature and, in so doing, being released from the grips of machines and technology.

From Laban's perspective, the movement of the human body was the key to this ideal, because movement acts as the conduit between the body, mind, and psyche. It was believed that without the recognition of the movement of the body and what that feels like, we would have less chance of feeling, sensing, expressing, imagining, thinking, and, thus, changing the world we live in. Our bodies, and therefore the movement of our bodies, act as a link between ourselves and the world we live in; hence, Laban's theories and practice, and therefore analysis of the movement of the human body, provided a way to explore this relationship.

LABAN'S CONTRIBUTIONS TO THE FIELD OF DANCE EDUCATION

Rudolph von Laban contributed greatly to the field of both movement and dance education. His serious and in-depth study of movement was astounding and he provided some necessary and crucial language to describe the intricate and complex movement of the body. In fact, his study was so vast and profound the language used for movement covered a very broad base of all the movements the body could perform. Because of the intricate nature of Laban's movement theories, his system of observing, describing, and recording human movement also facilitated the development of a complex form of notation, otherwise known as Labanotation, which enabled the recording and replication of human movement and, consequently, set or choreographed dances. This became part of Laban's main contribution to the field of dance and continues to be studied today. This was prime material for dancers because it opened up new ways of describing— especially for the purposes of choreographic replication—movement in such detail (before the advent of video) that dancers could literally transfer the original movements of dances onto their own bodies and recreate the dances.

What is particularly pertinent here in relation to the field of education is Laban's contribution to the place and purpose of dance education. After the Second World War, Laban moved to and lived in Great Britain, where he reconceptualized the role of dance in education. Based on his belief that children, particularly youth, would benefit from learning self-control and self-discipline, he considered that practice in the control of physical movement as well as the encouragement of creative forms of movement were necessary during the school years. These two aspects of learning about the movement of the body were both important from Laban's point of view and were considered to be part of modern educational dance. Laban believed ardently that dance, in some form, should be available to everyone and that movement formed the basis of all human endeavors using both the body and the mind.

Laban's purpose was to develop a new form of dance education in schools beyond the traditional forms of dance found in schools such as folk dance and historical or period dances. By drawing on what he could find out about the origin of traditional dance forms, as well as studying the everyday working habits of people in general, Laban worked to develop a comprehensive theory about the movement of the human body, which was noticeably lacking in comparison to the other arts, where much was written about the art form.

By its very form, movement, or dance, particularly from a historical perspective, leaves no trace beyond descriptions provided in words or in occasional etchings and photographs (which, in these other forms, become works of art beyond the art of dance) and, thus, is less permanent or visible when compared to other art forms such as painting, music, architecture, sculpture, poetry, and literature. For this reason, much of the history of dance has been lost.

While society continued to change, transformation in dance was less noticeable because there was little evidence recorded of such change. Thus, Laban set about creating a language for the "art of movement," or what was otherwise known, particularly in the United States and the United Kingdom, "modern dance." This "modern" dance was a newer, "freer" form of dance, which reflected the time as people began to release themselves from the restrictions of excessive clothing and industrialized working habits.

During this time there was also an emphasis on a distinct disconnect between the body and the mind, where the body was reserved for leisurely pursuits devoid of serious contemplation, and the mind was occupied in the far more important realm of work and study. Consequently, according to Laban, children in schools knew little of the richness and value that a life imbued by movement could bring. This is where Laban's belief in counterbalancing the industrialization of society needed to be activated in education based on a sound foundation of understanding the movement of the human body. From this arose the language used today in dance education, which was based on the effort elements that underpin all forms of human movement such as weight, space, time, and flow. It is this knowledge of human effort that formed the basis of Laban's theories of the "art of movement." With an emphasis on all the movement the human body could do, the notion of dance, or the "art of movement" changed from being seen as just a set of technically executed steps to a flow of movement arising from all parts of the body. Hence, we have the study of movement and its elements, or what is more commonly known as the elements of movement.

This effectively provided education with an approach to dance that could be systematically studied on the basis of what was considered the "universal" principles of human movement. This new approach to dance served several purposes. Firstly, it was seen as a way to capitalize on the children's "natural" propensity to move while providing them with a form of exercise and increasing their sense of expression. The preservation of spontaneity and creativity were important considerations for Laban as was the fostering of artistic expression. Ultimately, from Laban's perspective, this would lead to an awareness of a broader outlook of the way we, as humans, live our lives.

While also considering the observation of movement deficiencies and, thus, using these observations to improve upon both the weaknesses as well as the strengths exhibited by students, Laban believed that these new dance theories would lead to an integration of the intellect with creativity, both of which he saw as equally important in education.

Thus, Laban's theories of movement brought about a new way to view dance in education and provided a sound basis and language that could be explored in all forms of dance. Dancers and dance educators alike embraced his work, but his vision or theories of human movement extended beyond dance as they expressed the way humans operated both physically and mentally in everyday life. For this reason, Laban's contribution to the field of the study of human movement is used by a diverse group of people such as athletes, actors, sociologists, physiotherapists, educators, and psychologists, as well as dancers. One of the early disciples of Laban was Irmgard Bartenieff, who had learned dance with Laban, and then went on to develop what is now known as Bartenieff Fundamentals. Laban's theories also contributed to the work of other dance educators such as Lisa Ullman, Joan Russell, Joyce Boorman, Valerie Preston-Dunlop, and Anne Hutchinson-Guest, to name just a few. Ultimately, all of those involved in dance education are influenced in some way by the work of Rudolf von Laban.

In general terms, the legacy Laban left behind after his death in 1958 has continued to be developed by students and devotees of Laban movement theories, and what followed was the creation of a codified language for movement, which became known as Laban Movement Analysis. This has commonly been referred to as LMA, which is the acronym I will use throughout the rest of this chapter. The terminology and, therefore, ideology behind LMA as it is practiced today encompasses four main categories: Body, Effort, Shape, and Space (BESS). Each of what I will now refer to as the BESS components can be studied in further depth, and it is these BESS components that form the basis of the terminology used in dance education.

Thus, LMA has become an acceptable codified language for movement and a valuable tool for observing and understanding "body language" or the information or stories the movement of the body conveys. When used by those trained as movement analysts, LMA can be used to describe and interpret all forms of human movement in any area where we use or take care of the human body.

WHAT IS LMA? THE THEORY AND PRACTICE OF LABAN MOVEMENT ANALYSIS

Briefly, these four main categories of BESS deal with the spectrum of movement the body can perform as observed and codified by Laban. For the purposes of describing something of what the codified language or terminology refers to related to dance, the following is an explanation of each of the categories under the acronym BESS

- The Body aspect of BESS deals with principles such as the initiation of movement from specific body parts, the connection of different body parts to each other, and the sequencing of movement between parts of the body.
- The Effort dimension is concerned with movement qualities and dynamics, and is subdivided into Weight, Space, Time, and Flow factors.
- Shape is about the way the body interacts with its environment. There are three Modes of Shape Change: Shapeflow (growing and shrinking, folding and unfolding, etc.), Directional (Spokelike and Arclike), or Shaping (molding, carving, and adapting).
- Space involves the study of moving in connection with the environment and is based on spatial patterns, pathways, and lines of spatial tension. (Sandlos, 1999)

Perhaps, what one can see here is that, even by the choice of words used to describe Laban's work, there is a form of rationalization or clinical analysis applied to the concept of movement, which was Laban's intention because his movement theories had a broader application than just covering the rudiments of dance. He also wanted to address the basics of everyday working and sports movements so that his theories had a wider range of application. Of course, for dancers, whose work often arises from a passion or evocation of wanting to express some ideas/thoughts and feelings in movement, a clinical approach can appear to be somewhat devoid of that inner passion. Having said this, however, we can also look at classical ballet, and some other dance forms that have since been codified as a technique, such as the Graham or Cunningham technique, which, when separated out from the actual creation of a dancework, acts as a way to define and perform specified movements that can be devoid of—or separate from—the actual reason for creating the dance in the first place.

The techniques, in other words, become the tools we use for dance, but sometimes in a way that can hinder that actual passion, or desire, of dancing as well as accessibility to dance for everyone when set within a Western paradigm and discourse. Certainly, given the time Laban developed his theories, it is conceivable that the language he used had particular nuances that reflected that time. Much of Laban's work has been revised in later years, often because the original language used was viewed as being somewhat awkward and seen to be obscuring the original intent or meaning of Laban's work.

It is this issue that expresses something of the dilemma I have with the "language" used in dance education drawn from Laban's comprehensive observation and analysis of human movement and subsequently developed into LMA. This is the reason why I want to attempt to offer another perspective or reconceptualization of a way to use or read Laban's theory in dance education today.

If you flip through a "modern educational dance" text, you will encounter words such as *angle, bound flow, contracting, dabbing, direct, dragging, effort, expanding, falling, firm, flexible, flicking, floating, fluttering, free flow, gathering, gesture, gliding, grasping, growing, hovering, jerking, light, locomotion, motor sensations, patting, penetrating, piercing, plucking, poking, pressing, punching, rising, shooting, shoving, shrinking, slashing, sphere, streaming, sudden, sustained, traversing, throwing, thrusting, vibrating, whipping, wringing,* and *zone.* Although these "words" convey a comprehensive and diverse list of descriptive language that can be used to describe the almost infinite possibilities of movement of the human body, they are also open to an incredibly wide range of interpretations, seem to be somewhat abstract, particularly when disconnected to the contextual nature of the situation, and, from my perspective, many terms are strongly masculine in nature.

As a dance educator myself, and knowing full well how useful this language is, I am obviously not advocating for the eradication of such mindfully considered language used to describe the depth and breadth of human movement, but what I am questioning is the transmission of such language into any given context where dance is being taught without the consideration of "changing," adapting, or adding to the language in a way that connects to the "audience" or specific learners so as to be seen as a viable and meaningful way of both learning and understanding dance.

Often when language, or a particular discourse, is presented within the parameters of "academia" or education, and already given the seal of acceptability by the "powers that be," namely "white males," there appears to be little attempt made to alter that language. It is as if the language is "set in stone" and there is a fear that if certain language is changed or adapted (or even added to) the original intention of the theorist will be diluted, or misunderstood. Now, don't get me wrong! I am not calling for a complete overhaul of the incredibly rich language Laban has (and others have) already established for dance education. What I am suggesting is that the established and, therefore, accepted language should not be immune to, or eschew the introduction of, other terminology or ways of interpreting movement, especially when we consider the limited geographical and cultural climes the predominant language used in dance education originated from. This is so despite claims that the origins of dance, and therefore, language for dance, were drawn from all corners of the globe. I have noted that Laban discounted the dance movements of "native" people, or what he termed as primitive forms of communal dance because he deemed that these forms did not provide a sufficient source of inspiration. It is interesting to note that when "primitive" forms of dance are mentioned; they are used to compare to the initial or fundamental movements of infants and toddlers.

A POSTFORMAL CRITIQUE: THE IMPETUS FOR SEEKING A RECONCEPTUALIZATION OF THE LANGUAGE OF DANCE EDUCATION

Some years ago a colleague said to me that she felt some of the language we use in dance education could do with a facelift, or, in other words, a change. She posed the question as to why, as educators, we continue to hold onto somewhat outdated/limited/abstract words (or language) for the purposes of teaching dance education? Why, she continued, could we not introduce other language to assist the students in their exploration and understanding of dance education?

On top of this question came yet another question, this time from a different source. Another colleague in the field of dance education queried a student's remark that the language commonly used in dance education was somewhat exclusive because it generally relied upon the language drawn from a Eurocentric base and excluded other languages and, thus, concepts from countries and cultures outside Europe where dance also existed. The reply or response from this particular colleague was that dance, no matter where it took place, or of what style it was, still involved a vocabulary to describe the basic elements used, such as space, time, effort (energy/force), and body.

When I began to examine these questions from a postformal perspective I realized that it was important to remember that postformal thinking draws from a wide range of theories, which involves critical theory and feminist theory, as well as critical multiculturalism, cultural studies, together with postmodernist epistemologies, indigenous knowledges, and contextual or situated cognition (Kincheloe and Steinberg, 1993). This means that we can no longer apply the theories of one predominant culture, or way of thinking, without considering other ways of thinking if we want to create a holistic educational psychology that is ethically and culturally grounded so as to form the basis of a democratic educational psychology. This necessitates that I raise the argument that we need to examine the language of LMA more carefully and consider alternative discourses/approaches to dance education.

While not actually interrogating either of these two points of view, because there is more depth to them than I have actually outlined here, what intrigued me was the fact that the language we do use for dance education tends to have remained unchanged for many years. The list of descriptive words I provided previously are clearly drawn from Laban's theories of movement, and, as such, have become somewhat universal in their usage no matter what the context, such as the culture, language, age, and experience.

I also began to wonder if the language used could actually be detrimental to the acceptance of dance, particularly given the fact that dance aficionados would like to see dance as something all people could do in education. This concern relates not only to the teachers (aka adults) but also to the students/children, to whom this language would be imparted as a way to promote dance in schools. This language also filters down to early childhood environments, where, I know from experience, the language or vocabulary used is, or at least should be, gradually sidelined in favor of more meaningful terms and approaches to engage the young child's interest in dance.

What I started to see in this analysis was the fixation to hold onto certain language that was once codified by a theorist without considering that other language, vocabulary, or points of view about what constitutes dance could be used. It was almost as if there was a fear, or even a guilt, that if one did not heed what a now-well-known theorist espoused (and so thoughtfully too, in that time considering little other form of codifiying dance was done apart from ballet), it was seen as sacrilegious to dare to alter or add to the already established and well-thought-out vocabulary, or theory.

Now, I am obviously not the first person to have considered this question of the appropriateness of language, because evidence is already offered in the initial openings to this query. I also know that there are other dance texts that expand upon the language used in dance, while still acknowledging the origins of the dance vocabulary used in most educational settings. For me, nevertheless, this has larger ramifications than the actual language being used, although this is obviously important because it not only is the crux of the matter being explored here, but it also speaks of privileging some ways or approaches (languages) over others, as if the other ways of speaking about dance (the child's, different cultures, minorities, or the "other") were not seen as worthy or valuable in a predominantly Westernized/Eurocentric approach to education.

On the one hand, I value having a language for the area I teach; without the language there would be a somewhat limited approach to teaching this subject. Also, without the language, there would be little to help students with learning some of the basic and essential, or necessary, components of dance education. A codified language, with some sound basis, is vital, particularly in an area where it is seen that you do not actually have to think to move the body. The language or literacy of dance provides at least some evidence of the fact that dance, too, requires some thought and learning, beyond just using the body or copying movements that someone else demonstrates.

From a postmodern as well as postformal perspective, it is important, nevertheless, to remember that these ways of thinking encourage the unearthing or uncovering of what is or what has been taken for granted. These states of thinking promote continual growth and movement or change, and, for this reason, applying a static approach to understanding the languages or legacies we have inherited would exclude the development of new ways of thinking or seeing the world, which was the very impetus that inspired Laban to develop his theories. I associate this perspective or way of thinking with the notion of fluidity and flexibility (interestingly enough, two words Laban uses in his analysis of movement), where nothing is set but is forever changing, as it is being created by those involved in the process of learning and teaching. When one is involved in their learning, this brings in different approaches drawn from diverse backgrounds where new and more meaningful knowledge or understanding can emerge and add to the already rich body of knowledge that has been established.

Because the educator's/teacher's/instructor's approach to teaching will effectively influence what will be taught, and, consequently, learned, as well as how this learning will take place, it would be important to address the ways in which dance can or may be taught in educational settings by critically examining the language used in dance education. By doing this, we open up the possibilities of multiple approaches and thwart the perpetuation of the status quo through one approach to learning in dance. This links with a critical and postmodern approach to knowing where there is the need to look beyond a Westernized, Eurocentric perspective as the only epistemology to draw upon.

The language mainly used for the educational elements of dance carry one predominant view of "knowing" as opposed to exploring other languages and art forms, which can provide multidimensional understandings. We need to be aware of how the use of one predominant language for dance education can hinder as well as enhance what we come to know as dance and look at whether this raises issues of universalizing or generalizing, and provides, at best, somewhat abstract concepts/approaches to teaching dance. From a pluralistic and multicultural perspective, we need to promote the interrelationship between other cultural art forms and the Eurocentric/Westernized language and methodology used primarily in dance education today considering the students/children we teach and the diverse cultures they embody.

Ultimately, this leaves me with some questions that I think are worthy for all of us to consider from a postmodern and postformal perspective. Can these abstract and somewhat universalized concepts transfer across different dance styles/processes from other cultures/countries? Is this language still relevant in a multinational, multicultural society? Is it meaningful to children/students as a language for dance? Does it connect to students'/children's lives today? Is there still a place for a commonly accepted vocabulary for dance education that can be used universally and applied to any/all cultures?

CONCLUSION

In many ways Laban's theories were the antithesis of what ailed society, yet, as with many things in society, those who inherit such legacies fail to adequately apply the same visionary foresight to the ongoing sustenance of such legacies. Of course, I do not want to be misunderstood here, because I truly believe that Laban's theories and contribution to education have been mammoth, and for this reason, have been given worthy consideration in many fields (although in some fields concerning the body more than in others). Nevertheless, as with any visionary, we must continue to envision the possibilities, as well as the limitations, for the generations that follow.

Ultimately, I want to continue to honor the legacy Laban left us related to his theories of movement and its application to the field of dance education, but even more so I want to see it develop and grow as our world and people change and exchange different ways of being in the world. What can be more worthy of consideration than understanding ourselves as human beings and, thus, understanding others and the world we live in? Movement, or the way the body moves, is vital to this quest, especially where, in dance, the body and the person become one in a way that provides a means of celebrating who we are as human beings. Coming to know ourselves and answering the age-old question "Who am I?" is something that one begins to discover through being in touch with what makes us tick, namely the movement of the body and its interrelation with the mind and spirit. It is through the body that we experience the sensations of life, the pulse of our heartbeat, the weight and balance of bodily matter, the force of gravity, the tension and relaxation of everyday events, and the energy of life itself.

This was Laban's legacy, and something that we need to keep alive so as to never forget the treasure he left us with. This is perhaps best expressed in his own words: "Motion is an essential of existence. The stars wandering across the sky, are born and die. Everywhere is change. This ceaseless motion throughout measureless space and endless time has its parallel in the smaller motion of shorter duration, that occurs on our earth. This motion becomes movement in living beings" (Lewitzky, 1989). This belief in the power of movement is important to me and is something we all possess as breathing, living beings on this earth, and it is for this reason that I posit that all people, from all walks of life, from all cultures, and from all parts of the world, have their voices heard too, so as to add to the rich inheritance we have garnered from Rudolph von Laban. I cannot envision that such a forward-thinking theorist and visionary as Laban would not want his ideas expanded upon and, thus, critiqued. Nothing new comes without change, and change, which is meaningful and purposeful, comes from thoughtful and critical consideration of those things that have gone before.

REFERENCES

Kincheloe, J., and Steinberg, S. (1993). A tentative description of post-formal thinking: The critical confrontation with cognitive theory. *Harvard Educational Review,* 63 (3), 296–320.

Laban, R. (1988). *Modern Educational Dance* (3rd ed.). Revised by Lisa Ullmann. Plymouth, UK: Northcote Publishers Ltd.

Lewitzky, B. (1989). Why Art? From University of California, San Diego Regent's Lecture, May 31, 1989. Retrieved May 11, 2005, from http://www.perspicacity.com/dancesite/lewitzky/whyart.htm.

Sandlos, L. (1999). Laban Movement Analysis. Retrieved May 11, 2005, from http://www.xoe.com/LisaSandlos/lma.html. Retrieved 5/11/2005.

CHAPTER 34

Lev Vygotsky

KATE E. O'HARA

Lev Semonovich Vygotsky was born on November 5, 1896, in the small Russian town of Orsche. Within the first year of his life, his family moved to Gomel, one of the few designated provinces reserved for those of Jewish descent in tsarist Russia. Vygotsky's parents were both well educated and spoke several languages fluently. The second oldest child of eight children, Vygotsky frequently helped in the upkeep of the household and care of the younger siblings. The family was very tightly knit, and often joined together in discussions about history, literature, theater, and art. It was these family discussions that exposed Vygotsky to a wide range of interests.

His elementary education was received at home, studying independently and having a tutor for consultation. After passing an exam for the first five years of grade school, he entered into a private all boys secondary school known as a gymnasium—a secondary school that prepared students for the university. There he was a consistent student, and did equally well in all subjects. He graduated in 1913, with hopes of becoming a teacher, but unfortunately training for this profession was not an option. Teaching in public schools was a position not available for Jews in prerevolutionary Russia, and therefore his parents suggested he become a doctor because this would allow him more freedom.

Acting on the advice of his parents, Vygotsky sent an application to the Medical School of Moscow University and was accepted. After studying at the school for about a month, he realized that medicine was far from his true interest and transferred to the Law School of the same university.

And so again he began to study intensely, but like medicine, law was not pleasing to him. He was intent upon studying his true interests: literature, art, philosophy, and philosophical analyses of art. As a result, he decided in 1914, without interrupting his education at the law school, to enroll in the historical–philosophical division of Shanavsky University, a Jewish public university. The level of instruction at this university was very high, taught by leading scientists and scholars of that time; however, the degrees awarded were not accepted by the government, and graduates received no official recognition.

In December of 1917, the year of the Russian revolution, Vygotsky returned to Gomel after completing his education at both universities, and graduating from Moscow University with a degree in law. Upon returning home, Vygotsky was met by unfortunate family circumstances. His mother was recovering from a bout with tuberculosis and his younger brother, who also contracted the disease, was in a critical condition. Within the year, Vygotsky's younger brother died, and tragically a second brother died of typhoid. Before the end of the year, his mother relapsed and once again he had to care for her. It was in 1920 that Vygotsky himself experienced the first of a number of attacks from the same illness that struck his family members—tuberculosis.

Throughout his short life, Vygotsky battled numerous times with the disease before succumbing to it on June 10, 1934, at the young age of thirty-seven. Prior to his death, Vygotsky completed 270 scientific articles, numerous lectures, and ten books based on a wide range of Marxist-based psychological and teaching theories as well as in the areas of pedagogy, art and aesthetics, and sociology. His collaboration with Alexander Luria and Alexei Leontiev produced a completely new approach to psychology that emphasized the importance of social interaction in human development. Vygotsky's work did not become known in the West until 1958, and was not published there until 1962 (Hansen-Reid, 2001).

Despite this, once recognized, Vygotsky's theories greatly influenced modern constructivist thinking. He contended that humans, unlike animals who react only to the environment, have the capacity to alter the environment for their own purposes. It is this adaptive capacity that distinguishes humans from lower forms of life. One of his central contributions to educational psychology is his emphasis on socially meaningful activity as an important influence on human consciousness. Vygotsky's "sociocultural theory" suggests that social interaction leads to continuous changes in children's thought and behavior. These thoughts and behaviors would vary between cultures and that the development depends on interaction with people and the tools that the culture provides to help form one's own view of the world. There are several ways in which a cultural tool can be passed from one individual to another. One is by imitative learning, where one person tries to imitate or copy another. Another way is by instructed learning, which involves remembering the instructions of the "teacher" and then using these instructions to self-regulate. And lastly, a cultural tool can be passed to others through collaborative learning, which involves a group of peers who work together to learn a specific skill (Gallagher, 1999).

Vygotsky also differentiated between a person's higher and lower mental functions. Lower or elementary functions are genetically inherited; they are our natural mental abilities. In contrast, our higher mental functions develop through social interaction, being socially or culturally mediated.

Our behavioral options are limited when functioning occurs at an elementary level. Without the learning that occurs as a result of social interaction, without self-awareness or the use of signs and symbols that allow us to think in more complex ways, we would remain slaves to the situation, responding directly to the environment. In contrast, higher mental functions allow us to move from impulsive behavior to instrumental action. Again, it is noted that mediation occurs through the use of tools or signs of a culture. Language and symbolism are used initially to mediate contact with the social environment, then within ourselves. When the cultural artifacts become internalized, humans acquire the capacity for higher-order thinking (Goldfarb, 2001).

This cognitive development is a process in which language is a crucial tool for determining how a child will learn how to think because advanced modes of thought are transmitted to the child by means of words. Once the child realizes that everything has a name, each new object presents the child with a problem situation, and he solves the problem by naming the object. When he lacks "the word" for the new object, he demands it from adults. The early word meanings thus acquired will be the embryos of concept formation. During the course of development, everything occurs twice. For example, in the learning of language, our first utterances with peers or adults are for the purpose of communication, but once mastered they become internalized and allow "inner speech." Vygotsky believed that thought undergoes many changes as it turns into speech (Goldfarb, 2001).

There are several core principles of development at the heart of Vygotsky's sociocultural theory. They are as follows: (a) children construct their knowledge, (b) development cannot be separated from its social context, (c) learning can lead development, and (d) language plays a central role in mental development (Gallagher, 1999).

In addition, the sociocultural theory contains another widely recognized element called the zone of proximal development (ZPD). Vygotsky believed that any pedagogy creates learning processes that lead to development and thus this sequence results in "zones of proximal development." It's the concept that a child will accomplish a task that he or she cannot do alone, with help from a more skilled person. Vygotsky also described the ZPD as the difference between the actual development level as determined by individual problem solving and the level of potential development as determined through problem solving under adult guidance or collaboration with more knowledgeable peers (Gallagher, 1999).

In order for the ZPD to be such a success, it must contain two features. The first is called subjectivity. This term describes the process in which two individuals begin a task with different understanding but then eventually arrive at a shared understanding despite original differences in thought or thought process. The second feature is scaffolding, which refers to a change in the social support over the course of a teaching session. If scaffolding is successful, a child's mastery or level of performance can change, which means that it can increase a child's performance on a particular task (Gallagher, 1999).

It should be noted that Vygotsky's ideas and theories are often compared to those of Jean Piaget, especially his cognitive–developmental theory. Opposing Vygotsky's zone of proximal development, Piaget believed that the most important source of cognition rests with children themselves as individuals. But Vygotsky argued that the social environment could catalyze the child's cognitive development. The social environment is an important factor that helps the child culturally adapt to new situations when needed. Both Vygotsky and Piaget had the common goal of finding out how children master ideas and then translate them into speech. Piaget found that children act independently in the physical world to discover what it has to offer. Vygotsky, on the other hand, wrote in *Thought and Language* that human mental activity is the result of social learning. As children master tasks they will engage in cooperative dialogues with others, which led Vygotsky to believe that acquisition of language is the most influential moment in a child's life. Piaget, however, emphasized universal cognitive change while Vygotsky's theory leads to expect a highly variable development, depending on the child's cultural experiences to the environment. Piaget's theory emphasized the natural line of development, while Vygotsky favored the cultural line (Gallagher, 1999). It was Vygotsky's idea of culturally influenced development that has been central to changing the history of educational psychology.

Indisputably, Vygotsky's ideas have left behind a world of thought and theory based on objective and scientific notions. He has opened the door to postformal thinking, with a major impact, in particular, on the field of education. The principals of his sociocultural theory remind us that we can cease our search for one "true truth." His ideas reiterate the notion that our capacity for learning, our cognitive development, is ultimately a reflective, ongoing, and never-ending process.

We can use his concept of the zone of proximal development to explore the ramifications of being at our "actual development level" when we are performing tasks without help from another person. We must ask the question, "How did we get to the point of 'actualization'?" We surely did not inherit this stage or miraculously become placed in it; we must have had to develop through our social and cultural interactions. But, these interactions need not be another person. For example, various forms of media may have helped us self-create our zone so that we are able to engage in individual problem solving. In recent times, computer technology has become a powerful cultural tool, which can be used to mediate and internalize learning. Computers and related technologies change our learning contexts, thus creating meaningful learning activities. This developmental level is a fluid, ongoing process; the actual developmental level is forever changing. What a child can do with assistance one moment will be something that he or she will be able to accomplish independently in the next. In a pedagogical context, this theory supports the concept that when used effectively, technology can aid in the development of multiple literacies. In addition, we understand from Vygotsky that a cultural tool may be passed to another through collaborative learning. In this new context, peer instruction no longer needs a shared physical space. Learning communities may be formed over great distances via the Internet.

Vygotsky's zone of proximal development also has implications in the area of student testing and assessment, especially concerning children with learning and behavior problems. Acting on Vygotsky's ideas, one would have to question if ability and achievement tests are valid measures of a child's capacity to learn. Two children can differ substantially in the ZPDs. One child may do his or her best independently, while another may need some assistance. Therefore, the ZPD is crucial for identifying each child's readiness to benefit from instruction (Gallagher, 1999). Also, by viewing the purpose of standardized testing through Vygotsky's framework, we clearly discover the test's negative ramifications. Although standardized testing may allow for success of the "average developmental level" of the students being tested, it does not necessarily allow for the success of students whose developmental pace is different. The results of standardized tests and the pressure on them to perform well may greatly influence instruction. Low test scores can unfortunately move classroom practice away from child-centered approaches toward curriculum-driven ones. Curriculum then moves from a collaborative one, with hands-on learning, to one of a specific structure—one that is "drill driven." Classroom practice operates on the goal of bringing everybody up to the same level at the same time, regardless of social and cultural contexts. This disregard of the existence of the continued fluidity of developmental zones ultimately hinders the process of higher mental functions.

It is important to note that Vygotsky's ideas have also laid the foundation for those educational psychologists others working from the constructivist perspective. His notion of scaffolding, in which a person's mastery level changes with the assistance of another, is a concept that was later developed by Jerome Bruner and influenced Bruner's related concept of "instructional scaffolding." It is through the concept of "scaffolding" that we see Vygotsky's theory perpetuating an effective form of instruction that enables teachers to accommodate individual student needs and helps them develop into independent learners.

Scaffolding requires the teacher to provide students the opportunity to extend their current skills and knowledge. The teacher must engage students' interest and motivate students to pursue the instructional goal. Many times this type of teaching allows for interactive dialogue between students and teachers. In this way, communication becomes an instructional strategy by encouraging students to go beyond answering questions and engage in the discourse.

Currently, much of classroom teaching is dominated by a teacher lecturing and students listening. "Knowledge" is viewed as something that is to be transferred to the students. It is often decontextualized, neither socially constructed nor applied. By using Vygotsky's and Bruner's notions of instruction, teachers can help students develop new learning strategies, thus enabling students to eventually complete the task on their own. This is achieved when the teacher provides materials and "tools" to aid the student in developing beyond their current capabilities. Therefore, the teacher's role is not to simplify the content, but rather to provide unfamiliar content in a context that enables the student to move from their current level to a higher level of understanding.

Vygotsky also believed that an essential feature of learning is that it awakens a variety of internal developmental processes that are able to operate only when the child is in the action of interacting with people in his environment and in cooperation with his peers. Therefore, when it comes to language learning, the authenticity of the environment and the affinity between its participants are essential elements to make the learner feel part of this environment. These elements are rarely predominant in conventional classrooms (Schütz, 2004).

Many times classroom-based language development strategies include vocabulary lists, rote learning, and recitation. When classroom settings deny non–English-speaking students the opportunity to interact in social settings with English-speaking peers, the possibility for those students to develop academically and socially is substantially limited. Many word meanings are determined within linguistic and cultural settings. Therefore, in order for English learners to fully understand the language they not only need to learn the words in English, but using Vygotsky's principles as a basis, they must also learn the cultural background that gives the words their English meaning. The vocabulary and terms must be learned in context.

In a broader sense, Vygotsky's ideas enable us to construct new ways of teaching and thinking about learning. With his theories in mind, educators must consider students' cultures and their subsequent effects on the ways students learn. As educators, we must examine our own cultural expectations surrounding teaching and strive to create learning environments that are optimal for presenting new information, concepts, and ideas. This means that each child brings with him knowledge as well as a conception of learning from his family, cultural background, and social context. In order for children to succeed, we must help by making associations between the learning in a school context and learning in a socially constructed cultural context.

Drawing from Vygotsky's sociocultural theory, educators must aim to construct developmentally appropriate curriculum while keeping in mind our students' social experience and level of collaboration. Effective collaboration aids in the development of learning strategies when learners are given the opportunity to work together in heterogeneous groups to discuss, analyze, and solve problems. In order to do this we must offer our students "tools" that are not solely the words and thoughts of the teacher, tools that encompass symbolic systems we use to communicate and analyze reality. We must expand beyond the language of the teacher to include signs, books, videos, photographs, musical pieces, wall displays, charts, maps, scientific equipment, and computers in order to support independent and assisted learning. The use of these cultural tools helps students develop abilities and mental habits needed to be successful in particular intellectual or creative domains. The development of abilities has a marked impact on the development of individual personalities. As students make decisions, plan, organize, express their point of view, provide solutions for problems, and interact with others, they continually develop cognitively in the social world.

Vygotsky's theory has also made an impact on the physical classroom. Traditionally rooms are designed so that the teacher is situated in the room in front of students who are seated in rows, one behind the other. From Vygotsky's perspective, a classroom would be redesigned to provide students with desks or tables to be used as a work space for peer instruction, teamwork, and teacher-facilitated small-group instruction. Like the physical environment, once again the instructional design of material would be varied in order to promote and encourage student interaction and collaboration; thus the classroom becomes a community of learning that allows for or encourages the co-construction of knowledge.

In addition, we must actively ask ourselves to determine specific ways in which Vygotsky's zone of proximal development concept can be used to improve students' learning. We must move from teaching methods that rely on recitation and direct instruction, and begin to generate procedures that are based on postformal thought, such as Vygotsky's scaffolding strategy, which supports students as they are introduced to advanced concepts, synthesize information, and adopt individual reasoning about their social and cognitive world.

And perhaps most important, we must recognize that students socially construct knowledge and concepts through experiences within their cultures and we must alter our teaching strategies accordingly to create a connection between their cultural foundations of knowledge and their school-based experiences.

Despite the time that has elapsed since we first read Vygotsky's thoughts, his influence on the way we look at knowledge and learning are monumental. His impact in the present day is best described in the words of his daughter Gita: "Even though so many years have passed, Vygotsky's thoughts, ideas, and works not only belong to history, but they still interest people. In one of his articles, A. Leontiev wrote of Vygotsky as a man decades ahead of his time. Probably that is why that he is for us not a historic figure but a living contemporary" (Vygodskaya, 2001).

And so, almost a century later, Vygotsky continues to influence the field of educational psychology. His theories aid in our understanding of how children and adults learn, and, in our understanding of these theories, we are able to apply various strategies and tactics within educational settings. It is through his works and guidance that we can continue to socially construct knowledge, respond reflectively, think critically and thus become lifelong learners.

REFERENCES

Gallagher, C. (1999, May). Lev Semonovich Vygotsky. Psychology Department, Muskingum College. Retrieved March 2, 2005, from http://www.muskingum.edu/~psych/psycweb/history/vygotsky.htm.

Goldfarb, M. E. (2001, March 12). The Educational Theory of Lev Semenovich Vygotsky (1896–1934). *NewFoundations.com* (G. K. Clabaugh and E.G. Rozycki, Eds.). Retrieved March 5, 2005, from http://www.newfoundations.com/GALLERY/Vygotsky.html.

Hansen-Reid, M. (2001). Lev Semonovich Vygotsky. Massey University Virtual Faculty (A. J. Lock, Ed.), Department of Psychology, Massey University, New Zealand. Retrieved March 2, 2005, from http://evolution.massey.ac.nz/assign2/MHR/indexvyg.html (a site cataloguing resources on Lev Semenovich Vygotsky inaugurated for the centenary of Vygotsky's birth by providing a Web conference on various aspects of Vygotsky's collected works. Academic papers and other resources on Vygotsky are continually added.).

Schütz, R. (2004, December 5). Vygotsky and Language Acquisition. *English Made in Brazil*. Retrieved March 5, 2005, from http://www.sk.com.br/sk-vygot.html.

Vygodskaya, G. (2001, December). His Life. *The Vygotsky Project*. Retrieved March 3, 2005, from http://webpages.charter.net/schmolze1/vygotsky/gita.html.

CHAPTER 35

Valerie Walkerdine

RACHEL BAILEY JONES

In a time of questioning traditional assumptions in many academic disciplines, Valerie Walkerdine is a critical educational psychologist working today reconsidering the "truths" of psychology. She has focused her research on the ways that gender, class, and the media affect the formation of how we see each other and how we understand ideas of the "self." How do working-class girls come to know themselves in different ways than middle-class girls or both working-class and middle-class boys? How does class location affect the educational and career opportunities of girls? Walkerdine has worked throughout her career to answer these seemingly simple questions. Often collaborating with other psychologists, she has researched the gender gap in mathematics, the educational gap between middle-class and working-class girls in Britain, images of working-class girls in the media, and the creation of the "masses" by the media. By deconstructing, or taking apart, several traditionally accepted truths of psychology, Valerie Walkerdine attempts to build a new foundation for evaluating the development of children in relation to their gender and class. Her work in psychology complements the recent movement in child development known as "postformal" theory. I will examine how Walkerdine's concern with multiple narratives and subjective ideas of truth mirrors the questions of power and truth taken up by those who reconsider the traditionally accepted formal theories of development.

Valerie Walkerdine grew up in a working-class family in England during the turbulent post–World War II era. Growing up, Walkerdine watched movies like *My Fair Lady* and *Gigi* that represented the working-class girls who are transformed by education and love into upper-class women. She claims that the character of Eliza Doolittle in *My Fair Lady* inspired her to dream of higher education to escape a life of poverty. It was the popular-culture fantasies of success that drove her to become an intellectual. She became the first of her family to succeed in higher education and enter into the professional middle class by becoming a college professor. Her personal history is very important for Walkerdine, because it informs her research into the area of the feminine working-class development. Unlike traditional psychologists, who attempt to achieve objectivity by denying any personal attachment to their work, Walkerdine accepts the fact that psychologists are humans who have personal connections to the subjects of their research. In the many articles and books that she has written, Walkerdine often mentions her own biographical experience and how it influences her view of the research subjects. The reality of her working-class upbringing led Walkerdine to question traditional assumptions about links between class, gender, and innate intelligence. She understands that being a detached observer is impossible and believes that revealing the researcher's subjectivity ultimately strengthens the academic integrity of the research.

Walkerdine places her own history and subjectivity within the history of psychology as a scientific discipline. In order to question the modern framework of her discipline, Walkerdine lays out the way in which the "normal" psychological model was constructed. In the 1800s there was a growing belief that science could explain everything. Psychology was formed as a discipline in the late nineteenth century to create an objective and scientific framework to study the truth about human nature. Reflecting the rapid development of scientific research and discovery of the time, psychology was based on the idea that there were universal "truths" not only in the natural world, but also about the human mind. The discipline of psychology developed as a social science and claimed to have objective truth on its side. Early psychologists were primarily European males and they used their own standards to develop "scientific" models of normal behavior. Psychology, like biology, was used to justify colonialism, racism, and sexism through a form of social evolution based on the work of Charles Darwin. This evolution placed the white, European, middle-class male at the top of the evolutionary ladder, with women, children and all nonwhite colonial people lower on the ladder. The psychologically "normal" subject was created in the image of the rational white man. This placed all others as less than psychologically normal, somehow pathological, or mentally lesser. Early forms of psychiatry were used to adjust the deviant behavior of those whose behavior was outside the norm. Many racist and sexist ideas were supported by this culturally constructed psychological idea of "truth."

Valerie Walkerdine is engaged in a critical form of psychology that questions the history of the discipline and its claims to scientific truth. Postmodern researchers reveal their own subjectivity and connection to their research. Understanding that psychology was and is culturally constructed by human subjects helps one to realize that all psychological truths have to be reexamined within the cultural framework in which they were created. By questioning the modern psychology, with its idea of a single truth and objective research, Walkerdine belongs to the postmodern branch, which refutes the idea of objectivity and universal truth. It is through the idea of questioning traditional truths about the psychology of class, gender, and the media that we will examine Walkerdine's research into these three areas and their complex connections.

The consistent focus of Valerie Walkerdine's work is on the intersection of gender and class. She uses her biographical history of a growing up girl in a working-class family for the foundation of her inquiry. Some of her published work into these areas was on the socially accepted idea of male rationality. In *Counting Girls Out: Girls & Mathematics* (1998), Walkerdine describes her research (begun in 1978) into the question of why boys consistently outperform girls in the school subject of mathematics. The subject of math represents, for many, the highest form of rational thought. Rational thought has historically been attributed to the biological superiority of men. Women have been constructed as too emotional and irrational to excel in the rational discipline of mathematics. Walkerdine conducted research into girls' performance in mathematics by looking into the attitudes of teachers and of girls, as well as the cultural expectations for gender. She studied how these factors affected the performance of girls in mathematics. While traditionally the performance of students in math was researched quantitatively, or through analyzing test scores and number of passing grades, Walkerdine used observation of classroom dynamics and interviews of students and teachers to construct a picture of why girls struggle in math. Walkerdine found that the negative expectations of teachers and the poor expectations of the girls themselves had quite an impact on academic performance. Those expected to perform poorly often do. She also found that class was a factor in performance. Middle-class girls who did well in school generally did well in math. Those girls in the studies from the working-class, with much lower expectations, generally did worse than boys and middle-class girls.

While her research into math performance focused on gender, Walkerdine's work in the book *Growing Up Girl: Psychosocial Explorations of Gender and Class* (2001), written with Helen Lucey and June Melody, evaluates the relationship between difference class and the academic expectations and performance of girls in contemporary Britain. This work questions the use of the middle class as the "normal" academic and psychological subject. It also questions the idea of the upwardly mobile individual and the idea that anyone can succeed as long as they work hard. The idea of "equal opportunity" crumbles when Walkerdine compares the achievement of working and middle-class girls. Parental and teacher expectations and support for middle-class girls will not allow them to fail, or even to be academically mediocre. The expectations for working-class girls are much lower and the opportunities are much harder to find. Academic failure is accepted and in many ways expected in the working-class families. The few girls of lower economic class in the research who did succeed in school had a difficult time leaving their families and felt more detached from their family and class roots as they attained higher academic success. As educated, upwardly mobile young women, they were received with apprehension by their parents, who lacked higher education. The middle-class girls who succeeded were reproducing the success of their parents and did not experience the disconnect felt by the working-class girls. In much of Walkerdine's psychological research, she finds that academic performance is greatly determined by your economic status and the education of your family because of culturally acceptable roles. Girls and the working class are expected to do poorly in the "rational" academic subjects because the system was set up for them to fail. She dispels the "truth" of innately inferior classes of people; all psychology is based in the cultural norms of its time.

In addition to her work on the psychology of creating academic subjects, Walkerdine is interested in how representations in the media of girlhood and the working class create and limit opportunities. In *Daddy's Girl* (1998), she uses the pop cultural representations of Lil' Orphan Annie and the roles played by Shirley Temple to illustrate how identities of working-class girls are constructed. Walkerdine argues that the media regulates behavior through negative representations of poverty and expectations of what a girl should be and how she should act. Going one step further, she argues that the media creates the very way we can know ourselves as individuals. It creates the words and images we choose from when we create our selfhood. Working-class girls see very few options for themselves in the media. One of the few routes to success for these girls is through performing and looking cute, like Shirley Temple's many characters that were poor, but unthreatening and charming.

Walkerdine also works with the sexualized images of girls in the media. She takes issue with liberal critiques of the media that victimize the girls and give them no agency or fantasy of their own. It is not only an adult male fantasy that places young girls in make-up and short skirts. There is a lure in the glamor and success of beautiful women in the media, and for young working-class girls, the fantasy of being a glamorous object of desire is a way out of poverty. While observing her young, working-class subjects watching movies and singing pop songs, Walkerdine clearly identifies with her own childhood. This identification gives her a unique insight into the psychology of these girls. It is not the clinical objective observation of traditional psychology, but a new type of research that begins with admission of the researcher's own formation as a subject.

The creation of group psychology, knowledge of the self as part of the mass of people, is the subject of Blackman and Walkerdine's further research into the media. In *Mass Hysteria* (2001), written with fellow critical psychologist Lisa Blackman, the authors look into the creation of the "mass" in psychology and the way the media constructs mass identity. In traditional psychology, any group of people acting together has been called either a mass or a mob, both with negative connotations. A large group of people involved in protest or movement is labeled with "mass hysteria." It is assumed that people in a mass are unable to make independent decisions and they have lost their individual identities to the group. Those in the mass are assumed to be of lower class and therefore less rational and more susceptible to suggestion. Walkerdine and Blackman describe how psychologists such as Sigmund Freud view the mass as mentally simple and irrational. Karl Marx, who argued for the masses to unite and overcome the oppression of class, believed that an enlightened intellectual was needed to lead the process of understanding and revolt. He believed that the working class needed to change and they needed a leader to show the path to revolution. The overall impression is that the working class, when viewed as the mass, is inferior mentally to the upper and middle classes.

In questioning the tradition of group psychology, Walkerdine questions the idea of the "self" as we have come to think of it. She draws on the work of Jacques Lacan and his theories of language. He wrote about how language can take the role of a set of cultural symbols. The words, as symbols, not only describe reality, they shape how we view reality and help to form ideas of the self. The way we think of ourselves, using the culturally available words, shapes who we are. In this view, the "self" cannot be viewed as independent from society. The intellectual elite of society, the professors, scientists, and doctors among others, use their expertise to create vocabulary that defines normality, intelligence, and illness. A large part of the construction of the self is based on the science of psychology and its claim to truth. I have written already about the racist and sexist history of psychological truths. In this light, the subjects created in our culture, using the language of science and the tools of media representation, have been based on the fiction of a naturally superior white middle-class male subject. All other subjects are somehow "abnormal," or psychologically less stable. Walkerdine uses this context to bring up the issues of sexuality and race in terms of the creation of the "other" in psychological discourses.

Both heterosexuality and whiteness are set up as the "normal" ideal in traditional and modern texts. Homosexuality threatens our cultural image of normalcy, and must be made deviant to protect those who are "normal" and at the psychological center. It is the language of normalcy versus deviancy that controls our perception of sexuality. Psychological understanding of race, like gender, has been shaped by the history of the discipline. European colonial powers used psychology to defend their colonization and the often-horrible treatment of their subjects. They used the scientific language to maintain that nonwhite people were intellectually and biologically inferior and incapable of self-governance. Colonial peoples of Africa, Asia, and South America were constructed by the colonists as "primitive" and closer in mental functioning to children than European adults.

This is the same scientific language used to control a collection of individuals by calling them an "unthinking mob." The diagnosis based on psychological normalcy also diminished the perceived mental functioning of women by labeling women as "irrational" and "hysterical" by nature. The psychology that propped up oppression for years invented biological differences to ensure their "just" use of governmental power. Walkerdine uses the postcolonial writing of Homi Bhabha and Franz Fanon to help deconstruct the history of racism built into the language of psychology. These authors fight the notion that intelligence and race are linked in any way. Like the false claims of objectivity in psychology, intelligence testing that claims to be objective is in reality based on racist cultural ideas of what it means to be intelligent, that is, rational, Western, and white.

Walkerdine uses the postmodern philosophy of Michel Foucault to reveal the construction of false truths that have been claimed by those in power to be objectively proven. Foucault is an important French philosopher who evaluated traditional claims of truth and revealed how people are controlled by powerful claims to knowledge. Walkerdine uses her perspective as a product of working-class upbringing to bring new insight into the issues of the masses. She does not pretend to be objective, and forms connections to the subjects of her research. Postmodern social science stresses the importance of the researcher's socioeconomic position to their work. Facts of wealth, poverty, and oppressions are central to the psychological development of a subject. Walkerdine and her fellow critical psychologists are the first to overtly connect their own experience to that of their subjects. This admission of subjectivity is an important factor in revealing the vast networks of ingrained ideas about the formation of the individual. Theories of development need to be reexamined in order to rethink what psychology could mean for the future of education.

The postmodern, critical psychological research and writing from Valerie Walkerdine mirror the ideas of postformal learning theory. Both schools of thought begin with the wish to deconstruct and reexamine the modern idea of pure scientific "truth." Postformal theory uses the formal operations work of Jean Piaget as the modern conception of learning. Piaget's theory of formal operations set up distinct stages of mental development in children. In this view, rational, abstract thinking is the highest form of mental functioning. Again, we see the use of the European, male, middle-class idea of intelligence at the center of modern theory. All other processes that involve emotion, issues of power, and questions of meaning are devalued in formal theory. Postformalism seeks to expose the political and cultural assumptions behind formalism and to disprove the idea of one right way and one set of rigid stages of development.

The work of the postformal theorists, led by Joe Kincheloe and Shirley Steinberg, asks educators to evaluate and question the assumptions on which they base their practice. The culturally constructed truths in education about natural intelligence and equal opportunity make us believe that all children have an equal chance at success in school. If children fail, it is because they are not intelligent or do not work hard enough. Postformal analysis reveals how the cultural constructions of race, class, and gender affect real educational opportunities and the views of what counts as intelligence. Standardized tests that determine the amount of intelligence a child possesses are not only flawed by their use of culturally skewed questions, they measure and value only a certain kind of intelligence. This is the ability to take knowledge that can be applied to a real-life situation and abstract this knowledge to answer test questions that have little to do with life outside the test. Walkerdine critiques the same limited modernist view of intelligence in her work with the working class and issues of gender. The culturally biased view of intelligence is so important because it has been convincingly sold as the truth. Many have been excluded from higher education and professions on the basis of this notion of innate intelligence.

By focusing on questions that undermine the modern history of psychology, Walkerdine reveals the sexist and bigoted assumptions that have been claimed as fact. Her work in postmodernism is in many ways the psychological branch of postformal thought. Both theories deny claims to objective truth and both hope to set the groundwork for reconceptualizing and re-thinking education. A new vision is sketched out for educational psychology and development that is based on issues of social equity and justice. It is not enough to deconstruct old claims to truth and reveal inequity in terms of gender, race, and class. New methods based on the postmodern and postformal work could value and reward multiple perspectives and achievements.

Through her research, Walkerdine shows clearly that the stratifying of society based on the constructions of class, race, and gender are cultural psychological formations and not due to differences in innate ability. Changes in expectation and attitude on the part of teachers, parents, and the media could go a long way in creating a more equitable education. Of course the psychologists who, under the guise of science, developed the evolutionary order of intelligence have formed expectation and attitude over centuries. The rethinking of educational psychology will not transform social structures overnight, but the work of Valerie Walkerdine contributes valuable research to the field of psychology. She adds to a dialogue that is leading in the direction of social change and the reform of biased assumptions that for many decades have functioned as truth.

REFERENCES

Blackman, L., and Walkerdine, V. (2001). *Mass Hysteria: Critical Pychology and Media Studies.* New York: Palgrave Macmillan.

Walkerdine, V. (1997). *Daddy's Girl: Young Girl's and Popular Culture.* Cambridge, MA: Harvard University Press.

———. (1998). *Counting Girls Out: Girls & Mathematics.* London: Falmer Press.

———. (2001). *Growing Up Girl: Psychosocial Exploration of Gender and Class.* New York: New York University Press.

CHAPTER 36

John Watson

CHRIS EMDIN

The usual format of a description of a person's life is usually an incongruous mix of the chronological and the informational. We often receive broad strokes of the person's childhood and background, followed by the person's successes and their claim to fame. Born on a certain date and had a happy childhood; achieved notoriety at a certain age, lived and then died. In the case of John Watson, it is necessary to take a deeper look into specific times in his life and attempt to recreate the circumstances around these integral periods in order to get a firm grasp on his thoughts, ideas, and theories as they relate to the way we study learners in an educational setting. For the last hundred years, many of the perceptions of the general public on students' ability and aptitude have been shaped by Watson's theories. He has successfully ingrained a dismissal of subconscious motivations for success while impressing upon millions that repetition, the environment, and other external motivators hold the key to learning. These facts lead us to the activity of critically looking at why and how Watson shaped his ideas. We will begin this journey with a critical look at his childhood. Such a critical look provides us with a profound understanding of the man that revolutionized and certainly transfigured the inner workings and face of educational psychology. John Watson's life and work were intertwined in a dynamic inseparable manner and the issues that plagued his childhood and adulthood profoundly intersect with his work. Born into a family with deep idiosyncrasies, Watson constantly battled with dichotomies in his life and family. He had an exceptionally religious Baptist mother who encouraged cleanliness and morality in the lives of her children and a father who was a womanizer and an alcoholic. Although his family had a black nurse who helped raise John and established close emotional bonds with him, Watson often harassed black men and assaulted them as a hobby. These are the obvious dichotomies that exist in a study of Watson's childhood. His discomfort in these dichotomies led John to become a complicated student who exhibited an uncanny intelligence but also overt behavior problems. Such paradoxes in Watson's life led to his search for a universal, final truth in his academic work.

One of the most important concepts that personify the transformation from pre-behaviorism to behaviorism in the psychology of the era that encompassed John Watson's entry into and exodus from the academy was the shift from introspection as an acceptable belief to behaviorism. Watson created a need for an immediate shift from one philosophy to another. One could not be a behaviorist who believed in the possibilities of some salvageable introspective theories. There was an all-or-nothing approach to Watson's theories. He created a perception that a combination of theories would lead to a weakening of psychology because of the ambiguity of introspection. This belief is grounded in the mechanistic tradition of formalist thinking in educational psychology, which echoes a reliance on only one way of doing and knowing and is uncomfortable with the possibility of reliable information from arenas that are outside its domain.

HIGHER EDUCATIONAL JOURNEY

Watson's journey into higher education began with his acceptance into Furman College and his meeting with Gordon Moore, who was a philosophy professor there. Moore provided Watson with a model of an individual who had the ability to be an individual and thinker in the midst of the rigid Baptist environment of the college. Moore was someone who was able to have ideas and thoughts that were contradictory to the religious, Baptist tone that existed at the school. This situation further exemplifies the binarisms that were commonplace in Watson's life and interactions as Moore walked a fine line at Furman between his academic interests as a liberated philosopher and his role at the school as a lecturer who had to abide by Baptist principles. Moore later got a job as a faculty member at the University of Chicago and Watson followed his mentor to the school when he was admitted as a doctoral student. Under the guidance of his mentor, Watson began studying philosophy at Chicago. He eventually grew tired of the abstract nature of philosophy and decided to study psychology.

PSYCHOLOGY/ANIMAL BEHAVIOR BEGINS

Watson's research at Chicago began late in 1901 with his studies on how rats learn. This research would eventually lead to theories on how humans learn as comparative psychology was employed to discuss general principles of behavior between rats and humans. In the beginning of his research, he designed mazes with concealed entrances where food was stored in a wire box. He then studied the time it took rats to find the food. Various experiments were designed and executed. The scientific advancements that developed as a result of the physical work and new techniques that Watson developed were phenomenal. At a time when these experiments were practically unheard of, his techniques reflected his pure genius. He had rats run through labyrinths with food at one of four paths, with the path with the food covered, and studied the process. After drawing conclusions on the time it took the rats, more complex questions arose and, as a result, more complex experiments developed. After the study on how rats traveled through the labyrinth to find food, he decided to study at what age they could travel through the labyrinth. He created obstacles in a box between a litter of rats and their mother and studied the age at which the rats could find their way back to their mother. He studied the brains of the rats at certain ages to properly gauge their growth. Watson even studied the effects of the senses of the rat as they traveled through the maze by removing the eyes, middle ear, olfactory bulb and whiskers from different groups of mice to determine whether these effects changed the rats' learning of the maze. In essence, he designed and executed experiments that at the time were extraordinary and revolutionary and led to various new conclusions about rats.

Watson concluded that learning developed in an uneven manner over time until an optimal learning time was reached, and that rats at a certain age learned better than rats at other ages. He also discovered that regardless of the absence of certain senses, rats could still learn the maze. His work had seemed to provide him with what he perceived as concrete results about the nature of the rats learning processes. The problem with the results of these experiments was that they made Watson believe that he could use similar methods for studying humans. Comparative psychology in this and many other instances is a flawed approach to studying human learning. The quantifiable results of a study on rats cannot be applied to humans. As a matter of fact, the quantifiable results of observable phenomena in human beings cannot be compared to that of other human beings in different geographic areas. Imagine the differences when we simply compare socioeconomic backgrounds. In a comparison of individuals from different socioeconomic backgrounds, we discover emotional and cultural differences that are present but not necessarily visible. However, based on the assumptions that there were no aspects to his study of rats that were unconscious and that all of his conclusions were visible and verifiable, he was prepared to go one step further. He was ready to present his ideas on the nature of studying behavior in rats and express his belief that the results of his experiments could be used to draw conclusions about the nature of human beings. This method of observing, recording, and drawing conclusions based on the conclusions of specific observed phenomena were the spine of behaviorism's early beginnings.

Unfortunately, over time, the discipline of educational psychology has refused to evolve from its beliefs in universal data being applicable to specific groups as it is used to determine the ability, potential, and access to education of different groups of people. Watson hinted at his belief in the efficacy of a behaviorist theory to be used in humans and learning after his initial experiments with rats in 1901. His colleagues strongly disagreed with him because they understood the commonly held beliefs that humans were more spiritual and conscious beings. Despite their misgivings, he forged on with his work. While his work with rats was well received by intellectual journals, it was rejected by many popular magazines at the time. Watson had grown comfortable with these divergent opinions of his work and dealt with them as he had dealt with similar situations throughout his life. He forged on with his study and, as a result, laid the foundations for behaviorism in human psychology.

ANIMAL BEHAVIORIST TO HUMAN BEHAVIORIST

After moving into the position of Chair of the department of psychology at the Johns Hopkins University in 1908, Watson graduated from his study of rats to research on terns and monkeys. As he developed his research in these areas, he continued to theorize about the study of human behavior. In his early speeches on his take on psychology at Harvard and Columbia, Watson received negative responses to his provisional theories and ideas about human behavior, but continued with his study as he sought to remove the ambiguity of the prevalent consciousness movement of psychology by making it more scientific and observable. He was on a quest to discover specific answers to his questions on how human beings respond to certain stimuli. At this stage in his research, there was a need to find responses that could be consistent when a specific stimulus was presented. Utilizing the work of Pavlov and his work with dogs on "the conditioned reflex" Watson moved towards a study of conditioned motor reflexes in humans. Watson believed that similar to the dogs' salivating with the ringing of a bell in Pavlov's work, human behavior too functioned in this stimulus–response model.

This progression in Watson's thought led him to write many papers in publications that were not purely psychological, to share his work. Utilizing this media served as an opportunity to plant the seeds of behaviorism in the minds of the general public. This approach was and is still used to drive the mechanistic tenets of educational psychology into American and eventually international normal public discourse. As a result, there is a normalizing of preconceived notions that are not created by but end up enacted by the public. He argued on many occasions that human emotions, memory, attention and ways of being should be studied objectively. In Watson's thought there was no room for introspection because it had no observable, verifiable truths. Watson was also greatly concerned with the way that psychology competed with other sciences. Throughout his work, he criticized psychology for not having enough of a scientific approach to be considered a science. His mission was to give psychology a jolt of real science that was necessary in order for the subject to be considered valid in comparison to other sciences such as biology and chemistry. The ideas of behaviorism were therefore bound with the following tenets. First, psychology is a valid branch of natural science. Second, being a valid branch of natural science, its goal is simply to control human behavior without the auspices of introspection. Third, there are no divisions between human beings and animals in the study of behavior and response. Historically, these tenets laid the foundation for modern educational psychology and its statistics-based analysis of the stimulus–response model.

BEHAVIORIST WORK (EXPERIMENTS WITH CHILDREN)

In this section, I will describe two of the kinds of experiments that Watson routinely administered in order to create the evidence for the efficacy of behaviorism. One of the experiments that Watson is best known for is called the Little Albert Experiment. In this study, Watson conditioned an eleven-month-old boy (Albert) over a period of two months to fear certain objects. In order to show that fear was exhibited in an observable fashion, Albert was shown various objects and his response to these objects were observed and recorded. At nine months old, he was shown a white rat, a rabbit, a dog, a monkey, and objects such as masks and cotton wool. At this time Albert showed no response to/fear of any of these objects. Two months later, a bar was struck making a loud noise behind Albert's ear whenever he was shown a white rat. The loud noise caused Albert to cry. This process was repeated until Albert would cry at the sight of the rat without the loud noise. Watson used this experiment to demonstrate that emotional responses were conditioned. In another experiment Watson studied how a child reacted to an object that was dangled in front of her. He swung a piece of candy in front of the child and took notes on how and when she reached for the candy and put it in her mouth. After about 120 days of experimenting and observing, the child had shown perception and movement in a coordinated manner. She reached directly for the candy, quicker than she had when the experiment began. From this work Watson theorized about the time it took for children to develop physiologically. We are once again introduced to issues that surround the use of observable phenomena to draw broad conclusions. As the experiment progressed, Watson decided to light a candle and hold it one eighth of an inch away from the child's hand. He then moved the candle in a circle around the child. The child was then allowed to reach for the flame and touch it. She would get slightly seared by the flame each time she touched it. Watson noted that at 178 days there was an improvement of avoidance of the flame and that by 220 days the child would still reach for the flame but would not touch it. The conclusion of this experiment was that the child develops an avoidance reaction to the flame. Watson believed that this avoidance reaction could have taken a shorter period of time to develop if the child had been allowed to not just touch the flame and be slightly seared by it in the initial stages of the experiment, but be allowed to be burned by the flame when she initially touched it. The belief was that there could be training to avoid the flame.

With his own children, Watson found a great opportunity to put behaviorism into further practice. He closely studied his children and how they learned to respond to certain stimuli (this stimuli included himself and his wife). He then utilized his observations as further research to support his theories on behaviorism. In his experiments with his son, Watson attempted to condition his son's daily activities to occur on a specific daily routine. Behaviorism in practice included trying to condition his son's bowel movements to occur at specific times of the day. He attempted to condition his son's time to wake, eat, play, and sleep. The goal was to develop/train children that were self-reliant and free from emotional problems. This theory is apparent in educational psychology and functions under the premise that a set routine is necessary to have a "good student." It is also seen in the focus on interventions for behavior and learning problems that focus on training students to conform to preexisting norms. This mechanistic tradition also prevails in the lack of allowances for contextual delivery of instruction in classrooms. There is a reliance on a one-size-fits-all micro-managed curriculum that ignores issues that surround students with varying socioeconomic backgrounds.

WATSON'S THOUGHTS AND BELIEFS

The advent of Watson's work on behaviorism at Chicago represented an enormous shift from the functionalist psychology that his colleagues had supported. Functionalism gave the researcher an affective dimension by providing an opportunity for putting oneself in the place of the animal one was studying in an attempt to fully understand it. An entry into the affective dimension via functionalism and consciousness only added to Watson's consternation with the direction of psychology as a discipline. He firmly believed in the need for the scientific dimension of psychology. He attempted to reach this dimension through behaviorism. This search for scientific validation was important to Watson because it was the first step to having psychology held on par with other scientific disciplines. In an attempt to put forward his perspective on the field of psychology, he even proposed that the word *introspection* be banned from use in psychology. Watson's inability to accept critiques of his science is exemplified in his response to education scholars and philosophers and other critics of his work. In 1910, E. F. Buchner, a professor at Johns Hopkins who was renowned for his work in education and philosophy, critiqued behaviorism by questioning how the theory could remain devoted to being purely scientific and still maintain its practical use. Watson retorted by referring to Buchner as "a high-class Janitor" who came to Johns Hopkins "to coax these hayseed teachers to eat out of the University's hand, nothing more." When questioned about his thoughts on John Dewey, he said, "I never knew what he was talking about then, and unfortunately for me, I still don't know." These blanket dismissals of other paradigm's perspectives personified the stance of the pure behaviorists. Watson's belief was that if psychology would pursue the plan he suggested, "the educator, the physician, the jurist and the businessman could utilize our data in a practical way." He believed that behaviorism could and should be used in every possible arena. The practice of trying to make all things fit into one mold has been a long-lasting agenda of educational psychology. Its origins lie in Watson's attempt to use behaviorism in all arenas that involved human interaction. It remains today in the use of IQ testing as the criteria for measuring and judging human intelligence.

It is therefore also necessary for contemporary students of educational psychology to delve into a study of comparative psychology as it relates to Watson's movement from animal psychology to behaviorism. There is an obvious connection between these two areas of psychology, and each has exerted a powerful influence on the other. The natural progression usually discussed in the development from animal to human study by Watson was not necessarily a simple transition from the study of rats to the study of humans. There was not an end to the study of rats and then a new clear beginning to Watson's study on humans. The theoretical positions that ground behaviorism in humans were grounded in the experimental work that Watson conducted in animal psychology. Here we uncover the behaviorist belief that if experimentation is empirically verifiable for the rat, it would also be empirically verifiable in humans. As educational psychologists study Watson, we must view him not only as a behaviorist but also as an animal psychologist. There was no evolution, no change of interpretive frameworks from Watson the animal psychologist to Watson the behaviorist. He was both. Despite Watson's clamor for having psychology stand as an individual natural science, the nature of the science that he prescribed relied heavily on physiology because in essence it was a study of animals. This work can therefore be interpreted as a study in the earlier discovered and explored discipline of physiology. In letters and conversations with his colleagues, Watson often asked, "Am I a physiologist?" The dichotomies that were present in Watson's youth presented themselves in his academic work. He had to ask himself whether or not he was creating a valid new science or just doing an extensive study in animal physiology. I argue that this duality in his take on his work caused him to take such an unyielding stance publicly in his support for legitimizing behaviorism and denouncing introspection. Taking a mechanistic, formalist approach creates an arena where dichotomies are nonexistent. The way that Watson dealt with any ambiguity concerning his thoughts and philosophies was to attempt to scientifically validate them. The nature of the academic tradition is to create an arena where students blindly absorb a validated approved discipline without questioning it. The belief was that if behaviorism were scientifically validated, no more questions would arise.

Watson's take on educational psychology was simply an extension of his general beliefs on psychology. He stated that any investigator in experimental education would need to be an animal behaviorist. This belief transformed educational psychology, because many animal behaviorists began to enter into the study of educational psychology and brought their reductionist animal psychology theories and beliefs into the field of education. The advent and subsequent infiltration of these beliefs were accompanied by the absence of introspective methodologies and the popularization of less complex, reductionistic views of children. Watson's comparative psychology (animal-to-human comparisons) caused him to be sought after in education circles to explore experimental pedagogy. He did not fully enter into this arena until his exodus from academia (a departure forced by his affair with a student, whom he later married). At this point in his career, Watson sought to apply his theories to more popular issues like advertising and raising children.

UNDER THE BEHAVIORIST UMBRELLA

As the twentieth century progressed, Watson's comparative psychology and behaviorism became increasingly influential in the discourse of psychology. Throughout this process, Watson's allegiance to the denial of introspection and commitment to the formalist, natural scientific traits of psychology still remained. There is a thread that travels from the precursors of behaviorism in Pavlov's notion of stimulus and response through rats' learning their way around complicated mazes to the impact of behaviorism on theories of learning and the nature of educational psychology. There is an obvious marriage to the stimulus–response ideology that is undeniable in Watson's work. This strict model of interpreting human activity is austerely flawed on the basis of its derivation from practical human behavior and its lack of practicality in descriptions of complicated human responses. Watson's behaviorism is ultimately the most positivistic rendering of learning in the cosmos of educational psychology. In "Behaviorism: Modern Note in Psychology," a paper written by Watson in 1929, Watson expresses his belief that "we need nothing to explain behavior but the ordinary laws of physics and chemistry." A postformalist critique would argue that we have no criteria to describe the series of steps involved in complicated human acts, such as playing sports. We can see that the behaviorist model does not leave any room for the desire to score a touchdown and how that translates into throwing a ball. Watson's work does not account for the process of having a desire to do something and the process involved in actually doing it. In this example, we see that purely observing someone throwing a ball has its limitations. This lack of consideration for complex human processes such as desire can be further examined in actions that take place as a result of a belief. The belief that it is chilly outside would cause one to carry a jacket just as the desire to stay dry would cause someone to carry a jacket. The concept of belief described above is another example that does not fit into the model described by

Watson because it goes beyond his principle of predictable impulse reactions to a certain specific stimulus.

Watson's theories on thinking describe the extent of the limitations of his science. To avert the obvious introspective and internal dynamic of thinking, Watson posits that thinking is a behavior that consists of motor organization. According to Watson, thinking is talking that we have been conditioned to do in a concealed manner. This way of thinking leaves no room for the concept of imagination and imagery, which I would argue are essential dimensions of human existence. In the introduction to this encyclopedia, Joe Kincheloe describes the process of meaning making and its impact on human constructions of reality. The process of meaning or making meaning lies in a domain that is interpretive. In *Releasing the Imagination*, Maxine Greene (1995) describes the pre-reflective world that is an essential component of existing in the present. The notion of a pre-reflective world, which is created from our unquantifiable ideas, feelings, and expressions, approaches a level of complexity that cannot be accounted for from a Watsonian standpoint.

ANALYSIS AND IMPLICATIONS

The desire to make psychology an accepted and unquestionable natural science drove Watson to develop a science that was visible and verifiable. This desire coupled with Watson's strict adherence to the stimulus–response model in every facet of psychological analysis and observation was an apparent positivistic and narcissistic practice. The notion that there is only one way of knowing, doing, and learning (Watson's way of knowing and doing) impedes upon the natural progression of an individual or an academic discipline. It limits the possibility of expansion beyond what is known, thereby assuming that both the individual and the science are finite. We can therefore presuppose that Watson's thinking fosters an innate belief that at some point, all stimuli and responses will be observed and measured. Watson's dismissal of consciousness as an ineffectual method of practicing psychology served as an avenue to limit reality to what is observed and therefore known. This practice has become so embedded in the fabric of American culture and education that it lurks within the auspices of political programs and movements that are presented to the public as a way of recovering and improving the present state of sociopolitical affairs. Just as Watson's work provided a spotlight for a focus on human response, reaction, and performance and disregarded human thought and ways of being, the academic and reformatory institutions throughout the United States have turned on the high beams of the spotlight by convincing our society that intelligence and standardized tests are the only true measurement of students' abilities and intelligence. This notion is also accompanied with the assumption that institutionalizing at-risk youth will change their behavior and make them well-regulated members of society. The absence of sociopolitical, hegemonic, race, and class issues in any mechanistic educational psychological study delineates a reality that is insensitive to the implications of such defining factors. In lieu of the absence of these factors, an employment of a postformalist approach to educational psychology is as necessary as the discipline itself. Safe, preexistent notions are forced to face the reality of questions like why and what-if. The discipline's claim of objectivity in the use of and assessment by fixed bodies of knowledge is dismantled in the face of a postformalist approach that takes these "objective" notions and utilizes them as a springboard to expose the biases that underlie their claims to objectivity. A lack of such an approach will only attain a superficial analysis of educational psychology that maintains the flaws in thinking, theory, and practice that have been present since the advent of behaviorism. Watson's creation of such work should therefore be used as a tool for further critical study with a realization of its strengths and impact on psychology but also with an awareness of its shortcomings and implications.

REFERENCES

Greene, M. (1995). *Releasing the Imagination: Essays on Education, the Arts, and Social Change*. San Francisco: Jossey-Bass Publishers.

Watson, J. B. (1929). *Behaviorism: Modern Note in Psychology*. Retrieved August 4, 2006, from http://psychclassics.yorku.ca/Watson/Battle/watson.htm.